THE INDIANS OF TEXAS

From Prehistoric to Modern Times

W. W. Newcomb

The Indians of Texas

FROM PREHISTORIC TO MODERN TIMES

by W. W. NEWCOMB, JR.

with drawings by HAL M. STORY

 UNIVERSITY OF TEXAS PRESS, AUSTIN

INTERNATIONAL STANDARD BOOK NUMBER 0-292-73271-6

LIBRARY OF CONGRESS CATALOG CARD NO. 60-14312

COPYRIGHT © 1961 BY THE UNIVERSITY OF TEXAS PRESS

FIFTH PRINTING, 1973

MANUFACTURED IN THE UNITED STATES OF AMERICA

For Mary Elaine

FOREWORD

To MOST AMERICANS the life and livelihood of our Indian predecessors is a romantic and fascinating subject but often a sketchily understood one. The peoples who inhabited present-day Texas at the dawn of historic times are even less well known by the public than most North American Indians and consequently there are probably more myths, absurdities, and falsehoods connected with them than with the natives of any other state. There is good reason for this ignorance and misunderstanding: most Texas tribes disappeared many years ago, some before Americans entered what is now Texas. This has meant that ethnographers —those anthropologists who describe primitive cultures—have not been able to gather firsthand facts about most Texas Indians. What is known about their habits has to be gleaned from the written accounts left by the soldiers, missionaries, and explorers who first visited them. Ethnographers have had their hands so full describing the surviving North American Indian tribes it is no wonder that Indians who can never be known in the flesh have been neglected. As a result no one has written a comprehensive book about the natives of Texas.[1]

My own ignorance of Texas Indians and the conviction that as an anthropologist I should be able to answer questions about these bygone peoples started me on a search for this information. What I learned I have tried to put down in a nontechnical manner, yet this may sometimes be a difficult and unsatisfactory book to read. There are several reasons for this. The

[1] Mary Jourdan Atkinson's *The Texas Indians* (1935) and *Indians of the Southwest* (1958) do not deal comprehensively or extensively with Texas Indians. Mildred P. Mayhall's "The Indians of Texas: The Atakapa, the Karankawa, the Tonkawa" (unpublished Ph.D. dissertation, University of Texas, 1939) is likewise restricted in scope.

life of Texas Indians was often as different from our own as any to be found throughout the entire spectrum of human behavior—any time, any place. Because it was so different and because it is difficult at best mentally to shift gears and put yourself "inside" another culture, the reader, unless he is uncommonly imaginative and perceptive, may find himself unable to appreciate the nature and inner workings of Texas Indian cultures. He may come away puzzled and confused. It is also unfortunately true that some of the Texas Indians are so poorly known that only the major features and landmarks of their cultures can be described. Here the scantiness of details is also apt to leave the reader frustrated. Happily, some tribes intimately associated with Texas are well known. But here, too, the reader is asked to be indulgent, for there is so much information available about some tribes, the Comanches,[2] for example, that it is difficult to cram a balanced yet condensed account of their cultures into single chapters. Nor is this book in any sense an exhaustive, final study of Texas Indians. It is instead a first attempt to put together between two covers the fundamental facts about all Texas Indians. It is not a product of original research; it is a synthesis from many sources, including many modern authorities.

I must confess to having another reason for writing this book. It is the conviction, shared by other anthropologists, that by knowing and understanding tribes and nations far removed from ourselves in time or space, we can gain perspective and objectivity in evaluating ourselves and our age. Such knowledge also sets the stage for a more intelligent and rational appreciation of other peoples in the modern world. To some it may seem odd, even grotesque, that a knowledge of savage Karankawas or bloodthirsty Comanches can be of help in this respect. But it is. Knowledge of others forces us to realize that our ways, our beliefs and ideals, are only our own solutions to what may be common human problems. We come to see that there are many ways of thinking and acting, and that simply because other ways are different from our own does not inevitably make them inferior or wrong. In short, comparative studies of cultures help to lessen the provincial, parochial belief in the superiority of one's own culture. In a day when we are closer than ever before to the rest of the world, it is vital that we have the capacity to understand others and to appraise ourselves realistically.

It is all too obvious that in our shrunken, wrangling world the ways in

[2] Throughout this book I have followed Bernard De Voto's admirable departure from anthropological custom and pluralized tribal names where fitting.—See the Preface to *Across the Wide Missouri*, p. xiv.

which different groups of men live and die, think and dream, are tremendously varied. Men, insofar as they have been aware that there were other groups of men, have always attempted to explain these differences. But it has been only within the past century that a science seeking to investigate and appraise all of humanity in a relatively dispassionate way has developed. Since the Texas Indians are treated in this book from this special viewpoint it is necessary to explain briefly what it is. The special viewpoint and concepts are those of anthropology, the broad and inclusive science of human races and civilizations.

One possible answer to the question of why various groups of men—tribes or nations—customarily behave differently from one another (i.e., speak different languages, worship various gods, support different social systems, and prefer to eat different foods), is that they are innately different in their temperaments and biological being. Certainly men do differ from one another; some are short, some tall, some dark, others light, a few stupid, a few brilliant, ad infinitum. Moreover, various geographically distinct populations, such as the American Indians or the natives of Australia, often tend to be physically similar to one another and unlike others. These racial groups are real enough, that is, a number of subspecific, interfertile varieties of *Homo sapiens* can be distinguished (the number depending upon the criteria used to differentiate them). But the most significant fact about the varieties of mankind is that in important anatomical features (lungs, circulatory system, nervous system, etc.) all men are impressively similar. It is the minor details—hair form and color, skin color, nose shape, and so forth—that distinguish them. The numerous differences in custom and behavior that characterize various groups of men have never been traced to differences in the innate capacities of the races involved. All races seem to have intrinsically about the same capabilities. When groups of men do differ in their customary behavior—when, for instance, some avoid their mothers-in-law, believe that disease is caused by witches, and consider the bloody, raw liver of a buffalo the finest delicacy ever to cross the human palate—it is not attributable to their differing biological or racial affiliations. This does not necessarily mean that human races are exactly equal in inherent intellectual capabilities. The members of some races, on the average, may be inherently superior or better able to perform certain activities than the average members of another race. But even if this is so it is still of small moment, for the overlap between racial abilities, whatever they are, must be tremendous. If such differences do in fact exist, their nature is wholly unknown.

We are forced to assume that all groups of men, whatever their racial affiliations, have intrinsically about the same capabilities. Specifically, a Karankawa Indian acted, thought, and dreamed in a particular way not because he, as a representative Karankawa, was different in his biological or physical equipment from other men, whether German, Texan, Hottentot, or Comanche, but because he had learned to be a Karankawa from the moment of his birth. To state it another way, given the opportunity a normal child born of Karankawa parents could have grown up to be—to think and act—like a normal individual of any human society on earth. The Texas Indians are particularly pertinent to this discussion since, racially or biologically speaking, they are a rather homogeneous entity. All are members of the Mongoloid race and belong to its American Indian subdivision. The physical variations of Texas Indians were minor, being confined to slight differences in stature and skin color. If the differences in the behavior of various peoples were rooted in their varying race or biology, we should expect all Texas Indians to have had similar, if not identical, customs and patterns of behavior. Nothing could be further from the actual case. The various tribes of Texas Indians were about as diversified in their behavior as Texans, Frenchmen, Chinese, and Bantus are in theirs.

Since the varying biological make-up of various groups of men fails to explain why these groups can consistently behave so differently, what can? Some would immediately claim that the natural environment or habitat is responsible for the diverse behavior of tribes and nations. Surely the snow, ice, and cold do have a great deal to do with why the Eskimos behave like Eskimos and not like Tahitians. But is it as simple as this? Obviously not, for if the habitat determined how men live, could there ever have been a change from one way of life to some other in an unchanging habitat? The present denizens of Galveston are not Karankawas, not nearly. Yet this habitat has not changed perceptibly since the Karankawas roamed the region. There is a close and intimate relationship between habitats and the ways in which men live, but it is not a determinative one. Habitat I does not produce civilization A, nor habitat II nation B. For any habitat, even those that are restrictive and difficult, there are at least several different methods of living possible and usually a great many more. Anthropologists often dispose of this problem by stating that the habitat limits but does not determine the way of life of a people. To be more concrete, Eskimos cannot raise bananas or figs, and the Tahitians could not utilize the igloo for housing. A knowledge of a people's habitat is important in understanding some of the more immediate problems with which they are faced, and this is certainly so for Texas Indians. But it is not the key to understanding them; it is but the stage on which they tread.

Why, then, were Karankawas Karankawas? Why did they think and act differently from Comanches, Lipans, or for that matter, modern, urban Texans? The answer is their culture. The human organisms called Karankawas behaved in a distinctive Karankawan manner because of the culture that possessed them. This, of course, is not a real answer to our question; it merely gives a name to the phenomena responsible for distinctive Karankawan behavior. "Culture" is a word which is slowly seeping into the public vocabulary, but with a vague, shadowy meaning. It could hardly be otherwise when anthropologists themselves currently use the term in many different ways and with a variety of meanings. Originally most anthropologists embraced the definition set forth by the great English anthropologist Edward B. Tylor: "Culture or civilization, taken in its wide ethnographic sense, is that complex whole which includes knowledge, belief, art, morals, law, custom, and any other capabilities and habits acquired by man as a member of society,"[3] and this remains one of the more useful definitions of culture. For the purposes of this book *a* culture may be taken to mean that "organization of objects (tools, ritualistic paraphernalia, materials of art, etc.), acts (patterns of behavior, customs, rituals, institutions), ideas (belief, knowledge, lore), and sentiments (feelings, attitudes)"[4] which characterize a particular tribe or nation.

Every human organism is born into one culture or another, and quite literally it embraces and envelops him at the moment of birth. We may liken a human infant to a sponge with a thirst for liquids. What it does soak up—oil, salt water, vinegar, ditch water—is determined by the liquid in which it is immersed. Similarly, whether the child grows up to become preacher or cannibal, business tycoon or naked hunter, streetwalker or gleaner in the bush, is determined by the particular culture into which the fates drop him. Different individuals, because of their varied potentialities and the happenstances of their lives, respond in various ways to the cultures in which they find themselves. But a person born in Dallas, no matter what his or her inherent potentialities, cannot grow up there to be a Chinese peasant, a Tibetan lama, or an Eskimo hunter. The native-born

[3] Edward B. Tylor, *Primitive Culture*, Vol. I, p. 1.
[4] Leslie A. White, "Ethnological Theory," pp. 373–374, in *Philosophy for the Future.* For illuminating and detailed discussions of his concept of culture, see *The Science of Culture* and *The Evolution of Culture.*

Dallas youth learns to speak a variety of American English, drive an automobile, kiss girls, believe that polygamy is wrong, call his mother's brother "uncle," and so forth. If he does not learn to do and believe these things it is because he either is naturally defective or has learned otherwise from a foreign cultural source. He cannot, of course, help himself; the human sponge absorbs that culture of which he is a part. In most cultures, in fact, the beliefs, habits, and actions acquired as a member of society are so unquestioningly, unconsciously absorbed that a person does not realize he has "learned" them, nor that there may be alternatives to them. How many Americans (or Dallas youths, if you prefer) ever think that kissing is anything but a "natural" way for the human organism to express affection? Yet in many cultures people do not kiss at all. Much more could be said about the pervasiveness, the hold, which men's cultures have over them, but it is not necessary for our purposes to do so. It is enough to realize that from birth to death, awake or asleep, man is immersed in culture; that men are gripped by cultures which existed centuries before they were born and, barring nuclear annihilation, will continue after they are gone.

We may view culture, too, as something like a stream, flowing down through the ages, gaining mass and momentum as it moves, parting here, rivulets joining there, and farther on maybe an old oxbow, its waters stagnating in the sun. For the great enveloping blanket of culture, this design for living, is an accumulating, changing, moving product of the ages. A half million or a million years ago man's ancestors developed the unique capacity to be cultured, and humanity was born. Early cultures were crude; they did not equip men with effective, efficient ways of living. But as the ages coursed by, knowledge about the world accumulated, men learned how to live in it more efficiently and effectively. The transition from brutish, club-wielding cave dweller to well-fed, long-lived, literate modern has been a slow, arduous, though accelerating climb, a magnificent, overpowering tale of triumph. And today civilization stands on the threshold of even greater triumphs, of developing superior ways of harnessing the forces of nature, of achieving more effective ways of living.

The story of the Texas Indians concerns but a minute segment of human existence, a cupful taken in a moment from the stream of human events. For our interests lie in the nature of historic Texas Indian cultures (Plains tribes excepted) prior to the time they were greatly changed by the contagion of Western civilization.

The chapters have been arranged in an ascending order of technological productivity. Those tribes who, because of environmental restrictions or other reasons, produced the least amount of food and other useful goods have been placed first, the more productive, richer tribes later. Thus, the savages of the Western Gulf culture area—Coahuiltecans and Karankawas —are discussed before the Wichitas and Caddoes. It should be noted, too, that the terms "savage" and "barbaric" are used to indicate levels of technological productivity and are not meant in a disparaging sense.[5] The ranking used is, however, only of the roughest sort; convenience has also played a part. The Lipans should perhaps be placed above the Tonkawas, and the Atakapans, or at least some of them, might well be placed with the Karankawas.

W. W. NEWCOMB, JR.

[5] See Lewis H. Morgan, 1877, *Ancient Society*, Chapter 1.

ACKNOWLEDGMENTS

Many people have helped in various ways to make this book a reality, though only a few can be singled out for mention. Professor Leslie A. White, of the University of Michigan, teacher and friend, gave me the courage to face this task, as well as instilling whatever insight I possess into the nature of culture. The staff of the Texas Memorial Museum has been co-operative and long-suffering. Dr. E. H. Sellards, former director of the Museum, encouraged me in this project. Mrs. Willena Casey Adams, former Museum secretary, has typed the manuscript several times, provided editorial assistance, and always been optimistic about the worth of this endeavor. Hal M. Story, Museum artist, has spent many of his leisure hours working on illustrations. Their completion spurred me on to finish my writing task. Dr. T. N. Campbell, chairman of the Department of Anthropology, University of Texas, has generously given of his time and vast knowledge of Texas Indians. Finally, my wife, Gleny, has been patient and a source of constant encouragement. Without her this could never have been written.

W. W. N., JR.

Texas Memorial Museum
Austin, Texas

TABLE OF CONTENTS

ILLUSTRATIONS

Maps *(Drawn by Hal M. Story)*

xviii

PART I
Before the Written Record

CHAPTER I

The Beginnings

> .   .   .   . All that tread
> The globe are but a handful to the tribes
> That slumber in its bosom.   .   .   .   .   .
> William Cullen Bryant—Thanatopsis

THE DETAILS of the prehistoric past of the Texas Indians can never be fully known and only its barest outlines are suggested here. But no cultures or civilizations can ever be understood unless something is known of their past experiences and development. Could frogs be comprehended if we knew nothing of tadpoles, or butterflies really appreciated if we were ignorant of the caterpillars from which they developed? This outline of Texas Indian prehistory is aimed toward covering the essentials of this story and emphasizing the aged roots Indian cultures had in the soil of Texas.

It is curious but probably not a coincidence that the final chapters of man's evolution occurred during the Pleistocene—the Ice Age epoch which has taken up at most the last million years of earth history. A uniquely intelligent (symbol-using), erect, ground-living, gregarious primate appeared early in the Pleistocene. Before the epoch was over he had evolved his modern physique, and by virtue

3

of his capacity to be cultured had haltingly raised himself by his own bootstraps to become the most formidable, vicious, and successful mammal ever to adorn the face of the world. Toward the close of the Pleistocene, when man was finally able to penetrate the Western Hemisphere, he was already modern physically and had behind him hundreds of thousands of years of painfully slow cultural evolution. While he was by modern standards but a crudely-equipped hunter, he possessed fire, adequate clothing, and an efficient assortment of stone tools and probably some of bone. His material, social, and moral inheritance was such that he was able to withstand the most rugged circumstances a virgin land could impose. He was well equipped to conquer, exploit, and prosper in the New World.

Beginnings are often shrouded and obscure and so it is with the appearance of men in the Americas. Archeologists are just now commencing to uncover evidence which suggests that men first trod upon the North American continent at least several tens of thousands of years ago. But we can scarcely do more than guess what their existence was like, or from what people they sprang, or to whom they bequeathed their ways of living. Still, it is a fascinating pastime to speculate about the earliest Americans, to try to reconstruct their lives from the scattered bits of evidence we possess. That they were modern men in a physical sense is generally assumed. The few bones we have of early Americans (probably not the earliest) are wholly modern; nor would we expect it to be otherwise. The last of the more primitive men, such as the European Neanderthals, died out about a hundred thousand years ago, thousands of years before men gained access to this hemisphere; there were no higher primates from which they might have arisen, and no remains of near-man or physically primitive man have ever been discovered here. Beyond this we can scarcely go. The early Americans probably had affinities with the ancestors of present Mongoloid peoples (Chinese, Japanese, et al.) but it has not been proved. Later migrants surely did have, as is shown by the similarity of modern American Indians to Mongoloid peoples in skin color, hair color and form, and in other physical characters. Yet it is entirely possible that the earliest migrants had other racial connections, that they were destroyed or submerged by later waves of Asiatic, Mongoloid invaders. The racial connections of the early (or Paleo-Americans) would be interesting to know, but this knowledge is inconsequential to the understanding of their ways of living. They were human and that is enough; they were born with very nearly the same potentialities or range of capabilities that modern men are born with.

Most anthropologists are agreed that the earliest migrations to the Americas must have been by way of the Bering Strait between Siberia and Alaska. A map of the world readily shows that this was the only feasible route primitively-equipped people could take, discounting such theories as those which claim the Americas were populated from the mythical continents of Mu or Atlantis. It is also unlikely that ocean-going vessels had been invented at the time men first entered America. This not only bars seaborne invasions originating far away across vast expanses of either the Pacific or Atlantic Oceans, but it also seems improbable that island-hopping via the Komandorskie and Aleutian Islands in the North Pacific was utilized as a method of entry. This leaves but one easy avenue of approach to the Americas—the Bering Strait. Today the Bering Strait is approximately fifty-seven miles wide, but this expanse is broken by the Diomede Islands, and the longest water gap is about twenty-five miles, so land is normally in sight at all times for those who are crossing. During some phases of the Pleistocene ice ages the Bering Strait was considerably narrower and was at times nonexistent; hence Asia and America were at times connected by a land bridge. The alteration in sea levels and the appearance and disappearance of land bridges is an old an frequent occurrence in the earth's geologic history. One of the causes of sea-level fluctuation, and by far the most important so far as the first peopling of the Americas goes, were the ice ages. During glacial periods part of the earth's finite water supply is stored in glacial snow and ice instead of in the ocean reservoirs, and consequently sea levels are lowered. During warm climatic periods moisture which falls on the land is returned to the sea by runoff instead of being held on the land as snow or ice, so sea levels rise. When the various Pleistocene glacial periods reached a climax, sea levels must have been substantially lowered, but by just how much is a

5

matter of dispute. If the present Bering Sea was to be lowered about 150 feet a considerable land bridge connecting Siberia and America would emerge. It should also be pointed out that men could have crossed the ice-choked strait on the ice during cold winter months. This, incidentally, can still be done during particularly cold winters.

Although the earliest waves of American immigrants must have arrived via the Bering Strait, it does not follow that men in much later prehistoric times did not elect other routes. It is generally conceded that from time to time Polynesians and perhaps others may have been cast upon the Pacific shores of America, and it is common knowledge that the Vikings reached the Atlantic Coast of North America. Such chance landings, however, do not appear to have had any appreciable effect on the physical appearance of America's natives or upon the development or nature of their cultures.

The earliest Paleo-Americans known to archeologists were hunters, hunters who ceaselessly followed and stalked the herds of game of their day. Paleontologists know that a number of species of Pleistocene animals migrated back and forth between Asia and America, and necessarily by the Bering Strait route. A wandering, hunting people who stayed near game trails or hung on the fringes of the herds could by sheer accident wander into and so discover a vast new continent. How many times primitive hunters could have blundered across the Bering Strait it is impossible to say; it seems likely that it could have happened a number of times and over a span of thousands of years. After all, the Eskimos until recent, politically restrictive years, found the Bering Strait no physical barrier.

Once in North America, there were several possible avenues of migration into the heart of the continent—even at the height of glacial advances. This last point is important because the most favorable conditions for the formation of a land bridge naturally occurred during glaciations. In Alaska the great central plain, the lowlands bordering the Bering Sea, and the Arctic Coast seem never to have been glaciated, so passage up the Yukon River Valley and to the unglaciated Mackenzie River Valley was possible. From this region a southern migration along ice-free corridors may have been feasible as well. Men also may have been able to pass along the unglaciated

6

Arctic shores and eventually wander south along the Pacific and Atlantic Coasts. The probabilities would seem to be that diverse peoples at various times, bowing to altered conditions, pursued divergent routes once they had crossed the Bering Strait.

Three or four dozen places in America show unmistakable signs of some sort of occupancy by early or Paleo-American men, and the number is being augmented constantly.[1] The remains are confined to stone tools, a few of bone, man-made cutting marks on bone, and other odds and ends. With a few possible exceptions the remains of early man himself have not been surely found. The cultural remains occur frequently, in fact have often been recognized as early, by their association with the fossilized remains of various extinct animals—the mammoth, mastodon, horse, camel, sloth, and others. That fossilized remains of extinct animals are found in direct association with man's tools is a good indication that these tools have considerable antiquity, but exactly how great in terms of years is always a matter of doubt. Various Pleistocene animals became extinct at different times, and some members of every species may have lingered on long after others of their kind had disappeared in less favored regions.

Since the Second World War a more reliable way of dating ancient remains has been developed. This dating method rests upon the fact that every living organism absorbs, along with its normal complement of carbon, a radioactive isotope of carbon, called Carbon 14. It is thought that Carbon 14 is formed by the reaction of cosmic rays with atmospheric nitrogen, and that a constant amount is present in the atmosphere. Since living organisms constantly exchange carbon with the atmosphere, their Carbon 14 content is also constant. But following death no more carbon—and consequently no more Carbon 14—is ingested by an organism. Instead, the radioactive Carbon 14 atoms in the organism begin to decay or disintegrate at a known constant rate. Thus, by measuring the remaining radioactivity of an organic sample it is possible to compute the time elapsed since death. The combination of radiocarbon dates and paleontological and other evidence is permitting archeologists to speak with increasing assurance about the age and duration of prehistoric cultures.

[1] This section relies primarily on Sellards (1952) and Wormington (1957).

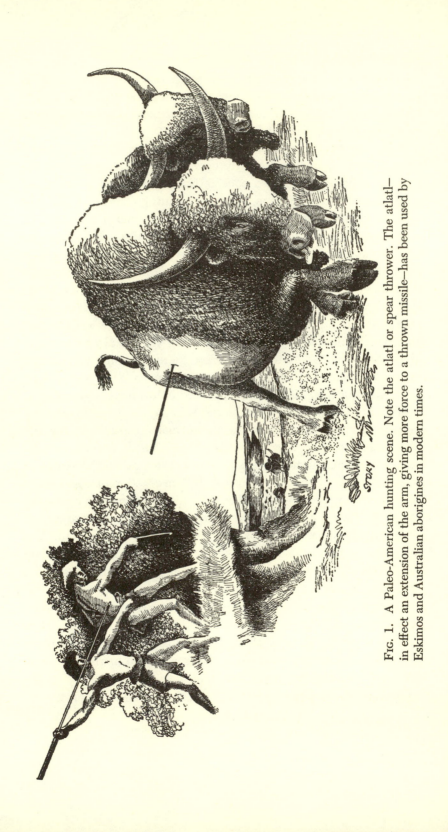

Fig. 1. A Paleo-American hunting scene. Note the atlatl or spear thrower. The atlatl—in effect an extension of the arm, giving more force to a thrown missile—has been used by Eskimos and Australian aborigines in modern times.

Cultural remains left by the Paleo-Americans have been found from the Pacific to the Atlantic Oceans and from Canada to South America, but with an apparent concentration of sites on the High Plains of North America. The earliest cultural relics so far discovered in Texas—and they are among the earliest so far found anywhere in the Americas—have been given the name Llano complex by E. H. Sellards. Llano man was a specialist in hunting an extinct species of elephant (*Elephas columbi*), and one of the favored habitats of this animal was on the Staked Plains (Llano Estacado) of Texas and New Mexico. The sites so far investigated seem to be near what were once water holes, probably spots where game was surprised, killed, and butchered. Several kinds of tools of stone and bone have been found at these places, but the characteristic implement is a flint spear or dart point known as the Clovis Fluted point (Fig. 2a). This type of point has been sporadically found from Alaska to the Texas coast, and one has even turned up in Costa Rica. No other type of projectile point, nor presumably the culture of which it was a part, has such a wide distribution in the New World. Some radiocarbon dates bearing on the time and duration of the Llano culture are beginning to appear. At present the earliest published date for man in America comes from a site near Lewisville in Denton County, Texas. Here members of the Dallas Archeological Society found a number of hearths in the floor of a borrow pit which had been excavated for the Garza–Little Elm Dam. These hearths (at least fourteen are known) contained the charred remains of both modern and extinct Pleistocene animals, shells, and hackberry seeds. A Clovis Fluted point was found in one of the hearths. Charred wood from the same hearth and from the same level, as well as another sample from another hearth, were submitted to a radiocarbon laboratory. It was found that the age of the samples was beyond the testing limits of the laboratory technique, and its limit was thirty-seven thousand years. (Crook and Harris, 1958) While such an early date is not unreasonable, other sites will have to yield comparable dates before this one can be accepted. Heretofore a date of about twelve thousand years ago was thought to be applicable to the Llano complex, and it may still apply to its more recent manifestations.

9

The Llano culture was succeeded on the southern High Plains by the well-known Folsom culture. It is the best known by virtue of being the first authenticated early-man site in America. In 1926, paleontologists from the Colorado Museum of Natural History discovered near the little town of Folsom, in northeastern New Mexico, a distinctive type of projectile point in association with fossil bison bones. The discovery of man-made tools with a long-extinct bison came as a violent shock to an archeological world that believed man to be a recent migrant to America. Acceptance was slow to come, but by the third year of excavation and the discovery of additional tools associated with bison bones, the evidence was convincing to the most skeptical. The nineteen projectile points, found in three seasons of work, were all of a distinctive type and are unlike more modern points. Named Folsom points, they are skillfully and artistically made. Most are about two inches long, somewhat leaf-shaped, with concave bases from which short projections, or ears, extend. Their most distinguishing feature, however, is the longitudinal flutes or channels present in the blade faces. Folsom points (Fig. 2b) are similar, though technically superior, to Clovis Fluted points. It may be that they are flinty descendants of them, adapted to hunting bison or designed to tip new types of weapons, or perhaps they are merely an alteration in style.

Men of Folsom, like the elephant hunters who preceded them, were hunters, but of a now-extinct form of bison (*Bison antiquus*). Folsom points found embedded in the vertebrae of these beasts leave no room to doubt that Folsom men hunted and killed them. Interesting too is the fact that no tail bones of these bison were recovered, suggesting that the animals were skinned, since the tail bone is often removed with the hide.

Since the original discovery many other Folsom points have been found. Compared to Clovis Fluted points, however, they have a more localized distribution, being confined principally to the Great Plains. In Texas, a Folsom site has been excavated by the Texas Memorial Museum near Lubbock, in the valley of the Yellowhouse Draw. Charred bones from the diatomite stratum, in which the Folsom points were found, yielded a radiocarbon date of 9,883 ± 350 years.

10

Snail shells from the diatomite were dated by the same technique and yielded approximately the same age. Another Folsom site has been excavated near Lipscomb, in Lipscomb County, and many Folsom points have turned up elsewhere in the state.

A third and apparently somewhat younger hunting culture came to light during a Texas Memorial Museum excavation of a fossil-bone bed within the city limits of Plainview in Hale County. Here the skeletons of approximately a hundred bison were found jammed together in an area about one foot deep and five hundred feet square. More than two dozen flint tools, including a distinctive projectile point, termed Plainview, were found in the bone bed. The Plainview point (Fig. 2c) is a spear or atlatl point (see Fig. 1) and is similar to the Clovis Fluted point except that it is not channeled or fluted. From the position of the bones and the geological conditions of the site it is clear that the bison had not bogged down in a swamp, and that they had died in a relatively short span of time. It is extremely likely that the men who fashioned the Plainview points either surrounded and killed this herd, or perhaps stampeded them into a gully, just as historic Plains Indians were wont to do. A radiocarbon date of 9,170 ± 500 years ago was obtained from some of the fresh-water snails of the excavation, making Plainview nearly as old as, and perhaps a close cultural relative or descendant of, the Llano culture and/or the Folsom culture. (Sellards, Evans, and Meade, 1947) We should also note that Plainview points are now known throughout the plains from Alaska to Mexico, as well as in Ontario.

There have been other discoveries in Texas of various vestiges of Paleo-American man, but space allows the mention of but two of the most interesting. The most peculiar and certainly the most exotic remains of Paleo-American man ever to turn up in Texas, and probably anywhere in the New World, are the three carved stone heads found in ancient gravels of the Trinity River near Malakoff and Trinidad in Henderson County (see Plate I). In 1929 the first of these carved heads was found by a gravel contractor at the bottom of a gravel pit. In 1935 the second and smallest head was recovered by another gravel contractor, and in 1939 the largest and most peculiar carving turned up in the course of a joint Texas Memorial Museum

11

and WPA excavation of Pleistocene fossils. The first head found weighs about 100 pounds and is roughly egg-shaped, being about 16 inches high and 14 inches wide. The second head is similar to the first, but it is smaller, weighing slightly more than 60 pounds. The third carving weighs 135 pounds; the marks and grooves on it are so crude that it may have been intended to represent some animal other than man. These crude carvings were made upon limestone concretions and lay at the bottom of the highest and oldest of the three terraces of the Trinity River, some 60 to 70 feet above the present flood plain of the river. Fossils taken from the gravel deposits of this terrace included a number of animals that lived before the close of the Pleistocene and have long since been extinct. Important among these were the elephant (*Elephas columbi*), mastodon (*Mastodon americanus*), an extinct horse (*Equus complicatus*), camel (*Camelops*), and ground sloth (*Megalonyx*). (Sellards, 1941) These fossils and the long period of time it must have required to lower the flood plain 60 to 70 feet suggest a considerable age for the carvings. Unfortunately no tools or other indications of humanity or cultural affiliation were found near them. These great stone images must be ancient, but what manner of men fashioned them and for what purpose, remains an unfathomed mystery.

In 1953 the fossilized physical remains of what appeared to be a Paleo-American were found in a "blowout" (a depression left by wind-shifted sands) on the Scharbauer Ranch near Midland. The skull fragments and the few other bones which were recovered were those of a woman, so she has appropriately been dubbed "Midland Minnie." Like many a mature woman, she has been reluctant to divulge her true age. At first she was reputed to be pre-Folsom, but later she was regarded by some archeologists as belonging to the Folsom horizon, maybe to a later one. One of the principal stumbling blocks to dating such a find is the fact that in a blowout all sorts of things could have happened to confuse and distort the true age. Blowing sand can move objects upward or drop them down out of their original positions; hence accurate interpretations are always difficult and seldom, if ever, indisputable. As is to be expected, whatever Midland Minnie's age, her remains are modern and are in no way primitive or less human than those of modern man. The skull is exceedingly longheaded, as are those of most other presumably early Americans, and if longheadedness turns out to be characteristic of Paleo-Americans, then it may have a bearing on their racial connections. (Wendorf, Krieger, Albritton, Stewart, 1955)

So little is known about these Paleo-American peoples that it is frustrating, but perhaps we should count ourselves lucky that we know as much as we do. All told, there never could have been many Paleo-Americans, and being a roving folk they left their own remains and their few imperishable tools scattered far and wide. No wonder that a hundred centuries later they are but poorly known! There are, however, several other pertinent comments which can be made about the Paleo-American pioneers. First, ten thousand years ago there were already in the Americas a number of different groups of people (perhaps they could be called tribes) who differed from one another at least to the extent that they used different kinds of tools and concentrated their hunts on different animals. They may have represented descendants of separate migrations, or they may have become differentiated after they arrived in America. Perhaps the true picture would be a combination of separate migrations of people bearing different cultures, who soon followed divergent routes to various environments in the wide spaces of America. It is certain that men were not long confined to North America, because a radiocarbon date of $8,639 \pm 450$ years has been obtained from some burned bones of sloth and horse in an inhabited cave near the Chile-Argentina boundary in South America. The fact that men had gained the farthest reaches of this hemisphere some nine thousand years ago does not necessarily mean that men occupied the territory nearer the point of entry thousands of years earlier than this. They may well have, but since the Paleo-Americans were nomadic hunters and gatherers, we might expect it to take but a short time—less than a thousand years—for them to spread throughout the hemisphere.

A second comment which may be made is that by our modern standards these early Americans were a courageous, fearless lot. Lacking bows and arrows, and equipped at best with spears and perhaps the spear thrower, they successfully, and by all appearances constantly, hunted the largest and most fearsome mammals in America. By way of illustration, some of the bison hunted by Paleo-Americans were half again as large and probably four times as heavy as our modern bison. It is not known whether they were more dangerous than the modern species, but in any case most people insist upon strong fences or heavy bars between themselves and our pampered, semitamed buffalo. No comment is needed about the awe-inspiring Columbian elephant. Some anthropologists have felt that since Paleo-Americans killed these formidable animals, a number of hunters must have worked in concert. Certainly the bone bed at Plainview suggests some sort of bison stampede, or perhaps a "surround" similar to some of the hunting customs of historic Plains Indians. There is little doubt that the co-operative efforts of a substantial number of hunters would be the most effective manner of hunting these big animals, but it should be remembered that a single African pygmy successfully slays the African elephant with a spear. It would seem reasonable to suppose that what a modern pygmy can do, a Paleo-American hunter could do also.

Lastly, in some fundamental attributes the hunters of Folsom and Plainview were similar to some of the hunting peoples on the plains ten thousand or so years later. Some Texas Indians, such as the pre-horse Tonkawas or Plains Apaches, also relied on the buffalo as their staple food. They too were nomadic, rather crudely-equipped hunters. The weapons of these modern Indians were superior to those of the Paleo-Americans, for they had the bow and arrow, but the remainder of their material culture was likely quite similar, and hence basically these cultures, separated by such a tremendous gulf of years, had much in common. In a sense, what is said about the pre-horse culture of the Tonkawas or Plains Apaches may be thought of as applying in a general way to the cultures of Folsom and Plainview.

The Paleo-American cultures waned along with the final withdrawal of the ice sheets, or perhaps more accurately, they changed so much that they became something else. (Krieger, 1953; Suhm, Krieger, and Jelks, 1954) Many of the animals they hunted became extinct, possibly assisted toward oblivion by these very hunters. As the mammoth, mastodon, ground sloth, giant bison, and others be-

14

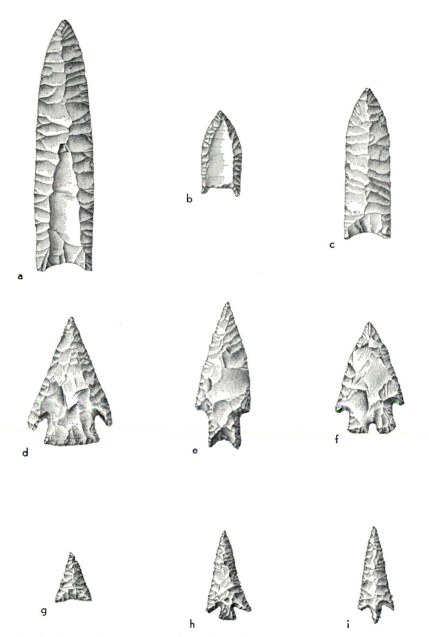

Fig. 2. Projectile points: *a*. Clovis, *b*. Folsom, *c*. Plainview—from Paleo-American stage; *d*. Castroville, *e*. Pedernales, *f*. Montell—from Archaic stage; *g*. Fresno, *h*. Scallorn, *i*. Perdiz—from Neo-American stage.

PLATE I. Carved stone heads from Texas. *Texas Memorial Museum photo-graph.*

came extinct, the hunter had to change his habits. He was forced to hunt other animals and he had to depend more and more upon berries, roots, seeds, and other plant foods. Although the details of what happened have gone dim with the passage of time the general outline of cultural development is clear. The relatively few cultures of the Paleo-Americans were replaced by what seems to have been hundreds of diverse local cultures. There is also archeological evidence for a considerable immigration into North America between 5000 and 2500 B.C. It is likely that there were other immigrants before and after this time who would have contributed to the diversity.

By about 5000 B.C. the Paleo-American cultures of Texas were giving way to these new cultures. How many distinct cultural types there were, their relationships to earlier groups, and their extent remains obscure. They are termed Archaic by archeologists and they lasted for many millenniums. Many of them were finally replaced or grew into the agricultural, pottery-making cultures of the Neo-American stage, from a few hundred to a thousand years after the birth of Christ. The Archaic cultures were typically hunting and gathering ones, as the Paleo-Americans had been, but with a difference. Instead of a small array of beautifully-made flint tools and a few other artifacts, they used an astonishingly large collection of stone tools. By way of illustration, the Edwards Plateau Aspect of the Archaic period is characterized by fifteen types of dart points, and another twelve are of minor or rare occurrence. (Suhm *et al.*, 1954:108) Besides this almost bewildering assortment of dart points, there were a large number of other stone tools: gravers, scrapers, knives, axes, choppers, picks, and drills. Polished stone tools appearing for the first time included pendants, tubular beads, pipes, and bannerstones (atlatl weights). Mortars and pestles also made their appearance, to say nothing of quantities of bone tools. The domestic dog had arrived by Archaic times, but the bow and arrow and its accompanying small, light bird points apparently were not introduced until shortly after the birth of Christ. The appearance of such items as mortars and pestles strongly suggests that the people were having to rely more heavily on seeds and other plant foods than was true in earlier times. The Texas Archaic (Fig. 2*d,e,f*) seems to be an elaboration upon earlier cultures, altered to fit different environments, and benefiting from the diffusion of foreign traits. The Archaic cultures were certainly richer, and they have an appearance of assurance and competence that the Paleo-American cultures lack. But it is to be doubted that life for the Archaic hunter and gatherer was substantially more rewarding than that of his predecessors.

If this were all there was to the prehistory of America, if cultural evolution had proceeded no further than the hunting and gathering level displayed by Archaic peoples, the story would be considerably easier to relate, but not very dramatic, perhaps not even very important. But this was not the case, for in some parts of the New World cultural development went far beyond this primitive stage. In fact, some of the native American civilizations rivaled in many respects those of fifteenth-century Europe. The crucial technological revolution upon which the great native American civilizations were reared was the farming revolution. At some place or places in Mexico and Central or South America, at least several millenniums before the beginning of the Christian era, men began to domesticate a large number of food plants as well as a few animals. Today the average city man takes his farm products—especially the cereals—pretty much for granted; perhaps familiarity breeds forgetfulness. Nevertheless, every great civilization of antiquity became great through the cultivation of some cereal. The world's great modern civilizations are, of course, based upon the efficient cultivation of wheat and allied grains, rice, and Indian corn or maize.

Just where and when Indian corn was first domesticated is a moot question, although it is known that it had a long period of development and accidental hybridization before it attained the form it has today. The earliest dated remains of corn so far reported are from Bat Cave in New Mexico and from caves near Ocampo, in Tamaulipas, Mexico. Primitive corn from both places yielded radiocarbon dates of approximately 2500 B.C. (Whitaker *et al.*, 1957:354) If corn originated somewhere in Central or South America, as is considered likely, a fairly long span of time has to be allowed for it to spread into Tamaulipas and New Mexico—far to the north.

By the time Europeans appeared on the scene, corn was being

cultivated just about to its environmental limits, limits which modern plant scientists have scarcely been able to extend. While corn was the most valuable domesticated plant in aboriginal America, there were a whole host of other domesticated plants of considerable importance. Among them were Irish potatoes, sweet potatoes, manioc (from which tapioca is made), several varieties of beans, squash, pumpkins, peanuts, tomatoes, chocolate, rubber, long-staple cotton, and tobacco. The value of these plants is shown by the fact that something like three-fifths of the modern world's agricultural wealth derives from plants first domesticated by American Indians. The domestication of these plants in the New World was, then, not only the cornerstone of Indian civilizations but was also basic and fundamental to modern American civilization. This tremendous debt owed to prehistoric American Indians is hardly ever mentioned; perhaps the debt is so great that the mere thought of it is embarrassing. It certainly should be to those who cling to the notion that American Indians were lazy, shiftless, indolent, and dull. The animals that the American Indians were able to tame were meager in comparison to their considerable number of domesticated plants. The llama, alpaca, guinea pig, and the Muscovy duck were domesticated in South America, and the turkey (for his feathers) was domesticated in Middle or North America. The economic importance of these animals is slight when compared to those domesticated in the Old World. But this lack can hardly be blamed on the Indians—there were no animals in America comparable to the horses, cattle, sheep, or swine of the Old World.

The American food-producing revolution meant essentially that with the same expenditure of energy and time more food and other useful things could be produced by farming than by hunting, gathering, or fishing. With the agricultural revolution, man began to nurture, to augment, and to control the productivity of his environment. Hunters and gatherers had no more control over the abundance of their food supply than does a pack of jackals; they had to be content with whatever nature provided. The far-reaching results of this technological revolution in America were similar to those that followed the Neolithic revolution in the Old World. Populations became larger and denser, for they no longer depended upon how many buffalo could be killed, or how abundant would be the harvest of roots and berries, but rather upon how many crops could be raised. It meant, too, that life was more secure, since survival no longer depended upon an unpredictable supply of wild foods. As soon as agriculture became fairly efficient only a portion of the population had to be producers of food. Some—the number depending upon the crops raised and the techniques possessed to raise them—could do other things; they could be priests, chiefs, traders, artisans, soldiers, artists, and so forth. No longer was nomadism a useful feature of life; men ordinarily had to stay in one place in order to plant, till, harvest, and protect their crops. Or perhaps it should be put the other way around: after men harvest a granary of grain they are not apt to go off and leave it, and it is too difficult to haul it around. Not only did the agricultural Indians settle down, but in some areas cities eventually came into being—like the native Mexico City—which were comparable in many respects to Ur, Memphis, Babylon, or Imperial Rome. Like these others, native American cities were characterized by a disciplined political organization, palaces, temples, and pyramids. In them the fine arts, mathematics, writing, and astronomy flourished. These were still essentially Stone Age civilizations, it is true, but ornaments of gold, silver, copper, and various alloys were worked with mastery and artistry by some Middle and South American Indians.

Only today are we beginning to appreciate the scale, the complexity, the host of accomplishments, and the long cultural evolution which marked the great cultures of the Americas. When Europeans began to overrun the Western Hemisphere in the last years of the fifteenth century they found the greatest civilizations—in terms of population, wealth, technological productivity, urbanization, advancement of political institutions, development of art, and the like —to be concentrated between the Valley of Mexico on the north, and the Peruvian Andes on the south. In the fifteenth century the peaks of native civilization lay with the Aztecs in the Valley of Mexico, the fading Maya in the Peninsula of Yucatán, and the Inca Empire of the South American Andes. This area of great civilizations has conveniently been termed Nuclear America. (Kroeber, 1948:

18

779–780) These nations had not always been in the forefront of cultural advance, any more than have the nations of western Europe always led the parade of technological progress. Many different civilizations developed at various times in this Nuclear region; they flourished at different times and waned or were replaced in different ages.

The Indian empires and nations of fifteenth-century Nuclear America and their cultural forebears were centers from which flowed all sorts of cultural stimuluses—ideas, material items, probably people—to the less advanced and more backward areas. Just how, when and from what places, and by what routes they spread into what is now the United States is as yet vague. The geographical position of Texas would lead a casual observer to expect that the Texas Indians, being relatively near the southern centers of development, would have shared some of the blessings of cultural advancement, or at least more of them than peoples farther away. Even if, for some reason, the Texas Indians themselves failed to benefit from their proximity to the center of things, it would be logical to expect that cultural impulses would have passed through Texas on their way to more receptive people and places. There is little evidence, however, that either of these expectations is correct. The more advanced historic tribes of Texas owed their status to cultural centers to the east and west, and only in an indirect and secondary way to the high civilizations to the south. The hypothesis that a migration passed through Texas, pipeline fashion, from Mexico to the southeastern section of what is now the United States, leaving no imprint whatsoever on the traversed region, is unbelievable. Almost certainly Texas was bypassed by the sporadic, episodic cultural ripples emanating from the south. The main reason for this is obvious: it was environmental. On the Gulf Coast, stretching for two hundred miles on either side of the Rio Grande and expanding inland to include a tremendous area in northeastern Mexico and southern and southwestern Texas, is an arid semidesert. Without irrigation agriculture is next to impossible throughout this inhospitable land. It would be an effective barrier to barbaric gardeners bent on colonization, plunder, or probably even exploration. The most logical hypothesis seems to be that

19

the influences which did trickle north from the centers of civilization circled Texas in a giant pincher movement. In the west, the slopes of the Mexican Sierra Madre Occidental provided a passageway for cultural influences to spread into the southwestern part of the United States. The first cultural stimulus was felt well before the beginning of the Christian era, and by the time the Spanish conquistadors overran what is now New Mexico and Arizona, the colorful, distinctive, and durable Puebloan cultural pattern was already of venerable age. In turn the Puebloan pattern affected, and to a minor degree had spread into, Texas.

To the east, an apparently seaborne movement from some unknown Caribbean shore spread another type of cultural pattern into the southeastern United States. In time it advanced into east Texas, where at the start of recorded history in this area the Caddoes possessed the richest and most advanced of Texas' Indian cultures. The archeology of the Southeast is not nearly so well understood as that of the Southwest, but it is known that a thousand or so years ago a culture with a strong Mexican bent had already spread from the Gulf Coast up the Mississippi virtually to the Great Lakes. These people were farmers as were the Southwesterners, but here the resemblance ended. Like the Aztecs, Toltecs, and Mayas, they were mound builders. But instead of stone-faced or plastered structures, theirs were simply earthen. Many were from forty to fifty feet high and were usually rectangular. On the flat tops of these mounds were wooden temples, priests' dwellings, and other structures. Log-faced stairs led from ceremonial courts or plazas to the tops of the impressive structures. These temple mounds—built by basketload after basketload of earth carried on the backs of the citizenry—are an expression of a developed technological base and an advanced and well-organized society which was probably focused upon a religion based on sun worship. Even in historic times these Southeasterners appear to have had a provincial watered-down version of the great Mexican culture. There are so many resemblances between the two areas, not only in fundamental cultural matters but also in such minor details as feather mantles, littters for chieftains, and the like, that there is no room to doubt the basic affiliation.

20

My hypothesis is not favored by many—perhaps most—archeologists, chiefly, it appears, because it requires a waterborne movement, and archeologists are morally committed to Mother Earth. They have labored mightily to trace a migration through Texas, or at least to find in central and south Texas some shred of evidence that an advanced civilization dwelled here or passed this way. Their fruitless efforts would seem to point all the more strongly to a seaborne entry into the Southeast.[2]

In this day of increasing conformity and standardization, the sprawling state of Texas remains the meeting ground and melting pot of the Old South, the Spanish Southwest, and the Midwest. So it was in Indian times, but magnified then many times over. The various tribes and nations of Texas Indians were not fashioned from the same cloth; in some cases they were not even vaguely similar. Some differed in their modes of living about as much as Texans do from Tibetans. Accidentally, so far as the rambling political boundaries of Texas are concerned, Texas Indians were members of one or another of four different cultural traditions. These regionally distinctive cultural types varied from each other in a manner roughly parallel to the differences in custom and tradition which distinguish modern Japan, China, Australia, and Pakistan.

Covering most of the coastal areas of the state and all of south Texas, as well as a large region in northeastern Mexico, were the Coahuiltecan and Karankawan tribes of the Western Gulf culture area. (Newcomb, 1956) This region has been traditionally thought of by anthropologists as a "cultural sink," apparently because so little was known about its original residents and because the cultures of the area were backward and "low" (meaning nonagricultural) as compared to the relatively nearby "high" (agricultural) cultures of highland Mexico, those of the Southeast culture area, and the somewhat more distant and less high Puebloan cultures of the Southwest cultural area. "Cultural sink" suggests some sort of cesspool where the cultural offal of many people has been discarded. This characterization is ridiculous and is a libelous slur on some fascinating

[2] For varying viewpoints, see Beals, 1932: 149–150; Krieger, 1948; 1953: 253; MacNeish, 1947; Mason, 1935; 1937; Newell and Krieger, 1949: 224–232.

Indians who do not deserve it. These aboriginal south Texans lived in a rugged area environmentally; the farming methods of the east Texas Caddoes simply would not work here, nor would the farmers of the Mexican highlands have found this a desirable land. Primitive cultures in harsh regions such as this are confined and restricted by the never-ending task of warding off starvation. They cannot display the frills and foibles of cultures in more abundant regions. Instead, their cultures are overwhelmingly oriented toward bare physical survival. The tale of how the poorly- and crudely-equipped savages of the Western Gulf region managed to wrest a scant living from their niggardly world is revealing, certainly from the point of view of the things to which the human system can become accustomed.

At the opening of the historic period a number of scattered bands of Indians, known today as Tonkawas, roamed over much of central Texas. Just where they belonged in a cultural sense has been difficult to decide, perhaps because they were truly transitional between two cultural types. Linguistically their affiliations seem to have been with the cultures of the Western Gulf area. By the eighteenth century, if not earlier, they were a buffalo-hunting, tepee-using, mounted Plains people, similar to other southern Plains tribes. Knowledge of the Tonkawas dates principally from this period, so they are considered here as being members of the Plains culture area. Probably adjoining the Tonkawas to the northwest in prehistoric times, and closely associated with them by the nineteenth century, were the ancestors of the Lipan Apaches. The Apaches of this eastern branch were also plainsmen; in fact, their Plains Apache forerunners were probably among the originators of much of the Plains culture which was followed by many western tribes during the eighteenth and nineteenth centuries. The other Plains tribes vitally associated with Texas in those early days were Kiowa Apaches, Kiowas, and especially Comanches. The Kiowa Apaches, close cultural relatives of the Lipan Apaches, joined the Kiowas at some unknown date. These confederated tribes, along with the Comanches, are often thought of as the real Texas Indians. In many respects their pre-eminent position is justified, yet the Comanches and Kiowas were not indigenous to the state and did not appear within its borders until after 1700.

In trans-Pecos Texas, and particularly in the Rio Grande Valley from El Paso downstream as far as the junction of the Rio Grande with the Mexican Rio Conchos, lived a people at the beginning of history who are known variously as the Patarabueye, Jumano, Suma, and by some other names. This culture type is the least known and the most enigmatic of all the far-flung Texas natives. Culturally the Jumanos were peripheral members of the Puebloan culture of the Southwest, but the exact nature of their culture and its relationships with other tribal cultures are for the most part a mystery.

Around 1700, Spanish Texas was invaded from the north by some groups of related Indians, known today as the Wichitas. These semi-sedentary tribes were the Wichita proper, including the Taovayas, Tawakonis, Wacos, and Kichais. Their settlements extended at times as far south as Waco and central Texas, but the Wichitas' headquarters, and the major crossroads of the eighteenth-century southern plains, was at Spanish Fort on the Red River. None of the Wichita peoples were in Texas in prehistoric days as far as is known, but their importance in the development of the state makes them an integral and important part of the story of Texas Indians. Linguistically and in other cultural respects the Wichitas had much in common with the Caddoes of the Southeast culture area. But during the eighteenth century following their adoption of horses, their culture became increasingly Plains-like. As a result, the Wichitas are sometimes classified as belonging to the Southeast culture area and sometimes to that of the Plains. (Kroeber, 1947:74–76)

At the dawn of historic times in east and northeast Texas and adjacent portions of Louisiana, Arkansas, and Oklahoma, lived about two dozen tribes of Caddo Indians. These were mostly joined together in confederacies, and the Kadohadacho and Hasinai confederacies particularly possessed the richest and most advanced cultures of all Texas Indians in terms of their techniques for exploiting the world. If the Comanches might be likened to the Asiatic Huns, the Caddoes might crudely be called the Romans of Texas. Culturally the Caddo confederacies were members of a Southeast culture area. The center and focal point of this cultural type was among the Natchez in the lower Mississippi Valley. The Natchez, in turn, and

23

the other peoples of the Southeast area, were linked to, if not a part of, a pattern of culture which has been termed Circum-Caribbean. (Steward, 1947) This civilization—and the term may be likened to the nations that make up European civilization—ranged from Colombia and Venezuela through the Greater Antilles to Florida. The Circum-Caribbean tribes were characterized as a farming and seafaring people. They were far enough advanced to have a class-structured society, based upon an intensive and productive agriculture. South of the Caddoes, on the coast and along the lower reaches of the Trinity River, were the Atakapans, dim reflections of the Caddoes' grandeur. These Atakapan tribes (Deadoses, Bidais, Patiris, Akokisas, and Atakapa proper) were in the hinterland, the sticks of the Southeast culture area, a relationship not altogether unlike the one which might be said to prevail between Muleshoe, Texas, and New York City.

These four basic culture patterns spanning the broad face of Texas at the beginning of history are convenient categories—pigeon holes—in which distinctive tribes may be grouped. In later years, too, Indians of tribes representative of all the major patterns of living in the eastern half of the United States ventured into Texas at one time or another—Delawares, Shawnees, members of the Five Civilized Tribes, Kickapoos, and others. The cultures of these migrant tribes and the vicissitudes of their history make an interesting story, but space limitations and the fact that their stay in Texas was usually so brief have meant that they have been excluded from further mention. Some migrant tribes succeeded in remaining in Texas. One is the Alabama-Coushatta, whose descendants live today on a reservation in Polk County in east Texas. The others are Puebloan fragments, Tigua, Piros, and perhaps others, brought to missions in and around El Paso at the end of the seventeenth century by Spaniards. They were thoroughly Mexicanized by the beginning of the twentieth century, and are presumably extinct today in a cultural sense. (Hodge, 1907a, Pt. 1: 624; Fewkes, 1902)

The cultures of the original inhabitants of Texas have long since been destroyed, often viciously. At best a few tribes have managed to be only critically wounded by a conquering, antagonistic white

24

world. Not one of the original Texas Indian cultures survives within the borders of the state. Some prolong the twilight of their existence on reservations in other states, but their story is no longer that of distinct cultures in our midst, but of a dispersed, insignificant minority. A handful of Lipan Apaches now dwell on the Mescalero Reservation in New Mexico; a few Tonkawas survive in Oklahoma. The Wichitas, Caddoes, and Comanches are concentrated on reservations in southwestern Oklahoma, shattered remnants of proud cultures. The others have disappeared—the Karankawas, Coahuiltecans, Atakapans, Jumanos—irrevocably, finally extinguished.

Despite the extinction of some Texas Indian cultures, and the dramatic alterations which have taken place in others, most if not all of the Texas Indians—in a genetic, biological sense—have managed in some degree to survive. It has become a truism to anthropologists that wherever and whenever peoples of alien cultures meet, they may fight one another, one people may even exterminate the other, or they may intermingle peaceably, but one thing they almost always do is interbreed. The collision of Texas Indians with Spaniards, Frenchmen, Mexicans, Texans, and Americans did not violate this rule. Many Coahuiltecans and Jumanos, some bands of Tonkawas, and no doubt others, were "tamed" by Spanish padres. They became Mission Indians, they forgot their old ways, and their descendants became part of the newly-emergent Spanish-Mexican civilization. There is no way of knowing how many of their descendants there are in Mexico, and how many continue as part of the Texas Latin-American minority. How much of a genetic contribution these and other Texas aborigines made to the white and Negro population of Texas is even more enigmatic. That it was made is certain; that it was greater than is generally believed seems likely.

PART II
Savages of the Western Gulf Culture Area

CHAPTER 2

The Coahuiltecans: South Texas

> I believe these people see and hear better, and have
> keener senses than any other in the world. They are
> great in hunger, thirst, and cold, as if they were made
> for the endurance of these more than other men, by
> habit and nature.
>
> Cabeza de Vaca (1528)

THE AREA from Galveston Bay south along the coast to the Rio
Grande, and westward from the mouth of the Trinity, passing near
San Antonio and crossing the Rio Grande somewhere below the
mouth of the Pecos, was the sixteenth-century Texas boundary of a
remarkable group of tribes, today long extinct.[1] The coastal bands
are known as Karankawas, the inland groups as Coahuiltecans, and
they are lumped together as the members of the Western Gulf culture area.(Newcomb, 1956) South of the Rio Grande the Western
Gulf cultures occupied a tremendous region, as far south on the coast
as the Rio Pánuco and encompassing inland the present Mexican
states of Tamaulipas, Nuevo León, the northeastern parts of Coahuila, northern San Luis Potosí, and northeastern Zacatecas. All the

[1] The principal sources for this chapter are the journal of Cabeza de Vaca
(Hodge, 1907b) and Ruecking, 1953, 1954a, 1954b, 1955.

29

peoples of this tremendous region in Texas and Mexico apparently spoke dialects or languages of a common linguistic stock, Coahuiltecan. While there were numerous minor cultural differences distinguishing various Coahuiltecan subgroups from one another and from the coastal Karankawas, they were all poorly-equipped, primitive hunters and gatherers.

South of the Balcones Escarpment and the San Antonio River lies an arid rolling plain. Much of it is covered with a dense, often impenetrable, growth of stunted trees and thorny shrubs; it is the land familiarly known as the Brush Country or the *Monte*. To the modern traveler streaking over its highways in chromeplated luxury, it seems incredible that this dry and rocky land with its thorny desert plants could yield enough wild food to support men. Yet it did for thousands of years. Even with modern technological know-how, agriculture is possible here only where irrigation can be practiced. Much of south Texas is ranch land today, but for the Indians, who had no domesticated animal other than a barkless dog, stock-raising was also impossible. Large game animals were scarce throughout the region, though a few bison wandered into south Texas, and deer, antelope, and javelina (collared peccary) were present. There were a number of small edible animals, including rabbits and other rodents, reptiles, birds, and bugs. No single animal species was plentiful enough to provide a continuing food supply, however, and all of them together could yield only a minor, though seasonally important, part of the foods eaten. Men had to rely mostly upon plant food to live here. And the uses to which the aborigines put various cacti, mesquite beans, nuts, sotol, agave, and other plants are the heart and soul of the story of the Coahuiltecans of south Texas. In short, for those who were wise to the possibilities of this land and catholic in their tastes, this was a livable and occasionally even a bountiful region.

Origins and Early History. Coahuiltecans were divided and subdivided into a large number of small tribes and bands, Swanton (1952:309–311) listing more than two hundred. While their exact number, location, and affiliation may never be known precisely, it appears that in south Texas there were four or five groups of tribes, each composed of an ill-known number of bands. In some cases bands seem to have been independent, autonomous units, lacking any formal political connections with other groups; in other instances they were at least temporarily united under tribal leaders.

San Pedro Springs, in present San Antonio, was the focal point of three or more affiliated Coahuiltecan bands known as the Payayas. How extensive their territory was in this neighborhood is unknown. To the southeast of the Payayas, between the San Antonio and Guadalupe Rivers, were the Aranamas. They and the associated Tamiques (Hodge, 1907a, Pt. 2:682–683) were linguistically distinct from the coastal Karankawas and seem to have formed a second Coahuiltecan grouping. Along the lower Nueces, south of the Aranamas, were a number of poorly-known Coahuiltecan bands termed Orejons. The evidence appears good that these dozen or more bands shared a common Coahuiltecan dialect. (Reucking, 1954b:3–4) Upstream, somewhere about the junction of the Frio with the Nueces, and occupying a large extent of territory, perhaps crossing the Rio Grande, were a number of bands termed the Pachal, named after the band that roamed near the junction of the Frio and the Nueces. Mexico-based bands that may have ranged into Texas were the Katuhanos, normally occupying the territory between the Rio Salado and Rio Grande, the Kesale-Terkodams, a large number of bands based in Coahuila but probably extending northward across the Rio Grande, and the Carrizos, a number of linguistically affiliated bands located along the lower Rio Grande and the San Juan of Tamaulipas (Map 1).

The prehistoric past of the south Texas Coahuiltecans is not well known, which is not surprising considering the fact that such crudely-equipped hunters and gatherers as these prehistoric peoples must have been, left behind few imperishable items for archeologists to find. And archeologists are notoriously reluctant to explore such sun-scorched, prickly, uninviting, and relatively unproductive regions. From excavations carried out in the Falcón Reservoir on the Rio Grande, however, it appears that this region was occupied for a very long time by nearly static cultures. Dart points, for example, which were characteristic of the area in Archaic times were found lying on the floors of Spanish-type houses built in the eighteenth century and presumably they were made by the Indians who occupied them. (Suhm *et al.*, 1954:138)

One reason for this curious state of affairs is that since this type of habitat limits and narrows the cultural patterns that are possible, once one method of survival has been worked out, the possibility that another and strikingly different mode of existence will be developed is remote. The people in such a culture are constantly busy supplying minimum needs; they cannot hazard the experiment of trying to find some new way of life. And in difficult habitats, such as the semideserts of south Texas, external influences which might stimulate cultural change are apt to be minimal. Outsiders are not attracted to such regions and its inhabitants are not likely to have surplus products to trade. But even on the basis of fragmentary evidence, south Texas has the appearance of a relict region, an isolated backwash in which cultures remained virtually unchanged for long periods.

Other evidence suggests that the Coahuiltecans of south Texas were anachronisms so far as other Texas Indians were concerned. Linguistically, Coahuiltecan-speaking peoples were related to the Hokan group of languages of California; in fact, Coahuiltecan is by many termed a Hokan language. (Sapir, 1920; Swanton, 1940; Ruecking, 1955) There were also some striking resemblances between the kinship system of the Yuman (Hokan-speaking) tribes of southern California and the Coahuiltecans (Ruecking, 1955), although some of them may be the natural result of a similar life rather than a common history. Between the Hokan-speaking peoples on the Pacific side of the continent and the Coahuiltecans of the Western Gulf culture area on the eastern side lay a tremendous gap. Two linguistic families occupied this intervening territory in early historic times: the Athapaskans, who are generally regarded as late-comers; and the speakers of Uto-Aztekan, a superlanguage stock whose members dwelled mostly in the deserts and plateaus extending from eastern Oregon to the Valley of Mexico. There are several ways in which the Hokan-Coahuiltecans could have become separated from one another in some dim, prehistoric era. One appealing hypothesis is that thousands of years ago the Hokan-Coahuiltecans were a contiguous or single people, perhaps occupying the entire breadth of the continent. Waves of invading Uto-Aztekan- or Athapaskan-speaking peoples split these early settlers into two groups or drove the two fragments into their historic ranges. Or, perhaps the wedge driven through their midst submerged and absorbed the groups in their immediate path, leaving untouched the outlying Hokan-speakers on the west and the Coahuiltecans on the east in their isolated, relatively unattractive lands. Swanton (1940: 145) asks: "May it not be that the aboriginal Californians and south Texans represented remnants of earlier waves, split in two by these late-comers and driven west and east respectively?"

This is conjectural but it has the ring of truth about it. The same sequence of events has occurred repeatedly in man's history; an invader with superior cultural equipment supplants and replaces a technologically inferior group. If the inferior culture survives, it frequently does so in marginal areas not coveted by the invader. A dominant Uto-Aztekan or Athapaskan culture may have supplanted an ancestral Hokan-Coahuiltecan culture, in much the same way that Americans replaced and relegated American Indians to marginal and generally unfavorable regions. Thus, the Coahuiltecans who were pushed into the Western Gulf culture area or merely survived there continued their primitive life for untold centuries, truly fossil cultures when encountered by Europeans in the sixteenth century.

The story of the sixteenth-century Coahuiltecans and Karankawas is intimately bound up with that fabulous Spaniard Cabeza de Vaca. He lived for eight years (1528–36) as a captive, trader, and medicine man among one or another group of south Texas Indians, passed entirely through their country, and undoubtedly knew them better than any other European or American ever did afterward. I have made considerable use of his journal here.[2] Álvar Núñez Cabeza de

[2] Anthropologists have never made much use of De Vaca's journal, principally because they were in doubt about where he was and to what people he alluded. Fortunately his route has been re-analyzed (Krieger, n.d., MS), and there is little doubt in my mind that this new interpretation is correct. (Also see Krieger, 1956: 47–58.) From the time the Spaniards were shipwrecked on

33

Vaca had been the treasurer of the expedition of Pánfilo de Narváez which had set out to conquer and colonize a vast area between eastern Mexico and Florida. His fleet had left a land party of three hundred men, including Cabeza de Vaca, on the Gulf Coast. After many difficulties this party escaped the inhospitable land by building five barges. With these they hoped to make their way along the coast to Pánuco, near present Tampico, but all were eventually lost. De Vaca's vessel was cast ashore on the Texas coast in the month of November, either on Galveston Island or on Velasco Peninsula just to the south (see Map 1). Eighty Spaniards were marooned on this bit of land, named by De Vaca the Island of Ill Fate. By the following spring only fifteen of this number remained; four had set out for Pánuco, and the rest had perished from disease or starvation. Only four of this number were ever to see civilization again: Dorantes, his Negro slave Estevánico, Castillo, and Cabeza de Vaca. By becoming a trader and later a medico-religious practitioner or shaman, De Vaca as well as his three companions was able to survive; in fact, after learning what was expected of them, they were accorded great deference and respect throughout the Coahuiltecan area. They turned aside sometime after crossing the Rio Grande and eventually emerged on the other side of the continent, on the Gulf of Lower California, from whence they proceeded to Mexico City and civilization.

After their meeting with the survivors of the Narváez Expedition, the south Texas Indians had little or no further contact with Spaniards until the seventeenth century. Luis de Carabajal had been authorized to found the kingdom of Nuevo León in 1579 and it was to extend into what is now Texas. By 1583 the capital city of León, now the pleasant little village of Cerralvo, was founded a few miles south of the Rio Grande. It remained the northeastern outpost of

---

the wild Texas coast, only one objective was in their minds—to get to Pánuco (Veracruz). That they wandered off in every direction but south is impossible. It is true that once across the Rio Grande, De Vaca turned aside, but it was not because he was lost, but probably because he was being treated so royally by the natives that he decided to salvage something from the horrors of those years. All citations from Cabeza de Vaca are from Hodge, 1907b, and throughout this chapter will be noted by page numbers only.

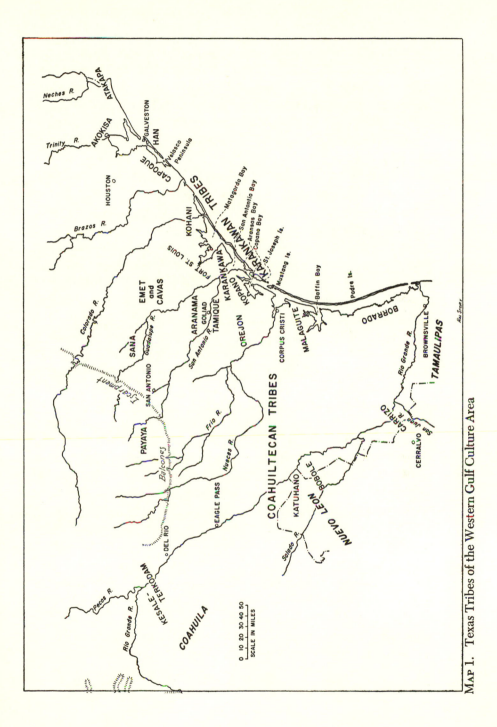

MAP 1. Texas Tribes of the Western Gulf Culture Area

Spanish dominion until after 1650. The Indians to the northward were hostile, and in 1655 a Spanish force of slightly more than a hundred men, accompanied by some three hundred Indian allies, and led by Fernande de Azcue, crossed the Rio Grande in pursuit of the Cacaxtles, an important subgroup of the Kesale-Terkodam Coahuiltecans. Some sixty miles beyond the Rio Grande they met these Indians, killed a hundred warriors and took seventy prisoners. (Bolton, 1916:283 ff.)

After 1670 the Spanish again attempted to push the frontier northward, this time principally through missionary activity. The pioneer in these efforts was Father Juan Larios, a Franciscan friar. In 1675, after five years' experience in the newly-founded province of Coahuila, Larios accompanied an expedition led by Fernando del Bosque across the Rio Grande. The expedition crossed the Rio Grande near Eagle Pass and traveled northward to the vicinity of present Edwards County. The Spaniards encountered three groups or tribes of native peoples. Smallpox had already spread to the Indians and was decimating their ranks. (Bolton, 1916: 298) Bosque's account reveals little else about the natives, however, other than that some of them were hunting bison and jerking meat and that various tribal groups were at war with one another. As a result of this expedition four Franciscan missions were established in the Coahuila district.

The mission of Santa Rosa de Nadadores was established in 1677, forty leagues northeast of Coahuila. In 1693 it was moved seven leagues northeast the better to minister to the Cotzales and Manos Prietos. (Swanton, 1940: 2) San Bernardo de la Candela ministered to the Catujanes, Tilijaes, and Milijaes, and other missions were begun toward the close of the seventeenth century for south Texas Indians.

The news that the Frenchman La Salle had built a fort on Matagorda Bay led to an expedition by Alonso de León in 1689 to destroy it. In the next year he led another expedition through Coahuiltecan territory, but neither of his accounts provides us with much knowledge of Coahuiltecans. In 1700 the mission of San Francisco Solano was established on the Rio Grande below present Eagle Pass. In

1718 it was moved to San Antonio where it became known as San Antonio de Valero—later to gain fame as the Alamo. In response to the presence of French traders and explorers in southeast Texas, in 1722 the Spaniards established a fort, La Bahía, and the mission of Espíritu Santo de Zuñiga in Karankawa territory. In 1726 the mission was moved to the lower San Antonio River among the Aranama Indians. In 1749 it was again moved, this time to a location opposite Goliad, where it served both Karankawa and Coahuiltecan remnants.

Other Franciscan missions were started for Coahuiltecans in the early years of the eighteenth century, and for a time they flourished and drew to them large numbers of Coahuiltecans. But introduced diseases rapidly diminished the native population, hostile Apaches and Comanches killed more and made life in the missions hazardous. By 1800 most of the south Texas Coahuiltecans had disappeared, having been destroyed by disease or absorbed into the Mexican populace, and many of the missions had been abandoned or secularized. By the time Anglo-Americans began to settle Texas the far-flung Coahuiltecans had dwindled almost to nothingness. In northern Mexico small acculturated groups persisted longer, but by the end of the nineteenth century they also had disappeared.

Appearance and Dress. Cabeza de Vaca found Coahuiltecans varied in appearance to the extent that different groups varied somewhat in skin pigmentation and in build. But he mentioned no particularly distinguishing physical characters as he did for the coastal Karankawas. Only one tribe did he single out (p. 65) for comment, the Yguazes: "This people are universally good archers and of a fine symmetry, although not so large as those [Karankawas] we left. They have a nipple and a lip bored." De Vaca was impressed, however, with the endurance and fortitude of Coahuiltecans. He noted, for instance, that the men could run after a deer for an entire day without resting and without apparent fatigue. It would be hard to give credence to such endurance if we did not know that equal vigor was true of other American Indians also. Even today the Tarahumaras of Mexico maintain this stamina to a remarkable degree. De Vaca (p. 86) was also impressed by the fact that they were so difficult to kill: ". . . often-times the body of an

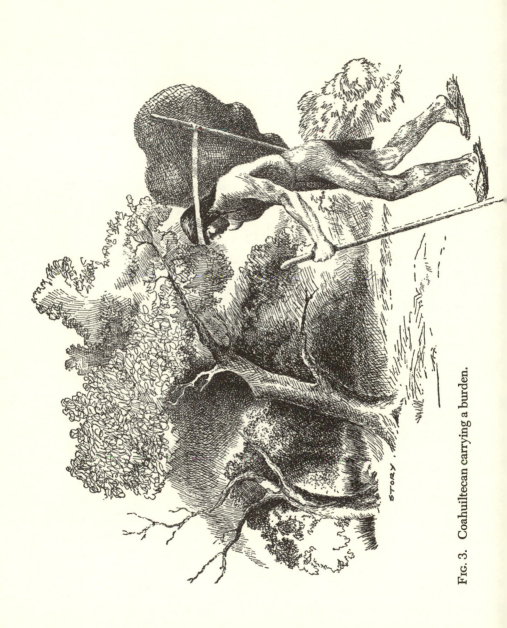

Fig. 3. Coahuiltecan carrying a burden.

Indian is traversed by an arrow; yet unless the entrails or the heart be struck, he does not die but recovers from the wound." De Solís (1931: 52), in an inspection tour of Spanish missions in Texas in 1768, noted that the mixed Coahuiltecan neophytes of Mission San Miguel Aguayo "are not ugly, and the Indian women are comely and very graceful, except one now and then who is surly and lazy." The men, and quite possibly the women, were tattooed for the purpose of denoting tribal affiliation and perhaps for other reasons. By way of illustration, while Fernando del Bosque was in Texas a Spanish captive was brought to him by a Kesale (Gueiquesale, Guesoles) Indian: "[He] appeared to be about twelve years old. He had a line on his face, marking him from his forehead to his nose, and two lines on his cheeks, one on each, and rows of them on his left arm and one on the right." (Martin, 1947: 14–15) What happened to the boy, incidentally, is not clear; he spoke no Spanish and Bosque does not indicate that he was taken from the Indians.

Coahuiltecans wore little clothing, a breechclout or loincloth, fiber sandals, and in inclement weather a cloak or robe, being sufficient for their needs. Breechclouts, at least among some bands, fell below the knees and were profusely decorated with animal teeth, seeds, and other ornaments. Some Coahuiltecan bands in Nuevo León tied or hung herbs near their genitals, which were covered by the breechclout. Rabbitskins were cut, twisted into ropelike strands, and sewn together to make blankets or robes. Cloaks were also made from coyotehides and probably any other hides they were able to obtain.

Subsistence and Material Culture. Of all the Texas Indians the Coahuiltecans had the fewest usable natural resources and consequently lived the harshest, most difficult life. Each Coahuiltecan band occupied a well-defined area which was considered to be its own; any and all trespassers were attacked. The wild foods available to various bands were quite varied—some bands in the vicinity of river valleys such as that of the Nueces were able to harvest pecans, others were able to make relatively great use of mesquite beans, and some, on the northern fringes of the Western Gulf culture area, were able to hunt bison. But all led a roving life, dictated by the availability and harvesttime of various wild foods.

39

Bands returned again and again to places occupied in earlier years, but their stay in any one locality was ordinarily brief—a few days generally, at most a few weeks. Summer was a season of relative plenty, winter a time when starvation often haunted the land. There seems to have been little that Coahuiltecans failed to eat which could be utilized by the human digestive apparatus. They killed the occasional buffalo that strayed into their land, more frequently hunted deer and javelinas, and made use of many smaller mammals and birds.

As mentioned, deer were often run down if they could not be shot and were sometimes taken by placing sharpened stakes behind barriers set along their trails. When a deer jumped such a barrier, particularly when hurried along by a hunter, he impaled himself on the stake. Javelinas were taken in cleverly concealed pitfalls, so dug that entrapped animals could not move freely. No doubt many other types of snares and traps were employed by hunters, too. But of more importance to the Coahuiltecan economy was the game supplied by communal hunting. Such animals as rabbits, but also the occasional bison herd, were most easily taken in number by "surrounds." In these a large group of hunters, perhaps all the able-bodied members of a band, surrounded a herd or encircled a likely piece of ground. Converging toward the center of the circle, the hunters slaughtered the animals as they attempted to break away or as they milled around seeking some avenue of escape. Brush and grass fires were also used to stampede game within range of hunters. De Vaca (p. 67) noted, for instance:

They [*Yguazes*] are accustomed also to kill deer by encircling them with fires. The pasturage is taken from the cattle [bison] by burning, that necessity may drive them to seek it in places where it is desired they should go. They encamp only where there are wood and water; and sometimes all carry loads of these when they go to hunt deer, which are usually found where neither is to be got.

Those bands situated near the large streams shot fish with bows and arrows, sometimes at night with the aid of torches to attract them, and they were also seined from shallow streams. Fish were sometimes dried and ground into flour, the grinding process being applied to virtually every edible substance the Coahuiltecans had. Fish were sometimes roasted without cleaning, and set aside for eight days, by which time the larvae of flies and other insects had developed in the rotting flesh. The larvae were then consumed as an epicure's delight, as also, apparently, was the remaining flesh.

Few living creatures were overlooked as a source of food, and for such peoples as the Yguazes, Cabeza de Vaca specifically mentioned spiders, ant eggs, worms, lizards, snakes—including rattlesnakes—earth, rotten wood, deer dung, and some "unmentionables" being eaten with relish. It is difficult to imagine the sort of food De Vaca declines to mention, but it may be that these Coahuiltecans followed a custom practiced by some of the natives of Baja California, incidentally in a similar habitat and perhaps deriving from the same cultural background. This practice, termed "second harvest," was the custom of removing seeds and the like from human feces, grinding them up, roasting, and eating them.

The principal Coahuiltecan foods were, however, from the vegetable kingdom. The bulbs of the agaves—maguey (*Agave americana*), lechuguilla (*Agave lecheguilla*), and sotol (*Dasylirion texanum*)—were roasted in pits, ground into flour, and eaten or stored for future use.[3] A drink, mescal, was made during the winter from the leaves of agave. It was said to be intoxicating and when mixed with the ground red beans of the Texas mountain laurel (*Sophora secundiflora*) was no doubt highly stimulating. The spineless, carrot-shaped, vision-producing cactus, peyote (*Lophophora williamsii*), was also dried, ground into powder, and used in a tea. The fruit or tuna of the prickly pear (*Opuntia*) was a favorite food, and even its unappetizing skins were dried, pounded into flour, and consumed.

Some of the south Texas Coahuiltecans were able to preserve prickly-pear tunas by squeezing out the juice, opening the fruit, and drying them. De Vaca (p. 66) said they were then put in "hampers like figs." They also preserved the tunas by roasting and subsequently storing them for future use. Prickly pears produced a thirst which

[3] See pp. 115–116 for a method of preparing sotol that was used by the Lipan Apaches. It was probably similar or identical to that used by Coahuiltecans.

these Indians were said to quench by collecting the juice of the fruit in pits in the earth and drinking from the pits. The lack of vessels was no doubt partly responsible for this custom, but in some areas of south Texas the earth itself was used to give added flavor and sweetness to various concoctions.

The mesquite thickets, common in the sixteenth century between the lower Nueces River and the lower Rio Grande, produced large quantities of beans used by the Coahuiltecan Indians whom De Vaca called Arbadaos or Acubadoes. The small tree called mesquite (*Prosopis juliflora*) is, of course, widely known in Texas and the Southwest generally. By stockmen it is often cordially detested, for it has taken over large areas of what were once good pasture lands. But one wonders whether the mesquite would have been able to spread to these new regions had they not already been overgrazed. The advance of the mesquite may also be laid partly to the ranchers' stock, which scattered mesquite beans through their droppings up and down every cattle trail in Texas. While the mesquite may be regarded as an obnoxious tree by modern man, by the Indian it was highly valued. The fruit is a bean, growing in a pod from four to seven inches long. In good harvest years the clusters of tan pods may bend the feathery-leafed branches almost to the ground. These beans are sweet and nutritious, an excellent food for man or beast. In the good years excess beans were dried, pounded into a coarse flour, and stored. This flour, often mixed with other seeds, berries, pulverized bones, and other oddments, was called *mesquitamal* by the Spaniards. Various Indian tribes prepared mesquite beans in different ways, and at least some of the Coahuiltecans had their own unique methods of preparing them. Cabeza de Vaca's Arbadaos dug a hole in the ground, threw in quantities of beans and used a wooden club to reduce them to a coarse flour. Not only did earth from the sides of the hole become mixed with the mesquite, but other, special earth was added. The mixture was repounded, thrown into some sort of container, and covered with water. If the broth was not considered sweet enough, more earth was added. When the concoction was ready, the Indians dipped in their hands and rapidly consumed this delicacy. The residue of hulls left in the container were thrown on a skin, then replaced in the receptacle, and the entire procedure repeated. The custom of consuming large quantities of earth and water greatly distended the belly, and the appearance of their bellies is reminiscent of those of modern, starving populations.

We feel repulsed, even nauseated, at some of the Coahuiltecan food habits, but not because ant eggs or deer dung are not wholesome and nutritious (for they may be), but because our culture has taught us from childhood that these things are not food. So strong are our feelings that many of us would starve in the midst of plenty —plenty, that is, of grubs, bugs, and offal. In a sense, then, while man's cultures provide all sorts of techniques and mechanisms for survival, cultures can also becloud the minds and restrict the acts of the human organism to the point of death.

The material equipment of these south Texans—the tools, the artifacts necessary for life—were few and uncomplicated. After all, only simple tools are needed to dig up sotol bulbs and snare jack rabbits, and the ceaseless nomadic mode of life of Coahuiltecans restricted their possessions to the durable and the transportable. Small movable huts or shelters were used throughout the Western Gulf culture area. These were made by placing reed mats and hides over bent saplings to form low, circular huts. Fires for cooking and heating were kindled in what must have been their acridly smoky interiors. But these dwellings were satisfactory for such a life, for mats and hides could be quickly rolled up and transported to the next camp. And for a people hardened to the burning sun of Texas summers and the freezing winter northers no more protection from the elements was needed. Coahuiltecan camps were filthy, refuse was piled about indiscriminately, and even the Spaniards, in an age when sanitation was conspicuous by its absence, recorded that they were dirty and smelled bad.

The principal weapon was the bow and arrows, the bow often being fashioned from a tough mesquite root and the bowstring from deer sinew or twisted lechuguilla fibers. Cane arrows, about twenty inches long, were made with a hardwood foreshaft and tipped with

43

flint points before iron became available. Arrows were feathered, and sinew and glue were used to join the various segments of an arrow. Cabeza de Vaca described the south Texas natives as superb archers.

Curved wooden "rabbit sticks" served as the chief, all-purpose digging, grubbing, prying, and throwing tool. Knives, scrapers, and hammers were made of flint. Gourds were used for storing such things as mesquite flour and water, and even the hollowed-out interiors of prickly pear "leaves" were used as receptacles. Some Coahuiltecan bands wove baskets and all seem to have manufactured net bags from fiber. A large net affixed to sticks, known as a *kakaxtle,* was used to carry heavy burdens. The cargo was carried on the back and, in common with many other American Indians, Coahuiltecans used a tumpline around the forehead to bear a good share of the load. Seines were also manufactured, as were woven mats. It may not be out of place to note here that the dry shelters and caves of Texas' Big Bend country have produced a wealth of netting, matting, basketry, and other items, left by their inhabitants ages ago, which have a distinct similarity to these material items of the Coahuiltecans.

Social Organization. It is difficult to speak of a "government" or a "political organization" for the Coahuiltecans of south Texas when the only kind of group that existed for a good part of the year was a small family-group, and during the harvest season was normally a band composed of these patrilineally-related groups. Yet this is precisely the point that must be recognized if we are to understand the social organization of these south Texans. It was the conjugal family or its patrilineally-reckoned extensions that took over nearly all the duties and activities we associate with courts, parliaments, congresses, and schools. Lawyers, judges, senators, policemen, whores, pimps, and preachers were wholly absent.

Each band, however, had a headman or chief, and at least occasionally there were chiefs whose authority extended over a number of bands. Presumably these leaders were the heads of the patrilineal kin groups. Band membership and band names were so shifting and impermanent, however, it would seem that leadership devolved upon

44

being a particularly able and outstanding man rather than upon being acquired through inheritance. Headmen seem usually to have been men who were exceptionally successful hunters and outstanding warriors—men who had time and again demonstrated their courage and bravery. They had limited authority, for band members could, if provoked, shift their band allegiance. Nor did extra wealth or goods accrue to headmen; on the contrary, in order to maintain the allegiance of a band's members a headman had to be generous, perhaps to the extent of impoverishing himself. To be successful, communal hunting required more people than the few individuals who comprised the family groups. Communal hunts were possible only during the summer harvest season, and at this time, presumably, headmen and chiefs temporarily assumed considerable authority over the specific location for the hunt and its exact time and execution.

Apart from the headmen and chiefs, the shamans were the only other individuals who were set off from their fellows, and even they had to spend most of their waking hours foraging for food. Shamans, and possibly headmen, were apt to have several wives, and they probably served as tokens of distinction and prestige, perhaps somewhat like Cadillacs in our society.

Band members lived together harmoniously for the most part. When arguments developed between two men the affair was settled by a fist fight. When one or both combatants were exhausted they separated. Sometimes the women parted them; the men never did. Bows and arrows or other lethal weapons were never used in a personal fracas. After a fight the disputants might take their mat houses and leave the band for a time, but when tempers had cooled they returned and friendships were re-established. Following a fight, a single man was, however, apt to leave a band permanently; he might even join an enemy band.

Small family-groups, apparently patrilineal lineages, composed of a man, his wife, sons and their wives, and unmarried daughters were the basic social and economic unit among Coahuiltecans. The animals a hunter brought into camp were shared by all, and there is evidence that the hunter consumed none of the game he killed, keeping only the hide. In short, as in many similar societies, the interdependence of the group was emphasized; personal gain or gain at the expense of the group was unknown. All the people a person lived with and worked with were his kin. Coahuiltecan society, then, as primitive society everywhere, was distinguished by (1) fraternity—all were kin; (2) equality—there were no full-time occupational specialists, much less various social classes; and (3) freedom—the resources of nature were free for the taking.

Duties were fairly evenly divided between the sexes, although Cabeza de Vaca felt that among the Coahuiltecan Yguazes the women had much the harder lot. They and the old men carried all the burdens while on their frequent journeys. Out of twenty-four hours, he claimed, the women rested only six; the remaining time was used to bake sotol roots, haul wood and water, perform household tasks, and care for children. During menstruation women ate by themselves and possibly were isolated in other ways. But the heavy work load of the women does not mean that men were lazy idlers who sat around the campfire telling tales and growing fat. On the contrary, most of their waking hours must have been spent in an onerous, often unsuccessful, quest for game or other sustenance.

Intermittent feuds, chronic small-scale warfare, and continual restive distrust characterized the relations between the many small Coahuiltecan tribes, and often even the neighboring bands of a single tribe. They did not have, however, the leisure, supplies, or organization necessary to conduct warfare in a fashion comparable to modern war. Warfare and feuding were mainly summertime activities, for the people were too scattered and busy in winter finding enough food to keep themselves alive to fight. Competition over tuna grounds and other sought-after natural resources was probably the basic cause of war; feuds and minor differences between the bands of a tribe were also occasioned by personal animosities, fights over women, and the like. Some bands resorted to female infanticide to prevent neighboring bands from increasing their strength. The picture, then, is that of many small, often impoverished, tribes and even bands embroiled in an almost perpetual bickering and skirmishing.

In only a few cases—and these were in the seventeenth century after original conditions had already been upset by Spanish conquerors —had the bands of any tribe been able to unite under a single leader in wars of conquest.

A number of measures were used to guard against surprise attacks. Huts were placed in dense thickets, trenches were dug around encampments, or brush was placed in trenches from which defenders could shoot their arrows. Attacks, of the hit-and-run variety, were made at night, and pitched battles were seldom if ever fought. Women often fomented attacks on an enemy, but often they were also the peacemakers. The older women would incite the men to war by gathering around a fire in camp one evening to chant and shout the band's grievances against some enemy, calling up thoughts of slain parents and captured children. When one woman subsided, another would take up the shout, taunting and goading the men to action. Eventually the men would begin to steal away to prepare themselves for battle, to paint themselves and to collect their weapons. They then would join the women in a wild dance, demonstrating their fitness and eagerness for battle.

Many, perhaps all, Coahuiltecan bands and tribes exchanged emissaries who bore challenges to war, offers of peace, or merely invitations to social functions. Those who went to initiate war presented themselves equipped for war to the headman of an enemy camp. The emissary shot his arrows into a tree and performed his war dance, challenging his enemies to war. They usually responded in kind, and the emissary quickly returned home to report the outcome of his challenge. Emissaries seeking peace likewise went to an enemy's camp, but they shot arrows into the air, and by other actions showed that they were desirous of peace.

Warriors returning from successful forays celebrated their victories with scalp dances. They halted before entering their camp, its populace swarming out to meet them. The scalps they had taken were placed on poles and the poles were set in a line. The jubilant warriors danced for a time around the poles, then the women, their bodies smeared with charcoal, removed them and themselves danced around with the poles. Captives were often roasted and eaten; Bosque recorded that there was ". . . great discord between them [various Coahuiltecans], from which they kill and eat each other and capture each other's children." (Bolton, 1916: 307) Both sexes and probably people of all ages took part in these feasts. They also ate members of their own band, but whether they actually killed these persons with cannibalism in mind is not clear. The probabilities are that they did not do so, that they ate fellow band members—and kinsmen—only after they had died from natural causes, and then for magical reasons. The men were barred from eating the flesh of fellow band members, but they did eat their powered bones along with peyote or *mesquitamal*.

As soon as a Coahuiltecan woman found herself pregnant her husband no longer slept with her, in fact, did not do so until two years after the birth of the child. Neither did he sleep with her during menstruation. At least some Coahuiltecans did not permit a pregnant woman to carry the customary heavy loads, and certain restrictions were imposed on the husbands of pregnant women. A friend accompanied the expectant mother to an isolated spot away from camp, and the birth took place in a squatting position. Mother and child were bathed as soon as possible. The placenta was tossed on a cactus, but if the child was stillborn, the placenta was burned.

Among some Coahuiltecan bands, apparently those on the Mexican side of the border, however, a custom known as the couvade was practiced. A new father retired to his pallet for about a week after the birth, to receive the congratulations of his friends; the mother went about her usual duties. This custom, while appearing silly to us, probably had a sensible, if unconscious motivation. It is a way by which a man can show the world that he is father of the child, or at least is going to perform the social role of father. Paternity among Coahuiltecans was no more obvious than it is among us.

Among some Coahuiltecans deformed babies and one member of a set of twins, whether alive or dead, were buried. If a woman died during childbirth the baby, living or dead, was buried with her. As already mentioned, feuding among bands of a tribe also led to infanticide, although this could not have been frequent. Cabeza de Vaca (pp. 64–65) alluded to it among the Mariames (probably the latter-day Aranamas):

They cast away their daughters at birth, and cause them to be eaten by dogs. The reason of their doing this, as they state, is because all the nations of the country are their foes; and as they have unceasing war with them, if they were to marry away their daughters, they would so greatly multiply their enemies that they must be overcome and made slaves; thus they prefer to destroy all, rather than that from them should come a single enemy. We asked why they did not themselves marry them; and they said it would be a disgustful thing to marry among relatives, and far better to kill than to give them either to their kindred or to their foes.

This is likewise the practice of their neighbors the Yguazes, but of no other people of that country.

Older children were also destroyed upon occasion, as were some of the Spanish castaways of the Narváez Expedition, because of in-auspicious dreams which certain people had. In common with many other primitive and not so primitive peoples, Coahuiltecans regarded their dream life as portentous and as real as, or more real than, reality itself. There may have been other reasons for infanticide—probably sheer economic necessity—but they have not been recorded.

Little is known about Coahuiltecan customs of child rearing, partly perhaps because there was little to distinguish their informal training methods. De Vaca's only remark (pp. 65–66) on the subject was that "they [Yguazes] have not so great love for their children as those [Karankawas] we have before spoken of." Infants were carried on a mother's back, their arms around her neck, and were probably se-cured by a robe or hide. At an early age children were provided with miniature bows and arrows and relatively soon were helping to pro-vide their daily sustenance. Boys were taken along on hunting ex-peditions and on war parties in which they served as look-outs and performed various menial chores. Passage from childhood to adult-hood was marked in some, perhaps all, Coahuiltecan tribes by shaman-directed ceremonies in the course of which children were tattooed. Tattooing was preceded by rubbing herbs that gave a cooling sensation on the parts to be tattooed. Long, shallow incisions were then made, into which charcoal and resin were rubbed. In these as in many other similar initiation rites, the children could not cry out and undoubtedly withstood the pain and emotional excitement stoically. Boys were apparently considered ready for adulthood—and hence tattooing—after they had proved themselves as hunters.

Premarital chastity was not important to Coahuiltecans, though virgins seem to have had somewhat more allure as potential wives. A marriage was arranged by the man and the girl's parents. The man gave the parents of his intended wife meat, hides, or other valuables. If he was invited to partake of the subsequent ceremonial feast it meant that his suit was accepted. If no invitation was forthcoming, it was a signal of rejection, a bitter pill to swallow for a young man who had labored hard to provide game and other things in what turned out to be a vain endeavor. Feuds between bands were occasionally traceable to spurned suitors. There seems to have been no marriage ceremony as such, a woman simply going to live with the man who was to be her husband. The men had to seek wives from other bands, as we have seen, and when bands of a tribe were feuding with one another the likelihood of obtaining marriage partners must have been slim. De Vaca (p. 65) remarked: "When the men would marry, they buy the women of their enemies: the price paid for a wife is a bow, the best that can be got, with two arrows: if it happens that the suitor should have no bow, then a net a fathom in length and another in breadth."

As is generally true in primitive society, divorce was frequent among childless couples, rare among those who had children. According to De Vaca (p. 65), "the marriage state continues no longer than while the parties are satisfied, and they separate for the slightest cause." Most men had but one wife (in cultures of such austerity it is difficult to support more than one), although shamans (medico-religious specialists) occasionally had more. And it is possible if not probable that the levirate (the system in which a man marries his brother's widow) and sororate (in which a woman marries her deceased sister's husband) were practiced. (Ruecking, 1955: 370) The men sometimes quarreled over women. Cabeza de Vaca (pp. 72–73) and his companions were separated by such a dispute:

. . . those among whom we were, quarrelled about a woman. After striking with fists, beating with sticks and bruising heads in great anger, each took his lodge and went his way, whence it became necessary that the Christians should also separate, and in no way could we come together until another year.

There was among Coahuiltecans a class of homosexual men, termed *berdaches* in the literature on American Indians, who dressed like women, did women's work, particularly carrying heavy loads, and lived with other men. They were often described as being more muscular and taller than the other men; they were also good archers. Some of these men appear to have been emasculated.

In the male-oriented society of the Coahuiltecans it is not surprising to learn that men, particularly vigorous young hunters, were mourned in a way that verged on desperation. A widow tore the hair from the crown of her head, cut short the rest of her hair, and rolling in the dust in paroxysms of grief, slashed herself time and again with a flint knife. Men, too, slashed themselves with stones over the loss of kinsmen; they did not, however, jerk out their hair. How long mourning continued is not known, nor is much information available on the disposition of corpses. Some, perhaps the shamans, were cremated; ordinary persons were buried away from the village or camp. De Vaca did note that all the people he encountered between the Island of Ill Fate and the Rio Grande mourned the death of close relatives, especially sons and brothers, by not leaving their dwellings to go after food for three months. Relatives and friends supplied the mourners with what food they could, but in time of scarcity no matter how hard over-taxed friends labored, some starved.

Supernaturalism. Belief in demons and spirits, elves and angels, gremlins and pixies flourishes best in those cultures that exercise the least control over the external world and have the most limited factual knowledge of it. Hence, the Coahuiltecans' conception of their universe and the forces that brought rain, supplied bountiful harvests of prickly pears, kept them healthy, and made the seasons come and go must have been one peopled with a multitude of powerful, more-than-natural beings and forces. This is precisely what their *mitotes* (dances and festivals) and other varied practices suggest, although their concept of the exact nature of such supernatural beings and forces is unknown. Coahuiltecan supernaturalism, like Coahuiltecan society, was probably not an entirely coherent or explicit mass of beliefs and practices. Much more likely every individual had his own vague concepts of the more-than-natural world and had his own personal ways, both magical and religious, of dealing with it, but all within a vague and, for us, mostly unknown social context. Probably, too, the belief systems of various Coahuiltecan tribes differed somewhat from one another.

Directing Coahuiltecan religious ceremonials, dealing with their supernatural world generally but chiefly treating the sick and ailing, were the shamans. Over most of the region they seem to have been elderly people of either sex, though only those who had had visionary or other out-of-the-ordinary experiences. Cures were attempted in several ways: by cauterizing wounds or even sores on the body (Cabeza de Vaca found this treatment effective), by sucking wounds and sores, and by blowing upon affected parts of the body. Shamans also practiced sleight-of-hand tricks, such as pretending to extract sticks, stones, and vermin from a patient's body. Patients were expected to pay for a shaman's services, and a patient and his family might be pauperized by a shaman. In some instances, a bereaved family put the shaman to death when he failed to cure the patient.

The feeling that a person who was different or had special qualities, and hence might be in contact with more-than-natural forces, should be a shaman is well exemplified by the experiences of Cabeza de Vaca and his companions. To Coahuiltecans these foreigners were extraordinary, they spoke an alien tongue and looked unlike any men they had ever seen. Consequently the natives soon coerced the Spaniards into attempting cures. When these proved successful the Indians were convinced of the soundness of their views. Even Cabeza de Vaca seems to have come to the conclusion that his laying on of

52

the hands was efficacious in the curing of various maladies, and this, naturally, was a great boon to faith healing.

Even before leaving the Karankawas, Cabeza de Vaca had been forced by the Indians to become a healer-shaman. But it was only after the four Spaniards had fled their captors that curing became their major occupation and their passport to travel almost triumphantly through south Texas. He reported (p. 74) that some people of the first tribe they stopped among, the Avavares [Chavavares]

came to Castillo and told him that they had great pain in the head, begging him to cure them. After he made over them the sign of the cross, and commended them to God, they instantly said that all the pain had left, and went to their houses bringing us prickly pears, with a piece of venison, a thing to us little known. As the report of Castillo's performances spread, many came to us that night sick, that we should heal them, each bringing a piece of venison, until the quantity became so great we knew not where to dispose of it. . . . After the sick were attended to, they began to dance and sing, making themselves festive, until sunrise; and because of our arrival, the rejoicing was continued for three days.

Not long after this Castillo cured five natives of cramps, for which he was given bows and arrows, but he was "a timid practitioner" and shortly afterward De Vaca also became a shaman. Although his first patient seemed to be already dead, he took off the mat which covered the body, prayed, and "breathed upon him many times." The Spaniard was given the man's bow and a basket of powdered prickly pears and went on to minister to other ailing people. He soon learned (p. 78) that the man he believed dead

had got up whole and walked, had eaten and spoken with them and that all to whom I had ministered were well and much pleased. This caused great wonder and fear, and throughout the land the people talked of nothing else. All to whom the fame of it reached, came to seek us that we should cure them and bless their children.

In time all four Spaniards became shamans, but Cabeza de Vaca by his own admission was the most successful.

Most if not all of the religious ceremonies or *mitotes* of south Texas (as well as the Mexican) Coahuiltecans involved the use of peyote. When eaten either green, dried, or drunk as tea, this spineless cactus has the property of seeming to heighten perceptions and of inducing hallucinations. Peyote is not habit-forming and does not induce sleep, so it is not properly classed as a narcotic. Peyote itself and quite possibly some of its ceremonial usages were borrowed from Coahuiltecans or related peoples by many reservation Indians of the United States toward the close of the last century. It came to them as a peaceful intertribal religious cult, and so great has been its appeal that it is the dominant religious cult of present-day Indian tribes west of the Mississippi.[4]

The usual Coahuiltecan *mitote* was an all-night dance and feast, during which peyote was eaten by both men and women. Some *mitotes*, probably those celebrating events such as puberty rites, were held by and for the members of a single band. Often, however, one band was host to another. These interband *mitotes*, and probably the others as well, were concentrated in the relatively bountiful summer months. It was during this season that boys were likely to kill their first deer and so be allowed to become "men." It was only during the summer, too, that enough food could be collected to feast the members of another band. A major purpose of these ceremonies was that of thanksgiving—to celebrate their good fortune at having full bellies for at least this one season of the year. *Mitotes* were also held to celebrate victories in war and probably other events and occurrences.

A fairly typical *mitote* went something like this. The guests, attired in their best finery, assembled sometime before dark. Soon after dark a large fire was started, meat was put on to roast, and music for dancing commenced. A drum, made by stretching a coyotehide over a wooden hoop, and a gourd rattle were used to accompany the singing onlookers. The dancers, both men and women, soon began to circle the fire in time to the pulsating music. They danced with their bodies close together, their shoulders moving slightly, their feet close together, from which position they progressed by a series of hops, all

---

[4] See La Barre, 1960, for an excellent summation of our knowledge about the peyote cult.

in time with the music. The dancing went on the entire night without pause. Peyote was passed at intervals, and occasionally some of the dancers fell into trances. Among some groups, those who had fallen into this peyote stupor were roused by being scratched with a sharp-toothed instrument until the blood flowed freely. In some ceremonies a shaman also addressed the participants. This ceremonial dance and the festivities were ended by daybreak, the guests departing with any remaining food.

To many Christians such a ceremony fails to sound like a religious activity, but as in other cultural matters it must be remembered that different cultures pursue the same ends by very different means. Part of the difficulty in this instance is also our lack of information—exactly what happened and why is unknown. We do know, however, that the stimulative power of peyote can rapidly provide the hallucinations by which a Coahuiltecan could come face to face with his God or Gods. And in common with that of many other primitive people, the Coahuiltecan approach to the supernatural world seems to have been a joyous one. There is no inevitable association between solemnity and dignity and the depth of religious feeling.

There were, of course, also many nonreligious aspects to interband *mitotes*. They were, after all, one of the few occasions during the year when people could see their friends and relatives from other bands. No wonder a feeling of festivity filters down to us across the chasm of time. This was the time for young men to find suitable girls to marry; now women might have the opportunity to visit with long-parted parents and kinfolk. This was a time, too, when exchanges of goods could be made, the more coastal bands exchanging shells and other products of the sea and shore for flint, projectile points, or red ocher for body painting. No doubt the *mitotes* were the high point of the year despite their brief duration.

Next to nothing is known of such things as origin tales and mythology for the south Texas Indians. De Vaca (pp. 78–79) did, however, relate a tantalizing tale told him by the Avavares:

They said that a man wandered through the country whom they called Badthing; he was small of body and wore a beard, and they never distinctly saw his features. When he came to the house where they lived, their hair stood up and they trembled. Presently a blazing torch shone at the door, when he entered and seized whom he chose, and giving him three great gashes in the side with a very sharp flint, the width of the hand and two palms in length, he put his hand through them, drawing forth the entrails, from one of which he would cut off a portion more or less, the length of a palm, and throw it on the embers. Then he would give three gashes to an arm, the second cut on the inside of an elbow, and would sever the limb. A little after this, he would begin to unite it, and putting his hands on the wounds, these would instantly become healed. They said that frequently in the dance he appeared among them, sometimes in the dress of a woman, at others in that of a man; that when it pleased him he would take a buhío, or house, and lifting it high, after a little he would come down with it in a heavy fall. They also stated that many times they offered him victuals, but that he never ate: they asked him whence he came and where was his abiding place, and he showed them a fissure in the earth and said that his house was there below. These things they told us of, we much laughed at and ridiculed; and they seeing our incredulity, brought us many of those they said he had seized; and we saw the marks of the gashes made in the places according to the manner they had described.

FEW AREAS in North America were more difficult for hunters and gatherers to exploit or yielded more stubbornly its niggardly harvest than the brush and cactus country of South Texas. But the Coahuiltecans made an admirable adjustment to the restrictions and privations of their land with but crude and primitive tools and exploitative techniques. Their success, in the last analysis, was compounded of a willingness to utilize virtually everything in their environment that the human organism could digest, which in turn depended upon an intimate knowledge of their land—what each plant was good for, when fruits in certain places would be ripe, where elusive game could be taken.

Our picture of the Texas Coahuiltecans is about as far removed from the romanticized version of the noble redskin as it is possible to get. Admittedly the harsh realities of their savage world and life are

56

more apt to repulse than attract. Yet the fact of their existence through perhaps a thousand years and more emphasizes again for soft-living moderns the adaptability, the toughness of humanity. The price of their survival may seem high to us, yet it was paid as willingly, as unquestioningly, as our own, and perhaps even more joyfully.

CHAPTER 3

The Karankawas: Gulf Coast

> The Karankaways are gone. Only bitter memories of
> them remain. In the minds of our people they are
> eternally damned, largely because they refused a
> culture we offered, resisting our proffered blessings
> to the last.
>
> Roy Bedichek—*Karánkaway Country*

THE HOMELAND of the Karankawas extended from the west side of
Galveston Bay southwestwards as far as the vicinity of Corpus
Christi Bay, including the offshore islands, the coast, and a narrow
strip of mainland. In early historic times there were at least five
groups or bands of Karankawas. The area from Galveston Bay to the
Brazos was the territory of the Capoques (Coaque, Coco) and the
Hans.[1] Next southward along the coast, at the mouth of the Colorado
River, were the Kohanis. The Karankawa proper—Korenkake, Clam-
coets, Carancaguacas—occupied Matagorda Bay and Matagorda

---

[1] Swanton, 1952: 320–322. The Hans may have been Atakapan linguistically,
but in other respects they seem to have differed not at all from Karankawas (see
Chap. 12). One of the principal sources for this chapter is the journal of Cabeza
de Vaca (Hodge, 1907b); when this source is used, it will be cited by page
number only. Other sources are Gatschet, 1891, and Schaedel, 1949.

59

Peninsula. The Karankawa proper were neither the largest nor the predominant Karankawan group. The Kopanos (Copane, Cobanes) dwelled along Copano Bay and on St. Joseph Island. There may have been others who should be classed with the Karankawas, but too few data are available to be sure. The significance of the name Karankawa is unknown, although it has been said to mean "dog-lovers." (Hodge, 1907a, Pt. 1: 657; Swanton, 1952: 320) Each of the Karankawa bands, so far as is known, was autonomous and independent, though sharing a common language and culture. (See Map 1.)

The coastal people south of Corpus Christi Bay and Mustang Island are poorly known; apparently they were Coahuiltecan, or what seems to have been a linguistic subdivision, the Tamaulipecan. The Borrados inhabited the coast from the Rio Grande to the vicinity of Baffin Bay, and a related group, the Malaquites, lived to the northward as far as Corpus Christi Bay. (Martin, 1936: 67) It is perhaps significant that these eighteenth-century names are vaguely similar phonetically to Cabeza de Vaca's Arbadaos and Maliacones.

The central section of the Texas coast, the territory of the Karankawas, is within what physiographers call the Coastal Prairie. It is flat country, rising little above the gulf, and there are many marshy regions. It is mostly grassland, but there are wooded regions on scattered sandy ridges and along the streams which cut through to the gulf. The thorny chaparral of the brush country becomes more frequent as you go south along the coast, but in early historic times it was not a prominent feature of Karankawa territory. There is little rainfall in winter, so little that in some years it would seem the Karankawas must have been hard pressed for drinkable water. Early Anglo-American settlers were perplexed by the fact that the Karankawas always seemed to have an ample water supply while they could find but little. In summer, rains are more frequent but rapid evaporation nullifies much of their effect. Rainfall increases northeastwards along the coast, yet even today much of the area is unprofitable for agriculture, either because of deficient rainfall or unsuitable soils.

The coastal prairies were frequented by many kinds of animals,

60

but no one species was numerous enough to be relied upon as the basis of subsistence. Deer were the most important and common big-game animal; buffalo stragglers were occasionally found, and javelinas, probably antelope, bears, and many smaller mammals were present.[2] The warm waters of the numerous lagoons and bays swarmed with fish and other marine life, and the many sand bars and low-lying offshore islands provided accessible bases for those in quest of seafood. Mussels and oysters, turtles, porpoises, many species of fish, ducks and other birds, marine plants, and other forms of life were present.

The varied food available to mankind—animal, plant, and seafood—would lead one to suppose that life for primitive folk along this coast was bountiful. But this was not the case. Most wild foods were obtainable only at certain seasons, of course, and although men had lived along this coast for thousands of years, they never came close to fully exploiting the riches of the gulf waters. Karankawa life was probably not as harsh or as grim a struggle as that of most Coahuiltecan groups, yet it was an arduous, often precarious, one.

Origins and Early History. Along the coast, from the mouth of the Brazos south to Baffin Bay, an archeological complex known as the Rockport Focus represents the archeological remains of the Karankawas. Since arrow points chipped from green bottle glass in traditional Rockport styles and glass trade beads have been recovered from Rockport sites, and since Karankawas were the only Indians in the area in early historic times, the association of the Rockport Focus with Karankawas seems assured. (Campbell, 1956; 1958a; Suhm *et al.*, 1954: 125–133) Metal tools, pipes of European manufacture, china made in England, musket balls, and other European objects have also been found in Rockport sites, but it is difficult to know whether these are a reflection of later European occupation or

---

[2] All of these animals, with the exception of the pronghorn antelope, either were reported by early visitors, or their remains are found in Karankawa archeological sites, or they are still present in the region. Antelope remains were found during the Texas Memorial Museum's excavation of La Salle's Fort St. Louis.

represent trade objects which the Karankawas had obtained. In general, Rockport Focus materials confirm many traits known about Karankawa culture and supply additional details about others.

The Rockport Focus was preceded along the coast by an Archaic complex—the Aransas Focus—sites of which have been located principally in the areas of Aransas and San Antonio Bays. (Campbell, 1947; 1952) Sites are shell middens and differ from other Archaic cultures in Texas—but not the later Rockport Focus—in the extensive use of shell for making tools and utensils. Dart points, of types found in central and south Texas, are present, and the absence of arrow points suggests that the use of the bow and arrow had not yet spread to the coast. There is no evidence of pottery in the Aransas Focus, but in most other respects it is much like the Rockport Focus and may be its ancestor. How many thousands of years ago the Aransas Focus began, how long it lasted, and when it was superseded by the Rockport Focus is unknown. Archeological consensus would make it a contemporary of other Texas Archaic cultures, a decision of small help, for none of them can yet be pinpointed in time, either.

The Karankawas entered historic times dramatically with the landing of the survivors of the Narváez Expedition on their coast in 1528. Their subsequent history is as turbulent, as marked by disaster, and as punctuated by encounters with the famous and infamous as that of any people anywhere. After Cabeza de Vaca's sojourn among them, the Karankawas were not visited again by Europeans for more than a century and a half. Then in 1685 the ill-fated expedition of the Frenchman Robert Cavelier, Sieur de La Salle accidentally landed at Matagorda Bay and established Fort St. Louis on Garcitas Creek in the heart of Karankawa territory.[3] Concern for south and east Texas flamed when the Spanish learned of the French colony, and an expedition was dispatched in 1689 to destroy it. But by the time Spaniards reached the fort the neighboring Karankawas had already massacred its remaining inhabitants, sparing but five colonists. In 1690, Alonso

[3] Historians have questioned the location of Fort St. Louis, but following the excavation of the Garcitas Creek site by the Texas Memorial Museum, little doubt remains that this is the correct location.

de León returned to burn the remains of the French fort and then continued on to east Texas and Caddo territory.

The Karankawas were ignored for a few years after La Salle's fiasco, but by 1720 interest in them—or in their land—was revived. In that year another French expedition, this time under Bernard de la Harpe, crossed Karankawa territory. In 1722 the Spaniards, probably in response to this fresh French sally, established the fort La Bahía, and the mission of Espíritu Santo de Zuñiga, in the vicinity of the old Fort St. Louis. In 1726 the presidio and mission were moved to the lower San Antonio River among the Aranama Indians, and in 1749 to a new location opposite Goliad. A new mission, Nuestra Señora del Refugio, was built in 1791 near the mouth of Mission River for these Indians, and it persisted until 1828. During the remainder of their stay in Texas the Spaniards were never able to establish entirely amicable relations with Karankawas. A few, it is true, were eventually gathered into missions, but most scorned such an existence. By the end of the Spanish reign in Texas, the effects of introduced diseases and other by-products of European invasion had reduced the Karankawas to a remnant of their former strength. They could still be formidable adversaries, but only fleetingly.

Appearance and Dress. It is hard to imagine the impact a Karankawa Indian would have upon modern sensibilities if a person were to be precipitated into their midst as were the survivors of the Narváez expedition. These Karankawas, whom Cabeza de Vaca designated Capoques and Hans, were magnificent creatures physically—tall, well-built, muscular, the men stark naked, but not unadorned. The nipple of each breast had been pierced through, as had been the lower lip, and pieces of cane were thrust through these perforations. The appearance of the women goes unrecorded except that they wore skirts of Spanish moss and deerskin. There are some hints in De Vaca's journal that the Spaniards found the women not entirely unattractive, although the castaways' standards of desirability and beauty may have altered in proportion to the time elapsed since they had last seen Spain.

The Karankawas, like other peoples of the Western Gulf culture area, painted and tattooed their bodies in a number of ways. Like the bodily ornamentation of other peoples, tattoos served to beautify the human body as well as symbolize age and sex categories. The Karankawas tattooed the French captives taken when they massacred the inhabitants of Fort St. Louis and this suggests that tattooing was for them a necessity. Their motivation may have been similar to that of Americans when a foreign waif is adopted—an American haircut and costume, frequently a cowboy outfit, are immediately mandatory. De Solís, who made an inspection of the Spanish missions in Texas in 1767–68 and held a low opinion of Karankawas, wrote:

Although the Indian men are so atrocious, the Indian women are very decent. From the time they are born they put on a *pabigo* or breech-clout of hay or grass which covers the body decently, and which they keep on until they die, renewing it when necessary. They paint themselves in stripes all over, different figures being formed with the stripes, now of animals, now of birds, now of flowers. These are the married women and the corrupt ones, but the maidens have only a small stripe on their foreheads as far as the chin which crosses through the point of the nose and through the middle of the lips. All of the Indian men and women are bad tempered and ungrateful except one now and then who is affectionate. In the woods and on the coast the Indian men go entirely naked, the Indian women always decently covered.[4]

Noah Smithwick (1900: 13), Texas Ranger and blacksmith, in the twilight of Karankawa existence in the nineteenth century, wrote:

They were the most savage looking human beings I ever saw. Many of the bucks were six feet in height, with bows and arrows in proportion. Their ugly faces were rendered hideous by the alligator grease and dirt with which they were besmeared from head to foot as a defense against mosquitoes.

Another Texas pioneer, John H. Jenkins (1958: 158–159), agrees with Smithwick about their stature, adding:

[4] De Solís, 1931: 42. De Solís' description of Karankawa life was written in 1767–68 following his inspection of the missions. Father Morfi's account was written a few years later and was derived, at least in part, from that of De Solís.

When on the warpath their costume and general appearance were quite peculiar and striking. Each warrior painted one-half his face black and the other red. Then he was entirely naked except for a breechclout or apron, with its long sash, bordered with tassels and fringes, almost touching the ground behind.

Their savage appearance to the contrary, when Karankawas had full bellies they were a happy, merry, and generous people. After Cabeza de Vaca and his companions had relaunched their shipwrecked vessel, it swamped, drowning three men. The survivors were naked and dying in the November cold when the Karankawas rescued and nursed them. The Indians gathered driftwood and hauled it toward their homes inland. They quickly returned and virtually carried the miserable, chilled survivors to their homes, halting along the way to warm them at fires they had thoughtfully laid. At the camp a shelter and fires awaited the Spaniards. That the Indians held a noisy dance of welcome and rejoicing which lasted the remainder of the night does not alter the fact that they were trying in their way to be good hosts. The relations between the Spaniards and Karankawas did not remain as friendly as these auspicious beginnings suggest. The enmity and harsh treatment to which the Spaniards were eventually treated cannot, however, be blamed more on the natives than on the Spaniards.

Cabeza de Vaca, himself a hardy individual, remarked upon the Karankawas' ability to withstand hunger, thirst, and cold, and two centuries later De Solís (1931: 44), while critical, was nevertheless in awe of their physical prowess:

They boast and brag of being strong and valiant, because of this they go naked in the most burning sun, they suffer and go around without covering themselves or taking refuge in the shade. In the winter when it snows and freezes so that the water in the rivers is solid and the pools, lakes, marshes and creeks are covered with ice they go out from the ranch at early dawn to take a bath, breaking the ice with their body.

Subsistence and Material Culture. From the waters of the gulf the Karankawas took oysters, clams, scallops, and other mollusks, turtles, undoubtedly a wide variety of fish, porpoises,

65

and an underwater plant, possibly the root of the water chinquapin or American lotus (*Nelumbo* species var.), and perhaps other marine plants. In creeks and estuaries they found alligators, whose grease, as we have seen, they were reputed to smear on themselves to discourage mosquitoes. On the mainland, as in the gulf, a variety of animals and plants contributed to Karankawa subsistence. Deer were hunted, as were bison when they appeared near the coast. Bear, peccary, and smaller mammals were also taken when the opportunity arose. Birds, particularly migratory water fowl, must have been frequent seasonally, but whether or not Karankawas hunted them to any extent is unknown. Berries, nuts, seeds, and other plant foods were gathered on the mainland shore.

To take advantage of such varied food sources each Karankawa band had to lead a roving, nomadic life, seldom spending more than a few weeks in any one campsite, but returning year after year to favored localities. Campsites were often on shell middens—refuse piles built up by years of intermittent occupation. If possible they were located near sources of fresh water, and were always accessible to lagoons or bays. The Capoques and Hans, with whom Cabeza de Vaca was so familiar, camped on the off-shore islands, catching fish in cane weirs and eating the root of an underwater plant in the fall. By midwinter these plants had begun to grow, making the root useless as food, and the bands were forced to move. They subsisted until spring exclusively upon oysters, which were found along the shore of the mainland; then for a month they ate blackberries. The summer months appeared to have again been spent on the lagoons and islands of the coast. Other bands probably followed a similar seasonal round, their movements being determined chiefly by the availability of foods and secondarily by climatic considerations. The bars and islands were cold and wet during the winter months, while the mainland shore was warmer and more attractive.

Karankawa subsistence was extremely varied, but no foods were continuously plentiful. It is difficult, in fact, not to think of Karankawas as harvesting a little here, then hastening to another spot to reap another minuscule harvest, and on to a third place, and so on continuously, seldom starving but never having a truly bountiful or fully

66

dependable subsistence, either. They were no more able to overlook a potential food source than were the Coahuiltecans, and when the harvest was good they gorged to repletion. Partly in consequence, Europeans were apt to sneer at their tastes and appetites, as did Father Morfi (1932: 49; see also De Solís, 1931: 43):

The coast tribes are unique in their gluttony. They eagerly eat locusts, lice and even human flesh. Their appetite does not require seasoning. They eat raw meat, tallow, bears' fat, and when they have them, are thankful. . . . With all of this they show a great passion for spoiled food. There arises from their bodies such a stench that it causes one who is little accustomed to them to become sick at the stomach.

The Karankawa's nomadic maritime existence was made possible by the use of dugout canoes. These they fashioned from tree trunks without bothering to remove the bark. One side of a log was trimmed flat, its ends blunted, and then it was hollowed out, probably with the aid of fire and much scraping. A solid section forming a triangular deck was left at either end of the canoe. Their size is but vaguely known, though they were large enough to hold a man, his wife, children, and household goods. Propelled by means of poles, these canoes were not sufficiently sturdy or trustworthy to allow their use in heavy weather or very far from the protection of the shore or the coastal islands. They were fit only for short voyages across the shallow, placid waters of lagoons and inlets. For such service they were attractive enough to make La Salle covetous of them, and the fact that he acquired several may well have been one of the factors which ultimately led to the massacre of his colony. Not surprisingly, the Karankawas are credited (Kuykendall, 1903: 324) with being "expert swimmers"; considering the nature of their dugout canoes, it would seem that they had to be.

The Karankawas' skill in handling dugout canoes gave them an advantage over Europeans which not only helped them to escape the harassments of white civilization but often allowed them to attack their enemies with impunity. Karankawas would suddenly appear along some shore, attack their Spanish or American adversaries, and almost magically disappear. The waters of lagoons and bays left no trail, a poled canoe was silent in an expert's hand, and the native's intimate knowledge of the coast and its innumerable places of concealment made pursuit fruitless and detection almost impossible.

The Karankawas' nomadic mode of life restricted their housing and household gear to the portable. Their hut or "ba-ak," for example, was made of a dozen or so slender willow poles, approximately eighteen feet long and pointed at one or both ends. The sharpened ends were forced into the ground in a circle, the upper ends interlaced and tied with thongs to form an oval framework over which skins and woven mats were thrown. Often only the windward side was covered, so it could as well be called a windbreak as a hut. Perhaps more care in construction was taken during particularly inclement weather and in places where they would remain for a relatively long time. The size of huts varied, but normally they were some ten or twelve feet in diameter and accommodated seven or eight people. Fires for cooking and for heat were built in the center of these huts, the smoke easily finding its way out. Skins were used to sit on and to wrap up in when sleeping. These huts could be rapidly dismantled by the women, who had a special knack for twisting the willow poles together to stow them in the dugouts.

Karankawas manufactured rather odd and distinctive pottery vessels which were frequently coated inside and decorated outside with asphaltum. They made wide-mouthed jars, globular ollas, bowls, and perhaps bottles. (Campbell, 1958a: 435–437) Meat, fish, and other foods were cooked in these vessels, their rounded bottoms being sunk in ashes and live coals. Oysters were thrown into the fire or live coals and were raked out and eaten when they began to open. Nuts and seeds were crushed with milling stones, but whether the resulting flour was used in gruels and stews, or was made into a paste or dough and baked in ashes is unknown. When corn meal and wheat flour became available to them they baked cakes in ashes.

Many small lumps of asphaltum (natural asphalt), which washed up on beaches, are also found in Karankawa (Rockport Focus) sites, a number of which bear impressions of twined basketry. Apparently, then, basketry, like pottery, was heavily coated with asphaltum for water-proofing. (Campbell, 1952: 74) Asphaltum was also used as an agent in affixing arrow points to shafts and for similar purposes.

The chief weapon of Karankawas, expertly used until their final extermination, was a long bow and arrows (Jenkins, 1958: 159):

He carried a bow as long as he was tall, with arrows of proportional length, with which he could kill game a hundred yards distant. I knew an instance of the terrible force of these arrows which is worthy of note. Aimed at a bear, three years old, that had taken refuge in the top of a tree, it went through the brute's body and was propelled forty or fifty yards beyond.

Kuykendall (1903: 324–325) records that in another instance arrows shot across a river at Americans

though impelled nearly two hundred yards, were driven to the feather in the alluvial bank. . . . every warrior's bow when strung, was precisely as long as his person and as useless in the hands of a man of ordinary strength as was the bow of Ulysses in the hands of the suitors. The arrow, formed of cane, was about a yard long, including a piece of solid wood the size of the cane and two or three inches in length, neatly fitted into it at each end. The larger piece of wood received the arrow head which was fastened with sinews; the smaller piece had a notch or groove to receive the bow-string.

Cedar is the wood reported to have been used for making bows, and bowstrings were of deer sinew, a quantity of fine sinews being twisted together. Arrows were feathered with three feathers. The bowstring was drawn to the left cheek in shooting, and a guard was worn on the left wrist. In addition to bows and arrows Karankawas used lances, clubs, and tomahawks. The bow and arrow was the chief weapon used in fishing, which may in part explain why they used an especially powerful bow, though cane weirs were also employed to trap fish. Their lack of seaworthy boats, fishhooks, and what may be described as a seafaring tradition limited severely their exploitation of the rich gulf waters.

Social Organization. The diversity of Karankawa subsistence, the modest harvest possible at any one time or place, and perhaps a limited water supply allowed Karankawas to forage through their territories only in small bands of thirty or forty people. And in some seasons even the bands seem to have been subdivided into smaller groups, probably individual family units. The bands were composed of relatives, apparently paternally-related kinsmen, our data being restricted to remarks like that of Cabeza de Vaca (p. 54), who said "all that are of a lineage keep together." The women presumably expended considerable energy in gathering plants and in hunting the smaller and slower animals. They were charged with most of the onerous chores of the camp—erecting and dismantling the huts, cooking, collecting firewood, and many other similar tasks. Many Europeans were shocked at the hard lot of Karankawa women, but such a condition as theirs is often a reflection of the economic importance of the men. The men bore the brunt of the hunting and fishing.

The small Karankawa bands were the largest social and political grouping these people ever achieved. And while there must have been considerable interchange between bands—intermarriage, visiting, and the like—it never resulted in tribal political units. Even a band's members were frequently, perhaps normally, scattered into smaller family-groups as they foraged by themselves. They could, however, quickly be brought together for social events, war, or other purposes through the use of a well-developed system of smoke-signaling.

Because of their unfriendly relations with inland tribes (Coahuiltecans and perhaps Tonkawas) Cabeza de Vaca (p. 56) was able, as an outsider, to act as a trader:

The Indians would beg me to go from one quarter to another for things of which they have need; for in consequence of incessant hostilities, they cannot traverse the country, nor make many exchanges. With my merchandise and trade I went into the interior as far as I pleased, and travelled along the coast forty or fifty leagues.

From the coastal region he took sea shells, "conchs used for cutting, and fruit like a bean of the highest value among them, which they use as a medicine and employ in their dances and festivities." (p. 56)

70

Just what this bean was is a puzzle. The "coral bean" or Texas mountain laurel immediately comes to mind as being widely used ceremonially and medicinally by Texas Indians. But this shrub more commonly grows inland than on the coast, so if it was the coral bean the trade should have been the other way round. De Vaca also carried an equally mysterious "sea bead" to the interior, as well as some other unspecified articles. In return he brought back to the coastal tribes skins, red ocher for painting the face and body, canes for arrows, sinew, flint for weapons and tools, "cement" with which to affix flint tools to handles and shafts, and deer hair, dyed and fixed into tassels.

Because of the small size of Karankawa bands and the fact that band members were a close-knit body of kinsmen, there was no necessity for the type of political institutions that are a part of larger, more segmented societies. Karankawa bands were headed by chiefs, Cabeza de Vaca to the contrary, who remarked (p. 54) that "they have no chief." It appears that to De Vaca a "chief" was an autocratic, dictatorial ruler, and since Karankawa chiefs did not have such powers, to him they were not chiefs. Gatschet (1891: 63), the first anthropologist to become interested in Karankawa culture, states:

What we know about their tribal rulers is, that they were ruled by two kinds of chiefs: they had chiefs for their civil government, whose succession was hereditary in the rule line, and war chiefs, appointed probably by civil chiefs. No women have ever been known to have acted as chiefs.

We do not know Gatschet's sources for this information, but having a peace chief and a war chief was common among North American Indian tribes and it would not be surprising if Karankawas made the distinction. If Karankawa bands were composed essentially of men descended from a common ancestor, then it is not unlikely that civil chieftainship fell to an elder of this group.

Eighteenth-century Spaniards described ordeals which men underwent in order to qualify for chieftainship, and perhaps these ordeals were used to select a chief from among several candidates. It should be remarked, however, that these ordeals are reminiscent of puberty rites or the initiation ceremonies for some kind of club or fraternity, and that the Spaniards could, in their ignorance, easily have been mistaken. De Solís (1931: 41) reported:

To this office [chieftainship] there are many Indian pretenders, and they administer extraordinary tests for admitting them, such as scarifying them from the back of the head with something like combs of the spine from seafish to the soles of the foot, making them shed much blood, and taking them off to a cane-break where they keep them fasting for many days, and they come out emaciated and thin and almost dead.

Despite occasional infanticide, the Karankawas were known to Cabeza de Vaca as being extremely fond of their children. He said (pp. 50–51) that the people of the Island of Ill Fate "love their offspring the most of any in the world, and treat them with the greatest mildness." De Vaca was amazed to learn that children were nursed until they were twelve years old, by which time they were able to fend for themselves. In answer to his question about this custom, the Indians told him that it was because of the frequent necessity to go several days without food that children had to be allowed to suckle for so long a time; otherwise they would starve or at best be weakly. Children were given two names, one a nickname which was used in public and to outsiders, the other a secret name, probably having magical significance. Infants spent much of their time fastened to cradle boards, which also served—apparently accidentally—to flatten their heads. Mothers carried their children "wrapped in the loop of the skin worn by her." (Gatschet, 1891: 122)

As soon as they were able, girls assisted their mothers in their various tasks and boys followed their fathers on the chase. Life was such that as soon as possible children had to contribute to their own support; the luxury of a leisure-class childhood could hardly be afforded. Among some of the Indians of the Western Gulf culture area there were puberty rites, ceremonies in which children were symbolically ushered from childhood into adulthood. Tattooing may have occurred at this time in shaman-conducted ceremonies.

Marriage was arranged between the man and the girl's parents.

Gifts presented by the suitor to the girl's parents were a traditional part of the nuptial arrangements, but what other customs, if any, were practiced have not come down to us. There is no record of any type of wedding ceremony and there probably was none. Apparently, a couple simply settled down in their own hut after the marriage arrangements had been made. Following marriage, Karankawas practiced a form of "bride service." For an unknown number of months a man gave all the fruits of the chase to his bride, who took them to her father's hut. Neither bride nor groom dared touch a morsel of this food, but the bride's parents in turn gave her food to take to her husband. At the conclusion of such service the recently-married pair normally joined the family or band of the husband. What may seem to us a curious custom could well have served the very practical purpose of strengthening the bonds between the two separate, perhaps basically antagonistic, groups from which the couple came. Since each band was composed of paternally-related kinsmen, probably rules of incest forced the men to find their wives in other bands.

An in-law taboo also existed between a man and his parents-in-law. He could not enter their dwelling nor they his or even his children's. They never spoke to one another. If persons in this relationship should happen to be in danger of coming face to face, both parties would turn aside and avert their eyes. A wife was under no such restrictions—probably a good thing since she lived with her father-in-law's family. Although in-law taboos are common in many parts of the world, many people are surprised to learn of them and are mildly amused by them. All people, of course, are faced by in-law problems, and many have found solutions to the frictions which inevitably arise between these relatives. The Karankawas' patterns of avoidance certainly solved this problem for them. It is interesting to note—as has been noted many times—that our culture has provided no solution for this problem. The mother-in-law joke may serve to relieve some of the aggressive feelings built up, but otherwise we are left to flounder as best we can. Perhaps the problem of in-laws is not serious enough with us to force a solution.

Karankawas were normally monogamous, but if no children were born, divorce was common. If a couple had children divorce was rare. It should be noted, too, that the Karankawas never seem to have been a fecund people. As is true of many, perhaps most, cultures, marriage was first and foremost an economic and reproductive union between two people or two kin groups, and was only in a minor way a romantic, primarily sexual, love match. Europeans who came to know the Karankawas frequently commented on their extramarital escapades. In the eighteenth century De Solís (1931: 42), for example, claimed that Karankawas

exchange or barter their wives. If one of them likes the wife of another better, he gives him his and something of value besides, and they exchange one for the other and barter them. They lend them to their friends in order that they may use them, they sell them for a horse, for gunpowder, balls, beads of glass and other things which they esteem.

Among Karankawas, as among Coahuiltecans and many other Texas Indians, were to be found *berdaches*, occupying a somewhat degraded status. De Solís (1931: 44) commented on them and Fray Morfi (1932: 55) also said:

It is not known whether they are actually hermaphrodites or not. These abominable people find and conduct themselves in every way like women. They accompany the warriors on their campaigns, not to fight, but to herd the horses which they steal from us, while they face and take whatever is given them; and principally, to lend their bodies to infamous and nefarious uses.

Death was attended by as much ceremony and ritual as any other phase of the life cycle, perhaps by more. This was particularly true for boys and young men; they were mourned for an entire year. Before dawn, at noon, and at sunset the parents and kin wept for the departed boy. When the year had passed, some sort of rite was performed after which the mourners purified themselves with smoke. Cabeza de Vaca also mentioned that when a son or brother died the members of his household did not attempt to supply themselves with food for three months. Relatives and neighbors attempted to do so, but when epidemics swept through their camps, as they did shortly

74

after the Spaniards were cast up on their shores, it meant extreme hardship and starvation. Only the aged were not mourned, for it was felt that they were a burden to others, got little pleasure from life, and so were better off dead. Ordinary persons were buried in shallow graves, on or near campsites; few tools or ornaments were interred with them. Shamans were not buried but were cremated during a ceremonial dance. One year later the shaman's ashes were mixed with water and drunk by his relatives. The motivation behind this custom probably falls into a category usually termed "contagious magic." The Karankawas apparently reasoned that by consuming his ashes they could acquire or perhaps retain within their own group the extraordinary qualities of their kinsman.

Apart from their various *mitotes*, some of which may well have been primarily social dances, Karankawas had a few other forms of diversion. Men and boys competed in shooting arrows at targets, in throwing knives and other weapons, and played some kind of ball games. They also held wrestling matches, a custom which distinguished them in the eyes of nearby tribes. Whether wrestling was merely a game or was used as a method of settling arguments is unknown.

When first encountered by survivors of the Narváez Expedition, Karankawas were trusting, friendly, and not particularly warlike, and as we have seen, their fear of inland enemies kept them near the coast. The actions of the Spaniards and French soon changed their ingenuous attitude and ways, however, and by the nineteenth century they had become dangerous and tenacious foes, requiring no provocation to attack strangers or others when the chances of success were bright. Looting ships wrecked along their treacherous coast became a favorite occupation.

Although not showing enmity toward early Europeans, the proud Karankawas were easily aroused to fury by a slight or an injury. Even the French, who among Europeans had a faculty for getting along with Indians, soon aroused the ire of the Karankawas, and La Salle's colonists were eventually destroyed by them. La Salle's difficulties began when a bale of blanketing from the wreck of one of his ships was picked up by the natives. La Salle sent a party to regain these goods peaceably, but the party's belligerent commander succeeded only in enraging the Indians. A few days later the Indians attacked the French, killing two, and from that time on stragglers and small groups were frequently ambushed. Finally La Salle (Cox, 1905, I: 218)

seeing himself constantly insulted by the savages, and wishing, moreover, to have some of their canoes, by force or consent, as he could not do without them, resolved to make open war on them in order to bring them to an advantageous peace. He set out with sixty men, armed with wooden corselets to protect them against arrows, and arrived where they had gathered. In different engagements, by day and night, he put some to flight, wounded several, killed some; others were taken, among the rest some children, one of whom, a girl, three or four years old, was baptized, and died some days after, as the first fruits of this mission and a sure conquest sent to heaven.

But a short time later the captain of La Salle's frigate and six of his men, while sleeping on shore, were surprised and killed by the natives. And the French were unable thereafter to subdue or come to terms with the Indians. When the Spanish arrived in 1690, Karankawas had shortly before massacred the last of the French remaining at the fort.

Karankawas would no more endure the insults—real or imagined—of the Spanish than of the French. The De León-Massanet Expedition of 1690, dispatched to uproot the French from Fort St. Louis, also ran afoul of Karankawa ire. In this case Captain De León with twenty men was seeking to take two young Frenchmen who had been captured by the Karankawas when they destroyed the fort (Bolton, 1916: 384–385):

The Indians were promised horses and clothing if they would give up the boys, and their reply was that they would do so promptly, and very willingly. The soldiers then began to enter the *ranchitos* [huts] of the Indians, peering with too much curiosity into their belongings, and committing other acts so that the Indians became resentful against the soldiers and distrustful of them when they found out who was guilty. Later, all being gathered together after the French boys had been delivered over to our men, the Indians commenced to shoot arrows among the soldiers. Two arrows struck Captain Leon in the side, but as he wore mail, they did not penetrate; also the horses were shot down under two other soldiers. There were four Indians killed and two wounded, and our men took the young Frenchmen and returned to the main body of the army, which was waiting by the Guadalupe River.

The eighteenth-century Spaniards knew the Karankawas less intimately than their forerunners, but said of their warfare (De Solís, 1931: 42):

They are cruel, inhuman and ferocious. When one nation makes war with another, the one that conquers puts all the old men and old women to the knife and carries off the little children for food to eat on the way; the other children are sold; the vagabonds and grown women and young girls are carried off to serve them, with the exception of some whom they reserve to sacrifice in the dance before their gods and saints.

Morfi (1932: 52) also commented on Karankawan ferocity.

The Indians of the Western Gulf culture area, and particularly Karankawas, are usually thought of as bloodthirsty cannibals. But the Karankawas who succored the shipwrecked Spaniards of the Narváez Expedition were horrified that the Spaniards ate the dead members of their own party. De Vaca said that if the Indians had known the Spaniards were going to behave in such a bestial way they would have slaughtered the Spaniards when they first met them. There is nothing further in Cabeza de Vaca's account of the Indians between the Island of Ill Fate and the Rio Grande which suggests cannibalism. In the eighteenth century both De Solís and Fray Morfi charged the Karankawas with cannibalism, but it must be remembered that they were not eyewitnesses to the custom. They alleged that captives were sacrificed (De Solís, 1931: 42–43):

. . . they set a nailed stake in the ground in the place where they are to dance the *mitote*; they light a big fire, tying the victim who is to be danced about or sacrificed to that stake. All assemble together and when the harsh instrument, the *caymán*, begins to play they begin to dance and to leap, making many gestures and very fierce grimaces with funereal and discordant cries, dancing with well sharpened knives in their hands. As they jump around they approach the victim and cut a piece of flesh off of his body, going to the fire and half roasting it in sight of the victim, they eat it with great relish, and so they go on cutting off pieces and quartering him until they take off all of the flesh and he dies. They take off his hair with the scalp and put it all on a pole in order to bring it to the dance as a trophy. They do not throw the bones away but distribute them, and each one whose turn it is to get one walks along sucking it until he is thus finished. They do the same thing with the priests and Spaniards if they catch any. Others they hang up by the feet and put fire underneath them and go on roasting them and eat them up. For others they make long poles of the thickness of an inch of resinous pine, of which there is a great deal, and set fire to them and torture the victim with them, and afterwards they set fire to him and half roast him and eat him up. For others they do not use a knife to cut them to pieces but they tear them to pieces with their teeth and eat them raw.

It should be said in defense of the peoples of the Western Gulf culture area that the cannibalism they practiced was distinct from the custom of eating human flesh simply as food. Many American Indians and most Texas natives ate bits and pieces of their dead or dying enemies. This custom was due not to hunger but was motivated by magic or revenge. Magically it was a way to gain an enemy's courage or fortitude, the logic being that an enemy's power, courage, and bravery were obtained—transferred—by eating selected portions of his body. It was also the ultimate vengeance one could visit upon an enemy, and for Karankawas was doubly enjoyed when they could consume parts of an enemy before the still-seeing eyes of the victim. It should also be remembered that the Europeans and Texans who charged the people of the Western Gulf culture area with cannibalism were not well acquainted with them. Some of the atrocities attributed to these Indians are undoubtedly rationalizations growing out of the inhuman, unfair treatment the Spaniards and Texans accorded them. It is much easier to slaughter men and appropriate their land if you can convince yourself that they are despicable, inferior, barely human creatures.

Supernaturalism. Karankawas are credited with a belief in two divinities. De Solís (1931: 41) mentions two, and Fray Morfi (1932: 21) said:

The Carancaguases [Karankawas] worship two divinities with the names of *Pichini* and *Mel*, and their dances, especially the funeral dances, are a kind of cult and rogation in which they pray for liberty, victory, prosperity in the chase, abundance in fishing, or happy results in their robberies. These deities have their ministers [shamans], whom they call *Comas*, who watch over their cult, promote, direct, and preside over their *mitotes*.

How many, if any, lesser beings, spirits, or supernatural forces there were is unknown.

The religious practices of Karankawas centered around their *mitotes*—ceremonies or festivals. There were several kinds, held for different purposes and involving different activities. One *mitote*, quite obviously considered to be of great religious importance, was a dance and drinking bout celebrated after successful fishing and hunting expeditions. It was a form of thanksgiving which very probably was also intended to ensure continued success in the quest for sustenance. A fire was made inside an enlarged hut, and on this fire large quantities of a yellow, frothy tea were prepared from the leaves of the yaupon shrub (*Ilex vomitoria*). According to Cabeza de Vaca (pp. 87–88) the yaupon tea was made by toasting the leaves in a pot over the fire. The vessel, while still on the fire, was then filled with water. It was boiled twice and the contents poured into another jar to cool. The pouring made the drink frothy and it was drunk as hot as possible. From the time it was first removed from the original pot, a chorus of "Who wishes to drink?" fell from the lips of the men. Upon hearing this cry, the women immediately stopped whatever they were doing and remained where they were. If a woman should ever move she was apt to be beaten with sticks by the men. If a woman chanced to pass by while the liquid was cooking and the pot happened to be uncovered, the contents had to be thrown away. Cabeza de Vaca was told that if the drink was contaminated in any of these ways by a woman, a man drinking it would fall sick and die. This drinking bout lasted three days, a man drinking in the neighborhood of five gallons daily!

De Solís (1931: 40–41) in the eighteenth century described Karan-

FIG. 4. Karankawa dancers.

kawan *mitotes,* one of which appears to resemble the drinking celebration mentioned by De Vaca:

They are very much given to dances they call *mitotes.* Some of these
dances are festive and happy, and others funereal and sad, being distinguished from one another by the instruments which they play for them.
For the festive ones they play a tamborine that is made of a tortoise shell,
or of a half gourd, or with a French pot, and a whistle of reeds and an
avacasele, for the sad ones they play certain instruments they call the *caymán.* This is very harsh and melancholy, and to the discordant notes they
add sad and horrible cries, accompanied by gestures, grimaces and extraordinary contortions and movements of the body, jumping and leaping in a
circle. For this *mitote* they light a fire, a big bon-fire and dance around it,
circling around the fire without ceasing day or night. These *mitotes* last
three days and three nights. The Indian women never dance in them; they
stand at a distance in sight of the *mitote,* with their hair over their faces,
confused and melancholy, shouting sadly and helping [*sic*]. In these
dances the Indians seem like demons because of the gestures that they
make. They adorn themselves, that is they paint themselves with vermil-
lion, and on some occasions with black, the eyes arched and reddened.

THE KARANKAWAS of the Texas Gulf Coast are
gone, yet they will forever stir our imaginations. Perhaps this is because, unlike ourselves, they faced daily and directly the stark realities of remaining alive. To those who have seldom been too cold, hot,
or wet, never really hungry, and confidently expect to see many
tomorrows, a people who had none of these advantages come as
something of a shock. Our civilization is like a great blanket cushion-
ing and protecting us from the raw world; the Karankawa blanket
was thin and patchy. Yet, they survived, even thrived, and were
happy with their ways. To Europeans and Texans it was astonishing
and insufferable that such a people should prefer their own gods,
food, and customs to civilization's blessings. But they did, and they
clung to these ancestral ways. And for this they perished. To per-
severe to such ultimate tragedy is a highway to continuing remem-
brance.

PART III
Nomads of the Plains

CHAPTER 4

From Foot to Horse

> The redman and the mustang formed an immediate partnership . . . and this union shook the life of the Great Plains, human and subhuman, like an earthquake.
>
> Roy Bedichek—*Educational Competition*, p. 7

THE HORSE-RIDING, buffalo-hunting, warlike Indians of the plains are among the most familiar of North American Indians, and their memory lingers more picturesquely in the public fancy than that of any other group of native tribes. In the nineteenth century there were more than thirty different tribes following this pattern of life, but most of them were recent invaders of the plains and none of them had been acquainted with the horse prior to the arrival of Europeans. In slightly less than three centuries this revolutionarily new kind of Indian culture came into existence, for a time blazed brightly, and suddenly was extinguished. It was conceived when Indians in the southern plains acquired Spanish horses, it established its form and became rich by hunting the buffalo on horseback, and it disappeared when the buffalo was exterminated and the American frontier overwhelmed it.

85

The problem of how and when Indians acquired horses has always been an intriguing one, especially since many Indians were bewildered and terrified by the first horses they saw. Several centuries later these same tribes were among the finest, most skilled equestrian people the world has ever known. For many years it was assumed that Indians had obtained horses abandoned or lost by the De Soto or Coronado Expedition in 1541.[1] Intensive study of the matter, however, has revealed that it is highly improbable that the Indians procured any horses from these expeditions. Even if some natives had acquired a few strays from early expeditions it is unlikely that they would have known what to do with them, apart from making a meal of them. The care and training of horses, the manufacture of riding equipment, and the skills and techniques of riding are a complicated, interrelated series of traits. They are not learned casually, certainly not by a fleeting glimpse of a mounted man. It was the early seventeenth-century Spanish settlements in New Mexico, particularly in the neighborhood of Santa Fe, that were the centers from which the horse complex spread to the Indians.

In 1598 the future governor and captain general of the colony of New Mexico, Don Juan de Oñate, rode into the Southwest. He brought some four hundred soldiers, priests, and families, and with them were seven thousand animals, including three hundred mares and colts. In a few years the capital had been established at Santa Fe and the surrounding country was dotted with ranches and villages. The Pueblo Indians had been conquered and temporarily cowed, and considerable trade had sprung up with the native peoples dwelling to the north and east. In these Spanish settlements the Indians were employed—or forced—to take care of horses. Soon these Indians were escaping from the Spaniards with considerable equine know-how, and often with the horseflesh as well. These escapees almost surely were the original bearers of horses and the equestrian art to the wild Indians. But the various traders who were soon supplying the new wants of the Indians may also have had a considerable part in teaching them to ride.

[1] The discussion on the acquisition of horses is derived primarily from Haines, 1938a, b, but also from Wissler, 1914; Webb, 1931; and Roe, 1955.

In the early years of the seventeenth century the spread of horses was slow, however, and it was not until the second half of the century that any tribes could be described as horse Indians. By 1659 the Spanish settlements of New Mexico were being raided by Apaches from the northeast, and this soon became a chronic and devastating habit; the Indians carried off as many as three hundred head of live-stock in a single raid. The Spanish expedition of Fernando del Bosque through Texas in 1675, which traveled from the mouth of the Conchos River northeastward as far as the vicinity of present Edwards County, encountered no horses, however, to say nothing of horse-using In-dians. The Mendoza-López expedition eight years later met no horses along the Rio Grande, but to the north on the Pecos, probably in present Crane County, they did meet Indians with horses, and Apaches even managed to steal some belonging to the expedition. (Bolton, 1916: 283–335) In 1680 the Pueblo Indians revolted; the Spanish settlers in New Mexico were driven out or killed, and the Pueblo Indians fell heir to large herds of sheep, cattle, and horses. They had little use for horses, wedded as they were to a settled, gardening existence, but the horses they acquired were eagerly sought by the wandering tribes. This temporarily successful rebellion seems to have done much to accelerate the spread of horses.

When the French explorer La Salle returned to Fort St. Louis in 1686, following an unsuccessful attempt to reach the Mississippi, he brought with him five horses he had secured from Caddoes in east Texas. Horses were scarce at this time, but when Henri de Tonti went in search of La Salle three years later, these Indians had a plentiful supply of them, which, attempting to imitate the Spanish, they called *cavalis*. (Cox, 1905, I: 44–50, 55, 60) From the various, sparse accounts it seems that the Apaches to the north and east of Santa Fe had learned about the usefulness of horses before 1650, and soon thereafter became thoroughgoing horse Indians. By the end of the century all Texas Indians had become familiar with horses, and their Southwestern source was acting like a magnet, drawing to it all sorts of footsore savages, eager to acquire this wonderful new animal. In 1705 the Comanches, in company with their linguistic relatives the Utes, appeared in New Mexico. They came begging peace, but on departing, they stole some horses, thus marking the arrival of the greatest horse thieves of them all. (Thomas, 1935: 105) By the eighteenth century the horse was spreading far beyond the borders of Texas, and by 1750 horses were common throughout the plains, even as far north as Saskatchewan.

Nobody could have planned an animal more suitable for the plains country, or better fitted to flourish under the hard usage of the Plains Indians, than the horses brought to the New World by the Spaniards. According to J. Frank Dobie in *The Mustangs,* these horses were of no single breed, nor of uniform quality, though the best of them were strong in Arabian blood, and many were of the Barb type, the North African version of the Arabian horse. For centuries the Arabian had been bred for several characters which eminently fitted his descendants for success in the New World—endurance, hardiness, swiftness. The Barbs varied considerably, and they seem "to have been somewhat larger than the Arabian, coarser in conformation," but like the Arabians they were "swift and exceedingly hardy and enduring." (1952: 7) In brief, even before he was brought to the New World the Spanish horse was a rigorously-selected animal. The hardships of the ocean voyage were a further culling factor, for something like a third of the horses that left Spain died without ever setting a hoof on an American shore. By the time these imported horses and their offspring reached the New Mexican settlements they indeed were hardy beasts, well-suited to the demands of Spaniard or Indian and capable of quickly going wild to found the immense mustang herds of the American West.

The horses the Plains Indians eventually came to have in such abundance were never known for their beauty, though there were exceptions, but they did retain the essentials of their Spanish, African, and Arabian ancestry—toughness, sturdiness, and tremendous powers of endurance. As Dobie remarks (1952: 16–17), "Their essence survived on the arid borders of Texas where the saying was common: 'A white man will ride the mustang until he is played out; a Mexican will take him and ride him another day until he thinks he is played out; then a Comanche will mount him, and ride him to where he is going.'" A full-grown mustang or an Indian pony was not large, averaging somewhat under fourteen hands high. He weighed only about seven hundred pounds and might be any color. Some of them were fast, and there are innumerable stories of how these small, shaggy, ill-formed, unkempt Indian ponies outran larger, stronger-looking American horses. One of the best and one which has often been repeated is told by Colonel Richard I. Dodge when he was at Fort Chadbourne (north of San Angelo in Coke County). Some officers at the fort teased a band of Comanches into a horse race. The Comanches did not appear to be eager for a race against the soldiers' thoroughbred Kentucky mare, and when they did agree to a race they brought out only a heavy-legged, long-haired "miserable sheep of a pony." At the sight of this pathetic beast, astride which was a 170-pound warrior brandishing a club, the soldiers substituted their third-best racer. In the race the Comanche, using the heavy club smartly, won. The Indians took the flour, sugar, and coffee that had been wagered against their buffalo robes. The soldiers immediately demanded another race, this time racing their second-best horse against this decrepit-looking, overburdened pony. Again the Indians won. The Kentucky mare was brought out, and the betting was furious. At the start of the race the Comanche jockey threw away his club and gave a yell; the horse bolted into the lead, and about fifty yards from the finish line the rider turned himself around on his steed, jeering and gesturing obscenely at the American. Dodge later learned that the Comanches had a short time before won a considerable number of horses from the Kickapoo Indians, using the same horse and approximately the same *modus operandi*. (Dodge, 1882: 341–342)

Just as the Indian pony was primarily of Spanish derivation, so too was the equipment of the Indian rider. The Plains Indians were technologically incapable of slavishly copying Spanish saddles, bridles, or other riding equipment. In general, their riding gear was a simple and primitive copy of Spanish or Mexican models. When, for example, Spanish bridles with their heavy snaffle bits were unobtainable, the Plains Indians substituted—and in many cases preferred—a "war bridle," formed from either a single length of rawhide, or braided rawhide, or hair, with a fixed loop (*honda*) at one end of the rein, through which the other rein passed. Several half hitches were taken with the rope around the lower jaw of the horse, and the free end of the rein was passed through the *honda*, with the surplus tucked under the rider's belt.[2] The end of the rein would pay out if the rider was thrown, and a nimble man could retrieve his mount and his seat in a moment. A long, dragging line was also occasionally used for the same purpose.

Most Plains tribes knew how to make crude saddles (apparently copied from Mexican or Spanish types) by stretching green buffalo hides over wooden frames, the shrinking of the hides tightening the framework. But also in common use, particularly for warriors and hunters, was a "pad" saddle, which was essentially a pillow stuffed with hair or grass, to which a girth and short stirrups were attached. The total weight of such a saddle was said to be less than three pounds. Comparable to our racing saddles, it doubtless added many extra miles to a day's ride or considerable speed to a short sprint.

Plains Indians showed no more originality and creativity in their methods of riding than they did in other equestrian aspects. They mounted their horses from the right side, aping the Spanish custom which had, in turn, been acquired from Moorish Arabs. (Roe, 1955: 63–64) Plains Indians did add a few innovations, such as a loop around a mount's neck, or a loop braided in the mane, from which they could suspend their bodies and so shield themselves behind their animals. The fascinating fact is not, then, that Plains Indians altered or bettered Spanish equipment or riding techniques but that they became—man, woman, and child—such incomparably magnificent horsemen. If not the best in the world, certainly they were among the finest. And there appear to have been no Indians who were more at home on a horse or who could perform more incredible feats of horsemanship than some of the Indians of the southern plains.

If the horse is thought of as the vehicle which bore the cultures of the Plains Indians, then the buffalo becomes the fuel which propelled it. The American bison (*Bison bison*), popularly misnamed "buffalo," is a gregarious relative of the European bison, our domes-

[2] See Ewers (1955) for a detailed discussion of the equipage that Plains Indians used on their horses.

ticated cattle, and other bovine ruminants. There have been bison in North America since at least Middle Pleistocene times, and as has been noted already, Paleo-Americans hunted forms of huge bison that are now extinct. Whether the modern buffalo is an evolutionary descendant of these Pleistocene giants, or a more recent emigrant from Asia is unknown; there is no question, however, that the natives of North America habitually hunted bison of these several species throughout their residence of more than ten thousand years on the plains.

Seldom has any other animal provided so many basic cultural requirements.[3] In one way or another, buffaloes provided food, both for immediate and future use, shelter, clothing, weapons, tools of various sorts, bedding, ropes, glue, cosmetics, fuel, and drink. It is almost unnecessary to remark that when the "inexhaustible" herds of buffalo became extinct the cultures which had come to lean so completely on them collapsed.

When Europeans came upon the scene bison roamed over much of North America east of the Rocky Mountains and north of Mexico, but the enormous herds were found primarily on the Great Plains. Here these herds wandered in tremendous tidal waves whose extent and number stagger the imagination. It was long supposed that their movement was a regular migration, but Roe (1951:674) has shown conclusively that "these wanderings were utterly erratic and unpredictable and might occur regardless of time, place or season, with any number, in any direction, in any manner, under any conditions, and for any reason—which is to say, for no 'reason' at all." Areas which had long had buffalo might suddenly be abandoned by them; on the other hand, regions which had never been favored might suddenly be overrun. Some of the reasons for the capricious movements of the herds are, however, understood. Roe has suggested that the dense, heavy coat of the buffalo indicates that it was adapted to cold climates, and that its extension to mild latitudes occurred in relatively recent times. Summer heat in the southern part of its range

[3] The discussion on bison is drawn from Roe, 1951; Hornaday, 1887; and Garretson, 1938. Roe's work is far and away the most comprehensive and exhaustive (also exhausting) study of this subject ever made.

91

rather than a lack of good grazing land often forced herds to move several hundred miles northward. This is particularly pertinent to the Texas Indian utilization of buffaloes, for the southern margin of the buffalo range passes through Texas. This means that in many parts of Texas winter may have been a better hunting season than summer, and that many buffalo hunters may have moved northward out of the state in the summer months.

Unfortunately no study has ever been made of the buffalo range in Texas prior to the nineteenth century. My impression is that large herds seldom crossed the mountain and desert barriers of trans-Pecos Texas, or south of the Edwards Plateau in early times. On the east, herds were found on the coastal prairies, but not in the piney woods of east Texas. In the first half of the nineteenth century buffalo seem to have disappeared generally from all but the Panhandle section of the state, only to reappear in the latter part of the century, apparently driven south by the concerted slaughter to the northward. But, as Roe suggests, the accuracy of such statements is open to question since their historic appearances and disappearances from parts of that state "appears to constitute little more than further corroborative evidence for the irregularity I have demonstrated throughout their habitat generally." (1951: 595–600) (See Map 2.)

Temperamentally, the bison was ill-suited for survival in a world of mounted hunters equipped with firearms. He was naturally sluggish, mild in disposition, and often incredibly stupid. His outstanding characteristic was his one-track mind—"whatever he did, he did with all his might." (Garretson, 1938: 44) Tales of his obstinacy and stupidity are legend. Both Indian and white hunters were sometimes able to shoot an entire standing herd if the animals were not alarmed, and the sight of other buffaloes dying did not necessarily arouse them. When on the move—or stampeding—few things could halt or turn bison, and there are many stories of their crossing rivers on the mired and trampled bodies of their fellows. From time immemorial the Indians took advantage of this trait of willy-nilly following the leader to run them over cliffs and precipices. While their stubbornness and lack of intelligence had much to do with their extinction as free, wild creatures, this is not to say that buffaloes were

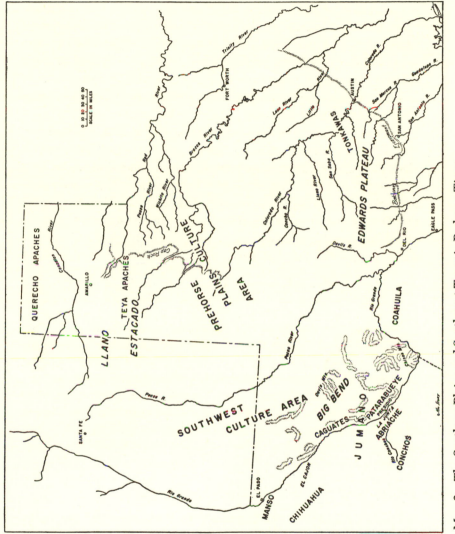

MAP 2.   The Southern Plains and Southwest Texas in Prehorse Times

completely harmless and inoffensive. They were the largest of the big-game animals in North America; bulls averaged about fourteen hundred pounds and might stand some six feet high at the shoulders. Despite this bulk and their somewhat awkward gait, they could move rapidly, and when enraged were extremely dangerous. They were fast enough to outrun good horses if they had a slight lead to begin with, and usually could outdistance an average horse. Add to these characteristics their temperamental unpredictability and it is easy to see why supposedly docile, tame buffaloes have frequently trampled and gored men to death.

As the number of buffaloes astounds us, so too does their wanton slaughter by nineteenth-century Americans. The year 1830 is generally taken as the demarcation before which their destruction was "desultory" and after which it was "systematic." The most prodigious slaughter took place, however, following the Civil War, with the introduction of repeating rifles and the rapid westward advance of the frontier. No one has ever improved on Hornaday's bitter remarks concerning this butchery (1887: 486–487):

The men who killed buffaloes for their tongues and those who shot them from the railway trains for sport were murderers. In no way does civilized man so quickly revert to his former state as when he is alone with the beasts of the field. Give him a gun and something which he may kill without getting himself in trouble, and, presto! he is instantly a savage again, finding exquisite delight in bloodshed, slaughter, and death, if not for gain, then solely for the joy and happiness of it. There is no kind of warfare against game animals too unfair, too disreputable, or too mean for white men to engage in if they can only do so with safety to their own precious carcasses. . . . Perhaps the most gigantic task ever undertaken on this continent in the line of game-slaughter was the extermination of the bison in the great pasture region by the hide-hunters. Probably the brilliant rapidity and success with which that lofty undertaking was accomplished was a matter of surprise even to those who participated in it.

I have no quarrel with Hornaday's feelings, only with the literal accuracy of his reference to man's savagery. The opposite proposition has probably more truth to it: "savages" act suspiciously like "civilized" men when they indulge in the wholesale, wanton butchery of wild creatures.

The destruction and extermination of the buffalo meant the end of Plains Indian cultures. This fact was clearly recognized by Americans, and at times was used to rationalize their slaughter of the herds. In 1875 a bill was introduced in the Texas Legislature which would have at last protected the buffalo. General Philip Sheridan was at that time commandant of the Military Department of the Southwest; he heard of the bill, appeared before a joint assemby of the House and Senate, and his speech killed the bill. In his speech he averred (Cook, 1907: 113) that the white buffalo hunters

are destroying the Indians' commissary; and it is a well-known fact that an army losing its base of supplies is placed at a great disadvantage. Send them powder and lead, if you will; but, for the sake of a lasting peace, let them kill, skin, and sell until the buffaloes are exterminated. Then your prairies can be covered with speckled cattle, and the festive cowboy, who follows the hunter as a second forerunner of advanced civilization.

Although Texas was at the southern edge of the buffalo range, parts of the state probably supported as heavy a concentration of these animals as was to be found anywhere, particularly the Staked Plains. The remarkable Llano Estacado is an eastward-sloping tableland, a part of the High Plains which sweep from Canada to southwest Texas. It lies south of the Canadian River, and is bounded on the north and east by the Cap Rock escarpment, and to the west in New Mexico by the eastern ranges of the Rocky Mountains. On the south the Llano Estacado passes onto the Edwards Plateau without any natural or noticeable barrier. To the eye the Llano Estacado is an incredibly flat plateau, broken only occasionally by shallow river valleys, playa lakes, and sand dunes. The Canadian River is the only river entrenched in a deep valley across the Texas Panhandle, but other shallow valleys cut across the plateau to form the upper reaches of some of the major rivers of Texas—the Red, Brazos, and Colorado. This is semiarid land, the average rainfall being less than twenty inches and fluctuating widely. The "normal" precipitation pattern is often broken by cycles of drought, devastating to the rancher and farmer—and equally unfortunate for the hunter whose quarry had forsaken a drought-stricken land. Winters are mild compared to those in the northern plains, the summers are hot, and the high evaporation rate rapidly reduces the potential benefits of summer rains. In late summer the Staked Plains often have the appearance of a sunscorched desert, but after spring or summer showers the land is transformed into a green carpet of grazing grasses. It was these grasses—buffalo, grama, needle, bunch, and others—which supported the incredible numbers of buffalo, pronghorn antelope, and deer.

South of the Llano Estacado the High Plains continue as the Edwards Plateau across the Pecos to the barren mountains of trans-Pecos Texas. Rimming the southern and eastern border of the Edwards Plateau is the Balcones Escarpment, curving in a vast semicircle from Del Rio to Austin and beyond. For roving hunters the Edwards Plateau was perhaps a shade less attractive than the Staked Plains, for there were more cedar brakes and brush land, and less grass for animals to graze, particularly bison. On the south and east sides of the plateau, streams have cut jagged canyons through the Balcones Escarpment, and up and down its margins innumerable springs break out. To judge from the archeological remains along it, prehistoric men must have found it a good place to live. To the east of the Cap Rock Escarpment and bounded on the east side by the western Cross Timbers (which extend from present Montague County west of Gainesville south to the west of Fort Worth) was a belt of oaks and brush forming a barrier to the east. This was predominantly prairie land in its native state, although in this century mesquite has taken over large areas, and it supported a rich store of buffalo and other grazing animals. These plains and prairies were the regions of Texas which supported the fantastically numerous buffalo. Here were found the pronghorn antelope, far beyond the numbers of the present day, skittering across the sun-drenched plains. And here too were deer, wolves, coyotes, and many other animals. These regions were made expressly, one might imagine, for the mounted Indian hunter. He gave the land up only when the buffalo had disappeared and his own life's blood had drained in vain into its sun-baked sands.

When the Indians of the southern plains acquired horses, it touched off a series of revolutionary changes in native cultures somewhat like those initiated by the automobile and electricity in our own. Horses immediately strengthened the economies and the military potential of Plains tribes. The possession of horses made a life primarily devoted to buffalo subsistence an easy and richly rewarding one. Before the spread of horses some peoples in the southern plains had depended upon the buffalo for their subsistence, and a number of agricultural tribes hunted them seasonally, but a buffalo-hunting existence was neither easy nor particularly rewarding. Pedestrian buffalo hunters were faced with difficult logistic problems, so difficult that even though buffalo were plentiful, hunters were hard pressed to keep their families and equipment in the vicinity of the herds. If the buffalo had remained in one locality throughout the year, or had even followed a regular pattern of seasonal migration, then prehistoric Indians could have relied more fully on them. But this was not the case, as we have seen. Even now, with our encyclopedic knowledge of the buffalo, the reasons for their erratic and unpredictable movements are not fully understood. It is no wonder there seem to have been only a few tribes who subsisted solely on the buffalo in pre-horse times.

The most successful prehorse adjustment on the plains apparently was one in which there was a combination of gardening and bison-hunting. With such an economy there was little danger that both the gardens and the supply of game would fail at the same time. Drought sometimes ruined the crops and the buffalo might vanish, but only infrequently would both food sources fail at once. There are some hints in the early Spanish literature that even those tribes that did not plant gardens carried on considerable trade with the agricultural Pueblo Indians. It follows that in poor hunting years they may have gotten "advances" from them, or resorted to raids and stealth to subsist until the game returned.

But horses changed all this; they allowed hunters to find the herds

97

even though they were ranging far from their usual pastures, and they provided quick and easy transport for people and their equipment so that they could remain near the herds. Horses rapidly transformed poorly-equipped hunters, who had likely lived a life of occasional feast and frequent famine, into rich, lordly nomads whose bellies seldom growled with hunger. Equipped with the horse, Plains Indians developed many of the characteristics of pastoral peoples of the Old World, despite the fact that the buffalo upon which they depended were never domesticated. The similarity can be pushed too far, but the raiders of Genghis Khan are paralleled in many respects by the Comanches, the Cheyennes, or the Sioux (Dakota).

The adoption of horses also increased greatly the incentives for southern Plains tribes to be warlike. To acquire an adequate number of horses they were forced to raid the Spanish settlements or other Indians who already had a supply. The horse-propelled, buffalo-hunting economy also made the southern plains hunting grounds a rich prize for the warlike, particularly since they were also adjacent to the original southwestern source of horses. Before the eighteenth century was well under way a dramatic and decisive conflict between the eastern Apaches and the Comanches was raging on the southern plains. Oddly, too, the horse, which did so much to make possible the Spanish conquests in the New World, was in the plains "an important factor in barring further expansion to the same nation." (Mishkin, 1940: 5) The southern plains Indians, particularly the Comanches, became so strong and aggressive that the Spanish were unable to subdue or conquer them. But southern plains tribes also blunted French penetration into the Southwest to the Spanish advantage, to say nothing of slowing down the American frontier's westward movement.

Although the Indians who adopted a mounted, buffalo-hunting livelihood had many diverse geographical and cultural origins, there developed besides the buffalo subsistence and horse complex a number of other distinctive cultural traits which characterized Plains cultures. The tepee (a skin-covered conical tent) was used by all these peoples for at least part of the year. It was transported from camp to camp by the horse-drawn travois, an improvised vehicle consisting of two trailing poles serving as shafts for the horse and bearing a platform or net piled high with camp gear, babies, etc. (see illustration facing p. 85). When on the move, or during communal hunting activities, the bands were usually controlled by some sort of "police" or soldier societies. Various bands or units of a tribe usually joined forces in the spring or early summer for a communal hunt, social festivities, and religious ceremonies, climaxed in many tribes by the sun dance. A special form of warfare—characterized by small war-parties utilizing essentially guerilla tactics, combined with an intricate system of counting coups (literally "blows" but often interpreted as merely touching the enemy) and other war honors—became one of the most distinctive features of Plains culture.

By the nineteenth century this cultural pattern had spread throughout the plains, and had been adopted by peoples of quite divergent cultural backgrounds. Where some of the distinctive traits of the Plains Indians cultures came from is a matter of speculation, although many characteristic Plains traits were clearly present in one or another of the prehorse tribes of the southern plains. Following the adoption of the horse these were synthesized to form a new cultural pattern. Many of the basic traits associated with horses, bison-hunting, and probably war undoubtedly originated with, and were first spread by, those tribes that were prehorse buffalo hunters and also were near the southwestern center of horse dispersion. Such people as Coronado encountered when he rode onto the Llano Estacado would fit the bill. The Spaniards called these Indians Querechos and Teyas. The Querechos—a term derived from a Pueblo word for those buffalo-hunting Indians east of New Mexico—are not surely associated with a later historic tribe. (Hodge, 1907a, 2: 338) But it is probable that they were an eastern Apache people, perhaps the ancestral group from which the Jicarillas, Lipans, and Kiowa Apaches developed. The Teyas may have been a Caddoan group who had partly or entirely forgone a settled, farming life for the excitement of the chase, but other evidence suggests that they too were Apaches. (Swanton, 1942: 35; Harrington, 1940: 512) Whoever their descendants were, the Querechos and Teyas were the prototypes for the historic, equestrian Plains Indians. They were buffalo hunters par excellence, their food was mainly buffalo flesh, their tepees were of buffalo hide, and much of their other equipment was once a part of this beast. They even communicated with strangers in sign language, a typical trait of the historic Plains Indians. A chronicler of the Coronado Expedition (Winship, 1896: 527–528) described these prehorse plainsmen as people who

follow the cows [buffaloes], hunting them and tanning the skins to take to the settlements in the winter to sell. . . . They travel like the Arabs, with their tents and troops of dogs loaded with poles and having Moorish pack-saddles with girths. When the load gets disarranged, the dogs howl, calling someone to fix them right. These people eat raw flesh and drink blood. They do not eat human flesh. They are a kind people and not cruel. They are faithful friends. They are able to make themselves very well understood by means of signs. They dry the flesh [of the buffalo] in the sun, cutting it thin like a leaf, and when dry they grind it like meal to keep it and make a sort of sea [sic] soup [mush] of it to eat. A handful thrown into a pot swells up so as to increase very much. They season it with fat, which they always try to secure when they kill a cow. They empty a large gut and fill it with blood, and carry this around the neck to drink when they are thirsty. When they open the belly of a cow they squeeze out the chewed grass and drink the juice that remains behind, because they say that this contains the essence of the stomach. They cut the hide open at the back and pull it off at the joints, using a flint as large as a finger, tied in a little stick with as much ease as if working with a good iron tool. They give it an edge with their own teeth. The quickness with which they do this is something worth seeing and noting.

ALTHOUGH THESE PREHORSE southern plains people (who were probably Apache) contributed some of the fundamental traits of historic Plains cultures, and were among the earliest Indians to adopt horses, as so often happens, others took up where they left off to become more successful and certainly better-known plainsmen. By the nineteenth century most Apaches had been driven from the rich hunting grounds of the southern plains by the Comanches, and with the exception of the Kiowa Apaches, were not even "typical" Plains people. Other customs which came to characterize the historic Plains tribes, such as the sun dance and soldier societies, were originated and put into their modern form by more northerly tribes, often with origins outside the plains. Southern plains tribes, then, particularly those of Texas, were not "typical" Plains Indians in an over-all, nineteenth-century sense, but in all probability they were the original Plains Indians: the precursors and perhaps originators of an important part of the fiber of later Plains culture.

CHAPTER 5

The Lipan Apaches:
Conquerors Dispossessed

> In some places we came across camps of people of the
> Apache nation, who are the ones who possess these
> plains, and who, having neither fixed place nor site of
> their own, go from place to place with the cattle al-
> ways following them.
>
> Don Juan Oñate (1601)

APACHE! A word burned deep in the heart of turbulent Southwestern history; a word which calls up thoughts of the frontier, of
ambush, of bravery and bloodshed. The people primarily responsible
for these connotations were the nineteenth-century western Apaches
of Arizona and New Mexico. They and their leaders—Geronimo,
Cochise, Mangus Colorado, Victorio—merit fully the attention that
has been paid them in novels, movies, and folklore. But they are
famous or infamous not because they were more savage, or braver,
or more bloodthirsty than many other Indians but because they were
among the last to be "pacified," and so their exploits are better recorded and are fresher in our minds.

These western Apaches (Navaho, San Carlos, Chiricahua, and Mescalero tribes), because of linguistic and cultural differences, are distinguished from an eastern group of Apache tribes. The modern eastern Apaches (Jicarilla, Lipan and Kiowa Apache) are the remnants of what was once a numerous, widespread, and powerful assemblage of tribes. (Hoijer, 1938) In contrast to their western brothers they are poorly known and unheralded, at least so far as the more recent history of the American Southwest goes. But during the sixteenth and seventeenth centuries and probably earlier, the eastern Apaches and the Mescaleros were the predominant people of the southern plains. The story of their subsequent downfall is important to the understanding of the culture of the nineteenth-century Texas Apaches—the Lipans. Without such a historic perspective their culture is distorted, even incomprehensible. (See Map 2.)

Origins and Early History. The prehistoric past of all these Apache people would doubtless make an exciting tale if only its full particulars could be told. At least the historic and linguistic facts are plentiful enough to lay the basis for some speculative and enticing theories. The Apache tribes of the Southwestern United States (both eastern and western divisions) are speakers of Athapaskan, geographically a widespread language family. The bulk of the Athapaskan-speakers are concentrated in the far Northwest—Canada and Alaska. Some of them are among the most primitive hunters in the New World, but others—the Tlingit and Haida of the Alaskan coast—are members of the relatively-advanced cultures of the Northwest Pacific Coast. But how and when did the southern Athapaskans become separated from their northern relatives? One popular hypothesis is that the southern Athapaskans are relatively recent newcomers to the Southwest, that small bands of nomadic Apaches filtered into the Southwest and southern plains by working their way south through the High Plains and against the eastern flanks of the Rocky Mountains. Here and there they may have met people already in possession of the land; they probably fought some of these and undoubtedly learned and borrowed cultural elements from them. They are often credited with being the nomadic raiders who caused the abandonment of some of the Pueblo towns several centuries before Spanish entry into the Southwest.

Regardless of the time Apaches arrived on the southern plains, virtually nothing is known of them archeologically. No Apache sites have been discovered in Texas, though it seems likely that they have been found but not recognized as Apache. Nor is the geographical extent of the eastern Apaches known, though it is probable that they roamed over vast reaches of the southern plains. The archeological assemblage known as the Dismal River culture, dated at 1700, give or take twenty-five years, and first discovered by A. T. Hill on the Dismal River fork of the Loup River in western Nebraska, is beyond any reasonable doubt Apache. Dismal River remains have since been found in scattered sites extending from western Nebraska south to western Kansas, but these Apaches had apparently moved from the Southwest to the plains in historic times, for no earlier stages of this culture have been identified or unearthed.[1]

The Spaniards were the first Europeans to encounter eastern Apache tribes, but they were never sufficiently familiar with them either to distinguish consistently between different groups or to provide much knowledge of their cultures. As we have seen, Coronado met one Apache tribe, possibly two, in 1541, the Querechos on the Llano Estacado of eastern New Mexico or the Texas Panhandle, and the Teyas somewhere about the headwaters of the Brazos. The next reference to Apaches in this vicinity was made by Vicente de Saldivar Mendoza in 1599, who had been sent by Oñate to procure buffalo fat on the plains. He first met Apaches in the vicinity of Las Vegas, New Mexico, and as he traveled eastward he encountered larger and

[1] Hill and Metcalf, 1941. Also see Strong, 1935, and Wedel, 1940: 291–352. In the Texas Panhandle and in northcentral Texas there are several late prehistoric archeological complexes which may prove to have been Apache, though so far as I know no archeologist has ever suggested any connections. The Henrietta Focus, for example, in the upper watershed of the Red, Trinity, and Brazos rivers should be examined thoroughly for Apache affiliations; it was not Wichita, Caddo, or Tonkawan. Bone fishhooks are found occasionally, the only element which seems to be definitely non-Apache.—See Krieger, 1946, and Suhm et al, 1954: 80–87.

larger concentrations of them, whom he termed Vaqueros. These were apparently the same people as Coronado's Querechos. (Gunnerson, 1956: 352) By the beginning of the seventeenth century the colonizer of New Mexico, Don Juan de Oñate, had turned his attention to the exploration of the plains. His account provides some interesting ethnographic tidbits, but it does nothing to straighten out the growing complexity in Apache names. His expedition in 1601 followed the Canadian River to the vicinity of the present boundary between Texas and Oklahoma and then turned to the northeast. Near the Arkansas River he encountered a *rancheria* (a term employed by the Spaniards with various meanings but usually meaning "village" or "camp") of Apaches numbering, he said, more than five thousand souls and called Escanjaques. (Bolton, 1916: 257) The Escanjaques guided Oñate's force to the Arkansas but would go no farther for fear of their Wichita enemies, who lived just north of the river. After an encounter with Wichitas, Oñate turned back but was forced to fight a major battle with the now-hostile Escanjaques.

Toward the close of the seventeenth century the Spanish began to refer to the Apaches east of the Rio Grande by specific band names. "Querecho," "Teya," "Vaquero," and "Escanjaque" were replaced by a confusing welter of names which often cannot be associated with later Apache peoples. The modern Jicarillas are recognizable in the Spanish documents of the early eighteenth century, however. And this is of considerable help in clarifying the lines of descent of modern Apaches, since the Jicarillas were closely related to the Cuartelejo Apaches, and at least one student has connected the latter with the Vaqueros. (Gunnerson, 1956: 352, 356; Wedel, 1959: 69–75) The Jicarillas, in turn, are closely related to Lipans, and in the eighteenth century there were probably even fewer differences separating them. In brief, there is a connection, if a somewhat tenuous one, between the sixteenth-century Querechos and the modern Lipans. The Cuartelejos were forced by Comanche invaders to unite with Paloma and Carlana Apaches under Spanish protection. Oddly, these united Apaches abruptly disappear from the pages of history in the mid-eighteenth century. (Thomas, 1935: 50)

The earlier associations of the Kiowa Apaches, or the eighteenth-century Spanish name for them, are still a mystery. It is entirely possible that they were unknown to the Spaniards. In the nineteenth century Kiowa Apaches ranged into Texas, but they were so closely associated with the Kiowas that they are discussed with them. Another group of Apaches mentioned frequently by the eighteenth-century Spaniards are the Faraones (or Pharaohs). They appear to have become the Mescaleros of later times, or at least a subdivision of them. Their original range included far west Texas, so they are quite properly regarded as Texas Indians. But because their land was soon pre-empted by Comanches, forcing them to flee the state, and because their culture was similar to that of the Lipans, no further mention of them will be made here. (Swanton, 1952: 329; Thomas, 1935: 80)

The early decades of the eighteenth century were critical years, in a sense fatal ones, for these eastern Apaches. They had begun to raid the Spanish settlements in New Mexico before the opening of the new century and the Spanish made their first retaliatory expedition against them in 1702. The Faraones were among the most audacious of these raiders, stealing horses, women, and children, both from the Pueblos and from the more settled Apaches. (Thomas, 1935: 23–24) The Spanish made numerous campaigns against nomadic Apaches in the first half of the century, and while they had little success in halting their forays they must have sapped their strength considerably. The Comanches and Utes had suddenly emerged from the isolation of their desolate plateau and mountain homeland to begin their attacks on the Spanish settlements and upon the eastern Apaches. Lastly, the Wichitas were soon supplied with French equipment, to say nothing of the desire for Spanish horses, and they also became more aggressive in their long-standing war with the eastern Apaches. In short, by the beginning of the eighteenth century all the neighbors of the eastern Apaches had become their actual or potential enemies. They were in the jaws of a vise, Comanches pressing against them from the north and Spaniards from the south. The character of some eastern Apache cultures played squarely into the hands of their enemies, particularly the Comanches. Many of the eastern Apaches had traditionally lived from spring until harvest time in *rancherías* (in this case meaning small villages) during which time they planted and harvested their crops. In the fall they embarked on a buffalo hunt which lasted until the following spring and the new planting season. These small gardening villages do not seem to have been actively linked together, so mounted bands of Comanches could sweep down on unsuspecting *rancherías* and destroy them one at a time, before their inhabitants could muster effective resistance.

By 1740 the Mallet brothers (French explorers) could remark that the Laitanes (Comanches) dominated the country between the Platte River and Sante Fe, although they also encountered bands of Padoka (the French term for Apaches prior to 1750), who were trying to hunt in this region without being detected by the Laitanes. To add to the misery of eastern Apaches, soon after 1740 their Indian enemies—Comanches, Utes, and Wichitas—began to acquire a fairly adequate supply of firearms from the French. But the Spanish denied firearms to the eastern Apaches, even when they were on friendly terms, so their plight rapidly became desperate.[2]

Many of the scattered eastern Apache bands must have been wiped out during the early years of the eighteenth century, but others, like the Jicarillas, took refuge among the Puebloan peoples, expecting protection to be provided them by the Spanish as it was for the Pueblos. They were disappointed in these expectations, and the modern Jicarillas are probably but a fragment of their former might, even though they likely include remnants from other eastern Apache tribes. (Thomas, 1932: 42–46, 58–59, 115, 194) Other Apaches, newly-mounted on their Spanish ponies, scattered over the southern plains. Some, who were to become the Kiowa Apaches, may have been isolated from their Southwestern relatives at this time by the Comanche wedge driven into the southern plains. In time this small and numerically weak fragment was forced to join the more powerful Kiowa tribe, and in the nineteenth century again reappeared on the plains of Texas. Other eastern Apaches, already on the southern

[2] Secoy (1953) contains a good discussion of this subject in *Changing Military Patterns on the Great Plains*. Also see Margry, 1879–88, VI: 457–461; Secoy, 1951.

margins of the High Plains, were forced farther into Texas and into Mexico, to become the often despised, renegade, and savage Lipans of recent Texas history. Their name is taken from *Ipa-n'de*—probably the personal name of a long-forgotten leader—to which the suffix *n'de* (signifying "people") has been added. (Swanton, 1952: 322; Brant, 1949; 1953) (See Map 3.)

By the nineteenth century the separate fates of these surviving eastern Apaches had produced three somewhat varying tribal cultures. The Jicarillas acquired to some extent a non-Plains, Puebloan-derived cultural orientation.[3] The Kiowa Apaches represent the other face of the coin, and have been termed one of the typical southern plains tribes. The Lipans remained a southern plains tribe, but they lacked some of the cultural frills which to many minds typify Plains Indians.

From the foregoing discussion it is apparent that the Lipans of the eighteenth and nineteenth centuries possessed a culture already much altered by the earlier historic disasters which had befallen it. What information we possess about their culture is derived from late nine-teenth- and twentieth-century sources—an account (edited by Dennis and Dennis, 1925; also see Sjoberg, 1953b) left by F. M. Buckelew, a white captive who spent eleven months in 1866 and 1867 with them, and a surprisingly large body of information gained from surviving Lipans. (Opler, 1936, 1940, 1945, 1959) I have also included some brief notes concerning the Vaquero and Escanjaque Apaches with my account of Lipan life. These sixteenth- and seventeenth-century accounts of Apache life on the plains supply an entrancing sketch, whether or not the Lipans are latter-day descendants of Vaqueros or Escanjaques.

Appearance and Dress. In Mendoza's time male Vaqueros customarily went naked, "but some are clothed with skins of buffalo and some with blankets. The women wear a sort of trousers made of buckskin, and shoes or leggins, after their own fashion." (Bolton, 1916: 225) Oñate's Escanjaques likewise "had large quantities of hides which, wrapped about their bodies, served them as clothing, but the weather being hot, all of the men went about nearly

[3] Opler (1946: 3) takes a very different viewpoint.

naked, the women being clothed from the waist down." (Bolton, 1916: 258) Essentially, Lipan costume in the nineteenth century remained as simple, for the most part, as that of earlier Apaches. In summer men wore a breechclout, leggings, and moccasins; in winter a buckskin shirt and a blanket were added. The women wore a knee-length deerskin skirt, snug-fitting leggings fastened to a belt around their waists, and high moccasins. By the nineteenth century their costume was topped by a Mother Hubbard sort of blouse fashioned from a complete doeskin. A hole was cut in the middle of the skin for the head to slip through, and the deer's tail, with the hair left on, was allowed to hang down the back. The younger girls beaded their dress elaborately and often fringed their garments with brass or tin ornaments. Children wore shirts of buckskin, and began to dress like adults only when they were nearly grown.

Warriors cut off the hair on the left side of the head even with the top of the ear and allowed the hair on the right side to grow long, sometimes almost reaching the ground. The long hair normally was folded up and tied with string so that it did not fall below shoulder level. Feathers and trinkets adorned the hair. The left ear was pierced with from six to eight holes, the right with one or more. On dress occasions earrings were worn in all these perforations. The men spent many spare moments plucking out their beard and eyebrows, the ideal masculine face being devoid of hair. Both face and body were smeared with several colors of paint. The women also wore earrings, made of copper wire and beads. Their hair usually was worn in one long plait down their back, but for special occasions was left unbound. Rings of polished copper were worn at the wrists and ankles, and highly-prized shells of river clams were made into finger-length bars, perforated, and worn around the neck. F. L. Olmsted, who briefly met the Lipans in the 1850's, was dazzled by Castro, a chief, who wore "a buckskin shirt, decorated profusely with bead-work" and had upon his head a *"wreath of fresh oak leaves."* Heavy brass rings fell from his ears, and a red stripe blazed across his face, "including the edge of the eyelids, whose motion had a horrid effect." Olmsted thought "his face was not without some natural dignity and force, but the predominant expression was wily and brutal"; his eye-

Fig. 5. Lipan warrior and his wife.

lashes and eyebrows had been plucked out. Olmstead seems to have been enchanted, on the other hand, by the "delicate features and slight proportions" and the "tolerably neat and pretty buckskin cape, with fringed leggins" of the girl who rode with Castro. (1860: 293) All in all a Lipan must have been a colorful sight when fully attired and ornamented. Their ideas of beauty and adornment were at great variance with our own, yet it is difficult to understand how they were any less rational.

By our standards Lipans were filthy, yet considering that they had no soap and frequently little water they did pretty well. Their one continual problem was lice (Dennis and Dennis, 1925: 98):

The lice laid their eggs, or nits, in the seams of their clothing. It was amusing to see them take a garment and fold it with the seam exposed and pass it between their teeth biting the nits. You could hear them pop, and from the greedy manner in which they would lick their lips it was evident that they liked the taste of the nits.

Subsistence and Material Culture. Throughout their known history the Lipans lived primarily upon the buffalo. The principal hunting seasons were fall and spring, at which times the buffalo were concentrated on the southern plains in huge herds. Frequently their fall hunt continued through the winter until spring, so that often their year was divided into two parts. Buffalo-hunting was usually a co-operative, group effort. Hunt leaders were especially chosen, and under them subleaders were selected to control small groups of men. After a suitable herd had been surrounded the hunters closed in from all sides and shot the animals with bows and arrows, the few guns they possessed, or even speared them. In earlier times these surrounds were conducted on foot, but as the Lipans came to possess horses their hunts were carried on more and more by mounted men and with more effective results. In the off season, and probably more often in the prehorse days, the individual hunt for buffalo was not uncommon. Mendoza in 1598 (Bolton, 1916: 230) while on the Llano Estacado noted that the Vaqueros killed buffalo "at the first shot with the greatest skill, while ambushed in brush blinds made at the watering places."

112

Many other animals were hunted in addition to bison, particularly in the nineteenth century, when the bison were approaching extinction. Wild cattle and the cattle of ranchers were treated much as were the bison, although their slaughter had little of the excitement of the bison hunt. Deer and antelope had always been valued for their skins, and smaller animals such as javelinas and rats were hunted. Wild turkeys were eaten, but other birds, particularly water birds, were not regarded as fit for human consumption. Buckelew took part in an antelope "surround" made somewhere between the Pecos and the Rio Grande in west Texas. All who could ride, including women and children, helped to surround a herd of antelope that were grazing unsuspecting in a natural basin. Those who did not have weapons took up positions from which they could drive back the antelope as they headed for the safety of hilly country. When everyone was in position a group of warriors rode into the basin and began to shoot the antelope, while the other hunters rode around the herd in ever-decreasing circles. The frantic animals would dash first to one side of the circle, to be met by a hail of arrows, then would turn and try to escape in some other direction, only to be met again by arrows. The hunt continued until all the antelope had been killed or had escaped; quite a few did find their way to freedom during the excitement of the chase. (Dennis and Dennis, 1925: 99–100)

As soon as a buffalo or some other big-game animal had been killed, the hunter opened the carcass and ate the raw, bloody liver. Small intestines of beeves and buffaloes were roasted whole and eaten; the large intestines were opened, washed, roasted, and also consumed. Heads were roasted together in pits and leg bones were also roasted, then split open for their marrow. Meat that was not immediately eaten was jerked—that is, cut into thin strips, placed on a rack of sticks, and smoked or sun-dried, after which it was stored in rawhide bags. Small animals such as rats were roasted whole, the burned fur and skin being peeled off before they were eaten.

While the Lipans always seem to have depended more upon bison for food than upon the women's gardens, the raising of maize, beans, squash, and pumpkins was an important, if secondary, subsistence activity in prehorse days. Some of the more horticulturally-inclined eastern Apaches, the Jicarillas for one, even irrigated their fields, but it is doubtful that the Lipans ever did so. Spanish documents indicate that those eastern Apaches who could not or did not raise their own crops made annual summer pilgrimages to the pueblos to trade for them. Mendoza in 1598 (Bolton, 1916: 226; also see Thomas, 1935: 142; map, 50), for example, mentioned that he had met Apaches "coming from trading with the Picuries and Taos, populous pueblos of this New Mexico, where they sell meat, hides, tallow, suet and salt in exchange for cotton blankets, pottery, maize and some small green stones which they use." In later years the annual visits to the Spanish pueblo settlements were clearly as much raiding ventures as trading journeys, and they may always have been so. The addition of horses to Lipan life (during the second half of the seventeenth century) enabled them to move camp, follow the herds, and kill the buffalo with much more dispatch and efficiency than they had ever been able to do afoot.

Mendoza witnessed a band of Vaqueros on the march, a sight which amused him but one which also gives us insight into the nature of prehorse transportation problems. These people were "driving great trains" of shaggy dogs which carried or dragged, by means of a travois, their tepee covers, food, and other belongings. The women loaded the dogs and adjusted their loads by holding the dogs' heads between their knees. Although the dogs snarled at one another, they traveled one after another "at a steady gait as if they had been trained by means of reins." (Bolton, 1916: 226–227) But no matter how well-trained their dogs, it is obvious that they could not compare to horses as beasts of burden.

When the Comanche onslaught began, early in the eighteenth century, horses must have already wrought many changes in Plains Apache life, not the least of which was the minimizing of gardening. Comanche attacks on Apache *rancherías*, and their frequent destruction, were further incentives to abandon their fields. Before the middle of the eighteenth century the Lipans had been forced into the more desolate reaches of western Texas and northern Mexico, to an environment even less conducive to agricultural pursuits. Throughout their later history gardening decreased in importance;

114

and even when the women did manage to plant gardens, camp likely was soon moved and the fields temporarily or permanently abandoned. By the time Buckelew was captured, Lipan women had forgotten many of their gardening techniques; they even asked him to show them how to plant corn. (Dennis and Dennis, 1925: 93)

Perhaps the most important wild-plant food of the Lipans, at least after they had come to frequent the drier regions of Texas and northern Mexico, was the various species of Agave. Agaves are widespread in the southwestern United States and adjacent Mexico, and there are something like a hundred species of this rather curious plant. The most familiar of the agaves is the century plant, frequently cultivated in American gardens; in present Mexico the best-known of the agaves is the maguey, the plant from which the fiery drink, pulque, is made. The tough, spiny, and fibrous leaves of the agaves grow from a central head or bulb. Most species are slow to mature and it may be fifteen years before a flower stalk is thrust upwards from the bulb or crown. This flower stalk grows rapidly and in some species may push upward twenty-five or thirty feet. Clusters of fragrant creamy-white flowers blossom from this stalk. In some species, as happens with salmon and some other animals, this reproductive act is the final one, for the plant dies forthwith. Texas Indians—Jumanos, Coahuiltecans, Lipans, and many of the prehistoric peoples—made extensive use of agave and sotol, a related plant. The fibers of the leaves were used in basketry and for sandals, and the more tender leaves could be roasted in the coals for a somewhat tough but tasty food. The flowers and the flower stalk, especially the bulb, were widely used for food. Preparation of the bulb was everywhere about the same; the following description is taken from Buckelew's detailed account of his captivity in 1867. By this date sotol had become one of the Lipans' most important foodstuffs and was in constant use. To prepare it, they put rocks into a roaring fire. Whether this fire was in a pit is not clear; Buckelew called it a "kiln." By the time the wood had burned down, the rocks had attained the desired temperature and the ashes were removed. The sotol bulbs were placed on the rocks and both rocks and sotol were covered with dirt. The bulbs were left for several days at the end of which time they were thoroughly cooked. The bulbs were raked out and left to cool, then were beaten into thin sheets and allowed to dry. Sotol could be eaten in this form, but the Lipans preferred to grind it into coarse flour from which they made small ashcakes. Buckelew said these cakes "made a very good substitute for bread." (Dennis and Dennis, 1925: 98) Besides agave, tunas of prickly pears, mesquite beans, datil (*Yucca baccata*), nuts, and wild fruits were utilized by Lipans.

Oñate's *sargento mayor*, Mendoza on the Canadian River in eastern New Mexico in 1598, gave an intriguing description of the Vaquero *ranchería* he visited. It was one

in which there were fifty tents made of tanned hides, very bright red and white in color and bell-shaped, with flaps and openings, and built as skillfully as those of Italy and so large that in the most ordinary ones four different mattresses and beds were easily accommodated. The tanning is so fine that although it should rain bucketfuls it will not pass through nor stiffen the hide, but rather upon drying it remains as soft and pliable as before. . . . The *sargento mayor* bartered for a tent and brought it to this camp, and although it was so very large, as has been stated, it did not weigh over two *arrobas* [fifty pounds].[4]

Nineteenth-century Lipans continued to dwell in bisonhide tepees, although they were less grand than those mentioned by Mendoza and Oñate. Their framework was of light poles, ordinarily sotol stalks, the heavier ends of which were placed in a circle, with the lighter ends tied together at the top. Hides were thrown over this framework except for a smoke hole at the top and a small entry hole, which could also be covered with a hide. The more capacious housed a dozen persons, the smaller only three or four. Beds were made by piling grass or cedar twigs to a depth of several inches and covering this with dressed hides, fur side up. Each person rolled up in a blanket and threw one of these hides over himself. Roemer (1935: 103), in Texas in the 1840's, inspected a Lipan camp at New Braunfels and was reminded "of a picture of the Orient."

[4] Bolton, 1916: 226–227. Oñate himself a few years later also mentioned large tents among the Escanjaques (*ibid.*, 257).

In the first tent that we visited lay a young Indian of effeminate, Bacchus-like appearance, stretched out on soft buffalo hides, holding a pipe, one and one-half feet long, from which he would take a few puffs from time to time. At his feet squatted a young Indian woman with rather broad, but otherwise not unpleasant features, who gave a little black-eyed two-year old boy white river pebbles to play with. At the same time she looked up to the young man with the greatest respect, obviously ready to do his slightest bidding. Not far from them sat an old woman with an ugly wrinkled face, apparently the mother of the young warrior or that of his wife.

Even in the second half of the nineteenth century, when firearms were more easily secured than they had been in Spanish times, the basic, trusted weapon of the warrior remained his bow and arrow. Lipan poverty was not the only reason for this. A bow and arrow, in comparison with a single-barreled, muzzle-loading rifle, was a very effective weapon for hunting buffalo or when making a charge. The Texas Ranger Noah Smithwick (1900: 220–221), reminiscing about Lipans, said that they "could discharge a dozen arrows while a man was loading a gun, and if they could manage to draw our fire all at once they had us at their mercy unless we had a safe retreat." Buckelew (Dennis and Dennis, 1925: 118) went so far as to assert that a Lipan "could present and string his bow, then shoot an arrow almost as quickly as we can shoot our modern rifles today."

Lipan bows were usually about four feet long and were made of seasoned mountain mulberry. Bowstrings were of split deer or bison sinews twisted together. The arrows were made of hard wood and were always kept dry; three feathers were tied on with sinew, and in historic times were tipped with iron points, generally obtained from barrel hoops. In pre-European times flint was used to tip weapons, and Mendoza (Bolton, 1916: 230) noted that the Vaqueros' weapons "consist of flint (tipped arrows) and very large bows, after the manner of the Turks. They saw some arrows with long thick points, although few, for the flint is better than spears to kill cattle [bison]."

It was necessary to take great care of bows and arrows; a damp bowstring had little snap, and warped arrows never flew true to their mark. Arrows were kept up by covering them with blood, though what good it would do is to be wondered at. The Lipans tested the trueness of an arrow by biting it. Quivers of calf or deerskin about four feet long were used to carry the bow, arrows, and fire-making equipment. Warriors also carried lances made with fine steel blades fastened to wooden handles. For protection they carried oval shields about three feet by two feet, made from thick, bull bisonhides. Arrows and even rifle bullets glanced off these shields unless the hit was dead center. Buckelew (Dennis and Dennis, 1925: 119) summed up the capabilities of the warrior and his equipment by saying that "the Indian with his powerful equipment of bow, arrows, lance, tomahawk and shield made him a good warrior. His knowledge of the open life and his power of endurance added to his cunning ability to take every advantage, and made him a very dangerous enemy."

Even in the second half of the nineteenth century, when flint and steel were available, Lipans preferred to light fires with the old-style fire drill. A long stick of sotol about the size of a broom handle, with a hole in its center and a notch cut in its side, was held on the ground with the feet. Another stick of dogwood (*Cornus* sp. var.) or wild china (*Sapindus drummondii*), known also as soapberry, about the size of an arrow was inserted in the hole and twirled rapidly in the fingers, producing a powdery dust which filtered down the groove onto a dry leaf. Soon the dust was smoking and in a moment was fanned into flame. If the twirler was rubbed in sand or grit, the fire could be made more rapidly.

In the arid country that the Lipans increasingly came to inhabit, several sorts of containers for water were necessary. Warriors carried a bag made from part of the stomach of a beef or buffalo. A drawstring closed this bag and it hung from the left hip. The continual ooze from it left the hip damp, but the evaporation kept the water cool. For camp use the familiar basketry water jug of the Southwestern Athapaskans, covered with pitch or rosin, was utilized. These containers held five or six gallons and were carried by the women with the help of a rawhide strap.

When Buckelew lived with the Lipans they had large herds of

horses, mules, and even cattle. The cattle were little valued except as food, and no attempt was made to breed or maintain them. It was so easy to steal cattle from ranches and to shoot wild ones that there was no incentive for them to become cattle raisers. Horses were a different proposition. The boys, often captives, took the horse herds to different pastures daily, and the entire camp moved at frequent intervals to find fresh pasturage. The favorite war horse was staked by a warrior's tepee at night and was always treated with care. The equipment used on the horses belied the expert quality of Lipan horseman. Crude saddles were made by fitting two hackberry forks to a horse's back and joining them together with two narrow hackberry laths two and one-half feet long. Two pieces of green rawhide with the hair left on were fitted snugly over the wooden members, sewed with buckskin thongs, and allowed to dry. The shrinkage of the rawhide assured a rigid, strong saddle. Riding saddles had a horn whittled on the front fork and stirrups were made to fit the entire foot. (Dennis and Dennis, 1925:74) Other accouterments for horses were similarly crude copies of Spanish or American models, or were obtained outright from their white neighbors.

Social Organization. Lipans believed that at birth both lightning and a small whirlwind entered the body by way of the throat. These were the mysterious forces which kept the body warm and alive. When they departed, so too did life. (Opler, 1945: 123) Childbirth took place within the tepee, with male members of the household excluded. Women gave birth in a kneeling position, a midwife holding the mother firmly by the shoulders. As soon as birth was accomplished the child's umbilical cord was cut about four inches from the body and tied close to it. The placenta was hidden where no animals could get to it. After mother and baby had been washed, the child was held up to the four points of the compass and was also "shown" to the sun—his introduction to the world. A mother was not supposed to nurse her new-born child for two days, and was confined to her tepee for four days. A few days after birth (probably four) the child's father named it after some natural object. And at the end of the four-day period the infant was placed on a cradleboard "made of buckskin stretched over a wooden frame and often beaded elaborately. It laced up the entire length of the front." (Dennis and Dennis, 1925: 92) During the day the mother paid scant attention to the tightly-confined baby; at night he was removed from the cradleboard and slept with his mother.

Like most other American Indians, Lipans seldom resorted to corporal punishment of children. Particularly unruly young people were doused with water but were seldom beaten. There was much familiarity between children and their grandparents, and a great deal of instruction about everyday behavior as well as information about the supernatural world was imparted by them. Little is known about the training and instruction of the nearly grown. The Jicarillas, for example, had puberty ceremonies, but there is no record of them among the Lipans. As was common among many North American Indians, as Lipan boys matured they were exposed to increasing hardships. They were made to do such things as roll naked in the snow and expose their bodies for long periods under a hot summer sun. They were also encouraged to become accustomed to danger, to court peril—all in all, a program designed to develop them into tough, eager warriors. By their late teens the youths usually had become warriors—meaning men—and were ready for marriage.

Lipan marriage was in concept and practice, quite distinct from our own. Marriage was a contract between two families, with each member of the partnership having duties and responsibilities not only to the mate but to the mate's family. When a young man desired to marry a girl he was expected to obtain permission from her father, or brother, or some other male relative. But even though marriage was "an understanding between families rather than between individuals" (Opler, 1945: 135) there was considerable courting of girls, and courting techniques included the use of a flute whose dulcet notes presumably softened the resistance of a maiden's heart. If the girl's parents agreed to the union, the bridegroom made them a gift of horses, firearms, and skins. The marriage ceremony was private; at least the young captive Buckelew had to hide while he watched the proceedings. Heated rocks were thrown on the flesh side of a large beefhide to make it curl up into a rough basin. It was then taken

120

to a secluded place and partly filled with water. The bride and groom appeared, stepped into the water hand in hand, and "marched around in the water for some time." Later their parents put in a solemn appearance, and after "a few other formal ceremonies the whole party marched back to the village" where a dance was held. (Dennis and Dennis, 1925: 113–114)

Marriage obligated a man to perform certain duties for his wife's family. As the wife's brothers left the extended family when they grew to manhood and married, the protection and breadwinning for the family fell to the husbands of daughters. Even when a man's wife died he was not released from his obligations, and he remained under the control of her family. Normally they would provide another wife for him, either a sister of his deceased wife or a cousin. If there was no woman available, or if the family so desired for some reason, they could dismiss the widower. The widespread custom of marrying a deceased wife's sister (sororate) is often a very effective and useful social mechanism. In the Lipans' case it meant that a family's economic well-being was not jeopardized by the departure of a provider. Nor was a widow released immediately from the obligations to her deceased husband's family. She had to observe carefully the period of mourning, often in the camp of her husband's family, and his family frequently produced a cousin or brother of her dead husband for her to marry. In recent times, the feeling that a man is not released from his obligations to his wife's family because of her death has led to a number of difficulties. One of Opler's informants, for example, told him about a maternal aunt of his mother's who had married a Mescalero. Without getting permission from her relatives, he married again after her death. His first wife's relatives did not forget this and "a long time afterward" one of them, a woman, stabbed him. He seized the knife and killed her, and in the ensuing fight two of his relatives were killed. (Opler, 1945: 138–139)

Among the Lipans, who, as we have seen, practiced not only the sororate but occasionally sororal polygyny (the state of a man's having several sisters as wives at the same time), a child who lost his mother either had another mother already (his mother's sister or one of her cousins) or his father would marry one of these women after his mother's death. Actually, however, the practice of polygyny seems to have been restricted to chiefs and outstanding warriors.

Husbands were extremely jealous, and in common with the custom of many other Plains Indians, an adulterous wife was punished by having her ears or the tip of her nose cut off, by a beating, or even by killing her. Some cuckolded husbands, however, simply abandoned their faithless spouses and their responsibilities to her family, and joined some other local group or band.

The Lipans (as well as the Kiowa Apaches) employed a kinship system which has been termed Matri-Hawaiian. (Murdock, 1949: 228–231) It is distinguished by the fact that all cousins—whether children of father's brothers or mother's sisters (known as "parallel cousins" to anthropologists), or children of a father's sister or a mother's brother ("cross-cousins")—were called by the same terms as those used for siblings. And Lipans had three sibling terms: older brother, older sister, and younger sibling. As might be expected, since the sororate was practiced, the same term was used for a mother's sister as for "mother," and the term for a father's brother was the same as that for "father."

A fascinating aspect of Lipan kinship was the respect and joking relation which prevailed among different categories of relatives. We have already noted the "educational" relation between grandparents and grandchildren. This relationship was also a "joking" one in which many vulgar remarks pertaining to sex and mating were passed. There was also a good deal of jesting with the spouse of any relative of the same generation and sex. On the other hand, siblings of opposite sex were treated with reserve if not by downright avoidance.

The central characteristic of Lipan beliefs and customs concerning death was a terror of ghosts.[5] This fear led to the quick burial of the deceased, destruction of the dead person's property, and to the immediate family's moving its tepee following burial. If it was a man who had died, shots were fired into the air to announce the unfortunate occurrence. (This custom may well have been initiated by seeing white soldiers shoot volleys in the air under similar circum-

[5] The discussion here is drawn from Opler, 1945.

122

stances.) Two elderly persons were immediately chosen to care for the corpse—elderly ones because they were less apt to be contaminated by death than young people. It was even better if one of the pair had some supernatural power by which ghosts might be controlled. These caretakers washed the body, combed its hair, and dressed it in its best clothes and ornaments. The possessions of the dead person were collected and tied with the body to a horse, which was led to the place of burial. Here a shallow grave had been dug and the body and possessions were lowered into it. The head of the body was placed toward the east, and before the grave was filled a caretaker addressed the corpse and commanded it to leave peacefully for the afterworld and not to return to bother its relatives. Food and water were placed with the corpse for its use during the journey to the other world. Normally the favorite horse of the deceased was killed over the grave by shooting an arrow into its neck.

The burial party took the precaution of returning to camp by a different route from the one they had taken with the corpse so that if the ghost tried to return to camp it would become confused and lost. The relatives of the deceased and those persons who had come in contact with him had to take all sorts of measures to rid themselves of contamination and to demonstrate their grief. Purification was by bathing, by sprinkling on pollen, and by smoke. Widows showed their grief by copious weeping, shaving the hair from their heads, and tearing their clothing or throwing it away. It was thought that ashes sprinkled at the head of the bed would discourage ghosts, and that a flint knife thrust into the ground at the head of the bed would prevent children from having nightmares and dreams brought on by prowling ghosts. Fasting was at least occasionally a part of mourning. Flacco, a Lipan chief who had been made a colonel by the Republic of Texas for his many services to it, had a son who was maliciously murdered by a Texan. Flacco and his wife appeared at Noah Smithwick's home sometime after they had learned of their son's death. They had starved themselves until they were like mummies. Smithwick finally persuaded them to break their fast with a meal especially prepared by his wife. (Smithwick, 1900: 223)

As soon as possible after burial the immediate family moved its camp in the opposite direction from the grave. It would be merely a token move, but, like the other customs surrounding death, it was yet another way of outwitting malevolent ghosts. Out of fear of contagion close relatives of a dead person kept away from other people for a number of days. After a week, more or less, friends invited them to rejoin the group. It is not surprising, considering the feelings Lipans had about death, that not only their own graves but all graves were scrupulously avoided. Even speaking the names of dead persons was avoided and thoughts of them were suppressed since they too were apt to draw the attention of ghosts. Sensibly, the death of the very young or the very old was not regarded as so catastrophic as the death of those in the prime of life. There was even a ceremony of the last blessing performed for the aged and dying in which no fear of death was shown.

The basic social unit among Lipans was a group of persons—termed an "extended" family—composed of parents, unmarried sons, daughters, and sons-in-law. A number of these family groups tended to remain together, and at least in early times moved within a restricted territory, after which the groups were often named. The most important man of a local group functioned as the leader to the extent that he was a chief advisor and director of local-group affairs. The largest social grouping of any real importance to the Lipans was the band. This was a confederation of local groups near enough geographically that they could unite for defensive or offensive purposes, and meet for social and ceremonial occasions. The most prominent and respected of the local-group leaders was the band chief. Beyond the bands there was no formal tribal organization. In fact, the Lipans were a tribe only in the sense that they were a distinct people culturally—a politically unorganized group of bands sharing a common life.

In later times, as the existence of the Lipans became more and more threatened by enemies, bands came to have war chiefs in addition to civil chiefs, although the civil chiefs appear to have retained their dominant position of leadership. Men became chiefs through their acknowledged bravery and experience. There was some tendency for chieftainship to become hereditary, but it could scarcely go further,

124

for poor leaders were quickly deposed, and band members could shift to another band if they were displeased with the leadership. The absence of any real political organization above the band level and the absence of any feeling of tribal unity, to say nothing of the shifting composition of the bands, suggest an explanation for the ease with which the eastern Apache, from the eve of historic times on, could become so divided and scattered. There was no internal force to keep them together—and hence strong.

As was true of other Plains Indian cultures, warfare was a major preoccupation of Lipan men, and in one way or another came to influence almost every phase of life. During the eighteenth and nineteenth centuries Lipans really had little choice in the matter: it was be warlike or perish. For more than a century the Comanches and their allies had carried on a war of extermination against the Lipans, the stakes being the richly rewarding bison plains of west Texas. The Comanches, better-equipped and more numerous, gained their objective; they won the bison lands. The Lipans were also frequent enemies of the Mexicans and occasionally of Americans, both of whom they raided when occasion permitted.

One of the principal ways of gaining prestige, not to mention wealth, was to become a successful warrior. Attaining chieftainship, as we have already seen, was in part a matter of demonstrated bravery and courage. Despite the accent on war there was seldom if ever a time when even an entire band of Lipans engaged in battle together. Typically, war parties consisted of from eight to a dozen men. Any warrior could lead a war party and only men who wished to do so joined the venture. All other southern plains Indians carried on their warlike activities in the same way, so there was no necessity for the Lipans to mass large numbers of men for defense. Americans and Mexicans were accustomed to fighting battles with large numbers of men, but the Lipans—like other Indians—merely refused to fight on these terms, and if possible carried on their guerrilla warfare. Frederick Law Olmsted (1860: 298) aptly remarked of the difficulties of Indian warfare, "Keeping a bull-dog to chase mosquitoes would be of no greater nonsense than the stationing of six-pounders, bayonets, and dragoons for the pursuit of these red wolves."

125

Buckelew (Dennis and Dennis, 1925:112) said that before a war party left for a raid

the old squaws would go some distance from camp, to some kind of evergreen trees, often in the cedar brakes. There they would spend a whole night in a weird mournful chant. This was a solemn time for all, but only the older squaws took part in their chanting ceremony. I suppose they were imploring the Great Spirit for success for their braves.

The morning after this ceremony the war party or parties left camp. On the raid in which Buckelew was captured the war party approached the farm on foot, leaving their ponies several days' journey back in the brush. Many other Plains tribes also raided afoot, a custom which is perhaps best viewed as a traditional holdover from prehorse days.

Attacks, under veil of night or early morning, were made quickly. If unable to surprise an enemy, the warriors were likely to postpone or call off the attack. Lipans were very adept at their own defense. If an attack was expected, relays of scouts were kept on duty watching the enemy, or on the lookout if he had not yet appeared. Smoke signals and messengers were also used to keep them informed about enemies. If an attack seemed imminent, the women and children were sent to the hills to hide while the men mounted their best war horses and headed for battle. Scalps were taken, and according to one of their myths, were prepared by holding the scalp by the hair and exposing its flesh side to a fire. After the flesh was burned and dried off, a stick, which would serve as a carrying handle, was run through two holes made in the scalp. (Opler, 1940: 49) Sjoberg (1953b: 95–96) has also discovered that parts of dead enemies, particularly Comanches, were cut off and eaten by victorious warriors. This custom may have been borrowed from their Tonkawa neighbors, but proof is lacking. War parties also took captives, who were either tortured and killed after the warriors had returned to camp, or were adopted. Captive children, particularly young boys, were used to herd horses. There were apparently many devices of torture, including slow burning, light stabbing, hacking off small pieces of flesh from living victims, and the like. Usually captives were turned over to older women whose menfolk had been slain by the enemy. Their revenge was no doubt sweet to them but horrible for us to contemplate.

When the returning war parties had been successful—which meant that they had lost no warriors and had captured horses, loot, or prisoners—they sang as they approached camp so that the people might come out and greet them. Once in camp the warriors sat in a circle, slapped their thighs, or in later times a sage-filled buckskin pillow, in time to their singing. (Opler, 1940: 48–49) This was the prelude to a victory dance, which included a scalp dance. No victory dance was held, however, if a warrior had been lost. According to Buckelew (Dennis and Dennis, 1925: 112), upon the return of a successful war party the old women "spent another night chanting their weird tunes. The tunes chanted now were not so mournful and seemed a little lively." Before resuming normal life, a Lipan who escaped from his captors had to undergo a ceremony which "brought him back"—cleansed him from his contamination.

Captives of Lipans who were to be adopted (as was Buckelew) were treated to a harrowing ceremony which was similar to the custom of "running the gantlet" of Eastern tribes. In Buckelew's case, as he and the war party approached camp a squaw came out, pulled him from his horse, threw his blanket aside, and began to whip him with a quirt. She whipped him until *she* was almost exhausted, then shoved him toward the camp. In camp the old squaws, boys, and girls were lined up awaiting the captive with quirts, sticks, and clubs while the warriors stood by to see that the boy could not escape. As he walked down the line everyone struck him at least once and the blows became heavier as he progressed, since the older youths and younger women were placed at the far end of the line. By the time he had reached the end of the line it had broken and a howling mob was following him. Suddenly, all became quiet and the old crone who had first whipped him approached with a murderous-looking knife, motioning for him to follow her. She led him beyond the camp to an open place where she sat on the ground. She forced him to lay his head in her lap. The women and children sat down in a circle around these two, the warriors standing beyond them. The women

127

began a mournful chant, and soon they were joined by the children. The captive was frozen with terror.

When the chanting ceased, the old woman forced the boy's head back until his throat was exposed, and raised her knife high in the air. But instead of plunging the knife into his neck, she slowly drew the blade back and forth across his throat, barely touching the skin. Several more times she flourished the knife and repeated the pantomime. Finally she motioned for him to rise, and the crowd followed woman and boy to her tepee. There she gave him supper and pointed out his pallet. But they were not done with him yet. In the morning a crowd again gathered in front of the tepee. The old squaw motioned him to the door, where without ceremony she stripped him of his tattered rags and dressed and painted him in Lipan style before the highly-entertained onlookers. After he was fully dressed the squaw began to examine his ears, and before the befuddled lad knew what was happening she had pierced one with a thorn. Then she forced him to stand still while she repeated the process on the other ear. The worst of the captive's ordeal was now over; as soon as his ears had healed, the old woman gave him a nice pair of earrings. He became the son of the warrior who had captured him, calling his captor "father" and this man's wife "mother."

Supernaturalism. The important supernatural personages so far as the average Lipan was concerned were a number of deities whom individuals could approach intimately, although they did hold vague beliefs in some sort of supreme power. The world of these supernatural figures has been clearly and interestingly pictured by Morris E. Opler in his *Myths and Legends of the Lipan Apache Indians.* In common with the mythology of other Southern Athapaskans, Lipan mythology included a culture hero—Killer-of-Enemies—who killed or otherwise disposed of various monsters and enemies. Before retiring from the affairs of men, he created deer, horses, other animals, and taught Lipans about warfare and raiding; in fact Killer-of-all Enemies founded all of Lipan culture.

Included in the cosmology of the Lipans is an origin tale about how they emerged from an underworld or perhaps an afterworld.

Souls also returned to this under- or afterworld at death. It was divided into a northern and a southern compartment; the spirits of sorcerers and the wicked went to the northern division, where fog and fire plagued them and snakes and lizards were their only food. Just where the underworld or afterworld was, is in doubt. Most stories refer to a "place below," but there are others which suggest that the dead went to a place near the camps of the living. Opler has recorded a number of tales in which persons have been wounded or otherwise injured and have visited (in delirium) the land of the dead, only to be returned, since their time had not yet come. Admittance into the land of the dead was almost universally by means of eating some sort of fruit (often tunas of the prickly pear); either the fruit was refused by those people who returned to life, or it was not offered to them by the dead.

Lipans feared the dead, or perhaps more accurately, the spirits of the dead. They believed, for example, that dead sorcerers might appear to the living as owls, and they were particularly afraid of dead relatives. Using the names of the dead was tabooed, so names died with their owners. This great fear of ghosts stemmed from the belief that they could return to this world and persecute or haunt those persons who had harmed them in some way. There was also the belief that the dead would like their relatives to be with them, so they were constantly exerting pressure to lead the living to the land of the dead.

A person became a shaman by having supernatural experiences. Theoretically anybody could have these mystical or visionary experiences, but they seem to have been uncommon. A shaman's power to control or predict events could be transferred from himself to another person. Normally he did not transfer his power until he was aged or felt that he was near death, the reason being that ceremonies and various rites, to be effective, had to be performed perfectly. If the power was used incorrectly or misused, the supernatural powers were apt to punish the original holder even though he had transferred it to another; hence shamans would not usually risk supernatural punishment or death by transferring their power until late in life.

The person seeking the power made a cigarette and presented it to the possessor of the power. If agreeable to the transfer, the power-possessor taught the neophyte his ritual and knowledge.

Shamanistic rites were conducted to cure the sick, help obtain game, bring misfortune to the enemy, foretell an enemy's approach, find lost objects, and control the weather. Shamans could also perform tricks, including the handling of snakes. They made various amulets and fetishes, often of stuffed skins, which were painted and were vaguely anthropomorphic in appearance. Most shamanistic rites were performed before small family groups, but there were larger gatherings in which the welfare of the whole people was at stake and in which all participated. Buckelew witnessed such a gathering, apparently of an entire band, assembled in this instance to deal with an eclipse of the moon. How the Lipans knew an eclipse was to occur is a puzzle, but at least Buckelew's description gives us some insight into important group ceremonials. Late one cloudless, moonlit night everybody—men, women, and children—gathered at the base of a low hill not far from camp. Here they sat in a great circle in the middle of which was a drum and "the long chain of disc-shaped bones and the smooth dry sticks." The musicians who were to play these instruments took their places, the spectators waiting, hushed, for them to begin. By signal they commenced to play, but differently from the music Buckelew had heard before. Soon the moon began to fade, became obscured, and occasionally the spectators accompanied the music with a low, mournful chant. The night darkened, the moon disappeared, but the music and chanting continued. Finally the moon began to emerge and shone again; the ceremony a success, the music stopped and the people returned to camp. "The music, the expression on their faces, in fact everything connected with the ceremony, depicted great solemnity." (Dennis and Dennis, 1925: 112–113)

AN AURA of the romantic and tragic clings to the Lipans, as it does to all Apaches. But apart from the intangibles of such a characterization, the dominant, recurring theme of later Lipan culture is its descent from something better. From their high estate as recent conquerors of the southern plains, they became dispossessed and harried remnants. Once a gardening and hunting people, they next became hunters, and finally poverty-stricken hunters and gleaners. From the proud and independent warriors Coronado met in the sixteenth century they became the skulking, beggarly riffraff of the Texas frontier.

CHAPTER 6

The Tonkawas: Central Texas

> Their huts were small and barely numbered thirty, all
> conical in shape, made of light branches, covered
> with the same material and an occasional buffalo skin.
> In the center of each is located the fireplace around
> which lie the male Indians in complete inaction, while
> the women are in constant motion either curing the
> meat of the game, or tanning the skins, or preparing
> the food, which consists chiefly of roast meat, or per-
> haps making arms for their indolent husbands.
>
> José María Sánchez (1828)

THE TERRITORY atop the Edwards Plateau and spilling over onto the
coastal plain to the south and the Brazos bottoms on the east and
northeast was the sixteenth-century homeland of a number of autonomous bands of Tonkawan Indians.[1] The word "Tonkawa" was

[1] For this chapter I have drawn heavily from Andrée F. Sjoberg's article on
this tribe (Sjoberg, 1953a). My interpretation of the ethnographic facts, however,
varies considerably from hers. She should not be charged, of course, with my
point of view.

133

derived from the Wacos' term for them, *tonkaweya,* which means "they all stay together." Tonkawas called themselves *tickanwatic,* meaning something similar to "the most human of people." The term appears in many forms, including Tonkawega, Tancaoye, Tancaguas, Toncahua, and Tonquaay. (Hoijer, 1952, II: 788–789) The independent bands were the Tonkawa proper—the Mayeye (or perhaps Meghey), Yojaune, Ervipiame—and a number of smaller, more obscure groups, the Cavas, Emet, Sana, Toho, and Tohaha. During the seventeenth and eighteenth centuries the scattered Tonkawan bands were reduced in numbers and by the beginning of the nineteenth century the surviving remnants had united to become a tribe, henceforth known as the Tonkawa. It is only after these groups became the Tonkawa tribe that a fairly full description of their habits and customs becomes possible. At this time the Tonkawa tribe was fairly typical of southern Plains Indians, with some rather close similarities to Lipan Apaches. What Tonkawan culture was like and what its affiliations were at an earlier date are uncertain, although the culture appears to have been then—as in later times—part of the southern Plains prehorse culture area. I have been unable to find support for the assertion that the archeological associations of the prehistoric central Texas peoples lay to the south. (Sjoberg, 1953a: 300; Krieger, 1946: 167) (See Map 2.)

Considerable linguistic data have been collected about the Tonkawas, but it has been difficult to relate their language to any other. (Hoijer, 1933; 1938) Swanton (1915; 1940) has suggested that the Tonkawa language belonged to the Coahuiltecan linguistic stock, but since there are no longer any speakers of Coahuiltecan this hypothesis is difficult to substantiate. It is unlikely that their language had no connection with that of any neighbor, and since their language was not Caddoan, Atakapan, or Athapaskan, Swanton's suggestion is attractive.

Origins and Early History. How long Tonkawan peoples roamed central Texas before the advent of Europeans is not known. The most recent archeological complex of central Texas—the Central Texas Aspect, and particularly one of its components, the

Toyah Focus—has been tentatively associated with Tonkawan peoples. (Suhm, 1956; 1957; 1959) But as sites of the Toyah Focus intermixed with identifiable historic material have not been found, this association remains somewhat speculative. Nonetheless, there is not the slightest particle of evidence which would suggest that the Tonkawan peoples recently came from somewhere else, so it is assumed that their ancestors were the people whose cultural remains are known (or partly known) to archeologists as the Toyah Focus of the Central Texas Aspect. The area of the Central Texas Aspect is roughly duplicated by the territory of the historic Tonkawas, and the archeological remains are about what one would expect for Tonkawan peoples. Peoples of the Central Texas Aspect lived by hunting, gathering, and fishing; they practiced no agriculture. Their sites are concentrated along the streams and rivers of central Texas, and they often seem to have camped on the burnt-rock middens of the earlier Archaic cultures (Edwards Plateau Aspect), their probable ancestors. They seem to have manufactured some rather plain pottery and obtained some from Caddo tribes to the east. (Jelks, 1953: 206; Suhm, 1955) All these traits are also applicable to the early historic Tonkawas.

It is barely possible that Cabeza de Vaca met Tonkawan peoples, and De Soto's successor, Luis de Moscoso, may also have encountered them. The first definite information Europeans had about Tonkawan peoples, however, comes from Henri Joutel, La Salle's follower, who heard of the Meghey (Mayeye) in 1687. Father Douay, on one of the French sorties from La Salle's Fort St. Louis, also met some Indians who may have been Tonkawan. Some of these people were mounted, and they galloped up to the French "booted and spurred and seated on saddles." (Cox, 1905, I: 223; Bolton, 1914b) They invited the French to their "town" but since it was not in the direction the French were taking they did not visit it. These Indians had been in contact with Spaniards, and if they were in fact Tonkawas they must have been ranging far to the west, into New Mexico, a quite considerable distance from their usual territory.

But it was Alonso de León's expedition in 1690 that marked the

135

beginning of continued European contact with Tonkawas. This expedition encountered Tonkawas in Victoria and Lavaca Counties; the more southerly group Massanet called Emets and Lavas (Cavas). (Bolton, 1916: 359) It may be significant that when the Spaniards approached a Tonkawa encampment the Indians "made for the wood, leaving to us the *rancheria, together with the laden dogs,* which they had not been able to drive fast enough when they fled." (Bolton, 1916: 359. Italics mine.) Using dogs to pack buffalohides, as these Indians were doing, is a typical Plains Indian custom. Besides the Emets and Cavas this expedition also met the Toxo (Toho) and Toaa (Tohaha) Indians.

By 1698 a mission had been established in northeastern Mexico for the Ervipiame, and throughout the eighteenth century various Tonkawan bands requested that missions be established among them. A number were, and Tonkawas and other Indians were gathered together in them. The reasons behind these requests are obscure, although we can be confident that the Tonkawas were not seeking religious succor from Spaniards. Then, as later, the militarily weak Tonkawas stood to profit by any kind of alliance they could make with powerful European invaders. The number of Tonkawas must have declined considerably during the eighteenth century, too, although information is sparse on this point. Introduced diseases were undoubtedly the major cause of decline, but their strength was also reduced by the fact that scattered Tonkawan bands sometimes joined other groups. It is known, for example, that by 1778 some of the Mayeyes had joined the Karankawan Cocos on the Gulf Coast and had intermarried with them. (Sjoberg, 1953a: 282) By the nineteenth century the remnants of the various Tonkawan bands had become the Tonkawa tribe. Their consolidation into a relatively well-organized and cohesive tribe served to slow their decline but it does not appear to have halted it.

Appearance and Dress. The physical characteristics of the Tonkawas are not well known; they do not seem to have been outstanding among Texas Indians because of any noticeable physical attribute. If they had been tall like the Karankawas or dark

136

as were the Caddoes, the fact would surely have been recorded. One nineteenth-century settler in the Bastrop vicinity, John H. Jenkins, (1958: 9–10, 161–162), does, however, give us a clue to their appearance, contrasting a Tonkawa captive to his Comanche captors:

He was very slender, indeed was much smaller than the Comanches, as well as different from them in form and feature. . . . he ran a footrace with one of the Comanches, and such running we had never before seen. The Tonkawa came out ahead and was pronounced winner, but both were most wonderfully fleet, nimble, and light, the race being one hundred yards.

Tonkawas seem to have shared with many other Texas Indians the general custom of wearing clothing mainly for protection from the elements and not to enhance the appearance or indicate status. On the other hand, the body—particularly the male torso—was richly adorned by painting and tattooing, and the head and neck were bedecked with earrings and necklaces. The one unique feature of Tonkawan attire was the extremely long breechclout in vogue among the men; otherwise they wore buckskin or bisonhide moccasins, leggings, skin shirts (in later times), and bisonhide robes, as the weather dictated. Women's clothing is poorly known, partly because there was so little of it. Their principal garment was a short skin skirt. In warm weather children wore little if any clothing, and the Texas Ranger Noah Smithwick (1900: 248) recalled a case in point. The Tonkawas were keenly interested in the settlers' social affairs, appearing uninvited at every wedding or "preaching." At one of the latter events the Tonkawas, as usual, had come,

watching and listening as intently as if fully understanding all that was being said. At last a squaw, weary of holding a chubby baby boy in her arms, stood him up in the door where his highly original costume, consisting of tiny bow of pink ribbon in lieu of the traditional fig leaf, attracted much attention.

Even in the nineteenth century, after several hundred years of exposure to mission influence and European custom, Tonkawas con-

137

tinued much of what must have been their native habits in clothing and bodily ornamentation. The men still wore ornaments in their hair, earrings, and necklaces of shell, bone, and feathers. Women perpetuated the short and dirty skin skirt, while continuing to decorate their bodies by painting "black stripes on their mouth, nose, back, and breast. On the breast the stripes are painted in concentric circles from the nipple to the base of each breast."[2]

The men parted their long hair in the middle and either let it flow loose, or braided it, or tied in with beaver fur. The women also parted their hair in the middle, but at least some of them wore it short. The warrior, in typical Plains fashion, donned feathered and horned head-dresses and lavishly painted himself and his horse red, yellow, green, and black. His facial designs were his personal possessions and, like those of our clowns, were not copied by others without permission.

Subsistence and Material Culture. Although the historic range of the Tonkawas was not in the heart of the buffalo country and despite the fact that the buffalo disappeared relatively early in central Texas, this animal provided their principal food source as well as much of the raw material for clothing and other equipment. Unquestionably the Tonkawas, once they were mounted on horses, would have abandoned central Texas for the richer buffalo plains to the north and west had they been able to do so. But early in the eighteenth century the powerful Comanches and other Plains tribes pre-empted this bountiful land. The numerically weak Tonkawas could only remain where they were and eke out an existence as best they could. It was inevitable, of course, that their dependence on other animals should increase as the buffalo vanished; deer, always valued, took on added worth since their hides could be traded to white settlers. Noah Smithwick (1900: 247–248) was acquainted with the trade in deerskins and venison and adds an anecdote concerning turkeys:

A lady who was in the habit of buying game once asked the vendor why he didn't bring in turkeys, they being quite numerous.

[2] Sánchez, 1926: 269. This citation is also the source of the quotation at the head of this chapter.

"Oh," said he, "turkey too hard to kill. Injun crawl along in the grass, [and] deer, he say, 'Maybe so, Injun; maybe so, stump,' and then he go on eat. Injun crawl a little closer and shoot him. Turkey look, 'Injun, by God,' and he duck his head and run." That was a fair illustration of the difference between the deer and turkey. I have seen an Indian crawling upon deer, holding his head just far enough above the grass to watch the motions of the game, and whenever the deer threw up its head, instead of ducking his own, the Indian would remain perfectly still. While the quarry gazed suspiciously at him for a few minutes until apparently reassured, and then put down its head and went on feeding; but let a turkey catch sight of a suspicious object he didn't wait to investigate it; it was "Injun, by God," and he was off.

Many other animals, including rabbits, skunks, rats, and land tortoises, were hunted for food. Rattlesnakes were considered an especial delicacy. Apparently the only mammals Tonkawas barred from their iron-lined stomachs were wolves and their coyote relatives —and these only because of religious proscriptions. Dogs, horses, and all sorts of carrion were devoured avidly. Unlike typical Plains Indians, the Tonkawas ate fish and oysters. These nomadic people even seem to have given gardening a try in the latter part of the eighteenth century, but they were never successful in this radical departure from their hunting and gathering tradition. Like their Coahuiltecan and Karankawan neighbors, they also utilized a large assortment of plant foods, including herbs, roots, fruit, and seeds. Tunas of the prickly pear were gathered in season, as were acorns and particularly pecans from along the river bottoms. By the nineteenth century the importance of pecans was enhanced, for they too had become an item of barter with the settlers. Unquestionably some of these dietary habits are reminiscent of cultures in the Western Gulf culture area, but the similarity may be the result of similar habitat and an increasing poverty, which forced the Tonkawas to rely more and more upon foods previously ignored.

Most meat was prepared by simply roasting it over a fire. In common with other Plains Indians, the Tonkawas preserved surplus buffalo, venison, or other meat either as jerky or pemmican. Pemmican was prepared by drying and pounding the meat, mixing it with other ingredients, such as pecan meal, and stuffing the mixture into a length of intestine from one of these animals. Pemmican provided a rich and nutritious food for the skulking warrior or weary traveler, and must have served as the Indian equivalent for a can of Spam.

The wandering Tonkawas used the bisonhide tepee until toward the close of the eighteenth century, when the supply of bison had dwindled so drastically that other materials had to be used for their homes. Like those of other southern plains Indians, Tonkawan tepees were small, squat, and crude, never the tall, imposing, and beautiful lodges typical of northern plains tribes. Temporary brush arbors or windscreens were used as auxiliary dwellings—as shelters for isolating menstruating women, as parturition lodges, and for ceremonial purposes. Even after the traditional tepee had been abandoned the brush-shelter replacements were patterned after them. A conical framework of branches and poles was set in place, just as it had been for the tepee, but now it was covered with any usable material handy —grass, brush, branches. Toward the end of the independent existence of the Tonkawas in the nineteenth century, flat-topped huts or arbors covered with brush, cloth, or skin replaced the vestigial brush tepee and became their typical, miserable homes.

As must all nomadic hunters and gatherers, these Indians kept their tools and other material possessions to a crude and simple minimum. The most important weapon, in hunting and in warfare, was the bow and arrow. There are no data on the type of bow used, but it was probably a simple self-bow. Arrows were originally stone-tipped, but metal points were substituted as soon as metal was made available by Europeans. Arrows were poisoned—or so the warriors erroneously thought—with juice of the mistletoe leaf. When the Tonkawas obtained firearms they continued the practice by putting the juice in the barrels of their guns. Lances were also used in war and in hunting, and it is said that in addition to the bisonhide shields, jackets and helmets of tough hide were used. Much of their other equipment came from the bison: glue for hafting arrows and other purposes was obtained from the hoofs; sinews were used for thread and bowstrings; the hair was fashioned into ropes and belts and the horns into cups and spoons. Baskets and mats were woven of grass and other fibres. As mentioned earlier, pottery was made or obtained from the Caddo area to the eastward, and the custom of manufacturing a crude cloth from the inner bark of mulberry trees was probably derived from the same source.

Social Organization. The extent of our knowledge of the pretribal social organization of the Tonkawas leaves something to be desired, and since the nineteenth-century tribe may have drawn some of its membership from non-Tonkawan sources, we must be cautious of projecting later data backward in time lest we get a distorted picture of the earlier Tonkawas.

In pretribal days the various autonomous Tonkawan bands seem to have inhabited specific areas of central Texas. Each of the bands was directed by a chief, and in time of war there may have been special war leaders. After tribal consolidation the bands continued to have chiefs, but there was now at least a titular head chief for the tribe. The consolidation into a tribe appears to have increased their strength somewhat, for the Spanish padre Morfi (1932: 7) was able to say in the 1750's that they were a "terrible and bellicose nation" who were "divided into *rancherías*, or bands, each with its own captain. These are roaming people, who do the bidding of their leaders. They live for warfare, robbery and chase." Upon the death of a principal chief the men of the tribe elected his successor. Though definite information is lacking, it seems probable that the pretribal band chiefs were chosen in the same democratic manner.

Kenney (1897) asserted that the tribe was split into two divisions, each composed of a large number of totemic clans (groups of relatives who traced their descent through one parental line back to a remote and mythical ancestor). In tribal council the two divisions were said to sit opposite each other around the council fire, but whether this separation represents some holdover from or an elaboration upon a pretribal social grouping is unknown. Each clan had a specific name, such as bear, wolf, buffalo, "a kind of short snake," "the real Tonkaways," "mouth open," "blinking with the eyelids," "long genitals," "Meyei" (meaning "dizziness"), and acorn. The name of the Sanux clan may be derived from the division called Sana, and that of the Meyei looks suspiciously like the name of the subgroup known as Mayeye. Children were born into the clan of their mother; in other words, Tonkawa clans were matrilineal. This meant that all the children of a married couple belonged to the same clan—their mother's—and were never members of their father's. The children of a daughter would, of course, belong to their mother's and their maternal grandmother's clan, but children of sons, according to the same social rules, belonged to *their* mother's clan. Since all clan members felt a close relationship, marriage within the clan was considered incestuous. The matrilineal reckoning of descent ordinarily implies that women are apt to be treated as equals of men, and in any case seldom have an inferior position in society. It is not known exactly what the Tonkawa situation was, although women, at least in some instances, were not above putting their men in their proper places. Smithwick (1900: 248), for example, recalled a time when a group of Tonkawas were in a store. One of the women became angry with her husband, Smithwick thought because of his gambling losses. She

proceeded to give him a genuine tongue lashing, to judge by the volume and intensity of it. The buck only laughed at first, but becoming weary of the harangue, lit out at the door and started on a dead run. His long queue floating back was grasped by the squaw and away they went, followed by the applause of the spectators.

Clans were the basic and vital units of Tonkawa society. Clan members lived together and assisted one another in their daily activities. Among other social customs associated with maternal clans (and true of Tonkawas) was the one whereby orphans and children of divorced parents were taken care of and provided for by their mother's clan. A man's property, at least that part of it which was not buried with him or burned at his death, passed not to his own children (and so out of his clan) but to his brother or his sister's offspring. After marriage the couple lived with the wife's group (a practice termed "matrilocality").

142

PLATE II. Tonkawas: *above*—Grant Richards, a chief, born in 1850 (left); Winnie Richards, his wife (right); *below*—Sherman Niles (left); William Stevens, born in 1874 (right). All photographed at the Omaha Exposition, 1898. *Courtesy of the Smithsonian Institution, Bureau of American Ethnology.*

PLATE III. A group of Tonkawas, some of whom are seen in PLATE II. Photographed at the Omaha Exposition of 1898. *Courtesy of the Smithsonian Institution, Bureau of American Ethnology.*

The kinship system of the Tonkawas is a fascinating one, particularly as it was strikingly different from our own. The Tonkawas had what anthropologists call a Crow system of kinship nomenclature, a name taken from another tribe of Plains Indians but having no connection with the Tonkawas. The key to understanding this system and its rationale is the feeling and practice of brotherhood among clan members, and the levirate (a practice whereby a man marries his deceased brother's widow). In the Crow system a man and his sister's son (nephew) are members of the same clan. If, as occasionally happens, this man dies and has no blood brother who can marry and fend for his widow, some other man must perform this necessary social duty. The son of the deceased man's sister is both a close relative and a fellow clansman. What if he "really" is a nephew (by our reckoning) and of another generation! The logic of the system now becomes apparent: a man was a brother to his sister's son, and by extending the levirate, if he died his widow might become the wife of his sister's son. It goes almost without saying that a wife's children are the husband's children too, so that in a Crow system the children of a mother's brother are termed "son" and "daughter." By the same social convention, a man's mother might, in the event of his father's death, be required to marry his father's sister's son (to us the man's "cousin") but logically enough—since this cousin could become his mother's husband—he is called "father." The remainder of Crow terminology follows this logic, ignoring differences of generation so that all collateral relatives through a man's maternal uncle are dropped a generation, while all descendants of a man's paternal aunt are raised a generation.

Actually the Tonkawas' system of kinship is not as completely known as the foregoing discussion of a Crow system might imply. Their terminology which points unmistakably to a Crow system, however, was the practice of using the same term for a father's sister's daughter as for a father's sister, and of using the same term for a mother's brother's daughter as for a brother's daughter. A mother's sister was also called "mother," and this custom was natural enough, considering the fact that Tonkawas practiced both the sororate (in

143

which a woman married her dead sister's husband, or, in which a bereaved husband wed his deceased wife's sister) and probably sororal polygyny (in which a man had as wives several sisters at the same time). In other words, sisters might be co-wives of a man, and an unmarried girl was a potential wife of her sister's husband. The Tonkawas also used the same term for "father" and "father's brother," and this seems to imply that the levirate was practiced.

At first glance a kinship system of this nature is apt to seem unduly complex and perhaps even to serve no useful purpose. But one of the first things to remember when dealing with the customs of other cultures is that seeming complexity is often merely a matter of strangeness. If we were to put ourselves for a moment in the moccasins of a Tonkawa who is examining, say, the modern American kinship system, we can appreciate why he would likely think it illogical, complex, and bewildering. He would find the term "uncle," for example, used for brothers or brothers-in-law of either a father or a mother. He could not possibly tell from this term whether a person's uncles were relatives only by marriage (affinal relatives) or were "blood" relatives, nor could he tell whether they were maternal or paternal relatives. Is this more logical than a Crow system? If a Tonkawa was really perceptive he might find out that to many people the most important uncles were rich ones whose genealogical connections might be vague indeed. If our Tonkawa was confused by the "uncle" terminology, think of his bewilderment when he turned to our "cousin" terms! Here, even we are confused by the perplexing variety of relatives dumped into this category. Is Cousin Cora's baby a "first cousin once removed" or a second cousin?

Not only was the Tonkawa kinship system no less natural than our own or any other, but it reflects the importance of kinship ties in primitive society. Unlike ourselves they had no life insurance policies or benevolent government to take care of widows and orphans. In a primitive society, such as the Tonkawas', such social problems were solved within and by kinship groups. Clearly the levirate is an effective way of providing for widows, and in such a system there is no such thing as an orphan. It may strain our culture-bound minds to

144

equate an aunt (father's sister) with her daughter (a cousin to us), but it is apparent that the behavior which is associated with such relationships can be highly beneficial.

In almost all cultures certain stages in the life cycle are emphasized or are deemed to be particularly significant, while others are minimized or ignored. The biological facts are of course the same for all men. We are born, grow up, become reproductively mature, grow old, and finally die. But different cultures attach very different meanings to the various phases of life. In our civilization, for example, marriage and funeral rites receive an elaboration conspicuously absent for puberty rites. Many primitive cultures, on the other hand, emphasize the transition from childhood to adulthood and fail to attach much significance to, or spend much ceremonial time upon, the transition from a single to a married state. It is always puzzling to know why one culture picks one or several phases of the life cycle as being crucial and minimizes others. It is certainly important that the individual be ushered through the vital and critical phases of life in ways which will effectively fit him into the new roles he will be playing. It is also important for society to prepare its members for the arrival of new members, their transition from role to role, and for their ultimate departure. But why various cultures vary so widely in which phases of life are emphasized remains highly speculative. It is understandable that cultures possessing the crudest of technologies and functioning in harsh or restrictive environmental situations simply cannot take time from their daily labors to develop elaborate *rites du passage*. But the technologically rich, or those who do have ample leisure, frequently do not elaborate all the transitional periods of life.

As with so many other facets of Tonkawan life, only a bare framework of facts is known about most of their life cycle. Before a child was born, the father was not supposed to touch any bird, nor was he allowed to break open the bones of animals for the marrow lest the child be born with weak legs. Whether or not there were similar do's and don't's connected with a pregnant woman is unknown. It is likely that there were, although a woman's association with her child is obvious enough, whereas taboos of this sort are an effective social way of proclaiming a man's fatherhood. Women bore their children alone in special brush huts, from the center of which hung a rope for them to cling to during labor. They bathed in a stream within a day after childbirth, and they also were said to apply white clay to their faces. The parents of a new-born child did not smoke or use firearms for four days after birth. This again was a magical taboo; it was believed that smoke would cause the child to have weak eyes.

Very little is known about infancy and the training of children. Presumably a baby was placed on a cradleboard soon after birth, and it is known that the child's head was flattened by tying a piece of wood to it. This beautifying treatment is more easily accomplished when used with an unyielding cradleboard. By the time he was about a year and a half old his head was sufficiently flattened and he was allowed to toddle around the camp. When the child was several years old he was named, but whether this was done in a formal ceremony or whether names or nicknames were informally bestowed is unknown. Children gradually learned the duties of their sex and what was required of them. There was little or no physical punishment meted out for misbehavior.

There is simply no knowledge of when or how the Tonkawas got married; the gap itself suggests that this transition in the life cycle did not receive special emphasis; or if it did, it was of a secret nature and was kept from the eyes of Europeans, who surely would have left a record of a rite so important to them.

The Tonkawas emphasized and elaborated upon the final crisis of life—death—if the amount of information available is any valid criterion. When a person was thought to be on the verge of death his friends and relatives entered the tepee where he lay. Some of them formed a circle around the ailing man and put their hands on his body. Around these, others formed a concentric circle and placed their hands upon the shoulders of those in the first circle. If the tepee was a large one there might be several such circles around the pallet. Swaying and chanting, they hovered around the dying person throughout the night; in the morning the ailing one presumably died.

146

Fig. 6. Tonkawa burial scene.

Generally the dead were buried immediately, although chiefs and particularly important people lay in state for a time. The hair of the corpse was cut, the face painted yellow, and the body wrapped in bisonskin robes. Kinfolk and friends did not eat until after the burial and friends brought gifts to be buried with the body. These presents were placed in the grave with the corpse, as well as some of his treasured possessions, such as guns, saddles, clothing, and enemy scalps. If the dead person was a woman, beads were ripped off her garments and heaped together in her grave. Other possessions were burned, and the ashes from a man's pipes were hidden. In accordance with the custom of many other Plains Indians, a favorite horse of the deceased was shot over his grave at least occasionally, and sometimes a pet dog was also put to death.

Burial itself was ritualized to the extent that an old man standing at the west end of the grave briefly addressed the band members and the corpse. Following his speech he cast a pinch of dirt across the grave, then moved to the east end of the grave and repeated this performance. For three days the band to which the deceased had belonged mourned. No singing was allowed and at sunrise and dusk the entire band vented its sorrow by prolonged wailing. Near relatives apparently mourned their dead more violently and for a longer time. Mothers, for example, wailed, and slashed their breasts with knives. If their sons had been lost in battle they sliced off their nipples. At the end of the mourning period the band chief addressed the deceased's people, and henceforward his name was never used again. Even names which sounded similar to the dead person's were tabooed. This practice sprang from the belief that the use of the deceased's name would so disturb and anger his spirit that he might come back to plague the living. In the nineteenth century when the Tonkawas were rapidly dying off, they began to borrow Comanche and white names, apparently because their stock of names was so depleted. Following the mourning period a four-day smoking ceremony was held. The ceremony was directed by a leader, probably a shaman, and the people quietly talked and blew smoke skyward. During this time relatives and friends brought gifts of food, clothing, household furnishings, and other things to replace those which had been buried or burned at the funeral. This four-day period seems to have been a time of purification for those who had been contaminated by death, a pause in which society was realigned and reintegrated.

Supernaturalism. Considering the other gaps in our knowledge of Tonkawan culture, it is not surprising that very little of a coherent nature is known about the religious beliefs and practices of these Indians. Part of the difficulty may stem from the very nature of their beliefs—they may not have been organized into a concrete, explicit system. And religious belief and practice does seem to have been individualized to the extent that within a broad cultural framework every person worshiped his own private spirits or gods in his own idiosyncratic way. There were shamans, but what they did, apart from curing, is not known. In curing ceremonies or medicine dances a special tepee was erected facing east. A small hole was dug in the center of the tepee and a fire was built in it. The patient entered the tepee and walked around the fire on the south side to sit on a blanket which had been spread on the ground. The shaman then performed his rites of rubbing the patient's affected parts, applying medicines, and calling to the forces of the supernatural world to effect a cure. When he had finished, the patient left the tepee by the same route he had used when entering.

Scattered data suggest that the Tonkawas believed that there was an omnipotent god or gods. But the most important supernaturals in terms of their direct effect on men seems to have been the spirits of the dead. These spirits journeyed to a home in the west. As a result the dead were buried with their heads placed towards the west, and the living slept with their feet in this direction for fear their spirit might commence its journey prematurely. Souls of women were thought to go directly to the home in the west, singing as they went; souls of men, however, were apt to hang around watching their living relatives and calling to them. If the dead were not properly buried, their spirits would remain to haunt the miscreants. These spirits took the form of owls and wolves—and it was said that the Tonkawas would not kill these creatures. Certain places were avoided, particularly at night, because strange sounds attributed to the souls of the dead were heard there. It was thought that if spirits haunted a place where people were living the people would soon die, and if a dead relative called to a person in a dream that person's days were surely numbered. Small bags containing roots and other medical items were worn next to the body to ward off illness that these malignant spirits were capable of causing.

The world must have appeared far different to a Tonkawa than it does to a modern Westerner, filtered through his secularistic, naturalistic eyes. It is difficult for us to feel empathy for a people whose world is literally aquiver with various sorts of spirits, ready at any moment to harm the living.

The Tonkawas have been traditionally characterized as savage and treacherous cannibals. The allegation is true to the extent that on occasion they did *ritually* consume the flesh of their enemies. So far as I have been able to determine, however, they never ate human flesh simply as food, like venison or pecans. The nearest approach to the latter type of cannibalism I have run across is in the account by Noah Smithwick (1900: 245–246). After killing and scalping a Comanche, the Tonkawas

fleeced off the flesh of the dead Comanche, [and] they borrowed a big wash kettle from Puss Weber, into which they put the Comanche meat, together with a lot of corn and potatoes—the most revolting mess my eyes ever rested on. When the stew was sufficiently cooked and cooled to allow of its being ladled out with the hands the whole tribe gathered around, dipping it up with their hands and eating it as greedily as hogs. Having gorged themselves on this delectable feast they lay down and slept till night, when the entertainment was concluded with the scalp dance.

So far the feast seems to be a feast and no more, but as Smithwick continues, it becomes plain that his recollections of this occasion were distorted in some respects:

Gotten up in all the hideousness of war paint and best breech-clouts, the warriors gathered around in a ring, each one armed with some ear-torturing instrument, which they operated in unison with a drum made of dried

150

deer skin stretched tightly over a hoop, at the same time keeping up a monotonous "ha, ah, ha!" raising and lowering their bodies in time that would have delighted a French dancing master, every muscle seeming to twitch in harmony. Meanwhile some old hag of a squaw would present to each in turn an arm or leg of the dead foe, which they would bite at viciously, catching it in their teeth and shaking it like savage dogs. And high over all waved from the point of a lance the scalp, dressed and painted, held aloft by a patriotic squaw. The orgies were kept up till the performers were forced to desist from sheer exhaustion.

It sounds as though the Tonkawas had learned how to have their cake (in this case a ritual dance) and eat it too (Comanche stew), if we are to believe Smithwick. Whatever the facts in this instance, there seems to be little doubt that the scalp dance was the focal point —the ceremonially significant part—of the day's activities.

John H. Jenkins (1958: 77–78), describing Tonkawa cannibalism in the same period as did Smithwick, clearly indicates the ritual overtones of the custom. In this instance the Tonkawas had persuaded Jenkins to lead them to the body of a Waco (Wichita) warrior he had shot:

When they discovered the body, they seemed wild with delight or frenzy. They sprang upon the body, scalped him, cut off both legs at the knees, both hands at the wrists, pulled out his fingernails and toenails, strung them around their necks, and then motioned for me to move aside. Seeing they meant further violence to the body, already horribly mutilated, I demanded why I must move. They said, "We must shoot him through the head for good luck." [To destroy his soul?] I tried to stop them, but they would hear nothing, said they were *compelled* to shoot him for luck.

I moved aside and they shot, tearing the head literally in pieces. They then went back to the house and camped, getting me to furnish them some beef. They boiled their beef, and the hands and feet of the dead Waco together, turning them with the same hands. Upon inquiry, I found they intended having a dance, and would feed their squaws on the hands and feet of the dead Indian, believing that this would make them bring forth brave men who would hate their enemies and be able to endure hardness and face dangers. They erected a pole, to which they attached the scalp, hands, and feet of the Waco, and then with horrible yells and gestures, all danced around it, while the squaws constantly danced up to the pole and took bites from the hands and feet and then would go back and dance again. They would prolong these dances three, five, and sometimes ten days.

It is not strange, considering the importance which the world of the dead played in Tonkawa belief, that ritual cannibalism was practiced. The reasoning is logical, given their beliefs about spirits. If a portion of a dead enemy's body was eaten it would do either or perhaps both of two things. First, by consuming parts of the enemy the cannibal might acquire part or perhaps even all of his spirit or spirit power. If the enemy was courageous he would thus acquire his courage, if brave, braveness, and so on. Second, consuming an enemy's body might also have been considered a way of insulting and reviling the souls of the enemy, as well as the living enemy. Souls of the dead might be expected to vent their displeasure upon their fellow kinsmen who had not been brave or courageous enough to prevent the death of one of their number. Or, the act of eating an enemy may have been thought to destroy the enemy's soul completely, and hence secure for the Tonkawas the greatest victory possible.

TODAY THE TONKAWAS are all but forgotten, yet less than a century ago they wandered free over large reaches of Texas. Somehow they were all but overlooked by early Texans. Perhaps if they had been more belligerent, or had their customs (apart from cannibalism) been more spectacular or strangely exotic, the settlers would have been compelled to take more notice of them. But their shattered culture was not one that appealed to Texans for its distinctiveness or strength. And perhaps this is the clue to the real nature of the Tonkawas. Their culture did not have the slant, the orientation which would fix its qualities in the minds—and so in the journals and diaries—of strangers.

The geographical location of the Tonkawas and the accidents of history were also not in their favor. The southern plains were pre-

152

empted by the Comanches, and soon the mission-weakened Tonkawas were between a Comanche anvil on the west and the advancing
hammer of the American frontier on the east. Some other people
might have made a better show of resistance, but such was not the
nature of the timid Tonkawas.

CHAPTER 7

Comanches: Terror of the Southern Plains

> Where all are such magnificent thieves, it is difficult
> to decide which of the Plains tribes deserves the
> palm for stealing. The Indians themselves give it to
> the Comanches, whose designation in the sign lan-
> guage is a backward, wriggling motion of the index
> finger, signifying a snake, and indicating the silent
> stealth of that tribe. For crawling into a camp, cutting
> hopples and lariat ropes, and getting off undiscovered
> with the animals, they are unsurpassed and unsurpass-
> able.
>
> Colonel Richard I. Dodge—*Our Wild Indians*

To MANY TEXANS the word *Comanche* is synonymous with *Indian*,
and with good reason. From the beginnings of Anglo-American Texas
until 1875 the Comanches were the principal and most stubborn adversaries the Texans had. Until the last years of their independence
they raided through much of the state, to say nothing of Mexico, and
killed or captured men, women, and children, carried off what loot
they could, and burned the rest. Not only did Comanches valiantly

155

battle Spaniards, Mexicans, Texans, and Americans but they conquered the original Indian residents of the southern plains—the eastern Apaches, Tonkawas, and others.

The Comanches are speakers of the Shoshonean branch of Uto-Aztekan, one of the most widespread of American Indian linguistic families. The Shoshonean-speaking tribes, centered in the Great Basin country of the western United States, are further subdivided into three mutually unintelligible language branches. One of these subdivisions is the Shoshone proper, which includes Comanche. (Zingg, 1939:3) If there were no other evidence to go on, the Comanche tongue would have to be associated with that of the Northern Shoshones because the two are virtually identical. But there is other evidence which confirms that the Comanches are a historic offshoot of the Northern Shoshones. There are many cultural similarities between the two peoples, and Comanche traditions agree that the Comanches came from somewhere north of the headwaters of the Arkansas River, probably the mountainous country of what is now Colorado and Wyoming.

Origins and Early History. The precise form of prehistoric Comanche culture is unknown, but there is little doubt that it was similar, if not identical, to that of the Northern Shoshones. Culturally, Northern Shoshones were rather crudely-equipped hunters and gatherers. Their rugged mountain and plateau environment provided a meager supply of wild foods—though likely richer than that of the Texas Coahuiltecans. Small bands, occupying well-defined territories, wandered through their land in a seasonally-prescribed rhythm in search of roots, seeds, jack rabbits, insects, and other wild products. Their shelters, tools, and general way of life were crude and primitive. Sometime during the seventeenth century some of the proto-Comanches, or a segment of the Northern Shoshones if you prefer, became acquainted with horses. By 1700 they had appeared on the plains of eastern Colorado and western Kansas, apparently having followed down the Arkansas River from their highland homes. By 1705 they were in New Mexico and before the century was half over were militarily in control of much of the southern plains. (Thomas, 1932: 57) The changes in their culture were revolutionary: from a scrounging, poor, militarily weak rabble, they became in less than a century a mounted, well-equipped, and powerful people.

The Comanches did not descend upon the plains in a body; they came in family groups and bands at different times.[1] The band type of organization persisted throughout the Comanches' national existence, and, like so many other Texas Indians, they were never a tribe in a political sense. Our term for them is not their own designation for themselves but is a Ute word meaning "enemy." The Spanish adopted the word *Komantcia* from the Utes and the Americans followed their lead. The Comanches' term for themselves means "human beings,"—not that other people were less human but they were, unfortunately, just not Comanches.

There were at one time more than a dozen Comanche bands, varying in size, territory occupied, and in some minor cultural respects. Some bands were exterminated in various conflicts, others probably grew large and new bands budded from them, and some changed their names. The largest and best-known Comanche band was the Penatekas or Honey-Eaters, known also as the Wasps and by some other names. They were the southernmost Comanche band and apparently led the advance into the southern plains. Their principal range during the nineteenth century was west of the Cross Timbers, generally between the headwaters of the Colorado and Brazos. Another well-known band was the Wanderers. This one, as the name implies, was even more nomadic than the other restless Comanche bands. During the nineteenth century they were generally found occupying the territory immediately north of the Wasp band. The Wanderers and two other bands, the Tanimas (Liver-eaters) and the Tanawas, comprised the Middle Comanches. One of the most warlike bands was known as the Buffalo-eaters; the northernmost, and one of the largest bands, was the Yap-eaters, so called from a root eaten by Shoshones and Comanches. The Yap-eaters and the Antelopes (Quahadi) drifted south about the same time, the Antelopes coming to dominate the Llano Estacado. They were one of the fiercest bands

---

[1] The discussion here, as is true of much of the remainder of this chapter, draws heavily upon Wallace and Hoebel's excellent book *The Comanches, Lords of the South Plains* (1952).

of Comanches and constantly raided the Texas frontier. They were also the last to surrender to United States domination. While these and the other less important or more transitory bands differed slightly from one another culturally, individuals and family groups could desert their bands at will and join others. That there were no qualifications for membership other than to be a Comanche was an important reason for their shifting number and nature. (See Map 3.)

Appearance and Dress. The Comanches are quite varied physically and may always have been so, though their habit of intermarrying with captives—Mexican, white, and Indian—is probably responsible for much of their diversity. George Catlin, the artist who accompanied the Dragoon Expedition to Comanche country, described them as short, heavy ("often approaching corpulency"), and ungainly in their movements, all in all a "most unattractive and slovenly-looking race of Indians." (1841, II: 66) On the other hand, the Texas pioneer John H. Jenkins (1958: 8), saw them quite differently:

The warriors were almost without exception large, fine-looking men, displaying to the very best advantage their erect, graceful, well-knit frames and finely proportioned figures, being entirely naked, with the exception of a small apron attached to a belt or girdle, which was made of cloth of all textures and colors, with fringes and tassels at the ends. They had keen black eyes without lashes, and long plaits of coarse black hair hanging from their bare heads down to the very ground behind them.

The truth probably lies between these extremes, and in any event, it was not the physiques of the Comanches that are so noteworthy as what they did to their bodies.

The traditional dress of the Comanches was about as far removed from the popular conception of the way an Indian dressed as it is possible to be. Quite young boys wore no clothes at all during warm weather; when about eight or nine they donned the standard breechclout, leggings, and moccasins. Girls, however, always wore some sort of covering. In cold weather buffalo robes were used, both with the hair removed and for extremely cold weather with it left on. Knee-high boots, or overshoes, made from bisonhide were worn over

PLATE IV. Comanche warriors: *above*—unidentified; *below*—Otter Belt, a Quahadi chief. *A. B. Stephenson Collection, courtesy Barker Texas History Center.*

PLATE V. A Quahadi Comanche camp. A. B. Stephenson Collection, courtesy Barker Texas History Center.

leggings and moccasins. Skin shirts also seem to have been used in cold weather. Their buffalo robes and buffalohide overshoes equipped them to withstand the coldest gales of the plains. While Comanche attire was ordinarily drab and limited to what the weather dictated, for festive occasions, and in later times after they had benefited from white example, they were as gaudily dressed and ornamented as any other people.

War parties, particularly, were a resplendent sight. Roemer, the visiting German scientist, for example, saw a war party just before it left for a raid into Mexico. The warriors had painted their faces red and most of them wore headdresses of buffalo horn. Their long lances had also been painted red, and each warrior carried a shield of tanned buffalohide "painted in gaudy colors and decorated with a circle of feathers" which fluttered whenever the shields were moved, perhaps serving to spoil an enemy's aim. Even the horses shared in their riders' adornment, their heads and tails being painted "carmine red." (Roemer, 1935: 270) Jenkins, a participant in the battle of Plum Creek near Lockhart in 1840, which took place after a successful Comanche raid to the coast, was astounded at their appearance. Warriors had attached red ribbons to their horses' tails; many wore headdresses of buffalo horns or deer antlers, one wore a headdress made "of a large white crane with red eyes," and others wore all sorts of looted plunder. One huge warrior "wore a stovepipe hat" and another "a fine pigeon-tailed cloth coat, buttoned up *behind.*" (Jenkins, 1958: 64–65)

Feather war bonnets were adopted late in the nineteenth century, apparently at the expense of the horn headdress, but never attained the vogue which they had among the northern Plains tribes. Painting the face and body was always an important part of ornamentation for special occasions. Red was the most popular color, but black, yellow, olive, green, and blue were also much used. All kinds of designs were used and so far as is known followed no particular style. Men lavished as much attention upon their hair as upon any part of their toilet, encouraging it to grow long. They even begged for the locks that women in mourning cut off in order to braid it into their own. The hair was parted in the center, with the part painted, and worn in braids on either side of the head. A scalp lock fell from the top of the head. The side braids were wrapped with fur, cloth, or other materials, and a lone yellow or black feather was usually worn in the scalp lock. (Wallace and Hoebel, 1952: 83) Other face and body hair, including the eyebrows, was plucked out by the fastidious warrior. Tattooing of faces and bodies was occasionally practiced by both men and women. Men also had their ears pierced in a number of places for earrings of shell, or rings of brass or silver.

In later historic times the women wore carefully-sewn and richly-ornamented buckskin dresses. Skirts made from two pieces of buckskin fell with an uneven hemline to the ankles. Blouses were of the loose, Mother Hubbard type, made of a single skin with a slit in the middle for the head. Moccasins and buckskin clothing were richly ornamented with beads, fringes, and the little bits of iron and tin known today as "tinklers." The women's hair was cut—perhaps "hacked off" would be a better term, since unlike the men, the women ignored this aspect of their appearance. It was parted in the middle, the part daubed with color, and allowed to hang loose. Although the hair received no special attention, the face was painted and cared for with as much attention as that of any modern Jezebel. "Her eyes were accentuated with red or yellow lines above and below the lids and sometimes crossing at the corners. Her ears were painted red inside, and both cheeks were daubed with a solid red-orange circle or triangle." (Wallace and Hoebel, 1952: 86)

Subsistence and Material Culture. As was true of the culture of other Plains Indians, the buffalo was the lifeblood of Comanche culture; its near-extermination sounded the death knell for the kind of life Comanches had come to know. They had always known the buffalo and hunted the few stragglers that penetrated their mountain and plateau home, but it was not until they swarmed out onto the plains that this animal loomed large in their way of living. While there was desultory bison-hunting throughout the year, it was in the summer, when the animals were fat and had shed their winter hair, and in the fall, when hides reached their prime, that Comanches went on large-scale communal hunts. Time and place of hunts was decided in an informal, general assembly of the band, with

160

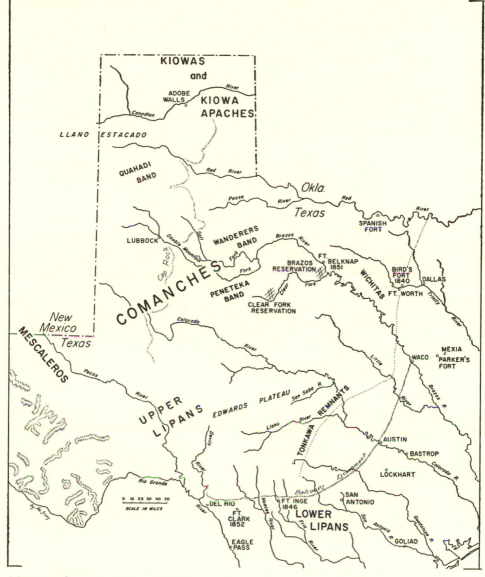

MAP 3.   The Texas Plains, 19th Century

war leaders making final decisions. Temporary camps near wood and water were set up in the vicinity of the herds; then all able-bodied persons, including women, moved nearer the herds. Communal hunts meant hard labor for all, but they were occasions for joy and a feeling of well-being, too. Dances were held nightly before flickering fires, with a large section, perhaps most of a band, present; it was a time for eating, rejoicing, and merriment. It was the Comanche harvesttime.

Like Tonkawas and eastern Apaches, Comanches had no military societies to direct and police their communal hunts. But a responsible hunt leader would be chosen, and he functioned as a co-ordinator and director. Every hunter knew what he had to do for the common welfare, and their hunts were efficiently executed with few visible controls. After locating a suitable herd the hunting party approached from downwind, and slowly encircling the herd, closed the gap on the upwind side last. Once they had surrounded the herd, the mounted hunters circled it and constricted it to as small an area as possible. If the herd could be made to mill around, their slaughter was that much easier. Once within range the riders approached the bison from its right side. When within a few feet the hunter loosed his arrow into the flank of the running creature, aiming behind the last ribs and downwards so that the arrow would penetrate the heart. "They kill them very fast, and will even shoot an arrow entirely through one of these large animals." (Plummer, 1926: 100) Another method of killing the buffalo was with a long-handled spear or lance. A hunter rode up to the bison in the same way, and with both hands grasping the spear, tried to drive it home. When the bison felt the spear point he generally tried to run faster, but sometimes would turn and gore the horse or rider. If the buffalo turned, the rider had to hold the lance firm against the charge in the hope of letting the wounded creature drive the lance deeper. This type of surround, utilizing bows and arrows and lances, was always the favorite way of hunting buffalo even after Comanches were well equipped with firearms.

When a herd could not be surrounded, a line of hunters might be formed downwind and the herd simply charged. Buffalo were also

162

stampeded over cliffs, often with the aid of an agile boy who, disguised in a bison robe equipped with horns and ears, lured the beasts on. Individual hunters also stalked herds, often disguised, and were frequently able to kill a considerable number before the herd took alarm. Butchering took place wherever the animals fell, the women coming up to help at the task if they were near. The hide was cut along the spinal column, pulled down the sides, and the carcass disjointed and cut up. The meat was wrapped in the hides and packed to camp on horses or mules.

While bison were the main source of food, elk were hunted in the river valleys, black bears were found in the Cross Timbers and were hunted for their oil, antelope were plentiful on the Llano Estacado, and deer were hunted as the opportunity arose. When war parties did not have time to hunt, they ate their ponies, and mustangs were hunted at least in some regions. In the brush country of south Texas in the 1840's, William Bollaert, an English traveler, heard that the Comanches had eaten twenty thousand mustangs in five years' time. Sometimes whole mustangs, and often portions such as heads, appear to have been cooked in earth ovens in a fashion similar to that which Lipans used for sotol. (Hollon and Butler [eds.], 1956: 361)

Longhorn cattle were always welcome since they tasted somewhat like buffalo, and being stolen from Texans probably sweetened their flavor. Comanches did not eat fish, wild fowl, dogs, or coyotes unless sorely pressed by hunger. When starving, they would eat virtually everything—rats, skunks, lizards, grasshoppers, decayed meat.

Comanches always collected a considerable number of wild-plant products in order to vary their predominantly meat diet. These included plums, grapes, currants, juniper berries, mulberries, persimmons, tunas of the prickly pear, and other fruits. Pecans, acorns, various roots, and tubers were also used. Corn and tobacco were never grown, but were secured by stealth or trade. As with other Plains Indians, pemmican was a great favorite and a nutritious ration for war parties or travelers. Berries or nuts were generally used to flavor dried bison meat, as was tallow, which was stored in intestines, bison paunches, and parfleche bags—rawhide bags of buffalo from which the hair had been removed.

Ordinarily Comanches ate a light meal on rising in the morning and a heavier meal in the evening. During the day people ate when they felt hungry or when it was convenient. As did many other Indians, Comanches always offered food to their visitors regardless of the time of their visit, and this has probably led to a belief that Comanches had no regular mealtimes. Meat was often eaten raw, although it usually was roasted to some degree. After the Comanches obtained pots and kettles, meat and other food were frequently boiled, but never was a meal "broiled and boiled on the same fire at the same time." This was considered the worst sort of bad luck—as bad as if someone's shadow happened to fall over food that was cooking. (Plummer, 1926: 111) Noah Smithwick (1900: 179), who spent some time with a band of Comanches and could hardly have been a fastidious feeder, found some of their delicacies too much for his trail-hardened stomach. He could not eat "the curdled milk taken from the stomachs of suckling fawns and buffalo calves," nor did he relish tripe "which they broiled without even taking the trouble to wash it, merely dragging it over the grass to wipe off the thickest of the filth." Other delights which graced the Comanche table were marrow, raw liver flavored with the contents of the gall bladder, warm blood from a freshly-killed buffalo, deer, bear, elk, or antelope, or milk and blood sucked from the slashed udders of one of these animals.

Comanche tepees were of the familiar Plains type, easily moved and set up—ideal homes for nomadic people. Made of tanned buffalohides, they stood from twelve to fourteen feet high when erected upon their framework of sixteen or eighteen poles. The door was usually covered by a bearskin, and an ingenious flap at the peak provided a vent for smoke. Both the door and vent faced away from the prevailing wind. The tepee was given added stability by tying a leather rope to the poles where they crossed overhead and attaching it to a stake driven into the ground near the center of the dwelling. Roemer (1935: 244–255) commented that Comanche tepees "afford more protection in inclement weather than many of the ordinary log houses found in Texas." A fire in the center was used both for cooking and for warmth. Skins were used to sit on and for sleeping.

164

If possible, Comanche camps were located near running water, and a large camp might extend along a stream for several miles. Within a camp the tepees were not arranged according to any set plan, although they were likely to be clustered near the lodges of the chiefs. The tepees of chiefs were larger than the others because public meetings were held in them.

The sight of a Comanche band on the move was an unforgettable one, particularly to travelers like Roemer (1935: 195), who had recently arrived from Europe:

According to Indian custom, they rode single file, the men in advance, dressed in their best, looking about, dignified and grave; the lively squaws following, sitting astride like the men, each usually carrying a black-eyed little papoose on her back and another in front of the saddle. At the same time they kept a watchful eye on the pack horses which carried the skins and the various household goods.

Once the Comanches were committed to a mounted, nomadic life, their possessions were restricted to things durable enough to be moved. The most useful and valued tool of the men was, of course, the bow and arrow. Comanches made good bows and were excellent archers. Bows were made preferably of seasoned Osage orange (*bois d'arc* [*Maclura pomifera*], colloquially "bodark"); when this wood was unobtainable, hickory or other wood was substituted. Bows made by Comanches in recent times have been about three feet long, the shorter length being easier to use while riding. Some Comanche bows were sinew-backed, and a few compound ones were made of horn. They were strung with bull buffalo or deer sinew which had been split, twisted together, and glued to make an extraordinarily strong bowstring. Arrows, preferably of dogwood, were made very carefully and tipped with iron and steel.

Warriors carried bisonhide shields, hardened, often paper-stuffed, and constructed with a convex outer surface to turn enemy arrows, blows, and often bullets. They were decorated with bears' teeth, to show the owner was a great hunter; with scalps, to suggest his status as a warrior; and horse tails, to symbolize his prowess as a raider. The shield also had on the rim a number of feathers, whose chief purpose was to throw off the enemy's aim. While shields originally had a practical purpose, some of them in later times came to have magical attributes, and hence had a number of taboos associated with them. Lances were used not only for buffalo-hunting but also in war. A short battle-ax was also used in war.

Social Organization. As is true among many peoples, to Comanches the mystery, strangeness, and uncertainness of birth, combined with the fact that a new and possibly much-needed member was to be added to society, made the act of childbirth a momentous occasion. If a woman owned her own tepee her child was born in it, but if she shared a tepee with others, a temporary lodge of brush was built. Within the lodge or tepee two holes were dug, one to receive the afterbirth, the other for steam-bathing. Stakes about four feet long were driven into the ground for the woman to grasp during the pangs of childbirth. An elderly medicine woman and several other women assisted the mother. Men stayed away from the birth lodge except in cases of difficult delivery, when a shaman might be called in. The shamans seemed to have performed only imitative magic to speed birth; the women assistants massaged and kneaded the woman's abdomen, burned sage to purify the lodge, and the like. Comanche women did not normally have many children, and death at childbirth was not rare.

As soon as a baby was born the umbilical cord was cut and the medicine woman hung it, if possible, on a nearby hackberry tree. The baby was bathed, wrapped in soft skins, and placed on a cradleboard, where it was to remain during the daylight hours for eight or nine months. The midwife set the time a woman had to remain in bed after childbirth. Sometimes a woman was up and about immediately, but in recent times ten days' rest has been the normal recovery period. In early days babies who were in any way defective or abnormal were abandoned to die, and one or both twins, especially if they were girls, were also abandoned. Children of either sex were welcomed and loved, but a baby boy brought the greatest joy to a family's heart. Comanches reasoned that since boys became the warriors, were the sex that defended the home, provided its chief sustenance, and—because of these duties—were likely to die while yet young, they were superior to and more desirable than girls.

There was no set time for formally naming a child, and until this event took place pet names were used. The father usually asked some prominent person to name his offspring, and this was done in a public ceremony in which a shaman puffed smoke toward heaven, earth, and the four directions and prayed for the infant. The child was held up to symbolize the fervent desire that he would grow up. Still holding him aloft the shaman announced his name. The parents then paid the name-giver or promised that payment would be made at a later date. Like Lipans, Comanches believed names had magical power. If a child was sickly or had some sort of ill-fortune, his name was changed.

Until a baby was nine or ten months old his physical activity was strictly limited. During the daytime he was strapped to a cradle-board; at night he slept between his parents in a stiff rawhide container. When he was about ten months old he was allowed some freedom to crawl and scramble about, and was carried on his mother's back. Children learned the ways of Comanche life informally and by precept rather than by any formal schooling. Girls were soon toddling after their mothers and when strong and big enough were given womanly tasks to perform. Boys likewise soon began to practice the arts of shooting, hunting, and riding. Children were not punished by whipping; generally persuasion and object lessons were used instead. An older sister was normally the disciplinarian, but if really harsh measures were called for, someone outside the immediate family was summoned.

There were virtually no puberty rites for girls, though some families might celebrate by giving a feast and having a daughter run wildly behind a fast pony, hanging onto its tail, so that she would be active and agile in life. As boys approached adolescence they began to congregate in gangs, avoiding girls. No laborious tasks were expected of them in camp, and their life was a continual, if playful, rehearsal of their coming adult life. The avoidance of sisters was particularly severe, and at about puberty boys were isolated from their sisters by being assigned to separate tepees. If a girl persisted in being familiar with her brother, he had the right to kill her. About the same time that a boy took to his own tepee he went on his first major buffalo hunt. But before he was qualified to go with a war party on a raid, he had to obtain supernatural power—a common Plains custom. This "medicine," as the Comanches called it, was revealed to a person in an eagerly-sought visionary quest. For if a vision was obtained, a man had a supernatural guardian who assisted him throughout life. Once a boy was spiritually equipped and had proved himself an able hunter, he was qualified to go on the warpath.

Following a boy's success on the warpath, a Giveaway Dance in his honor was often arranged by his father. A family might give away all of its possessions at such a dance, becoming poverty-stricken. But this showed the world that they had strong power—that they could obtain more material goods—and it greatly enhanced their social prestige.

A boy's return from his first war party, and the dance which often celebrated it, marked the beginning of adulthood (Wallace and Hoebel, 1952:132):

He was supposed to know by this time that to gain the approbation and respect of his people he must be brave and courageous in war, wise in council, cool and fearless in the midst of danger, ardent in his friendship, charitable to the less fortunate of his community, hospitable to strangers, and enthusiastic in his patriotism and devotion to the welfare of his tribe.

He was now eligible to marry and sometimes did so, although marriage usually was postponed for a few years. He wanted first to gain a reputation as a hunter and warrior. By so doing he would be in a favorable position to acquire as a wife the girl of his choice. Horses and other plunder were also needed to win a desirable girl, and acquiring these articles by raiding was more respectable and esteemed than wheedling them out of a doting father or other relative. As a result of these social pressures girls were married young, about the age of sixteen, to men who were often more than thirty.

Premarital sexual relations were not punished or considered to be morally wrong, but they were not encouraged either. Oddly, from our point of view, it was not the young boys who made advances toward the girls, but the other way round. It was common, apparently, for the more mature unmarried girls to slip into a boy's tepee at night and introduce him to the art of love-making. It was customary for these girls to keep their identity as much of a secret as possible since such initiative did their reputations little good. Theoretically young couples were not to be seen together in public, so there were all sorts of clandestine meetings. When girls went for water their lovers, or would-be lovers, commonly intercepted them. Young men also might slip into their lovers' tepees at night or persuade them to slip away with them into the shadows.

When a man had decided he wanted to marry a certain girl, the ordinary procedure was to give her father, brother, or some other close relative a present, preferably a horse. If the suitor had planned his campaign well in advance, he would already have cultivated the friendship of the girl's brother or some other near relative, and perhaps have given the girl herself some horses. A man was not apt to give horses or other presents unless he felt fairly sure of success, and of course the recipients knew the purpose of such gifts. A suitor's campaign was climaxed when he sent an uncle, some other older relative, or perhaps a friend to the lodge of the girl's parents with additional gifts. The intermediary's purpose was to make an offer of these gifts to the family in compensation for the girl. He stated his case and left without an answer. The girl's wishes might be deferred to, but in any case she usually abided by whatever decision her family made. If the suit was rejected the horses, with the gifts loaded upon them, were simply turned loose; if the suitor was accepted, the horses were driven into the herd of the girl's father or brother. Normally there was no further ceremony; the successful suitor simply took his bride to his tepee.

Some Comanche bands may have varied slightly in their marriage customs, and there were some less common ways of marrying. When girls learned, for example, that they were to be married to some wealthy but repugnant suitor they sometimes eloped with their young lovers. In such instances a boy, if he became well-to-do, was apt to recompense his wife's relatives. His relatives also might come forward with presents in order to make the marriage conform as much as possible to traditional custom. Occasionally, too, a man and a woman simply started living together, and so were in time considered to be married. More unusual was the custom of a girl's parents approaching some promising and industrious warrior with gifts. If he accepted them he married the girl. This form of marriage was beneath the dignity of—and somewhat of a disgrace for—a true Comanche warrior. It was usually reserved for captives—white, Mexican, and Indian—who had been adopted by the tribe.

Sons-in-law were obligated to provide meat for their wives' parents, but this duty was likely not onerous in the days when buffalo were plentiful. But since a son-in-law was expected to provide meat, a family tried to arrange for their daughter's marriage to a man of their own band. Interband marriages did occur, and in such cases a girl joined her husband and his band.

Normally a man inherited his wife's younger sisters as additional wives, and he might take other women, especially captives, as wives too. Sororal polygyny was an effective way of reinforcing the economic responsibilities a man had for his parents-in-law, and the assistance of sisters in the burdensome household tasks was a blessing for hard-pressed wives. The custom of the sororate, as might be expected, was also in vogue among Comanches. The related custom, the levirate (by which a man married his deceased brother's widow) was also practiced. In a society such as this one, where the life expectancy of warriors was not high, such a custom provided an immediate replacement so that the family could continue as before. The levirate led the Comanches to the verge of polyandry and a custom known as "anticipatory levirate," in which brothers lent each other their wives. Brothers were expected to be very close to one another and to display no sexual jealousy. They gave one another everything they could—and a temporary gift of a wife was a precious gift to bestow—one which clearly indicated the high esteem a man had for his brother. Wives, of course, could not undertake such liaisons on their own initiative or in secret, for such behavior would naturally enough be considered adulterous. When a man was on the warpath, it was normal procedure for his brother to sleep with his wife. One odd twist to wife-lending was the custom of a cuckolded man's calling his wife's seducer a "brother" while attempting at the same time to collect substantial damages from him.

These marriage customs provide the basis for understanding the kinship system of the Comanches. Since brothers by means of the anticipatory levirate formed a marriage group of sorts, and sisters through the operation of the sororate and sororal polygyny also formed a marriage grouping, kinship behavior and terminology were based on this arrangement. For example, a person called his mother's sister by the same term he used for his mother, and behaved toward her essentially as he did toward his mother. After all, she was apt to be a wife of his father already, and in any case was a potential wife of his father in the event his mother died. When this logic was extended, it is apparent that the children of his mother's sister were his brothers and sisters. Similarly, since his father's brothers could take the place of the father in the event of his death—and during the absence of the father already functioned in this capacity—it follows that these uncles were accorded the status and terminology of the father. It was only natural that children of his father's brothers were also termed his brothers and sisters. Unlike other Plains tribes—Lipans, for example—the Comanches had no in-law taboos. A son-in-law helped his mother-in-law and held her in considerable respect, but he did not avoid her. She could even joke with him, though she was never excessively familiar.

To Comanches the wonderful age, the age which was accorded the highest status, was that of the warrior. As we have seen, the transition from boy to warrior was marked by the test of battle, but passage from warrior to old man was a gradual one. The ideal warrior was a vainglorious, somewhat egotistical, aggressive, and independent person. But when he became an old man he was expected to be gentle, considerate, and thoughtful; he had to endure the pranks and the jokes of the youngsters. These senior citizens attempted to prevent bickering and quarreling within the tribe, and tried to restrain the younger men from embarking on the more foolhardy ventures of the warpath. All in all the personalities of the old men were supposed to be completely different from those they had had as warriors. No

171

wonder many men considered this metamorphosis so difficult they preferred to die while still young. The old men formed a sort of club in every camp, even having their own tepee where they met, gossiped, and fought again their old battles.

For the women the transition to old age was far easier. Before menopause a number of restrictions had limited their activities. During menstruation they had been isolated; if their husbands had "medicine," and virtually all of them did (i.e., had received supernatural assistance in a vision, and had certain magical paraphernalia strewn around the tepee), they were not allowed to sleep in their husbands' tepees, but moved back to their parents' lodge. Menstruating women could eat no meat, nor could they wash their faces or comb their hair. When confinement was over, no matter what the weather, they had to bathe before they could resume their normal lives with their husbands. After a woman had passed the menopause, she was naturally freed from these restrictions; she now could handle sacred objects, acquire supernatural powers through dreams, and even become a shaman. In a sense, old age was a release for the women, but for the men it was a deflating, downhill, restricting slide.

When an elderly person was obviously approaching death he was apt to be "thrown away" by his friends and relatives, not for want of affection but out of fear of evil spirits and his possibly malevolent soul. His kinfolk simply abandoned him. When a man was dying but had still some physical strength, he gave away his property and retired to an isolated spot to await death. He might take his own life after making the proper and final arrangements with his personal guardian spirits. Burial took place as soon after death as possible. Near relatives or close friends prepared the corpse with care, men attending to men and women to their own. The corpse was bathed, the face painted red, and the eyes sealed shut with clay. It was dressed in fine clothing, some of it donated by friends and relatives. The knees of the body were drawn up to the chest, the head was bent forward on it, and the flexed body was tied in this position. A blanket was wrapped and tied around the body which was then placed on a horse. Women, riding on either side or behind the corpse, took it to the place of burial, weeping and wailing as they went. Inaccessible

172

crevices, washes, and similar spots were preferred for graves. The flexed and bound corpse was placed in a sitting position or on its side in the crevice, facing the rising sun. Bands that moved far away from mountainous and hilly country occasionally used the tree or scaffold burial common to many Plains tribes. In the scaffold burial, scaffolds were constructed of poles and the bodies were placed upon them; in tree burial, the bodies were wedged into the crotches of trees.

When young and valuable warriors died, the mourning was intense and long-lasting; for the aged, it was moderate and brief. Female relatives of the deceased wept, wailed, tore off their clothing, and went about in rags as a token of mourning. They also might gash their bodies with knives, broken glass, and the like—often so severely that they fainted from loss of blood. These wounds were kept raw and bloody during the mourning period. Women often cut off their hair and on occasion chopped off a finger. The self-inflicted torture seems to be a vestige of the old Shoshonean custom of killing widows at their husbands' graves. The duration of mourning varied widely, but usually there was intense mourning for several weeks, followed by a year or more of milder mourning. The men might cut their hair and even gash their bodies if the death was that of a close relative or of a comrade, and they also smoked and prayed at such times.

Traditionally the inheritance of a deceased person's property presented no problem. In prehorse times there was practically no property, and by the time Comanches became Plains Indians it was customary to give away much before death. Personal equipment (knives, bows, etc.) was buried with the corpse, and articles like tepees were burned. Sacred paraphernalia were thrown in a stream or left in a bush or tree. A favorite horse—perhaps even several or more—belonging to the dead warrior was often shot at the grave. In 1816 smallpox raged among the Comanches and it has been estimated that five thousand horses and mules were destroyed as a result of this custom. (Hollon and Butler [eds.], 1956: 375) In later times the actual destruction of valuable horses was circumvented by cutting off the tails and manes and depositing them on the grave. But families that did this were regarded as stingy.

173

After a death the proper behavior was to destroy or give away all the property of the dead, in fact, to dispose of all the property of the entire family if the deceased was a young warrior. People who had no claim on a family's possessions could trump up one by providing some sort of goods to be buried with the deceased. Then they would wail and mourn so loudly and obviously that the relatives of the dead person were practically forced to give them something, perhaps a horse they coveted. Families were often left utterly destitute after such a giveaway and had to depend upon the largess of others until the mourning period was concluded.

Unlike Lipans, Comanches did not live in terror of the dead, but their deep concern with death is demonstrated by their many activities associated with the rites for the dead. Like Lipans, they avoided using the names of the dead, and when a prominent person died the entire camp moved away, but from a motivation different from that which caused Lipans to do the same thing. Comanches did not wish to remind mourning relatives of the dead by using their names, and they could escape thinking about a prominent leader, and perhaps the influence of his powerful ghost, too, by a hasty departure.

The stress placed upon individual independence and freedom of action, and also the strength of the many-purposed kinship groups, meant that formal governmental institutions were mostly absent. They would not have been welcomed or perhaps even tolerated by proud and haughty warriors. In pre-Plains days there had been even less need of governmental bodies, and their life on the Plains did not force them to modify greatly the pre-existing social patterns. In common with many other American Indians, Comanches insisted upon a separation of civil and military leadership. Each family encampment had a headman or peace chief, who usually was a member of the group of older men. Often he was not formally recognized or given a title, but his advice was valued and his authority real enough. As might be expected, such civil leaders were elected to their posts in no specified manner, but rather by common consent. This position was not sought by open competition, for the ideal chief symbolized peace and tranquility rather than aggressiveness and conflict. The man who was wise, even-tempered, possessed knowledge of the land, and was generous, might in time succeed to this post. There was a tendency for the position of peace chief to become hereditary, but only because the son of a chief had a better opportunity to acquire the qualities and customs associated with leadership than did other boys, and because the people became accustomed to looking to a representative of a particular family for leadership.

The peace chiefs came to be regarded as fathers of their people—wise old patriarchs whose advice was highly valued but whose power was limited. They can best be thought of as highly respected mediators. Peace chiefs seem to have had more power than war chiefs, although a civil chief who was becoming old and enfeebled might be outshone by a successful and vigorous young war chief. It also may be that the importance of the peace chief was greater in the more peaceful prehorse days than it was after the Comanches became involved in the constant conflicts of the plains.

All important matters—such as moving camp, making war or peace, seeking alliances, time and place of communal hunts and religious ceremonies, public relief of the indigent, and the like—were decided, at least in theory, in council. Like the peace chiefs, council members attained their rank through recognized achievements. Late in Comanche cultural life the position of councilor came to be recognized by a buffalo robe, painted to symbolize the sun's rays, and the feather war bonnet worn by the militarily successful. In council most of the talking was done by experienced older men. When they had finished, middle-aged men might speak, and finally a few outstanding younger men might be asked to express their sentiments. The Comanches, like many other Indians, felt that decisions should be unanimous, so not infrequently clear-cut policies and decisions were not reached by the council. Council procedure was most dignified and polite; speakers were never heckled nor heard disrespectfully, however much their views differed from others'. After the council had arrived at important decisions a crier circulated through camp, making known the news. Decisions were seldom if ever contrary to public opinion, for council members had acquainted themselves with

175

the feelings and desires of their people. Warriors, not wishing to anger the chiefs and fearing the ire of supernatural powers, seldom disobeyed the rulings of the council.

Any principal chief could call a meeting of his own band, and several bands were sometimes called into joint council. But there was no tribal council or tribal chief, and probably never did all the Comanche bands ever meet in a single council. War chiefs gained their rank, of course, by military exploits. Each had demonstrated his bravery and his qualities of leadership in battle. Every band recognized one of its members as the paramount war chief, and he was formally recognized as such by the council, making concrete his position among the warriors.

Within the bands and camp groups there were no judges, courts, or police to maintain order—but not because Comanches did not become involved in all sorts of frictions and difficulties among themselves, for they did. The qualities considered essential for the desirable and common personality type among Comanches also led to wild and reckless men who were consciously apt to break the law despite their sure knowledge of its dire penalties. Perhaps the most frequent breach of social tranquility was made by adulterers. Customarily, adulterous wives would have the tips of their noses cut off by their offended husbands, or they could be further mutilated or even killed. Roemer (1935: 272) encountered some women "who had their noses cut off and had short cropped, bristly hair covered with vermin, which they were just picking from one another. Clad in filthy skins and with their long, wrinkled breast, they presented the most horrible picture of femininity I have ever seen."

The methods husbands used to ascertain the guilt of their wives were at times brutal, but the mutilation of women was kept in bounds by the fact that women were viewed as a sort of chattel, and defacement would reduce their value in case they were transferred to some other man. When a man had determined his wife was having or had had an affair with another man, it was his duty to prosecute the matter. If he failed to do so he would be ridiculed as a poor citizen and as a coward (Wallace and Hoebel, 1952: 226):

176

. . . although the aggrieved husband was in fact prosecuting a wrong against himself, he was also put in a position of maintaining the public standards, whether he wanted to or not. He was in a sense a public prosecutor as well as the protector of his own private interests.

The customary way to collect damages was to force a guilty man to make payment in four kinds of articles: horses, guns, blankets, and clothing. Usually damages were paid in horses up to the number of ten. It was not, however, so much the actual value of the articles that was important as it was maintaining the prestige of the offended party and debasing the guilty one. The offended man normally sought out the guilty one, stated his case, and said what he desired in the way of compensation. The amount paid depended upon the physical prowess and war records of the men involved. If a famous warrior confronted a weak, unknown man, the damages would be severe; on the other hand, a man lacking in military ability had a difficult time collecting any sort of payment from a powerful, aggressive adulterer. A man who was afraid of his wife's lover, however, could get the assistance of friends, or could obtain the services of a warrior champion. This meant that a rude sort of justice was always obtainable through the equalization of the opposed forces. Theoretically a man had the right to kill an adulterer if he would not come to terms, but this seems to have been unusual. Sometimes, of course, the accused denied any guilt, and would take an oath of his innocence asking supernatural powers to destroy him if he was guilty. It is probable that few guilty men would have dared to take refuge behind such an oath. After damages had been paid, a man might release his wife to the other party. If this was done the children remained with the father. Roemer, while among the Comanches on the San Saba, was witness to the aftereffects of adultery (1935: 271):

. . . an old man appeared before our camp and complained to the assembled chiefs with a doleful countenance, that these . . . young warriors . . . had stolen his wife and two of his best horses. The chiefs, to whom the misfortune of the old man seemed to appear ludicrous, advised him to pursue the young men and to recapture his stolen property. The old man returned in the evening with a satisfied look and related that he had

Fig. 7. Comanche warrior.

found the young warriors not far distant from the camp and surprised them, just as they were in the act of drying the flesh of both of his horses. He had taken two of their mules to replace his horses and had also regained his wife.

Murder of a fellow Comanche was almost unheard of, but when it did happen, the kinsmen of the victim killed the murderer. In many primitive societies this sort of behavior leads to blood feuds between two groups, but among the Comanches it went no further.

The only other act considered criminal by the Comanches was sorcery. Jealous old men who had been unable to make a successful transition from warrior to old man were capable of performing black magic for antisocial ends. No new knowledge was required; all they had to do was employ the supernatural powers that they already had. Most sorcery was done in secret, but occasionally two men pitted their powers against each other publicly. Victims of sorcerers could be anybody against whom they harbored resentment or jealousy, but their power might also be directed against innocent persons who had been pointed out in a sorcerer's dream. In treating a sick person, a medicine man strove to learn through revelation the identity of the sorcerer who was making his patient ill. The brothers of the sick person immediately went to the accused sorcerer and asked him to release the victim from his malevolent power. The accused normally denied his guilt, and the ill person's kin left, sometimes threatening the sorcerer, sometimes to employ another sorcerer to counteract this malevolent power. Accused sorcerers could prove their innocence by taking a conditional oath or invoking a curse, much like that which men suspected of adultery might invoke. The accused swore his innocence; if he was lying, supernatural powers would soon sit in judgment. Some men earned bad names as sorcerers and were eventually destroyed, normally by some backhanded, stealthy maneuver, since sorcerers were dangerous if assaulted directly.

Other matters which in a civilization such as ours are dealt with by special institutions either never came up among the Comanches, or were dealt with by the families of the individuals involved. Thievery, by way of illustration, was practically nonexistent. If a person desired something another owned, he had but to ask for it to receive it, for

179

generosity was a highly-regarded virtue. Among such people as the Comanches, or any cultures with primitive technologies and relatively homogeneous, undifferentiated societies, the problems of property, inheritance, and the contractual obligations are apt to be minimal. The only vital problem for which the Comanches never developed fixed rules was their new-found form of wealth—horses. Horses were individually-owned by both men and women, and successful raiders managed to secure large herds. They soon became a medium of exchange and, as we have seen, were used as compensation in damage suits. Their disposition at the death of their owners was never completely clarified.

Among those peoples who have oriented their life around warfare, few have done so more thoroughly and completely than the Comanches. For just under two hundred years they were constantly embroiled in wars. In a very literal sense Comanche culture came into being through military prowess, blossomed through raiding and brawling, and nearly every aspect of life became intertwined in one way or another with the art of war. To gain a foothold on the teeming buffalo plains the Comanches had to be willing to fight and fight hard, and once they had won their land they had to fight with equal vigor to defend themselves against a varied assortment of white and Indian enemies.

The cultural imperatives which moved the Comanches to emphasize war were the rewards to be gotten by conquering the rich hunting grounds of the southern plains. The new way of exploiting these lands was on horseback, and the acquiring of horses was a powerful incentive to war. A popular view of Plains warfare has been that it was a "game," indulged in for no, or slight, material and practical purposes. This is an illusion. These tribal cultures were under great pressure to go to war—to be warlike. If they had not been, they would have lost in the intense competition for the rich bison lands, because the horse—essential to their life—would have been taken from them. The misunderstanding of Plains warfare has arisen because some writers have mistakenly taken the motivation of individual warriors to be the same as that which drove their tribes to war. (See Newcomb, 1950, for a more detailed discussion of Plains warfare.) There is little doubt that the motives which led warriors into a life of warfare had some of the aspects of a game. They were after horses and plunder, and particularly they desired the prestige which accrued to the successful warrior; high status in Comanche society could be obtained only in this manner. No wonder the Comanche could bring himself to perform such reckless deeds! Every male Comanche was a warrior, and he was brought up to believe that the ideal way of life was that of the warrior, to believe in courage and bravery—before and above life itself. Noah Smithwick (1900: 190), who had good cause to know the character of the Comanche warrior, said that he "never knew a warrior to submit to capture; they fought to the death." Twice he saw a wounded warrior "lie flat on his back and fight till dead."

The most gamelike aspect of Comanche warfare was the practice of "counting coup," which did not originate with Comanches but spread to them from other Plains tribes. The recognition of coups was roughly parallel to our system of awarding various medals for various deeds of valor in battle. The highest coup was awarded for the act of greatest bravery, and it followed from this logic that the most courageous deed was to touch or strike a living enemy. Killing an enemy with a bullet or arrow from a distance was not such a great feat. Scalping an already-dead enemy hardly counted as a coup, but scalping an enemy (alive or dead) under perilous circumstances was appropriately rewarded. The entire scalp was taken if possible, although often only a part of it could be obtained. The scalp was tangible evidence of victory, and was used in a victory dance; later on, locks of hair from it were useful for fringing and otherwise ornamenting clothing. Stealing horses staked in an enemy camp, or under other equally dangerous circumstances, also rated high on the list of war honors. Boys, women, and even hunters came to count coup on animals they had killed or wounded. The women, for example, often would race to a downed buffalo to be the first to touch it.

There was apt to be argument over who had counted coup on a fallen enemy, and often there was no witness to some honorable deed claimed by a warrior. For a deed to count, it had to be recognized by other warriors, and after a battle the chief gathered the participants together so that the honors claimed could be adjudged. The bands decided their coup honors in varying ways, most of them employing some form of oath in combination with what others had witnessed. Comanches counted coup on a victim but twice, contrary to some of the other Plains tribes who counted three and four times.

In common with other Plains tribes and consonant with the individualistic emphasis in Comanche culture, these Indians considered warfare a matter of individual initiative. Anybody could lead a war or raiding party, and others would join or not, depending upon the status of the leader as a warrior, his past success in such ventures, and the whim of the individual. Men who had often led successful parties had little trouble in obtaining followers, while an inexperienced man, particularly one who had received no supernatural sanction in a vision, might be unable to organize any sort of foray. Men who were thinking of leading a war party or a raid usually had received some sort of supernatural message suggesting when and where it was to take place. They also talked over their plans with other men. Smoking, the singing of war songs, and parading through camp normally prefaced the departure of a war party. The night before a party was to leave a dance was held, the warriors departing before daylight. Such war dances can be thought of as somewhat akin to a pep rally on the eve of a college football game, the same excitement and emotions being aroused in each case. Even old warriors would get up and recite their coups, their days of glory, much as a former football hero inspires his younger comrades to greater glories on the gridiron. The war dance was concluded with the leader of the war or raiding party recounting the aim and the reason for the foray. He left shortly thereafter, his warriors soon following, dallying perhaps for a few moments in the darkness with their lovers before final departure.

Leaders of war or raiding parties were in full control of their ventures. The way in which they were organized and the realization by a leader's followers that disobeying orders might cause the destruction of the party led to this somewhat out-of-cast authority of a single man. Occasionally there was disagreement among the members of a party, and they simply returned home or went their own way.

182

Normally, scouts were sent out and kept from a half to a full day's ride ahead of the main body. If it was to be a large-scale raid or one of considerable duration, the women and their lodges might accompany the group. Every precaution was taken when camping. During these halts, the leader usually lighted his sacred pipe and, after suitable offerings to the powers, passed it to the warriors. He might also take the opportunity to discuss the venture further and to give additional instructions to his warriors.

There was little difference between the various types of expeditions. War parties seldom passed up an opportunity to steal horses, and raiding parties when faced by an enemy would fight. Only one type of expedition—that seeking vengeance for the slaying of a Comanche—was single-minded in purpose. When such a party had slain one enemy and secured his scalp, they turned homeward even though they could have slain more.

Like other Texas Indians, Comanches struck swiftly, looted, killed, and quickly withdrew. Often the enemy was not surprised; in such instances Comanches would attempt various ambushes, but they usually declined to make a concerted charge or to stand and take an enemy assault. If the enemy was weaker numerically, Comanches began their well-known expedient of circling, drawing closer and closer, hoping the enemy would exhaust their arrows, or that whites would fire a volley from their flintlocks. If the whites all fired at once, the Comanches would rush them before they had time to reload. Jenkins (1958: 64), a participant in the Plum Creek battle, adds an interesting footnote to these encircling tactics:

It was a strange spectacle never to be forgotten, the wild, fantastic band as they stood in battle array, or swept around us with all strategy of Indian warfare. Twenty or thirty warriors, mounted upon splendid horses, tried to ride around us, sixty or eighty yards distant, firing upon us as they went. It was a superstition among them, that if they could thus run around a force they could certainly vanquish it.

If a Comanche war party encountered a vastly superior force, they would simply withdraw. If the enemy pursued them, the Comanche force would scatter into smaller groups, and if pressed hard enough

183

each warrior would flee alone. It was virtually impossible for an attacking force to follow each fleeing warrior, but if the enemy too subdivided into groups and continued the pursuit, a group might itself be ambushed by a suddenly-reconstituted war party. The Comanches, of course, had an excellent system of communication based on smoke signals, imitating the calls of owls and coyotes, and other things. One of the reasons why Comanches were so successful in their raiding ventures against Mexicans and Americans is that once they had made a raid they could withdraw rapidly and keep going through country which exhausted their most determined pursuers.

As soon as possible a raiding party would halt and divide the spoils. In theory all loot belonged to the leader, but usually he kept little for himself. The success of a raid was due to its leader's "medicine," and to keep the spoils would be to admit that his powers were waning. Moreover, if he was stingy in dividing up the loot he would have a difficult time recruiting followers in the future. Throughout most of Comanche history the object of most of their raids was horses, but about the time of the Civil War Texas ranchers began to push into the fringes of Comanche country, and the Comanches were soon driving off Texas cattle. Before long a regular trade grew up with New Mexicans in stolen cattle. Several hundred thousand head in all were driven off—sufficient to enrage the cattlemen permanently against Comanches.

Successful war or raiding parties returned to a gala welcome, with scalp dances and much rejoicing. Amid shouting and yelling, the warriors paraded into camp with their scalps held high on poles and with their loot. In the evening there was a scalp dance if scalps had been taken, or a victory dance if the party had only been on a raid. Unsuccessful forays, or ones which had sustained loss, were a different matter. In these cases warriors came into camp singly with their faces blackened, and the tails of their horses shaved. If their loss was severe, that is, if several prominent warriors had been lost, the entire camp would vehemently mourn their dead. In these paroxysms of grief and anger captives might be abused or slain, and vengeance on the enemy was sworn.

Some Comanche bands had a number of impermanent and informal military fraternities, made up of warriors who were congenial and who had the common bond of having jointly participated in a number of raids. They had special insignia, dances, and songs, and some of them seem to have had special purposes. The men who wore the full-feathered war bonnets and were termed war leaders also constituted a special group. In a similar group, though of a lower status, were the buffalo-scalp bonnet-wearers. War leaders had certain obligations—such as retreating only under certain conditions, helping comrades, and the like. The buffalo-scalp bonnet could be worn by any warrior who so desired, provided he was willing to assume the obligations that went with it. Ordinarily this type of bonnet was given to a warrior by friends who thought highly of him, and expected him in the future to perform noble deeds in war. Many Plains tribes had "crazy" warriors, even fraternities of them, who did everything backward and were reckless and extraordinarily brave. Occasionally, this type of warrior turned up among Comanches, and probably this custom was picked up in relatively recent times from other Plains tribes.

Supernaturalism. The basic and outstanding characteristic of Comanche religious practice was a direct, individual appeal to the supernatural powers. Religious practices were a matter of individual concern; there were relatively few group observances. "There was no religious organization, no theocracy, no priestly class, no dogma." (Wallace and Hoebel, 1952: 155) To be a success in life—to gain repute as a warrior—a man had to have the aid of some supernatural force. This assistance came to a person in a vision, a mystic experience. It might come unsought, but ordinarily a young man who had about reached puberty tried desperately to have a psychic experience. A shaman prepared the youth for his quest by talking to him and making him bathe, symbolic of purification. The vision-seeker carried four things with him: a buffalo robe, a bone pipe, tobacco, and materials for lighting the pipe. Thus equipped, and dressed only in a breechclout and moccasins, he left camp and sought an isolated hill or other special place to await his vision. On the way he halted four times—the Comanches' mystic number—to smoke and pray. When the youth had found a suitable place, not so far from camp that he could not return when weakened, yet isolated and lonely, he smoked and prayed for power. During the night he kept himself covered with the robe, his face to the east, but as the new day dawned he rose to face the sun and to absorb its beneficial rays. And throughout his quest he fasted. The attitude of the supplicant was one of awe and respect for the omnipotent powers, but not of groveling before them. The spirits were glad to give their power, and the supplicant was happy and grateful when it was bestowed upon him. Usually a vision was received within the customary four-day and four-night vigil, although occasionally the quest was extended and sometimes it was unsuccessful.

When the vision came, the candidate learned about the special bond which existed between himself and his guardian spirit. He was told of the restrictions and taboo he must henceforth follow. If he failed to follow the prescriptions he was given, his medicine—the power for good he had acquired—would turn to evil. Specific foods were often forbidden, and others could be eaten only under certain conditions. All medicines, or the sacred paraphernalia the supplicant was told to make or acquire, had to be protected from menstruating women and grease. His things might even be kept in a special tepee away from these dangerous, contaminating things. Songs, which he had to be able to sing at any time, were also given to him during his vision.

The supernatural powers given to men in visions were powerful, even dangerous, and their possessors had a heavy responsibility to see that all regulations and injunctions concerning their use were carefully followed. They could not divulge the secrets of their powers without express permission of the spirits, and above all they had to have complete faith in their power, else it would not work. In addition to the songs and taboos received in visions, supplicants were usually told of certain magical medicines. These objects might be stones, bird claws, skins, feathers, or many other things. Almost all Comanches carried some amulet or charm, worn often because of these visions, though sometimes they were acquired from shamans.

The powers acquired in visions by various men were not of equal worth or strength. Some worked well, some did not, and those which proved to be of little assistance were thought to be less effectual either because the power was weak or its possessor had misused it in some way. Men sought visions on many occasions when special assistance was needed—for hunting, when going on the warpath, for curing illness, or when seeking revenge. Those who became particularly successful in healing the sick in time became shamans or medicine men. But virtually all old men and women had obtained some curative powers.

While power was essentially an individual possession, those who had great power were often called on to pass some of it along to other persons, and they had to do so if they were asked for it properly. Comanches felt that the men who had strong power should use it for the benefit of all and that they should teach others how to use at least some of it. The power itself could not be transferred, but other persons could be instructed so that they would be prepared to receive such power. Another convenient provision about the power was that if its possession became too burdensome because of the taboos and other restrictions associated with it, a man could return it. All he had to do was to go back to the place where he had acquired it, address the spirits, thank them for the use of the power, and declare that he no longer wished to have it. The sharing of power also meant that a primitive sort of medicine society, limited to twelve members, grew up. If power was shared by more persons than twelve it was thought to become too weak or diluted to be any good.

Women ordinarily acquired power through their husbands; they could not acquire it directly until after menopause. Thoughtful men, responding to approximately the same motives that encourage men in our society to have life-insurance policies, usually prepared their wives to assume their power after they had died. With this power a woman could ensure her family's good fortune, although of course she might refuse the power if she felt it to be too strong or dangerous.

For treating injuries such as broken bones, gunshot wounds, and the like, Comanche medicine men had crude but apparently effectual techniques. They knew the use of the tourniquet, practiced some surgery, and used a wide assortment of herbs and other medicines to cure other ills. Their most effective cures were probably of mild

187

psychosomatic illnesses. Besides curing and protecting people from evil, some shamans were thought to be able to make it rain, to foretell the position of buffalo herds, to ascertain what the fate of overdue war parties was, and other things.

Power was generally obtained from nonhuman spirits, but occasionally a particularly brave man would stand up to ghosts and receive very great power from them. Comanches had no fear of the dead—or their ghosts—as did the Lipans, but they were still regarded as possibly dangerous. Ghosts appeared to men, often when they were on a war party, as skeletons or as bloody, scalped bodies. Perhaps the most fascinating of Comanche supernatural spirits were the "little men," somewhat like the elves or pixies in our folklore, but very dangerous. These little creatures were only about a foot high, and went about armed with shields, bows, and stone-tipped arrows. Their arrows always killed. Some audacious shamans attempted to acquire power from these little men but it was exceedingly dangerous to have such power, for it was easily misdirected.

Practically all Comanche religious practice was carried on by the individual and not by groups of people. By the middle of the nineteenth century, however, the Comanches possessed the beaver ceremony and the eagle dance. The Plains sun dance was tried once unsuccessfully in 1874, and in reservation days the Comanche became ardent members of the peyote cult. The beaver ceremony was a curing ceremony possibly borrowed from the Pawnees, and it was never performed by all Comanche bands. The eagle dance seems to have been a genuine Comanche ceremony; it was given by a man for his son or nephew, to acquire power from a shaman with strong power.

The spirit creatures encountered in visions were by far the most important supernatural beings, at least so far as individuals were concerned. It is not to be expected that a people with such individualistic practices would have a universal or well-organized conception of supernatural beings or of the supernatural world. Comanches universally believed, however, in a life after death. Spirits journeyed to the land of the dead beyond the setting sun, and this land was similar to the world they had left behind, except that all the disagreeable features of that world were absent. Everybody was youthful in this perfect afterworld; there was no war and no darkness. There was plenty of game for the men to hunt, the horses were fast, pounded corn was always available, and there was no sorrow or suffering. There was no doubt in their minds about this wonderful afterworld, for some people (in delirium) had been there and had returned to tell of its splendors. Originally, Comanches seem to have felt that after death they all went to this heaven, with the exception of those persons who were scalped after death, were strangled, died in the dark, or were mutilated. It is interesting to note in this connection that Rachel Plummer was perplexed by the fact that Comanches mourned more the death of those warriors—at the hands of Osages—who had been scalped than those who had not. The reasons why Comanches scalped their enemies becomes clear with the knowledge of this belief: scalping an enemy prevented his gaining immortality, and perhaps his being reborn at some future date to again plague the Comanches. Comanches, like many other people, associated the soul with the breath; if a person died by strangulation, the soul could not make its escape from the body and was forever imprisoned within the lifeless corpse. Spirits that left the body in the dark were apt to become lost and be unable to find their way to the afterworld. Another common belief was that various indignities or mutilations performed on a body after death were borne by the soul in its afterlife.

The Comanches' ideas about important deities were always, it seems, vague. The sun, moon, and earth were considered to be supernatural beings, and in later times at least if not earlier, there was a hazy belief in an omnipotent power—the Great Spirit, or Our Sure Enough Father. The Great Spirit was the creator of the universe and naturally of Comanches. In prayer this diffuse but all-powerful force was always the first supernatural to be addressed. Some Comanches also seemed to believe in a counterpart to this benevolent god—the Evil Spirit. Persons who held both beliefs could more easily account for the disasters which befell man, but the concept of Evil Spirit does not fit in with their idea of a perfect afterworld. Persons believing in the dual powers, and of rivalry between them, sought the aid and blessing of Great Spirit and probably at the same time attempted to appease and placate Evil Spirit. The belief in an omnipotent power is common among Shoshones and other tribes of the Great Basin, so it would not be out of keeping for Comanches to have held similar views. The wolf is often equated with the benevolent creator being, whereas the coyote, wolf's younger brother, though not his antithesis, is a mischievous spoiler. Whether the Comanches thought of the wolf and coyote as an embodiment of these supernaturals is not clear; today's Comanches no longer so regard them.

Great Spirit was by some Comanches associated with the sun, or the sun was felt to be an embodiment of this omnipotent power. There is no question that the Comanches venerated the sun and that it was universally regarded as all-powerful. But their theology never made hard-and-fast distinctions between the sun and the Great Spirit. The earth, addressed as Mother, was also deified, as was the moon. But all of these deities were somewhat removed, and the individual Comanche was much more concerned with his own personal guardian spirit. The sun, earth, and moon never became individual guardian spirits and never bestowed power on individuals.

All the spirits who were capable of bestowing their powers on men spoke the language of men, and they could take the shape of, or reside in, almost any object. Furthermore, they could instantaneously transform themselves into something else and then back again. Spirits frequently lived in natural objects, such as rivers, springs, high places, and particularly odd or unusual topographic features. Medicine Mounds, a series of rounded hills in Hardeman County, Texas, between the Pease and the Red Rivers, and one of these mounds in particular—a flat-topped cap rock—was a special abode of spirits. (Wallace and Hoebel, 1952: 204–205) South of Lawton, Oklahoma, on Cache Creek not far from where it joins the Red River was Medicine Bluff, a high, crescent-shaped bluff, also especially regarded by Comanches as an abode of powerful spirits.

Power could reside also in natural phenomena, and perhaps the most dangerous of these was thunder. As did other Plains Indians, Comanches believed that thunder appeared as a bird, larger and more powerful than the eagle. This thunderbird produced thunder,

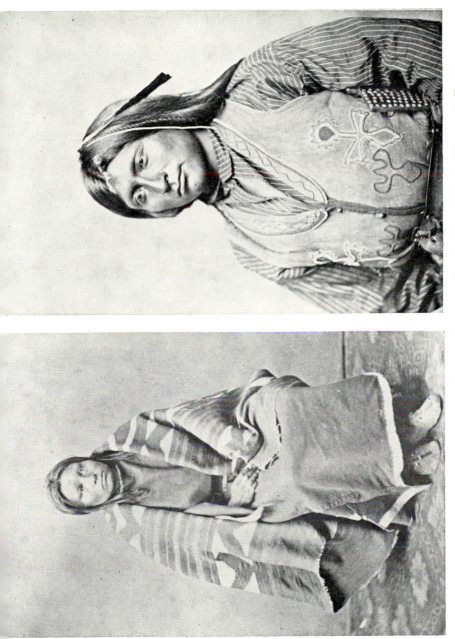

PLATE VI. A Comanche woman (left). Tabatoso, a Comanche (right). A. B. Stephenson Collection, courtey Barker Texas History Center.

PLATE VII. A Kiowa and his daughters. *A. B. Stephenson Collection, courtesy Barker Texas History Center.*

lightning, storms, and rain, and was feared more than any of the other powers of nature because it could do greater harm. Buffaloes were important supernaturally, as well as naturally; they could talk to people and occasionally they turned into people. A magical practice for attracting buffalo was to face old buffalo skulls found on the prairie in the direction of camp to induce the herds to approach. The coyote was thought of as a brother, and he often informed those who had power of both impending trouble and good fortune. Eagles had power, particularly in affairs of war; hence the use of eagle feathers in the hair and on shields and other equipment. The deer had considerable power, but it might be for good or evil. The elk was associated with strength and strong was the man who had this animal for a guardian spirit. The bear could cure wounds, but the skunk was even more powerful in curing. Actually, nearly all forms of life—even insects—could have special, more-than-natural powers, and might be guardian spirits. The only animals that never seem to have been regarded as potentially powerful were the Comanches' domestic animals—horses and dogs. In short, there was nothing in the Comanche world which for some person might not have become endowed with a power that transcended the ordinary.

THE DURATION OF Comanche existence on the Plains was short in comparison to many culture histories. It was a streaking comet in the nighttime skies, appearing from nowhere, blazing brightly for a time, meeting abrupt extinction. Its beginnings can only be described as humble, and while successful in the roistering struggle of Plains life, the rough corners of its culture were never smoothed enough to disguise these beginnings. Like a successful immigrant boy, Comanche culture could never quite hide its origins, and like him it was tough, enduring, boisterous, and aggressive.

CHAPTER 8

Kiowas and Kiowa Apaches:
Far-Ranging Raiders

You call yourselves white men,
But you all have red faces.
Come out and fight with us,
And we will see if your blood is red all over
The way it is in your faces.

Kiowa song

LIKE THE COMANCHES, the Kiowas and associated Kiowa Apaches were historically recent invaders of Texas.[1] And they can just barely be claimed as Texas Indians, for their principal nineteenth-century range lay to the north and east of the Texas Panhandle in the Wichita Mountains. The word *Kiowa* is probably a corruption of the tribe's name for itself, possibly meaning "a people who paint the two halves of the body or face different colors." In Comanche, *Kiowa* means "mouse"—not an apt characterization but a term Comanche warriors may well have taunted the Kiowas with in the days before the two

[1] This chapter is drawn primarily from Mooney, 1898; Marriott, 1945 (the song at the head of this chapter is from *ibid.*, pp. 32–33); Richardson, 1940; Battey, 1876; and Methvin, 1927.

193

tribes had become allies. The Kiowa Apaches, as we have seen in Chapter 4, appear to have become separated from their eastern or Plains Apache relatives, probably about the time the Comanches swept down upon the southern plains. In the warfare of the southern plains there was some measure of security in numbers, and the confederation of the Kiowas and Kiowa Apaches was undoubtedly of mutual advantage. Probably there were never more than two thousand Kiowas, and even fewer Kiowa Apaches. (See Map 3.)

Origins and Early History. The prehistory of the Kiowas is completely unknown, and their early historic location has long been in dispute. Kiowas speak a language related to Tanoan, and Tanoan-Kiowa appears to belong to the Uto-Aztekan family of languages. (Harrington, 1910; Sapir, 1949: 173) The other Tanoan-speakers are all Pueblo Indians—Tewa, Tano, Tigua, Jemez, and Piro—living along the Rio Grande in New Mexico, but nearer to the Plains than other Puebloans. The Tano and Piro are now extinct, and the Jemez have been joined by remnants from Pecos. Some of the prehistoric Tanoans could have foregone a settled, agricultural life for the pursuit of bison, but it is equally reasonable that nomadic hunters could have wandered into New Mexico, learned from its residents, and in time become the modern Puebloan Tanoans. The Kiowas' own traditions place their origins far to the north, near the sources of the Yellowstone and Missouri Rivers in western Montana. And historic documents confirm that they ranged as far north as the Yellowstone late in the seventeenth century. Kiowa tradition also asserts a close association with the Crow Indians while in the north, but "that these contacts were peculiarly intimate is demonstrated neither by Crow tradition, which fails to support Kiowa assertions, nor by a comparison of Kiowa with Crow culture." (Lowie, 1953: 365) Apparently the Kiowas had wandered far to the north in early, perhaps prehistoric, times, but that they remained there for any length of time is in serious doubt. By the nineteenth century they were southern Plains Indians, and, in fact, are often thought of as one of the most typical of these tribes.

About 1780 the Kiowas were in the Black Hills of present South Dakota, but by the end of the century they and their new confederates, the Kiowa Apaches, had been driven out by Dakotas (Sioux), who were moving in from the east, and Cheyennes, who were advancing from the northeast. Early in the nineteenth century the Kiowas and Kiowa Apaches were ranging between the forks of the Platte, but soon were moving south into eastern Colorado, and by 1832 were on the Arkansas. As the Kiowas and Kiowa Apaches pushed southward in front of the Cheyennes and Dakotas they met Comanches, and a warfare of many years' duration resulted.

About 1790 the Kiowas and Kiowa Apaches made peace with the Comanches, a peace which was to last throughout the bitter struggle with Americans for the southern plains. Tradition has it that a small party of Kiowas stopped at a house in a Spanish settlement, presumably in New Mexico, unaware that a party of Comanches was already there. Before a battle could break out, the Indians' host, acting as a mediator, proposed that the Kiowas and Comanches come to a peaceful settlement of their differences. After some discussion by both sides, the leader of the Kiowas' party, "Wolf-Lying-Down," went with the Comanches so that the matter could be further discussed by a larger and more representative segment of the Comanche tribe. He parted from his fellow Kiowas with the request that they avenge his death if he had not returned by fall. He did return, however, the Comanches having agreed to a cessation of hostilities. Whether or not this traditional history is entirely factual, it is true that the Comanches and Kiowas were afterwards at peace. They shared each other's hunting territories and often raided together. (Mooney, 1898: 162–164)

Appearance and Dress. George Catlin (1841, II: 74), the artist member of the Dragoon Expedition of 1834, wrote:

The Kioways are a much finer looking race of men, than either the Camanchees or Pawnees—are tall and erect, with an easy and graceful gait—with long hair, cultivated oftentimes so as to reach nearly to the ground. They have generally the fine and Roman outline of head, that is so frequently found at the North,—and decidedly distinct from that of the Camanchees and Pawnee Picts [Wichitas].

Intermarriage with whites and other Indians has undoubtedly reduced whatever homogeneity they once had, although a casual acquaintance with them a few years ago left with me the impression that they are often darker in skin color than many other Plains Indians. And Alice Marriott (1945: VIII), who probably knows the modern Kiowas better than anybody else, has described them as "dark-skinned" and "inclined to be short, stocky, and thick-chested." One of the Kiowa warriors whom Catlin drew would be outstanding in any population. He described him (1841, II: 75 and Plate 182) as extraordinary, "near seven feet in stature, and distinguished, not only as one of the greatest warriors, but the swiftest on foot, in the nation. This man, it is said, runs down a buffalo on foot, and slays it with his knife or his lance, as he runs by its side!"

The clothing and ornamentation of Kiowas and Kiowa Apaches were essentially like those of Comanches and other Plains Indians. The men wore deerskin moccasins, breechclouts, and shirts: the women wore high moccasins and dresses of deerskin also. Children wore little in warm weather, but dressed in adult fashions when clothing was in order. As with other Plains Indians buffalo robes served as a protection from winter storms. In the early days it was customary for warriors to cut their hair short on the right side in order to show off their various ear ornaments. The hair on the left was encouraged to grow as long as possible. It was normally tied or wrapped, and a scalp lock was also left hanging down behind. The women apparently followed the common Plains practice of parting their hair in the middle and plaiting it in two braids, or allowing it to fall free and securing it with a head band. Kiowas were extremely fond of any kind of metal ornamentation, and profusely decorated their bodies, clothing, and horses with silver and other metal trinkets.

The apparel of their war parties, like that of other southern Plains tribes, was elaborate. After a battle in 1874, for example, the apparel of several slain warriors was carefully examined. One wore a headdress of crow feathers "with black cow horns and a brow band of blue and white beads." Another wore a headdress of "owl feathers, colored yellow, with heifer horns, also stained yellow." (Nye, 1937: 236)

Subsistence and Material Culture. Kiowa and

Kiowa Apache hunting techniques were similar to those already discussed for Comanches, though communal bison hunts were more formally organized and controlled. In these the warrior societies acted as police in order to co-ordinate and restrain the hunters. They located the herds, surrounded them, and stood guard while hunters chased and shot the encircled beasts. Buffalo were sometimes also forced along converging driveways which led to cliffs or precipices over which they were driven. This procedure, we may recall, was an age-old way of hunting bison.

Other animals—deer, antelope, small game—were also hunted, but their over-all importance was relatively minor. A favorite method of hunting antelope was to impound them in a corral, made of upright logs stripped of their branches. From the opening of the corral two diverging lines of blanket-covered scarecrow posts were set up through which the antelope were driven. An antelope "surround" was also practiced by Kiowas, but only in the winter when the antelope were congregated in herds, or at other times when there was an extreme shortage of bison. In this surround an antelope medicineman performed a rather long and intricate ritual, much of it being a sort of imitative magic. Under his direction mounted hunters formed an immense semicircle on the prairie and slowly contracted it toward the women and others who completed the circle. Animals within the circle were captured with the hands or roped, for no shooting was allowed within the surrounded area. Animals that broke through, however, were shot. Many animals other than antelope were taken in such surrounds, one case being recorded in which "a woman caught a coyote by throwing her arms about its neck." (Mooney, 1898: 289) Antelope were also trapped by constructing concealed pitfalls along their trails. Wild horses were sometimes captured in corrals similar to those used for antelope, although these were set up near water holes where horses had to drink during hot summer months. After bison had become scarce the Kiowas ate horseflesh, but whether or not this was customary in earlier days is uncertain.

Kiowa traditions say nothing of their having raised crops, and this was not contradicted by their way of life during historic times. They did, however, obtain agricultural produce from other Indians by trade and stealth. And to break the monotony of a largely meat diet they utilized many wild-plant foods—fruits, berries, roots, nuts. They did not eat bears, birds, or fish.

Kiowas used bisonhide tepees, of course, erecting them upon a four-pole foundation. Twenty poles were added to complete the framework. Tanned bisonhides, sewn together and often decorated with paintings of remarkable artistry, were raised on the foundation poles. About eight hides were used for small tepees, and twelve were sufficient for an ordinary dwelling, but a headman might have a tepee up to twenty-five or thirty feet in diameter, requiring twenty hides. Pegs fastened the cover at the bottom. The entrance, facing toward the east except during the sun dance, was a round hole, about three or four feet in diameter and raised somewhat off the ground. It was closed with a stiff piece of painted skin, and so fastened on the windward side by buckskin strings that the doorway closed itself on windy days. In warm weather the sides of tepees could be rolled up to let in the breeze, and in the summer, brush arbors were also constructed.

The arrangement of the interior was simple; a fire pit was dug in the center, the sides away from the door were occupied by beds, and the entrance side was used as kitchen and pantry and for storage. Beds were made by placing light willow rods across several poles, over which were thrown buffaloskins and blankets; during the day they served as seats or couches.

As is true of all nomadic people, the material equipment of the Kiowas and Kiowa Apaches had to be restricted to durable, movable tools and equipment. The Kiowas, for example, had neither pottery nor basketry. Instead, they used hide bags and containers, horn spoons and utensils. Similar to the Lipan Apaches, they carried their water in buffalo or beef paunches (Methvin, 1927: 50–51):

When a jug is needed, a beef or buffalo is killed, the paunch is taken out and cut open, the rough inner lining is removed, the paunch is dried, and the edges are pinned together with smooth, wooden pins, which bring it together, looking, when filled with water, very much like a large, short-neck gourd. Two of these are filled with water and placed across a pack saddle and carried sometimes long distances.

The women tanned hides expertly; for tepee covers they scraped off the hair and removed bits of flesh from the inner side with bone fleshing tools. A great deal of hard labor was involved in tanning hides "but when done, they were as pliant as any leather manufactured after our most improved process. The hides intended for robes are of course dressed only on the inner side, but they are made very pliant and comfortable." (Methvin, 1927: 55)

Lances and bows and arrows were the chief weapons of the warriors before firearms were available, and these were not abandoned even after firearms were easily obtained. Kiowa quivers "were usually of panther skin or Mexican leather, but never of deer, antelope, or buffalo skin if it could be avoided." (Mooney, 1898: 276)

Social Organization. Normally children were named soon after birth, by a grandparent or some other relative. Occasionally they seem to have been taken to outstanding men for naming, and gifts of hides and horses were made for this service. Names were often drawn from some noteworthy incident, or they might refer to some great deed of war by an ancestor. Young men frequently took new names as a consequence of visions, and later in life new names might be adopted because of actions on the warpath, the hunt, or in domestic affairs. Older men or aged warriors who were drawing close to the end of life sometimes gave their names to promising younger warriors. They then adopted a new name or went nameless for the remainder of their lives. If the older men found no favor in any younger man they might simply throw away their names. Names of the dead were not used, or even spoken by their survivors. But this practice did not stem so much from a fear of the dead or their souls as from regard for the feelings of the deceased's family. The Kiowa Apaches retained the Athapaskan dread and terror of the dead and completely avoided any reference to their names.

Playing a prominent part in the instruction of boys was the Rabbit Society. All little Kiowa boys were automatically members of it. The Rabbits were instructed and drilled in their future duties as warriors by two grown-up men. The society may be thought of quite properly as the only formally-organized school the children ever attended. The Rabbits also held feasts and had dances in which their steps imitated the jumps and hops of their namesake. Rabbits wore at the back of their heads a piece of elkhide with the hair left on and an erect feather—the insignia of the society. The boys left the society when they were invited to join one of the adult warrior societies.

As the lads grew older they got the opportunity to join war parties, first only to herd the horses, later to participate as full-fledged warriors. It was during this phase of life, too, that young Kiowa men first sought to establish a beneficial relationship with more-than-natural forces. Power could be gotten anywhere if the supernatural forces were so disposed, but if a young man was unsure, if there had been no particular omen directing him to seek power, it was better to go to those places where people had received power before. These seem to have been usually hills, mesas, or bluffs. But the vision-seeker tried to find a place close enough to camp that in a weakened state it would not be difficult for him to return, yet isolated enough that other people would not bother him. When he had selected an appropriate spot he waited, praying, smoking, and fasting. The supplicant might have a vision soon, late, or perhaps not at all. But after a week or so under such lonely and trying circumstances it is not surprising that many men who had a sure conviction and faith in their quest secured guardian spirits.[2] There seems to have been no restrictions as to what might become a guardian spirit, one recorded spirit, for example, being that of the relatively insignificant mountain boomer (a lizard). (Marriott, 1945: 101)

These guardian spirits gave various instructions to the men—how to paint their faces, songs, sometimes dietary taboos, and certain magical amulets. At first glance it would be natural to dismiss the vision quest and guardian spirits as unimportant primitive superstitions. But when we realize that a man who had obtained such a helper had a tremendous psychological advantage over one who had not, we see that such beliefs were a great asset in an arduous, dangerous life. They gave the callow youth the confidence, the audacity, to embark on a warrior's career. Or, as sometimes happened, it

[2] Methvin (1927: 106) illuminates the psychological state of men embarking upon the vision quest.

emboldened a few to direct their activities toward less socially acceptable—if more peaceful—pursuits.

Girls reached a marriageable age soon after they became fourteen and boys by the time they were sixteen or so. There were no elaborate ceremonials to celebrate the marriage rite itself. A suitor proffered a girl's parents horses and other property as recompense for their loss. If an agreement was reached between the suitor and the girl's parents and her brother (who even after marriage continued as her guardian), the couple set up housekeeping. Occasionally girls were married against their will, and some girls escaped these disagreeable unions by eloping with men of their own choice. Marriott (1945: 101) recounts a case in which a girl wanted to marry a young man who unfortunately was both poor and part Wichita. But an older man whose wife was aging and needed help offered the girl's mother's brother (she had no father) eight horses—four for her uncle and four for her mother. The girl's family agreed to this marriage and in consequence she eloped with her poor sweetheart. Her family eventually became reconciled to the elopement, the uncle even helping the couple in making and furnishing their own tepee, and the mother giving her sanction by providing a feast for the women who worked on her daughter's tepee cover.

The residence of a newly-married couple was usually patrilocal, that is, with the husband's parents, but if a man was poor and of low rank he often joined his wife's family. Kiowas were polygynous, men of high status usually having several wives, though poor or low-status men had but one. By marrying the eldest daughter of a family a man had first claim upon her sisters, although he might or might not exercise it. But as a man's family grew, the work of caring for babies and camp chores was more easily accomplished by several women. And it should be emphasized that an Indian woman's life was in large part a matter of unremitting drudgery unless it was lightened by the help of other wives. It was the woman's task to skin and butcher the bison the hunters killed, pack the meat on ponies, and take it to camp. There she cured what meat she could for future use by slicing it thin, sun-drying it, and storing it in buffaloskin sacks or parfleches. She also tanned the hides, both for tepees and robes, pre-

201

pared the household food, erected and dismantled the lodges, cared for the children, and performed other household chores. A man's occupations, in contrast, can be described as violently active and serenely leisurely by turns. His hunting, fighting life was dangerous and frequently brief, but it was not boringly repetitious. Given these disparate economic responsibilities of men and women, and the drudgery of a woman's life, it is easy to understand why wives frequently persuaded their husbands to marry additional women.

The levirate was also in vogue among the Kiowas, a deceased husband's brother having an option to marry the widow. If he did not marry her or she refused to marry him, her brothers or sons supported her until she did remarry. When and if she did take this step, even if her brother-in-law had previously refused to marry her, an adjustment or agreement had to be reached with him in the form of a gift of horses or other property.

Adultery was the cause of considerable strife among Kiowas, not only because a man was in love with another man's wife and wanted to possess her but also because absconding with another's wife or seducing her was a way for a man to raise his status or to get even with a woman's husband. In short, wife-stealing was often the means to an end that was not mere carnal desire. And a woman herself might take the initiative and become an adulterer. This behavior was common when a man took a second wife and moved out of his first wife's tepee, instead of remaining in her tepee and only visiting his second wife, as was considered proper conduct. By running off with another man a woman would thus shame her husband. A man who ran off with a woman whose husband was of higher status could raise his own status: "If the lover could outface the husband and demonstrate thereby publicly his signal courage in the face of death, his reputation was enormously enhanced." (Richardson, 1940: 80) Punishment for adultery was quite varied, depending primarily upon the relative statuses of the men involved. An injured husband might collect damages, usually horses, from an adulterer, but if he was a weak, poor man of low status, he might get nothing. Unfaithful wives might be beaten, have their noses cut off, perhaps even be killed by their husbands. Then again there might be no retaliation.

An important aspect of the social life of the men was the six warrior societies, whose membership included all the male members of the tribe. The Rabbit Society for the young boys has already been discussed. The warrior societies in their increasing order of prestige were the Shepherds or Herders, who seem to have been composed mainly of younger men; the Horse Headdresses; the Black Legs or Black Feet; Berries or Skunkberry People (also known as Crazy Horses); and the Koisenko, meaning something similar to the "Real or Principal Dogs." Each society had two leaders and two sergeants-at-arms, known as whipbearers, and these officials controlled the behavior of their members. These societies were not formal age-groups, but since a person was apt to feel more natural in a society whose members shared his own interests, they were roughly grouped according to age categories. Each society had its own dance, songs, insignia, and duties, and was paralleled in many other Plains tribes by similar societies. Almost every man was invited to join one or another of the societies as he reached maturity, and in time he might move from one to another as invitations were extended to him and as his activities and interests changed.

Membership in the highest military order, the Koisenko, was restricted to the bravest warriors in the tribe. The number seems to have varied from about ten to forty members. It was their duty to lead the most dangerous charges, and they were not allowed to retreat in battle. Around his neck their leader wore an elkskin sash which trailed on the ground at his right side. In battle it was his duty to dismount in front of his comrades, thrust a ceremonial arrow through a hole in the elkskin and into the ground, and remain in this spot throughout the battle. If defeated and forced to retreat, members of his party could pull the arrow from the ground. But sometimes in the confusion of battle he might not be freed, and since he was also enjoined from avoiding danger, he was often lost. When such a man was killed another warrior from the Koisenko was chosen to take his place. But as the burdens of office were so awesome it is not surprising, to use Mooney's phrase, that "the office usually sought the man." (1898: 284)

Staking down the leader of the Koisenko with the ceremonial

arrow was used only, however, when a war expedition was prepared to fight to the bitter end. The sash-owner could join war parties as an ordinary warrior by not wearing the sash, and he might even lend it to another warrior if he was not going along. He could not, however, decline to take part in important war parties lest he be called a coward and be deposed from his high position. When a man became too old to go to war he resigned and passed his sash on to some worthy young warrior. Occasionally it was publicly taken from an old warrior, but this was not intended as an open rebuke.

The death of Sitting Bear, one of the last of the Koisenko, is tragic but is in the noble tradition of the society. In the summer of 1871 some young Kiowas had left their newly-formed reservation to raid in Texas, and they succeeded in killing several white persons (the number depending upon which version of the tale you read). Sitting Bear and two other chiefs confessed, though they seem not to have been guilty. They were arrested by soldiers at Fort Sill, and were to be transported to Texas for trial. The journey had barely begun when Sitting Bear, in chains in a wagon, managed to slip from his shackles and produce a knife. He began his death song (Marriott, 1945: 124):

> *I live, but I will not live forever.*
> *Mysterious moon, you only remain,*
> *Powerful sun, you alone remain,*
> *Wonderful earth, you remain forever.*

He stabbed his guard, who fell from the wagon. In falling, his gun went off, killing Sitting Bear, or (in other versions) the other soldiers fired, killing him (Mooney, 1898: 333; also Battey, 1876: 197; Methvin, 1927, 140–145):

. . . it is impossible not to admire the grim courage of the old man, as, true to his warrior oath to despise death, though laden with chains and surrounded by armed troops, he boldly sang his death song, and then, wrenching the manacles from his bleeding wrists, drove the guards from the wagon, picked up their abandoned guns, and coolly prepared to kill one more enemy of his race before he fell, shot to death.

As in many other things, the Kiowa Apaches' ceremonial organization was a somewhat distorted reflection of the Kiowas', and was

204

probably borrowed wholesale from them. The Kiowa Apaches had four ceremonial groups—a children's society known as the Rabbits, two adult warrior or military societies, and a society for old women. All children belonged to the Rabbit Society, but on growing up they frequently did not join the adult societies because membership carried with it heavy and unwanted responsibilities. (McAllister, 1935: 139–157)

The most important duty of the Kiowa societies was to police the sun-dance gathering, a different society being appointed each year by the *taime*keeper (the sun-dance leader, keeper of the sun-dance doll). They also policed the tribal buffalo hunt, saw that the vast circle of tepees was set up correctly, took part in sham battles and other ceremonial preparations for the sun dance, and generally enforced law and order. It was only during sun-dance time that all of a society's members met, however. For women there were but two societies. Membership in the Calf Old Women was by invitation, and only old women were members. They met for feasts, a woman becoming a member by giving four feasts, and they danced at one point in the sun dance. Their other activities, if any, and what purposes the society served are unknown. The Bear Women, the second society, is even less well known. This may have been primarily a religious society, since it was a secret or semisecret group, and people were afraid of them.

In addition to the dancing or warrior societies, there were a number of little-known religious societies. These included the Crazy Dogs, a society of great warriors; the Buffalo Doctors, who treated wounds and diseases associated with blood; the Eagle Shields, a shamanistic society treating diseases by sleight of hand and other magical measures; and the Sun Dance Shields, who guarded the sun-dance doll as well as its keeper.

Like Comanches, adult Kiowa males—the warriors—were the important personages in the society. But old men and elderly people generally did not occupy a degraded status. Only those who had no immediate relatives and could not support themselves were sometimes abandoned to die. Occasionally old men, perhaps in fear of abandonment, took their own lives. But abandonment of the aged, as we have seen before, was a matter of long-established custom functioning in a stringent, struggling economy, rather than of deliberate, hardhearted cruelty.

The dead were buried in high, inaccessible places, and a person's equipment was interred with him or burned. A warrior's horses and often a pet dog were killed over the grave. Kiowas mourned their dead in several ways. Women cut their hair close to their heads, gashed gaping wounds in their faces and arms, and some chopped a finger joint off in paroxysms of grief. Methvin (1927: 85–86) recounts that after Heap O' Bears, a chief, was killed on a raid, his wife on hearing the news

gathered up a whetstone and butcherknife lying near, stripped herself perfectly nude down to the waist, raked the knife back and forth over the stone, and then began cutting herself. She cut her arms from the shoulders down to her wrists, and gashed most horribly her breasts, and then smeared upon her face the blood that gushed forth from every wound. . . . [She] placed one of her fingers upon a rock and asked a friend to chop it off. And there she stood, bleeding and howling, accompanied with the howling of all the camp in such discord as can be portrayed only by emblems drawn from the world of fiends.

Men in mourning cut their hair to shoulder length and put away their fine ornaments and clothing, and sometimes they too lacerated their bodies. Mooney (1898: 363) visited the Kiowas during a measles epidemic in 1892, a disease all too often fatal to Indians who tried to wash off the red spots with cold water:

On one occasion, while driving near the camp, the author's attention was attracted by a low wail, and on looking for the cause he saw, sitting in the tall grass near the roadside, a bereaved father stripped to the breech-cloth, with his hair cropped close to the head and the blood dripping from gashes which covered his naked body; he did not look up or turn his head as the wagon passed, but continued the low wail, with his eyes cast to the ground. . . . Every night and morning the women went into the hills to wail for their lost ones, and returned to camp with the blood dripping from fresh gashes in their faces and arms; this continued for weeks and months, far into the fall.

The basic social unit in Kiowa life was a group of brothers, their

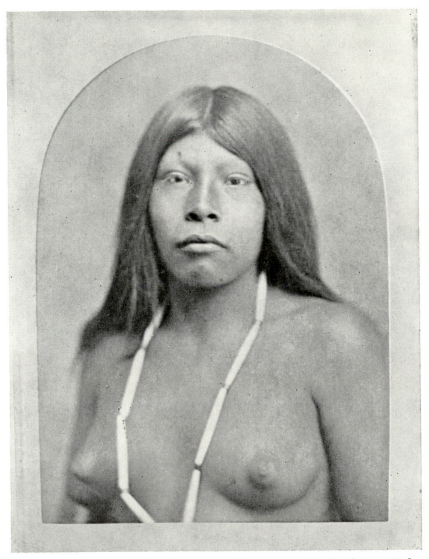

PLATE IX.   A Wichita girl, late nineteenth century. *A. B. Stephenson Collection, courtesy Barker Texas History Center.*

wives, and children. If one of the men was an important personage or a band chief, his sisters and their husbands, as well as other kinfolk, might be a part of this close-knit group. Usually the oldest brother was the head of this extended family. Depending upon the season and the supply of game, such groups might camp by themselves in a cluster of tepees or with other family groups. These family units were grouped into a somewhat variable number of bands, led by a headman or band chief. These bands were considered to be kin groups and the headman of each was spoken of as "father." Actually, it was only the core of the bands that could trace close genealogical connections—that is, the headman, his brothers, their wives and children, and a headman's sisters and their husbands and children. People grouped themselves around the most eminent and successful of headmen among their kinsmen. When a headman died, family units might join another band for a time, or until their kinsmen had joined forces in a reconstructed band.

Large bands were more successful than small ones because their communal hunts were more effective and they felt more secure from the attacks of their enemies. Because large bands were desirable there was competition between headmen to attract poor or unaffiliated people. And the principal way these people were attracted was by a headman's wisdom and generosity. But another way was by "giving a woman," that is, by supplying a wife for some poor but promising young man who would then live with the headman's band.

Since band membership was voluntary, the amount of power and authority a headman commanded was based on a realistic appraisal of his abilities. Headmen dared not impose harsh or unjust orders lest they be deserted by their followers. And any headman who was less than generous, made poor decisions, and failed to maintain internal peace might soon find himself without a band to direct. A headman functioned chiefly to preserve law and order within the band and to direct its hunting activities. He decided where to camp and when to move, and prevented open fighting insofar as he was able. He often joined with other headmen to settle disputes between bands.

In early summer the entire Kiowa tribe as well as the affiliated

207

Kiowa Apaches gathered for the annual sun dance. They camped in a giant circle around the sun-dance lodge, each band, including the Kiowa Apaches, having a designated position. Mooney listed a total of six bands plus the Kiowa Apaches late in the last century, but there were undoubtedly more in earlier times. The owner or keeper of the *taime*, the sun-dance doll, was the nominal head at this time. He selected the location for this religious festival, announced the program of events through a camp crier, and enjoined the tribe against quarreling or fighting throughout the sun-dance period. The *taime*keeper was assisted by the men's societies in running the sun-dance ceremonies, and was responsive to the advice of the band chiefs.

The Comanches are often thought of as far-ranging raiders, and they were, but Kiowa war parties covered distances as great or greater. In the second half of the nineteenth century, for instance, one raid carried far enough south for them to become acquainted with monkeys and parrots (perhaps British Honduras). From their Oklahoma-Texas home they also raided chronically throughout Texas and to the western border of New Mexico, as well as occasionally journeying to the northern plains. Those parties that undertook raids at great distances were, of course, mounted. Men going on shorter raids, and often those directed against Indian enemies, sometimes went on foot, returning if successful on the backs of "liberated" ponies.

War parties varied greatly in size—from small family groups to some that were virtually tribal operations. The women sometimes accompanied them. As was common with many Plains tribes, the leader was in absolute control, directing all phases of an attack, and all booty from a raid also belonged to him (but only to be later distributed among the members of the party). For large war parties "giving the pipe" was the ceremonial method of enlisting recruits. During the sun dance a prominent warrior contemplating leading a raid sent a pipe to each in turn of the leaders of the warrior societies. If they were favorably inclined they smoked it and when their societies next met the pipe was offered to the members. Smoking signified a desire to join the war party, but no one was forced to do so.

208

When a number of men had decided to embark on this type of foray, all other raids, no matter how small, were forbidden until its conclusion. (Mooney, 1898: 282)

For small war parties the pipe was not used, but the occasion was none the less ceremonial. A man wishing to lead such a party invited other warriors to join him. The night before leaving, he bent a stick into the shape of a hoop and placed it around the fire pit in his tepee. Alone, he began to sing the travel song, beating time on the hoop with a stick. Warriors who wished to accompany him came into the tepee and joined him, also beating in time on the hoop. Women came in to sit behind the men and sing, and after awhile the group moved outside to a buffalohide, which the men held up with one hand and beat time on with the other, continuing to sing the travel song, the traditional song sung by those going to war.

As was true among other Plains tribes, a successful raid was considered to be one in which no warrior was lost. If no losses had been sustained and the party returned loaded with scalps, horses, and booty there were great celebrations. The war party would enter camp at a run, simulating their attack on the enemy, firing guns and shooting arrows. They were dressed in their best attire and war bonnets, their faces painted black to signify they had slain an enemy. Such occasions were planned so that the camp would have time to prepare for the dance, the war party entering camp in the early afternoon, even though such timing meant they might have had to camp out an extra night. Once in camp the warriors took the women up on their horses behind them, riding around in a circle and singing, with the fresh scalps, painted red inside and stretched over small hoops, carried on six-foot poles by the women. At nightfall a fire was built, and the returned heroes and all the women danced. Such dances might be held every afternoon and evening for a month. The scalps were later offered—perhaps "sacrificed" is a better word—by placing them in some remote place with an offering and a prayer to the sun or other power with whom a warrior had reached an "understanding." Some scalps might also be kept by warriors, who "strung them upon sticks, by running a stick like an arrow, only larger and about two feet in length, through them, near one edge." (Battey, 1876: 241)

By performing four deeds out of a recognized number of about twelve, a man became a warrior, an honored title. Eminent warriors who had displayed outstanding bravery and skill were known as "great warriors." A man bragged about his war exploits—recited his brave deeds—at every opportunity. If questioned concerning the credibility of these exploits, he took an oath of veracity by smoking the pipe. While war to many of the men was a game—a sport—it must not be forgotten that to lose decisively in this "game" meant tribal annihilation.

Kiowas were not always, of course, the aggressors, and at various times they suffered heavily from attacks by other tribes, particularly Cheyennes, Arapahoes, and Osages. Unlike many other Plains Indians, Kiowas are known to have thrown up earthen breastworks for defense, and this apparently novel tactic was successful in repelling attacks on at least two occasions. (Mooney, 1898: 271, 273)

Supernaturalism. Kiowa beliefs about the supernatural world and their ways of dealing with it stand out as rich, intricate, and full of pageantry compared to those of such people as the Comanches. Kiowas believed there were a number of gods, the chief being the sun. All the forces of nature, even relatively insignificant creatures such as small plants and inanimate objects, might also be imbued with more-than-natural powers or qualities. Originally there may have been no belief in a heaven or hell, and perhaps the fate of human souls was only vaguely conceived. But Thomas Battey, a Quaker and the first teacher among the Kiowas in the 1870's, queried the Kiowas on this point and they described for him a heaven across a western ocean, where old friends met in joyous reunion, game was always plentiful, the horses were all "large, swift, and beautiful," and people were forever healthy and happy. (1876: 110–111) Presumably, hell would be the opposite of these ideal conditions.

By some, at least, owls and other nocturnal birds were regarded as possessed by the souls of the dead. As was indicated by the discussion of the vision quest, all kinds of supernaturally-regarded revelations—dreams, visions, hallucinations, and so forth—were regarded with great seriousness. Such revelations could induce a man to join a war party or abandon one; they could suggest the direction in which to hunt; and consciousness of one's failure to obey supernatural injunctions could and did induce death.

Adjustment to this complex, omnipresent supernatural world was attained on a tribal level by the annual sun dance, and through the medicine bundles—the Ten Grandmothers. For individuals, personal medicine bundles—amulets—were used, as well as prayer and sometimes sacrifice. For example, a horse might be sacrificed to the sun by tying it to a bush or tree in the hills, where it would perish. The Grandmothers controlled the welfare of the tribe and so were cared for devoutly. Each of the Grandmother bundles was guarded by a particular family, eldest sons learning from their fathers the rituals and taboos associated with their bundle. Care of the bundles involved giving them ceremonial sweat baths and keeping their containers in repair. But so sacred were the bundles that their guardians could not open them, this right being reserved for a priest. Annually the guardians of the bundles brought them to the priest in a special ceremonial tepee. The priest, who had inherited the right, opened and inspected them, then cleansed and purified them with smoke. Then, still alone, he closed them up and returned them to their guardian-owners. The last of the priests charged with caring for the bundles died before the turn of this century. The bundles, consequently, have not been opened since, although "the Ten Grandmothers have been as sacred and as valued as ever—offerings and prayers are still made to them." (Marriott, 1945: VIII)

Legends of the Kiowas associate the Ten Grandmother bundles with the twin culture heroes known as Half Boys. The myths about these boys will be taken up later in this chapter. It was customary to give presents to the bundles as well as to pray to them. Consequently their guardians materially benefited from their association with the bundles. Moreover, the possession of a Grandmother was felt to mean its guardian was in closer touch with the supernatural powers than most people, and so was apt to have more success in whatever ventures he undertook. As a matter of fact, many Kiowa chiefs and leaders were bundleowners. The ten tepees where the Grandmothers were kept were also sanctuaries where persons might seek refuge, as was the tepee where the sun-dance doll was kept. Keepers of the

Fig. 8. Kiowa sun dancer.

bundles also served as preservers of the peace, for they possessed peace pipes which when smoked by quarreling Kiowas enjoined them against further contentious words or actions. Smoking the pipe was not a judgment against either party, and involved no loss of prestige. It did serve to maintain internal peace.

The great annual religious festival, the sun dance, was generally held when "the down was on the cottonwoods," or about the middle of June, thus coinciding with the summer buffalo hunt.[3] It was considered to be so important to tribal welfare that every Kiowa was expected to attend. Its performance prevented sickness and disaster, and in a more positive sense, it was thought to bring happiness and prosperity in the form of a plentiful supply of bison, many children, and victory in war. In essence, the Kiowas' sun dance was a worship of the sun as the creator and regenerator of life through the sacred mediator, the *taime*.

The director of the sun dance and its principal performer was the shaman who owned the sacred image or idol, the *taime*. Theoretically its performance depended upon someone's dreaming of the sun dance, but the *taime*keeper was bound to dream of it if no one else did. Occasionally, in fact, more than one person dreamed of the festival— requiring two dances in one summer. But in the nineteenth century, with the disorganization brought about by the advance of the frontier, some summers passed without even one sun dance. After the keeper of the sacred image had been told of a dream, he hung the image in its case on his back and rode off to the various camps to announce the time and place of the dance. It might take him three or more days to ride to all the camps, and if his journey exceeded more than four days he took a ritual sweat bath on the fourth day so that he might break the fast required of him during his trip. His announcement was usually made just a few days before the dance was to take place, but sometimes it was made immediately after a sun dance for the following year.

During the latter part of the nineteenth century the central figure in the ceremony was a single *taime*, a small stone image less than

[3] This description of the sun dance relies on Spier, 1921; Battey, 1876; Mooney, 1898; Methvin, 1927; and Scott, 1911.

two feet tall, dressed in a white-feather robe, a headdress of a single feather, and ermineskin pendants. Blue beads encircled the neck, and the face and body were painted in designs symbolic of the sun and moon. The *taime* was kept in a rawhide box and never exposed to public view except during the sun dance. Then it was fastened to a stick set up at the west side of the medicine lodge. Originally the *taime* was a buckskin image and was left in the medicine lodge at the end of the sun dance. Early in the nineteenth century there were three *taimes*. These were carried on important war parties, and the present image is also thought of as an important war medicine. The three *taimes* were captured by Osage Indians in 1833, and were returned two years later when peace was made between the two tribes. Then the Utes captured two of them in 1868, and never returned them. Since then the Kiowas have had only the one *taime* described above.

Many other Plains Indians also had tribal "medicines" upon which ceremonial life was focused and the prosperity of the tribe depended. The Cheyennes had a bundle of sacred arrows, the Arapahoes a stone pipe, a turtle, and an ear of corn; and the Omahas a shell.

When the tribe had assembled at the site chosen by the *taime*keeper a series of varied activities commenced. The bands made camp, each in its designated spot in the camp circle, all the tepee entrances facing toward the center of the circle where the medicine lodge was to be constructed. At this time two young men from one of the military societies were selected by the *taime*keeper to scout for a tree which would serve as the center pole of the medicine lodge. And all the men who were going to dance were purifying themselves by taking sweat baths under the supervision of the *taime*keeper. As soon as the tree for the center pole had been selected, everybody followed the high priest, his family, and a number of elderly men to the area where the medicine lodge was to be erected. Guarding them on all sides were the military societies. The procession halted on its journey four times (the Kiowas' ritual and magical number) while the *taime*keeper smoked and prayed. After the fourth pause the military societies charged the central area and a pole which had been temporarily set up there, this performance apparently being a symbolic conquest of the area.

The following morning a man, who had inherited the right, set out with his wife to kill a young bull buffalo and secure parts of its hide. They were required to fast during the hunt, the buffalo was supposed to be killed by a single arrow (and if it was, it was a good omen), and the buffalo was supposed to fall on its belly with its head toward the east.

On the ensuing day the center pole for the medicine lodge was cut down. This was accomplished amid much pageantry, the military societies attacking in mock battle one of the societies that defended the tree destined to become the center pole. After the recitation of coups by outstanding warriors and prayers by the *taime*keeper— who had brought along the *taime*—the tree was chopped down by a captive girl. She was usually a Mexican who had been brought up in the tribe. After the twenty-foot, forked cottonwood had been cut, it was carried triumphantly to the site of the medicine lodge by a specially-designated military society. Once there, a shaman who had inherited the right to do so, placed it in a hole already dug. The buffalohide was then fastened in the forks of the cottonwood, with its head toward the east. Soon many offerings of cloth and clothing were also tied to it.

The completion of the ritual setting-up of the center pole was a signal for the military societies to organize the construction of the medicine lodge. This was a festive occasion, the work proceeding amid horseplay, music, and dancing. The women cut the cottonwood poles and branches necessary for the medicine lodge, attaching ropes to them, and climbing up behind the men on their horses, who then dragged them to camp. It has been reported that in "old times" this was an occasion of sexual license, that "there was more or less promiscuous intercourse between the sexes, married and single, but to this no stigma was attached." (Scott, 1911: 352)

The completed medicine lodge was some sixty feet in diameter, with an entrance to the east. Around the center post were seventeen equally-spaced cottonwood posts, twelve feet high or more. Small

215

cottonwoods were tied to these horizontally, and against them others were set up vertically to form a leafy wall. Here spectators would sit unobtrusively in the shade. More cottonwood limbs were laid from the center pole to the outer poles and other branches were placed across these to form a roof. All the ground inside this medicine lodge was cleared and covered with sand, and a mound several feet high and about five feet in diameter was thrown up around the center post. Another screen of cottonwoods and cedars was erected opposite the east entrance, several feet from the west wall, behind which the dancers readied themselves for dancing. In front of this screen the *taime* was placed, as well as an eagle-feather fan, shields, and other ceremonial equipment. As in the cutting of the center pole, a captive, but this time a male, was employed to open the *taime* bundle. Captives were trained for such purposes because the supernatural forces were so powerful and dangerous that if a mistake was made in dealing with them they might wreak sudden vengeance upon someone nearby, and it was better for this someone to be a captive than a Kiowa.

The completion of the medicine lodge precipitated a wild dance by the warrior societies and others, and that evening the sun dance proper got under way. The *taime*keeper, his four associates, and the members of the Sun Dance Shield Society were required to dance intermittently throughout the four-day period. Ordinary men who had vowed to dance might or might not continue throughout this period, but for however long they danced they did not eat, drink, or sleep. The four days of dancing was a stern physical ordeal; it was not undertaken lightly. But for those who believed it could cure or ward off sickness, or make them better warriors, or give them many children it was well worth the effort. And if they had vowed—if during a moment of sickness or while in mortal danger they had promised the mysterious powers—to dance, they dared not hedge on the vow lest some terrible calamity overtake them.

In one of the dances, vividly described by Battey (1876: 176–177), the upper part of the dancers' bodies was painted white and they wore ankle-length white buckskin skirts, over which they wore equally long blue breechclouts. Facing the *taime*, they danced to the beat of the drums and the singing of women. In their mouths they held bone whistles, their breath escaping through the whistle, to add to the confusion of sound already in Battey's ears, an eerie accompaniment to the music. Their eyes fixed on the *taime*, they were oblivious to all else. Finally, another dancer, apparently the head of their society, appeared from behind the screen. Painted white like the others and wearing a blue breechclout, he also wore a buffalo robe. He faced the entrance of the lodge, and for some time stood without the slightest movement, gazing intently at the sun. Then he began to move his head, from side to side, forward and backward, slowly at first, then faster and faster, at last so frantically that his robe fell off. Now he began to dance wildly, "he jumped and ran about the enclosure,—head, arms, and legs all equally participating in the violence of his gestures,—every joint of his body apparently loosened," but his eyes were still riveted to the sun. Sweat streaked his painted, glistening body, and finally, exhausted, he halted.

Every day in the late afternoon the dancers were pursued by the *taime*keeper, who, using a feather fan "fanned" them into unconsciousness. He wore a blue breechclout and the scalp of a white woman whose flowing hair was fixed into his scalp lock. In a series of half running-jumps, but in step with the music, he entered the arena and circled the dancers. They feigned not to notice him as he stretched his arm over their heads; then he approached the *taime*, examined it closely, danced again, and returned repeatedly to inspect the image. Finally he noticed the feather fan near the *taime*, reluctantly took it, fearfully held it up to the *taime*, and then waved it up and down and from side to side. Turning to the dancers and spectators he waved it from side to side near the ground, then in a sweeping motion around the dancers, and repeated the motion above his head. Then, as if to strike them in what seemed to be a rage, he pursued the terrified dancers around and around the dance area. Eventually he separated one of them, pursued him relentlessly until the dancer stumbled and fell, exhausted or unconscious. Then he cut out another dancer and pursued him until he fell, and so on until all had fallen under the spell of the fan. While unconscious or exhausted the dancers hoped to have visions. If successful they called for a pipe and related publicly what they had seen.

Several other kinds of dances occurred throughout the four-day period, and apart from the sun dance itself there were many purely social activities—feasts, meetings of societies, marriages, reunions, exchange of news and gossip. Sun-dance time was the one occasion during the whole year that the entire tribe was congregated in one location; no wonder it was Christmas, New Year's, county fair, and June wedding rolled into one.

At the end of the sun-dance ceremony, the dancers were given a small amount of a medicinal drink, the *taime* was carefully packed away, old clothing and occasionally a horse were tied to the center post as sacrifices, and the religious ceremonies were over. There was a great secular dance that evening, and the following morning the warriors usually rode off to war.

Unique among Texas Indians, though not among many other North American Indians, was the practice of keeping a tribal history or calendar by painting and drawing mnemonic devices on hides, or on paper when it became available. Mooney obtained from Kiowas three such calendars: the Sett'an, which began in 1833 and covered sixty years; the Anko yearly calendar, commencing in 1864 and covering twenty-nine years; and the Anko monthly calendar, covering thirty-seven months. He obtained a fourth from a cavalry officer at Fort Sill, who had gotten it from a Kiowa. Mooney also learned that there had been another, thought to date back farther than the others, which had been kept by a Kiowa Apache but was included among the other personal possessions that had been buried with him.

Usually, the pictographs which made up the calendars were arranged in a continuous spiral. They began at the lower right-hand corner of the paper or hide and ended near the center. Winter was shown by black bars, symbolizing dead vegetation, and summer by a drawing of the sun-dance medicine lodge. Whatever had been the outstanding event of the year was pictured beside the winter or summer mark. If it had been a measles epidemic, a generously-dotted figure would be shown; if a leading warrior had been killed while on a raid, his figure with an appropriate wound was drawn. In this way a fairly accurate account of history was kept, though the events portrayed would often not coincide with what historians would term the most important happenings. There is no way of knowing how ancient the practice of keeping calendar histories was, although there is no reason to suppose that it must have developed in recent, historic times. On long winter nights warriors would gather in a tepee, and, as the pipe was passed from man to man, each recounted, by turn, a tradition, myth, or great deed of war, or if one of them owned a calendar history he might recite the events it pictured.

A great omnipotent being was regarded as creator of the world—its lakes and streams, mountains and plains, animals and Kiowas, as well as the sun, night, and day. After he had created the cosmos and everything therein except the Kiowas, he traveled westward until he came upon a hollow tree lying on the ground. Three times he made as if to strike its trunk, the fourth time he hit it a hard blow, and out came the Kiowas—grown men and women who ran from him in fear. He called them back and told them they were his children, and seeing that they were not put together properly he corrected their defects and sent them away. He struck the log a second time and again grown men and women emerged. They too were frightened of their creator and ran away, only to be called back. But these were perfectly formed, so he sent them away as they were. A third time he smote the log, and this time children as well as adults came forth. This angered the creator, "and discovering indications that evil had been wrought by them while yet in the log, he became very angry, and told them that since they had done wrong before coming forth from the log, he should make no more Kiowas." (Battey, 1876: 107–108) This part of the legend sounds as if it were made up for the benefit of the good Quaker who recorded these legends. In another version the reason or rationalization accounting for the small number of Kiowas was that a pregnant woman became stuck in the opening of the log and blocked the way for those behind her. (Mooney, 1898: 153)

After bringing forth all the Kiowas the creator gave them their tools and weapons and instructed them in their use. He left them

219

then, and in one account met the Great White Man, the creator of Europeans. After this meeting he returned to the Kiowas and instructed them to treat white men who came to take their land as enemies. The creator retired then to become a group of stars, and the Great White Man became the moon. This last tale is undoubtedly a recent addition to their mythology, to account for the white men and to sanction Kiowa resistance and retaliation.

Besides the creator, there was a boy hero, whose mother was a Kiowa but whose father was the son of the sun. The myth relates that a girl while playing discovered a porcupine in a tree. She climbed the tree to catch the porcupine, but as she did the tree shot up, bearing her up into the sky and to the upper world. Once there the porcupine changed into his real self, the son of the sun. He and the girl were married and she bore him a son. Her husband had warned her not to go near a certain plant if it had been cropped by a buffalo, but like Eve and her yearning for the forbidden fruit, she grasped the plant at the first opportunity. Uprooting it she found a hole through which she could see the earth below, hitherto forgotten by her. Longing for her old world, she lowered herself and her child by means of a rope. Her husband, discovering her escaping, threw a stone down at her, hitting her head and killing her. But the child was uninjured, and after a time was adopted by Spider Woman. The boy became twins after being cut in two by a gaming wheel he had thrown into the air. These twins, Half-Boys, had many adventures, including the destruction of monsters. Eventually one of them walked into a lake and disappeared forever, and the other turned himself into the Kiowas' tribal medicine, the Ten Grandmothers. The medicine has, of course, been divided into ten parts.[4]

THE KIOWAS are marked off from the other Plains Indians by their linguistic uniqueness, by their close alliance and confederation with the Kiowa Apaches throughout most of historic times, and, with respect to other Texas Plains Indians, by their varied

[4] For Kiowa Apache mythology, see McAllister, 1949.

220

and complex social and ceremonial life. The richness of Kiowa life, reflected in their societies, traditions, and their artistic sense, seems somewhat out of place for a people who had always been nomadic hunters. This impression gives strength to the speculation that the Kiowas have not always been plainsmen, that their origins are to be sought in the Southwest.

PART IV
Barbaric Gardeners

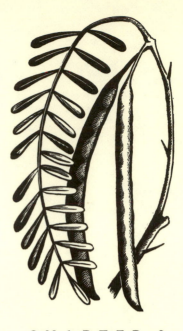

CHAPTER 9

The Jumanos: Southwestern Borders

> The men were very handsome and the women beauti-
> ful. . . . They are a striped people and very merry . . .
> they go about naked.
>
> Hernán Gallegos (1581)

IN 1535, Cabeza de Vaca and his trail-hardened companions crossed
the country of the Jumano Indians, and before the century was over
other Spanish explorers had repeatedly traversed their land. Despite
this early and continued acquaintance with the natives along the
southwestern borders of Texas, the Spanish never described—probably never knew—this people with anything approaching complete-
ness. Moreover, Jumano culture disintegrated during the eighteenth
century, so it was never adequately described, and is poorly known
today. Even the linguistic affiliations of the Jumanos are not known
with certainty, although indirect evidence seems to favor their being
speakers of a Uto-Aztecan tongue. (Sauer, 1934) To make matters
worse, the word *Jumano* and its variants were applied by the Spaniards at various times to the Wichita (Taovaya) Indians, to a Pueblo
group in eastern New Mexico, and even to some Indians in Arizona.

225

(Scholes and Mera, 1940: 269) The Spaniards first used the term for the natives of southwestern Texas, albeit somewhat ambiguously, and in time applied it to all of these other widespread and culturally distinct groups. The reason the Spaniards used the term *Jumano* so loosely was that all of these culturally diverse groups painted or tattooed the body. This custom was common, if not universal, throughout Texas and most of Indian America, so it is likely that all the people who at one time or another were labeled as Jumanos by the Spaniards shared some special or distinctive form of painting or tattooing. Fortunately, a number of anthropologists and historians have worked on Jumano history, so we at least have an accurate idea of who the original Jumanos were, and are able to distinguish them from other tribes also designated as Jumano. (Hackett, 1931–34: 137–139, 169–170, 424–427; Bandelier, 1890: 80–81, 84–86, 167–169; Bolton, 1911; Sauer, 1934; Scholes and Mera, 1940) *Jumano* is an Indian word of unknown meaning in Hispaniolized form. In Spanish documents it appears with numerous variants—Xumana, Jumana, Humana, Umana, Xoman, Sumana. While it is, unfortunately, an ambiguous and unsatisfactory term, it has come to be commonly applied to the Indians of southwestern Texas and parts of northern Chihuahua, Mexico, and for want of a better term this usage is continued here. (See Map 2.)

One of the more troublesome Jumano anomalies has been the fact that there were two geographically distinct groups, pursuing different modes of subsistence, both of whom have been called Jumano. One group lived as settled gardeners in the Puebloan tradition, wresting their living from garden plots in the valleys of the Rio Grande and the lower Rio Conchos. The other group lived, or at least hunted, beyond the Chisos and Davis Mountains on the southernmost plains of west Texas. It is presumed that they hunted throughout the summer in this region, but in the fall traveled to the valley villages to trade, visit, and await the return of the hunting season. Whether these two groups were essentially a single people, sharing a common language and common origins, is unknown. One student of the problem uses the term *Jumano* exclusively for the nomadic group.[1]

---

[1] J. Charles Kelley, in fact, claims that the "historical and archeological evi-

The earliest mention of the nomads—and the earliest usage of the term *Jumano*—was by members of the Espejo Expedition in 1582–83. Espejo himself used the appellation both for the natives in the vicinity of La Junta (the now-extinct name given the region about the junction of the Rio Conchos and the Rio Grande) and for the hunting Indians he met on the return journey from New Mexico, somewhere between the Pecos River and La Junta. The other chronicler of the expedition, Luxán, employed the term *Jumano* only for the hunting Indians, saying: "We met three Jumanas Indians who were hunting and we were able to understand them through Pedro, a Pataraguey [Patarabueye, a Jumano subdivision] Indian." These Indians led the Spaniards to their *ranchería*, and apparently supplied guides for the remainder of the journey. Luxán added: "On our way we found settled people of this nation, who in their clothing are similar to the Pataragueyes, except in their houses." (Hammond and Rey, 1929: 124–125)

Were these hunting Indians merely a branch of the more settled farming people, who were hunting or exploring in the southern plains? Or were they representatives of a distinct culture, known to the Patarabueyes only because they came to the La Junta villages to trade? We probably shall never know precisely, and it seems foolhardy to attempt to draw any hard-and-fast conclusions from such lean historic pickings. Still, it can be suggested that the archeological evidence for the abandonment of the valley home of the Jumano after 1400 implies that some of these dissatisfied and probably hungry Jumanos may well have wandered to the plains of west Texas and taken up a different kind of life. If they did do this, the separation may not have continued long enough for the two groups to become culturally distinct. And if the nomadic offshoot made annual visits to the settled group, possibly recruiting new members there, the differences between the two might be long blurred and deferred. Whatever the truth, the nomads are even less well known ethnographically

---

dence . . . demonstrates clearly that they were ethnically and to a large extent culturally distinct groups." (1955: 984) Recent archeological investigations cast considerable doubt upon his so-called "archeological evidence," however (Suhm, 1957: 55–56), and the historic facts allow several interpretations.

than the sedentary valley dwellers, and until something more concrete is discovered I shall employ the term *Jumano* for both groups.

The land of the Jumanos stretched from the vicinity of El Paso down the Rio Grande Valley as far as the Big Bend region of Texas, and a short way into Mexico up the Rio Conchos in Chihuahua. While their permanent villages were in these river valleys, all of Texas south and west of the Pecos may be considered as territory ranged to some extent by Jumanos or their nomadic relatives. Climatically trans-Pecos Texas is arid and large sections of it can be classified as desert. The land supports agriculture only where irrigation of one sort or another is possible. When these Indians were first encountered by Spaniards, their fields and gardens were situated in valleys, either in places where there was sufficient moisture from the runoff of an arroyo or ephemeral stream to raise crops, or on the flood plain of one of the few permanent streams of the region, where the chances of a good harvest were relatively high. The first type of farming has been termed "temporal" irrigation, the latter, "riverine." (Kelley, 1952: 358) The Jumanos, so far as is known, never practiced any sort of artificial irrigation, such as damming streams, digging ditches, or the like; they depended entirely upon these natural supplies. That they did not practice any kind of irrigation severely limited the productivity of Jumano agriculture, for droughts or even a slight diminution in the already-light rainfall would make many of the temporal fields unproductive. Riverine farming was more apt to be successful in this dry, hot land, but the shifting, errant nature of the Rio Grande must often have forced the Jumanos to shift their fields. There were also relatively few places where riverine irrigation was possible.

From New Mexico to the Big Bend region of Texas the Rio Grande flows through a narrow valley, flanked by brush and cactus-covered terraces and starkly barren mountains. There are stretches of valley land, generally narrow but sometimes running for tens of miles along the river, which could be used for riverine or temporal farming. In the valley, too, there were (and are) many groves—sometimes tangled and matted jungles—of willow, cottonwood, cane, and brush. These were useful for building purposes, but it is unlikely that these areas could easily have been cleared by Stone Age Indians for farming. The Rio Conchos is the only large tributary to enter the Rio Grande throughout this entire region, and the lower Conchos has essentially the same characteristics as the Rio Grande. The gravelly, dusty uplands and terraces away from the valleys, as well as the low mountains of the region, could be utilized by the Jumanos only for hunting and gathering. At the lower elevations desert flora, such as creosote bush, ocotillo, prickly pear, and other cacti, predominate, with a corresponding scarcity of the larger game animals. In the higher mountain elevations cedar, pine, and other trees grow, but it is doubtful whether Jumanos used the plants or animals of this zone to any great extent. The Jumanos, or the more nomadic groups of them, did considerable buffalo-hunting, however, and made long expeditions in search of them. Cabeza de Vaca (Hodge, 1907b: 103) even called them "the Cow nation," not because he witnessed them hunting buffalo but because these were the first people he had seen who had a plentiful supply of buffalo products—hides and presumably dried meat. Later accounts make it clear that good buffalo-hunting was normally to be found no closer than the plains north and east of the Davis and Chisos Mountains.

Origins and Early History. Archeological excavations have revealed that in relatively late prehistoric times the natives of this region were peripheral members of the Puebloan civilization of the Southwest, and they lend weight to the conclusion that historic Jumano culture was affiliated with it. The towns of the sedentary Puebloans were scattered over a wide area in the Southwest, through northern Arizona and New Mexico, into Colorado and Utah, and it is not surprising that this cultural pattern extended down the Rio Grande into Texas. The distinctive and rich Pueblo culture was based upon an intensive, well-developed agriculture. The men raised several varieties of corn, as well as beans, squash, sunflowers, and sometimes cotton and tobacco. While the men toiled in the fields, the women kept house, ground the corn, and made basketry and their justly famous pottery. Their villages or towns were built of stone or adobe, often in grand, many-roomed apartment buildings. The productive fields of the Pueblos made possible the performance of a number of intricate and colorful sacred pageants and ceremonials, all intimately interwoven with the social organization and agricultural pursuits. All in all, Puebloan culture was as advanced and highly developed as any native civilization north of Mexico, the cultures of the southeast possibly excepted.

Sometime around A.D. 1000 there was a rapid expansion of this Puebloan culture, technically called the Jornada Branch of the Mogollon (and Mogollon for our purposes may be called Puebloan), southward down the Rio Grande. (Lehmer, 1948; Kelley, 1949a,b; Suhm et al., 1954: 27–51) By A.D. 1200 farming villages had spread at least as far as El Cajon, a canyon barrier about 125 miles downstream from El Paso. These river-valley farms apparently depended upon temporal irrigation from very small watersheds which do not support any kind of farming today. Between 1200 and 1400 this farming culture spread on down the Rio Grande as far as Cañon Colorado, below present Redford, and up the Rio Conchos into Mexico some 40 miles. But "there was a more or less simultaneous disappearance of all these farming communities above the Presidio Valley, probably around 1400–1500 A.D." (Kelley, 1949b: 112–113; 1952: 361–362) Some villages survived in the vicinity of the junction of the Conchos and the Rio Grande, and during the sixteenth century there were scattered settlements up the valley to just below El Paso. Whether this was a reoccupation of the valley permitted by a favorable shift in the climate, or whether it represented hardy survivors who had never abandoned the area is unknown. At any rate, it was these people extending from the La Junta vicinity upstream almost to El Paso who became the main Jumano body of historic times.

As the Puebloan culture spread down the Rio Grande and into trans-Pecos Texas it did not enter a virgin, uninhabited land. There were local Archaic cultures in the region, and the culture of the historic Jumanos and their immediate archeologic forerunners suggests a mixture of the imported Puebloan with an indigenous hunting and gathering culture. With such a mixture it is difficult to determine whether there was a real migration of Puebloan people into this land,

230

who adopted some of the local customs, or whether the local folk learned of the cultural advances made upstream, borrowed some material items and techniques from them, and in time became for all intents and purposes Puebloan. Whichever the case, what little is known of the early historic Jumano culture suggests a provincial, watered-down, poor, and struggling Puebloan culture, including a number of non-Puebloan elements which were probably derived from earlier peoples of the immediate area.

The reasons for the sudden expansion and subsequent abandonment of much of this region are not fully understood. It has been argued that the expansion down the Rio Grande was "made possible, if not caused, by a temporary change in climatic conditions more favorable for farming." (Kelley, 1952: 362) Throughout the Pueblo area in the years between 1100 and 1400 there was generally a shifting and moving about. Climatic change may have been the chief cause of the unstability, although the appearance of Athapaskan (Apache) raiders, epidemics, internal strife, and other things, may have played a part. The contraction of the Jumano region after 1400 may also be linked to an influx of new people and to climatic change, especially as only a slight decrease in rainfall could easily have made temporal farming impossible over much of the area. The places which were not abandoned, incidentally, were mainly in the La Junta vicinity, and could depend upon riverine irrigation. Even when De Vaca entered the area the Jumanos were suffering from a drought: "We asked how it was they did not plant maize. They answered it was that they might not lose what they should put in the ground; that the rains had failed for two years in succession." (Hodge, 1907b: 104)

In the sixteenth and seventeenth centuries the shuffling, consolidation, and abandonment of settlements in the Jumano region continued, in fact was accelerated, as the presence of Spaniards, Apache raids, and an adverse climate combined to devastate the Jumanos. Toward the close of the sixteenth century the Spaniards had pushed their settlements northward on the central plateau of Mexico as far as Santa Bárbara in the southern part of the present state of Chihuahua.

231

Santa Bárbara became the center of a mining region and affected the Jumanos in several ways. It was on the present Rio Valle Allende, an upper branch of the Rio Conchos, and the easiest route to the north was down the Conchos, so before 1600 several Spanish expeditions had penetrated all of the Jumano country. The mines in the Santa Bárbara region needed laborers, and consequently slave-catching expeditions ranged far afield. As early as 1581, Hernán Gallegos, a member of the Rodríquez-Chamuscado Expedition to New Mexico, mentioned that slavers had already been among the Cabri (Pazaguates?) Indians, a tribe who lived between the Conchos Indians and the Jumanos on the Rio Conchos. (Hammond and Rey, 1927: 252) The next year Antonio de Espejo, himself a fugitive from a murder charge, led an expedition through the Jumano country in search of Father Rodríguez. Espejo and Diego Pérez de Luxán, a member of the expedition, left accounts of their sojourn among the Jumanos—the best descriptions of Jumano culture we possess. The first Jumano settlement this expedition reached on the Rio Conchos had already been named Patarabueyes by Spanish slave-hunters. Consequently, the expedition was not welcomed by the natives, who attacked the Spaniards' horses in the night, killing three and wounding six or seven others. Alert guards prevented additional casualties among the stock. The Indians seem not to have had any thought of trying to slay the Spaniards. (Hammond and Rey, 1929: 54)

While the Jumanos had suffered to some extent from these slave raids, tribes closer to the Mexican mines and settlements suffered much greater humiliation. These weakened tribes were soon dispersed and either joined other tribes or disappeared altogether from the pages of history. As one authority remarks, "Weak tribes were absorbed by stronger ones, and many faded out in the process of Mexicanization—the shift from *indio* to *gente de razón*, first by mingling of Indian stocks and breakdown of tribal consciousness, and later, increasingly by hybridization." (Sauer, 1934: 1) The Concho tribe, who appear to have been friendly and culturally similar to the Jumanos, were associated with, if not assimilated by, the Jumanos as early as 1683. This amalgamation could be traced partly to Spanish influence, but partly also to the effect of Apache raids.

232

By 1683, when the Spanish explorer Juan Dominguez de Mendoza came down the Rio Grande from El Paso to La Junta, he encountered only a few groups of Suma (Caguate) Indians in the vicinity of El Cajon. They were subsisting mainly on agaves, and all sought aid from the Spaniards in repulsing the Apache raiders who were forcing them to consolidate their numbers in these *rancheriás*. Below El Cajon and until he reached the La Junta neighborhood Mendoza found the valley empty of Indians. At La Junta he found the Jumanos "versed in the Mexican language" and asking for baptism. Complying with these requests, he baptized more than a hundred persons. (Bolton, 1916: 321–325)

In 1693 the Spaniards abandoned Texas, and until after 1715 had little further contact with Jumanos. When they did return they found to their amazement that their erstwhile friends had become allied with their Apache enemies. This bond had become so close that the Jumanos shortly thereafter were regarded simply as a segment or division of the Apaches, and were known as "los Apaches Jumanes." This drastic alteration in their relationship to Apaches would seem to have been the only course open to the weakened, benumbed, and bereft Jumanos. (Bolton, 1911: 80–82)

J. Charles Kelley (1952), who has made a careful study of later Jumano history, has shown that in the years between 1683 and 1715 there were fifteen Puebloan villages near La Junta and along the lower reaches of the Rio Conchos. By 1747 only seven of them survived, and their populace was of somewhat diverse origin. Fear of the Apaches on the one hand, and poor crops and perhaps continued drought on the other, seem to have forced the consolidation and abandonment of these villages. It should also be remembered that from the sixteenth century on, Jumano culture had been increasingly exposed to Spanish-Mexican culture. It had lost its essential integrity before the eighteenth century, and was unable to put up either a physical or moral barrier against Spanish or Apache encroachment. Some of the Jumanos, attracted to the mines and haciendas of Mexico where they became wageworkers, shortly disappeared into the general Mexican populace; others stayed in the few remaining ancestral pueblos. But they too lost their identity as Jumano Indians,

233

and likewise became a part of the local populace. The Jumanos had always hunted buffalo to some extent, and this old tradition plus their acquisition of horses apparently drew some Jumano remnants to the plains. In the 1770's at least some of the Jumanos were participating in raids with Apaches, and it is presumed that sometime after this date they lost their identity and merged entirely with one or more of the eastern Apache bands. (Bolton, 1911: 83–88; Sauer, 1934: 68)

In the sixteenth century there were five major Jumano villages or pueblos in the La Junta region. The first Jumano village Spanish explorers entered upon descending the Rio Conchos was on the left or north bank of the stream. It seems to have been only a dozen or so miles from La Junta, possibly at the site of the present hamlet of San Juan Bautista. It was called Amotomanco (or Otomoacos), apparently the native term for the language or dialect spoken there.[2] Spanish slave-raiders called this village Patarabuey, however, and the term came to be used to designate all five villages since "they are all interrelated with one another." On the Mexican side of the Rio Grande, above its junction with the Rio Conchos, were two settlements of Jumanos whom Luxán termed Abriache. The pueblo which was located near the junction of the two rivers was named Santo Tomás by the Espejo Expedition, and it contained "about six hundred persons, young and old." The present town of Ojinaga, Chihuahua, may be on or near the site of this pueblo. The other Abriache pueblo was situated about fifteen miles up the Rio Grande and was named San Bernardino by Espejo. Across the river from Santo Tomás was a pueblo that the same expedition named San Juan Evangelista. It "was on a high ridge with many flat-roofed houses; below were many other houses forming a sort of suburb." (Hammond and Rey, 1929: 58–62) A short distance downstream was the largest of all the Jumano pueblos, named Santiago by the Spaniards. The ruins of this pueblo lie on the outskirts of Presidio, Texas. (Kelley, 1952: 373)

[2] Hammond and Rey, 1927: 254. The excerpt at the beginning of this chapter is also derived from this citation.

Besides these five pueblos there were "many others and many *rancherías* along the river, all being settled, both up the Del Norte river [Rio Grande] and the Conchos." (Hammond and Rey, 1929: 63) Espejo (Bolton, 1916: 172), who was probably trying to impress the officials back home, claimed that the population of the five pueblos numbered "more than ten thousand Indians." This probably was too high an estimate for the Jumanos in the vicinity of La Junta, and probably too few for all the people we have called Jumano.

Although the sixteenth-century Jumanos were concentrated in the La Junta vicinity, Spanish expeditions found scattered groups of them all along the Rio Grande Valley almost to El Paso. Luxán, the most accurate chronicler of the Espejo Expedition, noted that Jumanos were encountered for sixteen days or a distance of about forty leagues up the Rio Grande from La Junta. Espejo himself said they extended for a distance of twelve days journey. (Hammond and Rey, 1929: 64–67; Bolton, 1916: 173) The reception given these Spaniards was uniformly friendly. Luxán (Hammond and Rey, 1929: 67), at a place he called La Deseada, remarked, for example:

Upon our arrival there came to us in procession and singing, more than two hundred Indians, men and women, from the same Otomoacos nation. They presented us with shawls, tanned deerskins, mescal, and ornaments like bonnets with colored feathers which they said they obtained from the direction of the sea.

More or less the same sort of welcome by comparable numbers of Jumanos was given the Espejo Expedition throughout the land.

The upstream Jumanos, dwelling as far north as the lowlands below El Paso, were called Caguate or Caguase. Culturally and linguistically they were similar to the other Jumanos, although they seem to have been somewhat more poverty-stricken. In the vicinity of El Paso the sixteenth-century Spaniards encountered a different but equally friendly people whom they called Tanpachoas. The Espejo Expedition rested here for about a week, the natives bringing them large quantities of "mesquite, maize, and fish, for they fish much in the pools by means of small dragnets." The only difference

235

the Spaniards could discern between these Indians and the Oto-moacos was that the male Tanpachoas had "their privy parts tied with a small ribbon." (Hammond and Rey, 1929: 67, 69; Sauer, 1934: 66–67) The adornment of the penis with ribbons or other finery is a South American Indian custom and was virtually absent among North American Indians. An occurrence of this kind brings to mind various speculations: Did penis sheaths diffuse from south to north? Was penis ornamentation independently begun?

In the seventeenth century the Indians in the El Paso vicinity were termed Mansos by the Spaniards, who founded a mission among them. These seem to be the same people who were earlier called Tanpachoas.

In 1535, Cabeza de Vaca and his companions approached the Jumano country from the south, probably following down the Rio Conchos, as was the custom of later Spanish explorers. They found the Jumanos different, at least in their manner of welcome, from any of the other tribes they had encountered. Instead of coming out to meet the Spaniards, they stayed in their houses. Nevertheless, the Spaniards were welcome, for houses had been prepared for their use and presents of skin blankets were given to them. In their houses the natives "were all seated with their faces turned to the wall, their heads down, the hair brought before their eyes, and their property placed in a heap in the middle of the house." (Hodge, 1907b: 103) This seems a queer greeting by any standard; could it have been the Jumanos thought that this little band of Spaniards were some sort of white gods? Men do not ordinarily greet terrestrial strangers with such a show of submissiveness. De Vaca compared these people, both in physique and near-nakedness, to Karankawas. He added that "the women are dressed with deer-skin, and some few men, mostly the aged, who are incapable of fighting. The country is very popu-lous." (Hodge, 1907b: 103–104)

Before the next recorded visit, in 1581, the Jumanos apparently had learned that Spaniards were only mortal, for there is no further mention of obsequious greetings. No slave raids had been pushed as far as the Jumanos' land at this time, but the "Cabri" (Pazaguates?)

just to the south had suffered from Spanish slavers, and the Jumanos likely had learned of this all-too-human custom from them.

Appearance and Dress. The Spaniards continued to be impressed with the appearance of the Jumanos, however. Gallegos, the chronicler of the Rodriguez Expedition of 1581–82, for example, thought the first Jumanos he encountered (Amotomanco) were a fine-looking people and, on the Rio Grande, he described other Jumanos as "very clean, handsome and warlike, the best featured we had encountered thus far." He also reported the Caguates to be "well inclined people and fine men who received us well and offered us of what they possessed in the same manner as the others had done before." (Hammond and Rey, 1927: 256, 260)

Diego Pérez de Luxán supplies a somewhat more detailed description of Jumano appearance in the La Junta vicinity (Hammond and Rey, 1929: 57–58):

These people are naked and have their privy parts uncovered. They cover themselves with well tanned skins of the cibula (bison). . . . The women wear some sort of tanned deerskin bodices [this was apparently similar to a present-day poncho] resembling scapularies which cover their breasts and other tanned deerskins as skirts, carrying as cloaks tanned skins of the cattle. These people wear their hair long and tied to the head. The men have their hair cut very short, up to the middle of their heads, and from there up they leave it two fingers long and curl it with minium paint in such a way that it resembles a small cap. They leave on the crown a large lock of hair to which they fasten feathers of white and black birds such as geese, cranes, and sparrow-hawks.

Gallegos also noted a few items of Jumano adornment (Hammond and Rey, 1927: 257):

. . . we saw a piece of copper which an Indian carried about his neck tied with some cotton threads. Another carried a copper sleigh-bell. . . . some of the Indians who came to meet and see us carried white and colored coral, although not of fine quality, suspended from the nose; they also had turquoises.

Subsistence and Material Culture. Despite the

237

many comments of sixteenth-century Spaniards, it is difficult to evaluate the nature of the Jumano subsistence. Small climatic changes could and undoubtedly did force major and perhaps frequent alterations in subsistence habits, as has been previously noted. It also seems that various Jumanos in different places, either along the Rio Grande or those scattered groups away from the river, lived in various ways. Perhaps the best summation of Jumano subsistence possible is to say that since farming endeavors were precarious even in the more favorable localities, there was a striking diversity in subsistence habits for a single but widespread people. While the benefits of intensive horticulture were bountiful for Puebloan people generally, they were at best meager for the peripheral Jumanos.

In good years those Jumanos who lived along the Rio Grande and Rio Conchos raised fairly ample crops of corn, beans, squash, perhaps some other vegetables, and possibly cotton. It is not entirely clear who worked in the fields—whether the men or women—though Luxán's account (Hammond and Rey, 1929: 61, 62) would seem to imply that the men did. If so, this would be in accordance with Pueblo custom.

Probably the most important wild foods, especially in drought years, were mesquite beans and the beans of its near relative, the screw bean or tornillo (*Prosopis pubescens*). These beans are removed from their pods only with great difficulty, as anyone knows who has tried to do so. But the pods are edible, and some Indians ate the pod and all. Generally, the Jumanos ground the dried pods of tornillo and mesquite to a coarse flour which could be stored, to be prepared later in a number of ways. Even today mesquite beans are recognized as a rich, nourishing food, though so far as I am aware they are not considered as food for human consumption. Mesquite beans are, however, used extensively as fodder, and an old tale has it that ancient horses, fit only for the glue factory, will act like young stallions when put on a mesquite-bean diet. Luxán (Hammond and Rey, 1929: 67–68), incidentally, tells what may well be the first recorded instance of men feeding mesquite beans to horses, as well as giving a good illustration of the attitude many Indians had for horses in early times. The Rodríguez Expedition had left a worn-out horse with the cacique of the Caguates nation. These Indians "had built a manger for it and gave it a large quantity of mesquite and talked to it as if it were a person." It had recovered to the extent that the next year Espejo's party appropriated it from the Indians. "When we were leading it as we were about to depart they took leave of it and gave it more mesquite to eat."

The bulbs of the various species of Agave, cooked in earth ovens, were also an important wild-plant food, as were the tunas of prickly pears and the fruits of other cacti, such as the delicious pitahaya.

It is doubtful that buffalo meat figured very prominently in the diet of the river-valley Jumanos before the advent of horses. The buffalo range was a long way off, so far that only dried meat could have been brought back. It could not have been plentiful enough to have been anything more than a desirable delicacy. Buffalohides were of greater importance to Jumanos, if the early reports of the Spaniards are valid. Dried flesh and hides had to be carried on men's backs, or hauled by dog travois (which we are not at all sure the Jumanos possessed) for a hundred miles or more, and through some rugged mountain country at that. It is certain that the Jumanos hunted buffalo, however, and it may well be that some of them had abandoned their river-valley homes for a nomadic hunting life on the southern plains. Espejo met Jumanos near the Pecos River, far to the north of La Junta, on his return trip from New Mexico. After meeting three Jumanos out hunting, the Spaniards were taken to their *ranchería* by a stream. "The Indians, men and women received us with music and rejoicing. As a sign of peace and happiness there was held a dance between the tents of the Indian men and women." (Hammond and Rey, 1929: 124) Whether these Jumanos were simply Amotomancos, Abriaches [Patarabueyes], or Caguates on a seasonal hunting expedition, or were a related hunting people who only visited the river-valley folk in the winter months is unknown.

Very little is known, too, about the Jumanos' method of preparing and cooking food. They possessed pottery, as archeological finds attest, so food could be boiled, but oddly and in keeping with other

Fig. 9. "Standing on top of their houses they showed great merriment on seeing us." (Hernán Gallegos)

perplexing aspects of Jumano culture, Cabeza de Vaca (Hodge, 1907b: 105) said that they did not have pottery and described a way of cooking known as stone-boiling.

They fill the half of a large calabash with water, and throw on the fire many stones of such as are most convenient and readily take the heat. When hot, they are taken up with tongs of sticks and dropped into the calabash until the water boils from the fervor of the stones. Then whatever is to be cooked is put in, and until it is done they continue taking out cooled stones and throwing in hot ones. Thus they boil their food.

Stone-boiling was widely practiced by Indian hunters and gatherers. But why the Jumanos should continue to cook by this method after they had obtained pottery is a mystery. Perhaps this was a case analogous to the American husband who broils—or burns—the family's steaks on a backyard grill, even though a modern, efficient electric or gas range is handy inside the kitchen door.

The sixteenth-century Spaniards must have been impressed by Jumano dwellings, especially in contrast to the rude huts they had previously seen in the Mexican deserts. The following description of the houses in the La Junta vicinity by Hernán Gallegos in 1581 (Hammond and Rey, 1927: 256) is one of the most complete, but practically all of the early explorers commented on them:

Standing on top of their houses they showed great merriment on seeing us. These houses resemble those of the Mexicans, except that they are made of paling. They build them square. They put up the bases and upon these they place timbers, the thickness of a man's thigh. Then they add the pales, and plaster them with mud. Close to them they have their granaries built of willow, after the fashion of the Mexicans, where they keep their provisions and their harvest of mesquite and other things.

Cabeza de Vaca, who had seen many strange sights, was moved to remark that "these habitations were the first seen, having the appearance and structure of houses." (Hodge, 1907b: 102)

Jumano towns were not made up of the many-roomed, multistoried dwellings often thought of as typical of the Pueblo Indians. Instead, their houses stood alone, though often clustered, like those

241

of San Juan Evangelista, "on a high ridge with many flat-roofed houses; below were many other houses forming a sort of suburb." (Hammond and Rey, 1929: 62) The houses were also "low and well arranged into pueblos" (Bolton, 1916: 172), and at San Juan Evangelista there apparently was a central plaza. In the fields were flat-roofed houses where they lived during harvest time. Upstream on the Rio Grande, presumably in the more temporary locations, Jumanos continued to dwell in their flat-roofed houses, but they also erected some kind of grass huts, perhaps similar to the open-sided, brush-covered *ramadas* of today. The Jumano hunters (if Jumanos they were) who were met by the Espejo Expedition in west Texas on their return to Mexico were living in tents in the manner of Plains Indians.

Archeological excavations have added considerable data concerning the houses of the Jumanos and their forerunners. Rectangular, they averaged twenty-eight feet by thirty feet, and, as the early Spaniards said, were built in pits, or, as Luxán put it, "half under and half above the ground." (Hammond and Rey, 1929: 59–60; Kelley *et al.*, 1940: 35) The lower parts of the walls of a house excavated near Redford, Texas, on the Rio Grande were "built up at least some distance above ground level. These walls were constructed of turtle-back-shaped adobe bricks laid up longitudinally and plastered together. The inside of the house was plastered and at least in places painted with red, yellow, black and perhaps white bands." (Kelley, 1951: 118) Above the adobe walls were presumably the mud-plastered palings. The flat roofs, too, were probably constructed of saplings and brush, over which a liberal coating of adobe was applied. These buildings were sturdy enough to support their occupants on the roofs, and entry may have been through an opening in the roof. These houses were unquestionably well suited to the long, hot summers in this part of the Rio Grande Valley. They must have been cool, and any damage infrequent rains did to them could be easily repaired.

Interestingly, the jacales encountered today in this region may be modern survivals derived from the old house type of the area. The modern jacal is usually small and normally is used only as a store-house or shed, but otherwise it duplicates many of the features of the prehistoric houses. A shallow floor is excavated, corner posts, usually of cottonwood, are raised, and horizontal stringers are lashed to them or rest in their crotches. The walls and the roof are normally made of prickly ocotillo stalks, laid vertically and tied together, over which a liberal coating of adobe is plastered. These structures are cheap to build and are surprisingly durable in this dry climate.

Very little can be said about the tools and other material equipment of Jumanos because so few data are available. Early Spanish explorers almost to a man, however, commented on Jumano weapons, suggesting that they warranted respect. (Hammond and Rey, 1929: 69; 1927: 255) Jumanos used what Spaniards described as "Turkish" bows, apparently meaning the Tartar bow, which is reinforced with horn or sinew. Bowstrings were of sinew; arrows must not have been out of the ordinary, for they go unremarked. Warriors also carried bludgeons of tornillo wood and buffalohide shields.

Buffalohides and deerhides were expertly tanned: "The Natives dress the hides of these cows as hides are dressed in Flanders, and make shoes of them. Others they dress in different ways, some of the natives using them for clothes." (Bolton, 1916: 173) Luxán added (Hammond and Rey, 1929: 57) that the hides were tanned and made pliant by "beating them with stones until they are soft." While among the Caguates branch of Jumanos, Gallegos said that "among the things presented they gave us two bonnets made of numerous macaw feathers." (Hammond and Rey, 1927: 260)

Social Organization. The nature of Jumano society goes undescribed, yet there are a few tantalizing hints about it to be found in the accounts left by Spanish explorers. Each village or pueblo had one cacique (chief), and sometimes two, one apparently a war chief, the other a peace chief. (Hammond and Rey, 1929: 58) Although there were dialectal distinctions and probably other minor differences distinguishing the various pueblos, they were friendly with one another, and at least at La Junta there was a paramount chief who held sway over several pueblos. We learn, for example,

243

that the Espejo Expedition, after visiting San Juan Evangelista, "went to another pueblo, the largest of all, whose cacique was called Q. Bisise and whom all other caciques respected." (Hammond and Rey, 1929: 62)

While we are ignorant of the basic social and ceremonial structure of Jumano culture, it must have been rich. The sixteenth-century Spanish expeditions were treated with ceremony and pomp. When the Espejo Expedition arrived at the La Junta pueblo called San Bernardino (Hammond and Rey, 1929: 60)

. . . there were only a few old Indians, as the others were in the sierra, owing to fear. After we had reassured them through the interpreter and the . . . Indian Juan Cantor all the people came down within half an hour, making musical sounds with their mouths similar to those of the flute. They kissed the hand of the Father named Fray Bernardino, whom we had along. And all, both young and old, offered everyone maize, beans, mescal, dry calabashes, gourd vessels, buffalo skins, and Turkish bows and arrows.

At every pueblo they visited, the Indians kissed the Father's hand and brought presents, and in all these pueblos the Spaniards "were received with much rejoicing and music which they made with their mouths as I have described above." Besides this peaceful and friendly greeting they were treated to elaborate dances and other celebrations. "They made music by beating their hands while sitting around a big fire. They sing, and in time with the singing they dance, a few rising from one side and others from the opposite, performing their dances two, four, and eight at a time." (Hammond and Rey, 1929: 62, 67)

OF ALL THE TEXAS INDIANS the Jumanos are the least known, and the few facts about their culture that we do possess seem to raise more questions than they answer. The facts tantalize, frustrate, and shed little light; yet an over-all image of Jumano culture does emerge, if only a skeletal one. The impression is of an outpost civilization, a pioneer people who had been temporarily successful in establishing settlements on the fringes of Puebloland. Their success had been greatest in prehistoric times: villages had appeared, perhaps linked together in political confederations, population was

244

relatively heavy, and the social and ceremonial life was rich and varied. But when drought came to this region which was already arid or semiarid, the fledgling settlements faltered and may have been on their way to failing completely when overtaken by Spanish colonialism. Some Jumanos appear to have remained near their often drought-parched lands, eking out a living on wild-plant foods and what their fields could be made to produce, perpetuating their old life as best they could. Others may have moved to better-watered districts, and some surely gave up their precarious gardening existence to become bison hunters on the southern plains.

CHAPTER 10

The Wichitas: Nations of the North

> Their foresight in supplying provisions shows them to
> be industrious, for there is no house in which at pres-
> ent there may not be seen four or five vessels full of
> maize, each one estimated at four and a half *fanegas*,
> besides a great quantity of beans and calabashes
> [pumpkins]. They preserve the latter from year to
> year, weaving them curiously like mats.
>
> Athanase de Mézières (1778)

WHEN CORONADO in 1541 visited the province of Quivira, in what
is now central Kansas, he was among the ancestors of the tribe known
today as the Wichitas. The territory from north of the Smoky Hill
River, in the vicinity of present Lindsborg, Kansas, south to the
Arkansas River was Coronado's Quivira. (Wedel, 1942: 21–22) During his visit of almost a month Coronado found more than two dozen
politically independent towns or villages. South of the Arkansas
River, perhaps extending into Oklahoma, lived close cultural relatives of these people, as well as their eventual confederates and in
time tribal cohorts—the Tawakonis and Wacos. Several other Spanish
expeditions visited Quivira during the sixteenth century, but they

247

were annihilated and consequently left no additional information about the natives. In 1601 the Spaniard Don Juan de Oñate stopped among the Quivirans of southcentral Kansas, and he left a brief account of his visit. When the people of Quivira were next encountered, by French traders in 1719, their southward drift into Texas was already well under way. The peoples of Quivira—the Wichitas—cannot, of course, be claimed as "native Texans." They were, however, within what became her borders long before she became a state and during the reign of Spain and France had a powerful and decisive influence upon the course of events in Texas.

Origins and Early History. The Wacos, Tawakonis, Taovayas, Wichita proper, and some minor groups are closely related linguistically, with only minor dialectal differences distinguishing them. Their essentially common language, termed Wichita, is one of the four languages of the Caddoan stock, the others being Pawnee, Caddo, and Kichai. If there were once cultural differences which distinguished these various Wichita subgroups they have long since been forgotten; what is said here about one subdivision is assumed to hold true for the other Wichita peoples as well. The ultimate origins of the Wichitas are generally considered to have been in the southeast somewhere around the lower Red River. They and the Pawnees are said to have migrated north, the Pawnees continuing north and the Wichitas turning back south to their Kansas home. According to the traditions of both Wichitas and Pawnees, the parting of the two groups took place in the vicinity of the Platte River. Caution is necessary when dealing with the notoriously inaccurate traditions of a people, but these at least seem reasonable.

Wichita peoples migrated southward during the seventeenth and eighteenth centuries for several reasons. One of the most powerful was the military pressure exerted from the north by the Osages—equipped with European weapons. Hostile Comanches were also pushing down from the headwaters of the Arkansas, and these formidable enemies soon made the scattered villages of the Wichitas untenable. (Wallace and Hoebel, 1952: 6) The Wichitas were acquiring horses during this period from the southwestern New Mexican source, and this too may have made a more southerly location desirable. The number of villages also declined as the dispersed Wichitas were forced by their enemies into larger, consolidated villages. Because of the abandonment of the old villages and consolidation in new locations, the names and number of Wichita subtribes are varied and somewhat confusing. Various European nations also had divergent names for the Wichitas, and one nation might even have varying names for them at different times.[1] The French called them "Panis," usually with a qualifying adjective, such as "Pani Pique" or "Panipiquets" (Tattooed Pawnees) and "Panis Noirs" (Black Pawnees) to distinguish them from the Pawnees whom they had previously encountered farther north. When Americans became acquainted with the Wichitas, they attempted to follow the French differentiation and, imitating the French pronunciation, called them Pawnee Picts, but sometimes they seem to have confused them with the Pawnee proper. When the Spaniards became reacquainted with the Wichitas in the eighteenth century, they termed them Taovayas, after the most important subtribal village on the Red River. Sometimes, however, they merely referred to Wichitas as "Norteños" (Peoples or Nations of the North), and the Spaniards in New Mexico persisted in calling them Jumanos. The name *Wichita* is not entirely apt, since it was taken from neither the largest nor the most important subdivision of this loose confederacy. The origin and meaning of the word is uncertain; it is not the Wichitas' term for themselves. (Hodge, 1910, II: 947)

In 1747, French traders succeeded in concluding a Wichita-Comanche alliance, and within a decade the Wichitas had founded a substantial settlement and trading center on the Red River. Their principal village was inhabited by the subtribe known as the Taovayas, the lesser village by the Wichita proper. In 1757, Athanase de Mézières, a Frenchman exceptionally successful in dealing with the native peoples of Spanish America for the Spanish Crown, visited these Red River villages. The Wichita settlements on the banks of the Red he named San Bernardo and San Teodoro. Today the unexcavated ruins on the Texas side of the river are known as Spanish

---

[1] Harper, 1953a. Harper (1953a, b, c) contains an excellent appraisal of Wichita history.

Fort, and are near the present town of Spanish Fort in Montague County (see Map 3).

The Tawakonis (Tahuacano[a]), Wacos (who appear to have been the Iscani of earlier times), and perhaps other subgroups, originally on the southern flank of the Wichita peoples, were in the vanguard of the southern migration. By 1772 they had settled on the Brazos at Waco and on the Trinity upstream from present Palestine. (Hodge, 1910, II: 702–704) By 1779 the village on the Trinity had been abandoned and its people had joined those on the Brazos. The Wacos (Iscani), it seems, comprised one of these Brazos River villages and were actually a subdivision of the Tawakonis. The word *Waco* does not appear in the early Spanish documents; it was first used by Americans in the nineteenth century. After other migrations into Texas and eventual difficulties with Texans, the Tawakonis and Wacos joined the Wichitas in 1859 on their reservation in the vicinity of Anadarko, Oklahoma. Today the Wichita tribe numbers about five hundred, and is considered to be composed of four subtribes: the Wichita proper, Tawakoni, Waco, and Kichai. The last are a poorly known tribe, speaking a separate Caddoan language and originally supporting a somewhat different, though unknown, culture.

Appearance and Dress. The Wichitas differed from many of their neighbors in the Plains in two noticeable ways. First, they were short, stockily built, and quite dark in skin color. George Catlin (1842, II: 73), the artist who accompanied the Dragoon Expedition led by Colonel Henry Dodge in 1834, and became famous for his Indian paintings, said:

The Pawnee Picts, as well as the Camanchees, are generally a very clumsy and ordinary looking set of men, when on their feet; but being fine horsemen, are equally improved in appearance as soon as they mount upon their horses' backs.

Amongst the women of this tribe, there were many that were exceedingly pretty in feature and in form; and also in expression, though their skins are very dark.

The second striking feature was the extensive tattooing on the face and body, a custom practiced by both sexes. Many North American

250

Indians tattooed themselves, but the Wichitas seem to have out-distanced most other tribes in this respect. The men were tattooed on both eyelids, and a short horizontal line extended from the out-side corner of the eye. Appropriately, their name for themselves was "raccoon-eyed people." The men also had two short tattoo lines extending downward from the corners of the mouth. On the back of their hands were clawlike designs, placed there after a boy had killed his first bird. Other marks, symbolizing war honors, were tattooed on the arms and chest. The men also pierced their ears, usually in four places, and suspended numerous ornaments from them.

Women's tattoos were all quite similar, though styles may have come and gone through the years. Commonly a tattooed line ran down the bridge of the nose to the upper lip. A line encircling the mouth was broken just below the lower lip and the ends extended downward to the chin. Between these two lines were two other parallel lines, and all four lines terminated at the chin and intersected with a line tattooed along the chin line. This chin-line tattoo ran from ear to ear, above which was tattooed a row of solid triangles. Other triangles were tattooed on the neck and upper breast and a series of parallel zigzag lines coursed up and down the arms. The breasts, including the nipples, were tattooed with several short lines, and around them were tattooed three concentric circles, said to prevent pendulous breasts in old age.[2] By Catlin's time the men had apparently given up tattooing, but the women, as shown in his plates, were still tattooed in traditional style. (Catlin, 1841, II: Plates 174–177)

When the first realization of what the Wichitas looked like strikes us we are apt to think their tastes savage and barbaric. But on re-flection and when we remove ourselves as much as possible from our own cultural bias, we have to admit that the paint, powder, dyes, and whatnot used by the ordinary female of Western culture are intrinsically no more beautiful nor less savage—though certainly less permanent—than the tattoos of a Wichita belle.

[2] Dorsey, 1904: 2–3. Much of the description of Wichita culture relies on this valuable source. Curtis (1930) has been used extensively, as has Schmitt and Schmitt (n.d.) for social organization.

FIG. 10. Tattooed Wichita women plaiting pumpkin fibers.

The clothing of the men consisted of moccasins, leggings, a loin cloth of either skins or fur, and a robe or a shirt.[3] In warm weather all clothing except the loin cloth and moccasins was discarded. The women wore a skirt of buckskin or buffalohide, tanned on both sides, wound around the waist and reaching below the knees. Catlin (1841, II: 74) said that the women

are always decently and comfortably clad, being covered generally with a gown or slip, that reaches from the chin quite down to the ancles, made of deer or elk skins; often garnished very prettily, and ornamented with long fringes of elk's teeth, which are fastened on them in rows, and more highly valued than any other ornament they can put upon them.

Subsistence and Material Culture. In prehorse times garden produce was more important to the economy than meat obtained in the hunt. Even after the Wichitas were mounted and were, of course, much more mobile, bison and other wild game remained supplementary to the produce of the gardens. At the opening of the seventeenth century Oñate (Bolton, 1916: 261) noted the importance of gardening:

. . . the villages were surrounded on all sides by fields of maize and crops of the Indians. The stalks of the maize were as high as that of New Spain and in many places higher. The land was so rich that, having harvested the maize, a new growth of a span in height had sprung up over a large portion of the same ground, without any cultivation or labor other than the removal of the weeds and the making of holes where they planted the maize. There were many beans, some gourds, and, between the fields, some plum trees. The crops were not irrigated but dependent on the rains. . . . Like the other settled Indians they utilize cattle in large numbers.

In the nineteenth century, when Catlin (1841, II: 70) visited them, there had been little change in the fecundity of their fields: "These people [were] cultivating quite extensive fields of corn (maize), pumpkins, melons, beans and squashes; so, with these aids, and an abundant supply of buffalo meat, they may be said to be living very

[3] Bolton, 1914a, II: 201. The excerpt at the head of this chapter is from this citation also.

well." Like many Plains Indians, the Wichitas did not eat fish, despite the multitude which might have been taken from the rivers and streams along which their villages were located.

The fact that the gardens were extensive and produced bumper crops meant that the Wichitas were a settled folk, allowing them to congregate in villages. Even in early times their villages were of considerable size, although Oñate (Bolton, 1916: 259) was undoubtedly exaggerating when he claimed to have visited "a settlement containing more than twelve hundred houses." In the eighteenth century De Mézières (Bolton, 1914a, II: 201–202) described the villages we know as Spanish Fort, on the Red River, in more believable terms:

The nation of the Taovayazes is divided into two villages, one situated on the northern bank of the Vermejo, or Natchitoches, River, the other opposite the first on the other bank. The former is composed of thirty-seven houses, the latter of one hundred twenty-three. Each dwelling contains from ten to twelve beds, considering which fact a conservative estimate places the number of men, including youths, at more than eight hundred, while that of the women and children of both sexes is very large.

Not only were these twin villages fairly large by Texas Indian standards, but they were well fortified. A Spanish force, following the sacking of the San Saba Mission by a combined force of Comanches and Wichitas in 1757, attempted a reprisal on Spanish Fort. To the surprise of the small Spanish army, composed largely of recruits and Indians, they found the village, and the path which led from the village to the river, surrounded by a stockade and moat. Within the village was a corral for the stock and beyond the village the Comanches had pitched their tepees. Upon the approach of the Spanish, the Indians, armed with guns, manned their fortifications. But the Spaniards never really had an opportunity to assault the fort, for the Indians made repeated sallies from the village to harass them. The Spaniards were soon forced to withdraw in humiliating defeat, and with the loss of two precious cannons. It must be admitted that the Wichitas had learned from the French something of defensive art, though just how much is difficult to ascertain. The Spanish noted that

254

a French flag flew over Spanish Fort, and Coronado had found no stockaded villages in Kansas two centuries earlier. (Harper, 1953a: 268–269)

The dwellings of the Wichitas—and the old type was used until this century—are generally known as "grass houses." This term is not intended to convey the impression that they were flimsy or temporary, for some were used for many years and were of sturdy construction. Early in the seventeenth century Oñate (Bolton, 1916: 260) described them as

all round, built of forked poles and bound with rods, and on the outside covered to the ground with dry grass. Within, on the sides, they had frameworks or platforms which served them as beds on which they slept. Most of them were large enough to hold eight or ten persons. They were two lance-lengths high.

The houses, from fifteen to thirty feet in diameter, were built over a circular framework of upright forked cedar posts. Other cedar logs were fixed in their crotches, joining the posts together. Long cedar poles were laid against this framework, with the butt ends resting on the ground and the upper ends tied together. Stripped willow poles were tied horizontally to these, and coarse grass was spread over the entire exterior, starting at the base of the structure. The grass was made secure from the prairie winds by more willow poles. Above the top of the lodge, where the cedar poles met, was a sort of false peak made from bundles of tightly-wrapped grass. From the base of this peak projected four poles, about three feet long, each pointing in a cardinal direction. In Wichita mythology, the peak was symbolic of the creator, and the four poles symbolized the gods of the four quarters of the world. Each house had two low and narrow doors, one on the east, the other on the west. The doors themselves were made of grass tied to a willow framework and were not hinged. Often there was a southern door, apparently a vestige from an earlier age when there was both a north and south door, used for ceremonial purposes. Not only was the process of erecting these grass houses a fairly complicated one, but it was also accompanied by an intricate ceremonial procedure.

255

In the center of the lodge was a slight excavation for the fire. A small smoke vent was provided near the top of the roof, but the lodges were still acridly smoky. About half a dozen beds (the number depending upon the size of the lodge) were arranged along the walls. They were made of light willow withes, covered with buffalohides, and were raised several feet off the floor. Buffalohide curtains, decorated with paintings of martial scenes, were hung around the beds to afford some privacy. Between the fire and the west doorway and sunk into the floor was a heavy, hollowed-out tree trunk on which the women ground the family's corn.

Nearby the family had an arbor, a structure similar to the grass lodge except that the sides were open and it was elongated, larger, and had a raised floor. Here the family rested and worked during the heat of summer. Another arbor, from ten to twenty feet square, was used to dry and store meat and vegetables. The top of this arbor, reached by a notched tree-trunk ladder, was used for drying meat and corn. From its sides and bottom were suspended the curiously-braided strips of pumpkins.

Another structure, a thatched hut, erected on a platform, was the sleeping quarters for the unmarried, carefully-guarded girls. After the girls had climbed into their upper berths for the night their mothers removed the log ladders. One is inclined to wonder whether such an arrangement would not but challenge amorous young warriors. The space under these raised huts was also used for drying produce from the fields. Oñate (Bolton, 1916: 260) was apparently referring to these when he noted that each house

had granaries or platforms, an *estado* [from five to six feet] high, which they must have used in summer, and which would hold three or four persons, being most appropriate for enjoying the fresh air. They entered them through a small grass door. They ascended to this platform by means of a movable wooden ladder. Not a house lacked these platforms.

The Wichitas manufactured pottery, but this skill was abandoned as soon as European equivalents were obtainable. They also manufactured handsome wooden vessels, small wooden mortars, and undoubtedly other articles of wood, until recent times. Granite slabs for corn-grinding and other tools and utensils of stone were made, as well as rawhide bags, parfleches, and other hide containers in the Plains Indian tradition. In short, the number and nature of their tools and utensils were much larger than those of any of the nomadic Texas tribes.

Social Organization. The Wichitas were similar to less productive hunting and gathering societies in that the division of labor was based almost wholly on sex and age distinctions. In the words of De Mézières (Bolton, 1914a, II: 203):

The women tan, sew, and paint the skins, fence the fields, care for the corn fields, harvest the crops, cut and fetch the fire-wood, prepare the food, build the houses, and rear the children, their constant care stopping at nothing that contributes to the comfort and pleasure of their husbands. The latter devote themselves wholly to the chase and to warfare.

There was a good deal of co-operation among relatives in performing various tasks. When a new house was to be built, the men who were to occupy it performed the hard work of cutting and raising the heavy cedar post framework. The women of the household and other women, who according to their method of reckoning kinship were called "sisters," all joined in thatching the house and feeding the workers. In the same way the women of a household co-operatively tilled and harvested their fields and in concert performed many other womanly duties. Although the women performed most of the burdensome chores and were responsible for the gardens which supplied the bulk of the food, since they worked together and for each other, their labor was not as onerous as it might seem. The life of the man when at home in his village was no doubt one of leisure; nonetheless this perhaps should be regarded as a reward for the heavy strain of the warpath and the hunt. From the late seventeenth century on, the military pressure of the Osages, and for a time the Comanches, Tonkawas, and Lipans, to say nothing of various European powers, kept the Wichita warrior constantly harried and busy.

The villages were inhabited from spring until fall while the women were planting, tending, and harvesting their crops. After the crops were harvested and stored in late fall or early winter, the Wichitas

257

abandoned the villages for a winter buffalo hunt. They lived in tepees while on the hunt, and in other respects behaved as Plains Indians until their return to the villages at planting time in the spring. It is likely that the winter hunt was less important in prehorse days, but how much so is not known. A hunting life for pedestrian Wichitas must have been more demanding, less rewarding, and all in all less satisfactory than it was after they had acquired horses.

After the Wichitas had become commercially oriented by French influence, and were moving into consolidated villages, slavery made its appearance, and the age-old communistic, equalitarian nature of society was shaken. It was replaced with a sketchy class system based on wealth, a few families becoming wealthy and powerful because of their trade connections with the French and Comanches. In the case of slavery, Lipan Apaches and other captives, instead of being killed and sometimes eaten, were sold to the French, who took them to Natchitoches for sale to Louisiana plantation owners. But in 1769, following the transfer of Louisiana from France to Spain, Indian slavery in Louisiana was abolished. Before captives became a useful article in trade, it is difficult to see how they could have been economically useful to the Wichitas. A slave is not apt to make a good hunter, or a hunter at all, as the freedom of movement necessary for a hunter would inevitably lead to his escape. It is conceivable that slaves might have been used as village drudges and field workers, but in prehorse times the Wichita economy was a subsistence-for-use one, not designed to create a salable surplus, so it is difficult to understand how a slave could have been used for these purposes.

As is common in many cultures, the Wichitas had a number of supernaturally-inspired customs associated with birth. An expectant mother pitched a tepee hard by her grass house where she was attended during delivery by an elderly, experienced midwife. A new father was prohibited from entering his wife's lodge for four days after birth because it was felt his presence might make both mother and child sick. Soon after the birth, another old woman, especially knowledgeable in the mythology of the moon (Bright Shining Woman), took the infant to the river and bathed it. At the river she prayed to the moon and another deity called Man-Never-Known-On-Earth that the child would grow as rapidly as did the moon in its monthly cycle. She sprinkled water on the infant's head, immersed it completely, and prayed to the spirit of the water. Afterward, when the moon next appeared, the child was again taken from the grass house and was held up and shown to the moon, again with the prayer that he would grow as surely as would the moon.

Many other rites associated with birth were built around a similar sort of hopeful imitative magic. The placenta, for example, was placed in a straight young elm tree in the belief that this would assist the child to grow straight. It never was thrown into the water for fear the fish would eat it and so cause the child's illness and death. Even the child's cradle was made ritually by a healthy woman who had grown rapidly. Cradles that had sheltered a succession of healthy children were carefully preserved and were much in demand.

Children were sometimes named prior to birth from auspicious dreams of the mother or other relatives. From our point of view, this led to some ridiculous names, as many dreams did not conform to the subsequent sex or character of the child. Dorsey (1904: 8), one of the authorities on the twentieth-century Wichitas, cites the case of a robust, fairly intelligent man whose name was "Ignorant-Woman." Names were normally given, however, after the child had indicated a suitable name for himself by some action or characteristic. If a child or an adult suffered bad luck or ill health his name was changed, perhaps many times. If a person had good fortune in life, even a most inappropriate name would be retained. Sometimes sickly children were allowed to choose their own names. A number of men were invited into the father's lodge, their names were pronounced, and the child was permitted to select the one he preferred. The possessor of this name then gave the child not his own name but a name which referred to some noteworthy act he had performed on the warpath. It was also customary for teenage boys and girls, particularly those of high-status families, to have their names changed. Elderly warriors suggested their new names. Men sometimes changed their own names if their offspring were ill or unfortunate in other respects. In this case they bought the name of some old man who had had a successful life. After the purchase the seller went nameless or

259

conferred a new name upon himself. As might be expected from the foregoing, if a man died on the warpath, or died young for some inexplicable reason or because of witchcraft practiced by him or against him, his name was no longer used in any connection. To the Wichitas there was a great deal in a name.

The absence of the father at the birth of his children was an indication of the part he would play in their early upbringing. It was the mother and her female relatives who played the major role in the education and training of young children. Although fathers fondled and played with their infant offspring, they were likely to be away from home for long periods of time—hunting, on the warpath, herding horses, or engaged in other male activities—so they normally had little opportunity to be with their children.

A mother nursed her child for two or three years unless she became pregnant again. During the child's first years of life he was seldom far from his mother. When he was not in her arms, he was in his cradle nearby or on a pallet beside her. The training of young children was by our standards permissive and was without much corporal punishment. Toilet training, for example, was casual. Toddling children wore no diapers or pants in the house, and when they made a mistake the mother simply cleaned up the floor and pointed out to the child the necessity to go outdoors. The idea was soon implanted in the child's mind that the grown-up thing to do was to go outside for elimination. Children were often toilet-trained before they learned to talk, apparently with little fuss or stress. There were few don't's for small children; they were kept from things which might harm them, such as the fire, and they were restrained from being too "grabby," and that was about all.

When a child was three or four years old, discipline became somewhat more strict. The mother usually disciplined by scolding, although she might occasionally resort to switching. She sometimes called in another person to punish an unruly child, infrequently a boy's older brother, a grandparent, or the mother's brother. Usually it was a nonrelative, preferably an ugly old man who threatened the child by pretending he was going to eat him. Boys were also often punished by throwing them in a creek or scratching their legs with

260

the point of a knife. If nonrelatives were asked to punish the children, they chose whatever punishment they liked, and although the punishment might be unduly harsh the mother could not interfere. It seems likely that the mere threat of punishment by a nonrelative "bogeyman," particularly if a child had once experienced it, was likely to produce the desired behavior.

As boys grew older, their fathers became more important in their training, while girls continued to be instructed primarily by their mothers. The father's role was to instruct his son in the duties of a good Wichita man, to instill in him bravery, modesty, and the ability to get along with others. He taught him horsemanship, how to hunt, how to play games, and made certain that he was hardened by daily baths in a cold stream. He made the lad participate in the rigorous activities of the young men. A man could also pass along to his son personal supernatural powers and magical medicine bundles. But the father did little more than lecture his daughters. It was the mother and other women of the household who taught them gardening, sewing, and housekeeping. Other aspects of learning how to become a Wichita were unconsciously, informally taught. Children grew up knowing about sex, for example, since in their intimate family life, they were bound to see the sexual activities of their parents and other relatives.

As a girl matured she was closely watched by her mother and other relatives, and was warned to stay away from men. Girls were married sometimes after their sixteenth birthday, by which time they knew how to look after a grass house, cook, and work in the fields. Boys were probably somewhat older when they married, for they had to be proved hunters and able to provide security for the family. Ordinarily the family of a marriageable boy initiated negotiations with a girl's family by sending a middle-aged member of their group to talk to them. If the go-between received a favorable reply the prospective bridegroom went to the girl's lodge the following evening. If her family still favored the match he remained there that evening. Until the marriage took place, the girl was closely guarded against the attentions of other men. If she misbehaved during this interval her father was apt to beat her severely. The marriage was formalized by the groom's relatives presenting horses and buffalo robes to the bride's father or brother, and by giving a feast for the bride's family. They also presented the bride with gifts of clothing, and during the feast the groom's relatives gave him what was probably unwelcome and embarrassing advice on how to get along with his in-laws, his bride, how to be a success in life, and so forth. While this was the socially correct marriage procedure, and was characteristic of well-to-do, upper-status families in more recent times, poorer families apparently abridged the gift-giving and held no feasts.

Traditionally, the residence of a newly-married couple was matri-local (with the family of the bride). Young men generally married, however, within their own village, so they did not move away from familiar surroundings or far from their families.[4] The new son-in-law performed a number of duties for his wife's family, the most important being to supply them with meat and to herd their horses. His esteem among his wife's family depended upon how well he fulfilled these obligations, and whether or not he acquired a successful war record. A bride ordinarily did not live with her parents-in-law and was not particularly obligated to them. She occasionally took her mother-in-law some special dish she had prepared, and often performed some service for her, such as carrying her firewood. There was also a marked "respect" relationship between parents-in-law and children-in-law, and it is often still followed by modern Wichitas despite the disintegration of most of the social structure. The relationship takes the form of formality and reserve. Schmitt and Schmitt (n.d.: 20–21) relates, for instance, that

if a person wished to communicate with his parent-in-law, he would do so through a third person, usually his spouse. Similarly, a parent-in-law might "talk" to his child-in-law through the latter's spouse, i.e., his child. Talking restrictions were less rigid in the *father-in-law—son-in-law* and *mother-in-law—daughter-in-law* relationships than in the cross-sexual relationships. A man and his father-in-law could and did converse about matters of "business" such as hunting and herding the horses, but a man was supposed to let his father-in-law initiate conversations.

[4] Murdock (1949: 63) has suggested that this endogamous, bilateral, kin group be called a "deme," the Greek term for an administrative unit.

When it appeared that a person was on the verge of death, all of his relatives began to assemble. There was some apprehension that the corpse's soul was apt to feel lonely and might attempt to get living relatives to join it. But this fear was minor compared to the horror with which the Athapaskans regarded their dead. A friend, not being likely to be lured by a departed soul, was asked to take charge of the last rites. And this person persuaded several of his own friends to assist him. The corpse was bathed, dressed in his finest attire, and his face painted with his own personal symbols. As soon as all relatives had gathered, the body was buried, the interval generally being from two to four days. Wichita cemeteries were located on hills, and the persons in charge of the funeral dug a shallow grave. The accouterments of war, with the exception of the shield, were placed in the grave of a warrior. The shield either was given to one of the deceased's friends, who understood the magical rites associated with it, or it was placed by the grave or hung in the limbs of a tree. Before the body was lowered into the grave the man in charge prayed to the Earth Mother (Dorsey, 1904: 13):

Now you have been made to contain all things, to produce all things, and for us to travel over. Also we have been told to take care of everything which has come from your bosom, and we have been told that in your body everything should be buried. I now come to bury this man.

The corpse was then placed in the grave with its head toward the east. The body was covered with earth and the grave encircled to a height of about four feet with logs or slabs of stone. For four days the relatives of the dead continued to mourn, unkempt and dressed in ragged clothing. Four times a day they purified themselves by bathing in a stream. On the fourth day a man of good character reminded the mourners, as well as the other members of the village, that the final rites of mourning were to take place. This man and several others of good character entered the mourners' lodge, where they gave the mourners, seated on robes, in turn a pipe to smoke to signalize the end of mourning. After the mourners had smoked they were addressed briefly by the leader of the delegation to the effect that the village should resume normal life and that the mourners should allow

263

it to do so. After assenting to this proposal everyone in the village wailed and wept for a few moments, after which the tears were wiped from the mourners' eyes and their faces were washed by the delegation's leader. A feast provided by friends of the bereaved family brought to a close these rites. (Dorsey, 1904: 14)

Relatives of the dead person cut or cropped their hair in mourning, the amount shorn off depending upon the nearness of the relationship to the deceased. A widow or widower continued to mourn after the other relatives had been released from their mourning rites. But finally, after several months, the family of the deceased decided that the surviving spouse had mourned enough. The mourner was released in a rite in which his hair was cut and his body washed, and he was dressed in new clothing by these relatives. They re-equipped the household of the deceased, for his property had been given away in mourning, and ceremonies similar to the one a surviving spouse went through were held for other close relatives so that they too could return to a normal life.

Before Wichita social life was disorganized by the intrusion of the French, Spaniards, and Americans, the ideal family was composed of a woman, her husband, unmarried children, daughters and their husbands, and children, and her sister or sisters (who might be co-wives of her husband). As was true in other societies of this type, the oldest competent woman, known as "mother of the house," was the director and dominant person in the family.[5] At death her oldest daughter replaced her. A matriarchal family such as this lived together in a grass house, were its owners, and formed the basic, co-operative economic unit of Wichita society. As is readily seen, a "mother of the house" might well have considerable control over a son-in-law, even though he was a chief or outstanding warrior. While on the hunt, this family group was broken up to some extent, as married women ordinarily had their own tepees, but the close-knit family camped together. Even the village pattern was duplicated while on the hunt, as the various family groups tried to camp near one another.

[5] Schmitt and Schmitt (n.d.: 11) contains an excellent discussion of Wichita kinship.

264

While the Wichitas were several jumps ahead of Karankawas, Tonkawas, and Comanches in their techniques for exploiting the world, the organization of their society remained rooted in kinship relationships. The way a person behaved and how he acted toward other people continued to be determined primarily by the way in which he was related to them. The Wichitas had a Matri-Hawaiian kinship system similar to that of the Kiowa Apaches and Lipan Apaches, differing from it mainly in minor details. It may be recalled (see p. 122) that a Hawaiian system is characterized by a person's terming all cousins (cross- and parallel) by sibling terms, and by bilateral descent. These features combined with matrilocal residence to form this social type. In such a kinship system generation is emphasized, and lineal and collateral relatives are largely merged or lumped into single categories. One can think of a generation system as one in which a number of horizontal layers, with some exceptions, were superimposed one upon another, like layers of a cake. Among the Wichitas all siblings of a person's father were termed "mother" or "father." A mother's sisters were "mothers," but a mother's brother was not called "father." And all cousins, whether children of father's or mother's siblings were merged as "brothers" or "sisters." In the first descending generation, a man termed his brother's children "our children," but his sister's children he called "nephew" and "niece." A woman termed both her brother's and sister's children "our children." Children of the second descending generation were all "grandchildren," and reciprocally, in the second ascending generation, all grandparents and their siblings were termed "grandparents." The relative age of certain relatives was also taken into account. A mother's sisters were "big" or "little" mothers, depending upon whether they were older or younger than the mother. Similarly, a father's brothers and sisters were "big" or "little" father or mother, depending upon the age relationship of the father to his siblings. Where the merging or lumping of generations is violated, as for a man's sister's children, it may be laid to the maternal emphasis in Wichita society. It is obvious from a glance at such a system that any Wichita was apt to have a large circle of relatives within a village. It is equally apparent that while the range of relationships is wide, relatives on the outer fringes of a person's kin were but vaguely defined.

Like members of a person's bilateral family, relatives by marriage (affinal relatives) were mostly lumped into one or another of two categories—male or female relatives-in-law. The reasons for the exceptions are obvious; a man's wife's sister or a brother's wife would normally be termed "wife," for such they might well become under the sororate and levirate. Interestingly, a wife's sister's husband was referred to as "rival" (Schmitt and Schmitt, n.d.: 7–8):

With matrilocal residence the two men inhabited the same house and were in competition for favors from members of the household; and, since each could call the other's wife, *wife*, they were in theoretical rivalry over spouses. . . . Two women who were married to brothers likewise called each other rival.

Broadly speaking, Wichitas also classified blood (consanguinal) and affinal relatives on the basis of "respect" or "joking" relationships. Persons in adjacent generations maintained a respect relationship, but individuals in the same or alternate generations displayed joking behavior. These contrasting modes of behavior were not of a black-and-white, either-or rigidity. Two blood brothers, for instance, maintained a mildly teasing and joking relationship, whereas a man and another person he called brother (a mother's sister's son, for example) enjoyed an extreme joking relationship. Schmitt and Schmitt gives an illustration of two brothers—in our system distant cousins—and the extreme joking behavior they showed for each other. An informant in the presence of this brother told the Schmitts (n.d.: 24):

I was sleeping up at O's [his brother's] arbor the other night. You know how a horse, when it pull hard, lets go sometimes? Well, I was awake and O and his wife were lying in bed. All of a sudden O let go with one. It made the bed springs go down and touch the ground. O's wife woke up and made a noise 'whiiiiii'. Then she said, 'Must be some mosquitoes around here!' . . . This highly exaggerated story told at the expense of a "brother" caused much amusement. O himself obviously enjoyed the story and did not deny it had happened.

266

Such social conventions generally serve as a means of maintaining social solidarity and effectiveness and achieving co-operation, although the infant science of anthropology cannot always adequately explain why. The joking relationship between a man and his wife's sister, (who was a potential wife through the operation of sororal polygyny and the sororate) for example—was an extensive and continual one. Perhaps this joking relationship presaged the marriage bond which at some future date might unite these people. Grandparents, for another example, were joking relatives, and as such their teasing and joking about sex gave their grandchildren a great deal of needed information about this subject. In the same manner, the respect relationship between a man and his mother-in-law, which amounted to almost complete avoidance, served to prevent possible conflict between these two individuals. Avoidance behavior between these relatives also forestalled the problem of any possible incestuous desires they might have had.

At the beginning of historic times the Wichitas' largest sociopolitical units were the villages. In later times, as the Wichitas were reduced in numbers, emigrated, and were harried by their enemies, the villages consolidated and the Wichita, Waco (Iscani), and Tawakoni tribes emerged. These, as well as the Kichai, continued the progression to become the modern Wichita tribe. Each village had a chief and a subchief, or a first and second chief. Each of these leaders had his own following, however, and in some cases villages may actually have had dual chiefs. These chiefs were elected by the eminent warriors, an informal but powerful group, who could and did restrict any autocratic tendencies on the part of the chiefs. A chief's son had to demonstrate his ability, bravery, generosity, and other virtues, else the warrior group would choose some other person to succeed as chief. Some Wichita myths also relate a political sort of Horatio Alger tale in which poor boys from uninfluential families achieved chieftainship through their bravery in war and other personal attainments and characteristics. The title of the subchief was The-One-Who-Locates, referring to his duty of selecting new or more advantageous village sites. Other village officials were shamans, some of whom were in charge of particular ceremonies, and one of

267

their number was the village crier or announcer. Lesser officials were known as "servants." Their duties were primarily ceremonial, and they were appointed by the chief or the medicine men. It should not be assumed that since there were chiefs—and hence a military aristocracy of sorts—that the desires and needs of ordinary people went unheeded. De Mézières (Bolton, 1914a, II: 203) noted that "their government is democratic, not even excluding the women, in consideration of what they contribute to the welfare of the republic." The duties of the first chief seem to have been primarily associated with those things we term foreign affairs. Officials of various kinds were hardly needed to keep order and harmony within the village, for these functions were performed by the extended maternal kinship units.

Agriculturalists are often thought of as an inherently peaceable folk, much more so than the hunter who lives by the chase and the kill. But to so characterize the Wichitas would be wrong. They entered history as warriors, and until they were finally settled on their Oklahoma reservation they continued as warriors. The Osages and eastern Apaches were probably prehistoric enemies, and Oñate (Bolton, 1916: 259) at the beginning of the seventeenth century noted their bellicose nature:

. . . we began to see people who appeared upon some elevations of a hill. Although hostile to this nation [Escanjaque Apaches] they [the Wichitas] came on, inviting us to battle and war, shouting and throwing dirt into the air, which is the sign used in all this region to proclaim cruel war. Three or four hundred people awaited us in peace, and by the signs which one side was able to make to the other we were assured of friendship. Peace being made, some of these people came to us, and throwing among us some beads which they wore about their necks, proclaimed themselves our friends.

In the eighteenth century and until the French negotiated a mutually advantageous treaty between Wichitas and Comanches, the Comanches were dangerous and feared enemies. When the Wichita peoples entered Texas they invaded the domain of the Lipan Apaches and Tonkawas, and these Indians became their bitter foes. No wonder the principal activity of the men was the warpath!

268

According to what little information is available, their customs of war were typical of those of Plains Indians. Small war parties were led by men who wanted to lead them. A successful warrior had no problem in recruiting men, but if a man was untried or had been previously unsuccessful, he might have difficulty in enlisting others. When a man had decided to lead a war party, he invited a number of his friends to his lodge and explained to them the nature of the expedition he was planning. Subleaders and spies or scouts were designated, and the group then dispersed to prepare for the warpath. The object of these war parties was to take scalps, captives, and horses. The Wichitas counted coup—that is, acquired warrior prestige through touching an enemy's body—but they also won recognition by stabbing and killing. The past deeds of a warrior were symbolized on his robe and tepee cover. The meaning of these symbols was understood by the other warriors, and falsifiers were quickly exposed. During winter evenings warriors also competed with one another in recounting their heroic deeds.

While a warrior was away with a war party, his wife was expected to dress in ragged clothing and avoid any festive social gatherings. If a woman did not respect these customs it was felt that something would happen to her husband. If she behaved decorously and the expedition was successful, her husband's female relatives honored her by washing and dressing her in new clothing. In general, the return of victorious parties set off many days of rejoicing, which included scalp and victory dances. And if a man had returned with an enemy scalp his mother and mother-in-law demonstrated their joy and pride by giving away many of their families' possessions.

As was true among other Plains tribes, the male Wichita was constantly exposed to powerful forces motivating him to enthusiastically embrace the game of war. The way for a man to acquire prestige, wealth, the plaudits of the opposite sex, and the good will of his in-laws was to become a successful warrior. For Wichita culture to survive amidst a host of ugly enemies, the members of its society *had* to want to fight. That they may have viewed it merely as a dangerously-glorified game does not make it less true that defeat would have spelled the doom of Wichita culture. In fact, the unorganized, small-scale, intermittent nature of Wichita warfare was crucial to their decline and eventual impotence. If the Wichitas had been able to marshal numbers of warriors under an organized leadership, how different might have been the history of Texas!

Supernaturalism. "They have no religion, or very little, the most noticeable feature of it being the veneration of fire, together with ridiculous superstitions." (Bolton, 1914a, II: 203–204) It would be difficult to reconcile De Mézières' eighteenth-century accusation with the extensive accounts of the Wichitas' religious system described by Dorsey and Curtis early in the twentieth century were it not for the realization that men often wrap themselves up in their heaviest blankets of provincialism and ethnocentrism when faced with what to them are strange religious beliefs and practices. De Mézières did so and he was wrong.

It is true, of course, that it is more difficult for an outsider to comprehend a people's conception of the supernatural world—the ideas about its gods and goddesses, spirits and demons—than it is for him to understand the forms they use in worship, for the rites observed for the worship, control, or pacification of the supernatural are visible; the beliefs prompting these observances are not. De Mézières saw crude sleight-of-hand tricks, gyrating shamans, and weird dances in which fire played a part. No wonder he thought the Wichita religious system a poor thing. No wonder he failed to realize the all-pervading nature of their beliefs.

The Wichitas believed in a pantheon of gods and goddesses, arranged in a somewhat vaguely-graded hierarchy, and divided into sky and earth, male and female dieties. Chief among the deities was Man-Never-Known-On-Earth, although "Not-Known-To-Man" is descriptively more accurate since he was beyond or above human comprehension or knowledge. It was this supreme power—Kinnikasus—who was responsible for the creation of the universe and all within it. While other deities were specifically invoked for certain purposes, Kinnikasus was generally included in every prayer. Next in importance seems to have been a sun god, known as Man-Reflecting-Light. He was sometimes associated with the supreme power, if not actually merged with him. Such vagueness is common in preliterate mythol-

270

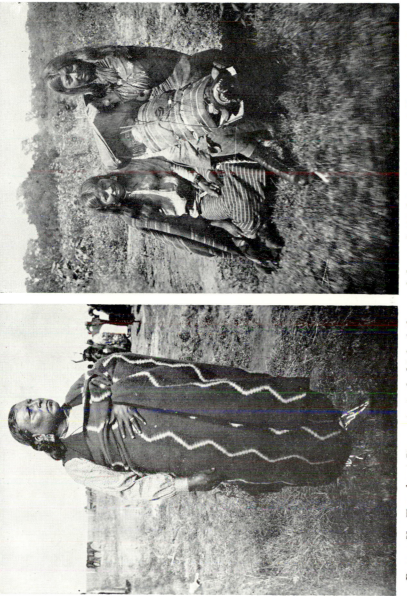

PLATE X. Tawakoni Jim, principal chief of the confederated Wichita, Waco, and Tawakoni tribes (left); Two Wichita women and a baby (right). *Photographs by James Mooney, about 1893. Courtesy of the Smithsonian Institution, Bureau of American Ethnology.*

PLATE XI. Sam Houston, a Caddo, born in 1838. *Photograph by Wells M. Sauyer, 1898. Courtesy of the Smithsonian Institution, Bureau of American Ethnology.*

ogies and theologies. The distress and confusion are ours, for the need for analyzing and drawing sharp distinctions may not be felt by those holding the beliefs. Standing next in the hierarchy was Morning Star—the spirit of the first man created, the deity who ushered in daylight and ruled the other stars. Following in importance were South Star, the guardian of warriors, and North Star, who allowed men to orient themselves on earth. But North Star, or The-Light-Which-Stands-Still, was also feared; he brought death—but in withholding death also bestowed life. Shamans acquired their power from North Star and initiated their ceremonies by smoking to him. The powers of Great Bear were similar to those of Sun and Morning Star; other sky deities of importance were Ghost Bear, Flint-Stone-Lying-Down-Above, The-Light-That-Flies (referring to meteors which were associated with the west and healing), and many other less important ones.

In addition to these celestial male gods or spirits, a moon goddess, Bright Shining Woman, was one of the most important figures in Wichita theology. Moon, the wife of Morning Star, was the first woman created, and so was mother of the universe. Bright Shining Woman was particularly important to women, for she controlled the forces of reproduction and procreation—of humans, animals, and crops. It was natural for women to turn to her as childbirth approached, and for them to hold their infants up joyfully for her blessing. But not all the important gods and goddesses were celestials; the goddess of water, Woman-Having-Powers-In-The-Water (or Woman-Forever-In-The-Water), was associated with Bright Shining Woman and was nearly as important. The water goddess was responsible for the cleansing and healing properties of water, and it was she who provided water to drink and for the crops. She also guarded the virtue of women, helping them to remain chaste while their husbands were away on the hunt or the warpath. During their husbands' absences, wives went to the river as Morning Star rose, to bathe and to pray to the water goddess. Dusk found them again at the riverbank supplicating her. Another terrestrial goddess, Earth Mother, was held to have given birth to everything. She nourished and preserved men, and provided the roots and tubers useful in curing the sick. Naturally enough, those who were about to commence a journey across her surface always directed a prayer to her. There was also a wind god, associated with breath and life, and with the soul. Sometimes, too, wind was thought of as the breath of the spirit of the Earth Mother.

The Wichitas' conception of the universe was very different from ours, for everything—animate and inanimate—possessed a soul or spirit. Some things, such as Bright Shining Woman, had more power— or power which could be influenced by men—than others, but all things contained or could contain more-than-natural attributes. A star could take on the guise of man and appear in a vision or hallucination in order to guide and assist a man in his life's undertakings. Animals often assumed supernatural power and appeared to men in dreams or revelations. But such guardian spirits and forces should not be confused with the great, universally-known sky gods and goddesses. The celestial gods and goddesses might be called social deities, whereas animal spirits appearing to individuals were purely personal. If Christians believed in both an all-powerful God and in personal spiritual helpers—call them personal angels—the situation would be roughly parallel to the beliefs of the Wichitas. They felt that all spiritual knowledge came from revelations, and even that all the knowledge of material advancement came from the supernatural powers.

While the Wichitas did not emphasize the idea of a life after death, they did believe that there would be some sort of continuing existence in a spirit world. Father Morfi (1932: 13) in the eighteenth century went so far as to say that "this belief is no unimportant cause for their valor, because they are persuaded that in the future life they will enjoy happiness in proportion to their deeds of this life on earth." The only people who did not enjoy a pleasant immortality, if we are to rely on more recent accounts of the Wichitas, were those who committed suicide. The souls of these persons hovered near the Wichita heaven, aware of its joys but never able to taste its pleasures.

Analytically Wichita religious practices can be divided into two categories. First, the more important deities who controlled tribal welfare were paid homage to by semisecret religious societies. Individuals propitiated their spiritual guardians in their own private ways by prayers and offerings. Anyone who chose to join these religious societies could do so; there were no other qualifications for membership. These societies performed certain ceremonies and dances which enlisted supernatural assistance in matters of general concern, particularly war. The most important ceremony was the deer dance, conducted by various shamanistic societies. The ceremony itself consisted mainly of the shamans' reciting in song the story of how they had acquired their magical powers. The various societies also demonstrated their powers—principally by sleight-of-hand tricks. During the course of the ceremony a red bean of some undisclosed variety, perhaps the coral bean (Howard, 1957; Campbell, 1958b), was given to those who were preparing to become shamans. This bean produced spasms and finally unconsciousness, during which time the rough jaws of a garfish were scraped over the body of the neophyte to demonstrate that he was insensible to pain. In his unconscious state he normally spoke to some savage animal, who instructed him in how to deal with the supernatural world and gave him power to use in curing. This guardian animal provided the basic material from which the future shaman's songs and practices would be derived. Other features of the deer dance consisted of offerings to various gods, violent purging on the part of the shamans, and a ceremonial foot race by all the members of the tribe to ensure endurance on the warpath. The deer dance was customarily held first in the spring when the green grass had appeared, next when the corn was ripening, and finally when the corn was harvested; it was never held in the winter. The general purpose of it was to purge evil influences and promote health, longevity, and prosperity.

Early in this century Wichitas still remembered fourteen dance societies, three of which were for women. (Curtis, 1930: 43–44) The exact nature of all of them is unknown. One of the more popular dances, performed by a secret society, was known as the Calumet Pipe Sticks. In it feathered pipe stems were borne to a prominent person, or even to some neighboring tribe. The dance was sanctioned by one of the old myths, and its performance was supposed to be of lasting benefit to the tribe. There were also Rain Bundle ceremonies, which apparently ensured the maturation of the corn and the increase of the buffalo. Chanting was the distinguishing feature of this ceremony. Surround-Fire and Small-Robes, both of a similar ritualistic nature, were ceremonies devoted to obtaining supernatural power from certain animals. There were also a number of ceremonies and dances, some performed by women, which ensured the successful return of war parties.

Dancing was the accepted method for supplicating supernatural forces, and as was true with many other American Indians, the games and dances of the Wichitas were held in a ceremonial manner with religious overtones. In common with many primitive agriculturalists, the Tawakoni and Waco subdivisions had first-fruits ceremonies. Sánchez (1926: 266) in the nineteenth century noted:

Among these tribes are found certain superstitious practices that do not exist among the others. The best known of these is the celebration of the so-called *feast of new fruits*. This is reduced to a gathering of all the men in one house, the women not being allowed to enter because they are considered incapable of participating in the sublimities of the mysteries. The men then take strong purgatives and do not partake of the fruits of the newly gathered harvest until their system is well cleansed.

Students of religion often make a distinction between practices that are religious and those that are magical. They define as religious those that are supplicating, worshiping, and beseeching, whereas practices that are magical are those believed to be able automatically to force supernatural powers to react in favorable ways. Certainly the dividing line between the two is a tenuous and vague one; assuredly the Wichitas drew no such line of demarcation. They attempted to influence the supernatural world both religiously and magically, though it may well be that they looked upon the performances of the semisecret societies as predominantly religious, whereas the individual, personal attempts they considered both religious and magical. The Wichitas' methods of witchcraft are instructive for one type of magical practice. Slow death of another person, for example, could be accomplished by obtaining a lock of the victim's hair and placing it in a hole of a tree. As the cavity of the tree slowly grew shut, so

274

would the victim slowly wither and die. A quicker way to kill was to place the lock of hair in the mouth of a toad and then kill the toad. This contagious magic is of course effective in a society where all believe in it; to die of magical witchcraft requires only that a person be firmly convinced of its efficacy, and that it is being used against him. Unfortunately, the pages of the past here become blank, so we are ignorant of the countermagical witchcraft which the Wichitas may have practiced.

A Wichita child learned about the many deities of the pantheon not in church or in school, but from an elderly man who was especially invited to the grass house to instruct him. This old man was a person who throughout his life had led an exemplary life—he had been brave, kind, modest, and decent. His recitation of the tales of the ancient world and its heroes was itself a form of prayer. The myths he related were divided into four parts: the first concerned the origin of the world; the second, its transformation; the third, its present existence; and last, the tales which foretold the end of the present world. The myths of the first two eras were thought of as the "old" or "true" tales, while the present existence was spoken of as the "new" era. The tales of the first era told of the creation of the world, in which the land appeared floating on the water. The first man and woman were created and they were given an ear of corn and bows and arrows. But the earth was still dark and it remained so until three deer had been slain by the man. As daylight flooded the world, populated villages and animals appeared. The first man and woman then went from village to village teaching the people how to conduct themselves, and when they had completed this task the first man became Morning Star, the first woman, Bright Shining Star (Moon).

In the second era the people scattered over the earth and they learned again of their powers. Various groups gave themselves names, and turned into the animals whose names they had taken. But this was a period of wrongdoing, and some forgot their duties, both animals and celestial beings. In culmination, a woman gave birth to four monsters whose heads reached to the sky. To destroy them and the wrong and wilful world, a deluge was sent. Two persons survived the flood, and they were once again given an ear of corn and bows and arrows. They were taught various skills, including the proper method of constructing the grass lodge. These two people taught their children about the ancient world, and their children carried out their instructions and were given power by the animals, and were taught the secrets of the animals. They were also told that they would die, but one person who had died returned from Spirit Land, so they learned about the other world, and thus obtained their belief in a life after death.

The Wichitas believed that the fourth period was rapidly approaching, and in a sense it was an accurate prediction of the decline of their culture. They believed that in this period the things needed for life would no longer be available, that people would no longer be able to get anything done. As the end approached, weeds would grow in place of corn, and the animals, trees, and even running water would talk to men. Incest would occur, no more children would be born, and—a sure indication of degeneracy—they would lose their judgment. The animals would also fail to reproduce, and ultimately the world would become uninhabitable. But when the end arrived it was believed that some great star would select an eminent man to explain to the people what was happening. All the stars and the sun would become human again as in the earliest days, and then another cycle of four eras would begin.

Up and down the eastern margins of the plains, in the prairies and in the river valleys, there had been a number of tribes who both farmed and hunted bison. Pawnees, Osages, the Central Siouans (Kansas, Missouri, Oto, Omaha, Ponca, and Iowa) were the southern tribes who practiced this economy (Kroeber, 1947: 84–86) And the Wichitas may be grouped with these, although their affiliations with the Southeastern Caddo were also close, as becomes apparent in the following chapter.

Their combination of hunting and gardening was apparently the most successful type of adjustment to be made in an environment marked by cyclic droughts. With the addition of the horse to Plains

Indian life, however, the advantages of their economy waned. What the inroads of the mounted hunters did not do to hasten the disintegration of their way of life, ravaging epidemics introduced by Europeans did. The story of the historic Wichitas, then, is one of almost continuous decline, of movement from old, scattered villages to new, consolidated ones, of tremendous population reduction, of eventual impotence before their conquerors.

CHAPTER II

The Caddo Confederacies: East Texas

> One of our Indians went on to announce our coming;
> the chiefs and youth, whom we met a league from the
> village, received us with the calumet, which they
> gave us to smoke; some led our horses by the bridle;
> others, as it were, carried us in triumph, taking us for
> spirits and people of another world.
>
> All the village being assembled, the women, as is
> their wont, washed our head and feet with warm
> water, and then placed us on a platform covered with
> a very neat, white mat; then followed banquets, calu-
> met-dances and other public rejoicings, day and
> night.
>
> Father Anastasius Douay (1687)

THE CADDO CONFEDERACIES of east Texas, despite their collapse
before Texas became a state, were the most important of the state's
natives from several points of view, and they deserve a prominent
place among Texas Indians. They achieved a level of cultural development unsurpassed by other Texas Indians, possessing compara-
tively advanced techniques and tools for exploiting the resources of
nature. In short, the Caddoes were highly successful agriculturalists,

279

a fact not true of other Texas Indians, with the possible exception of their Wichita relatives. The Caddoes' assured and abundant food supply made possible a relatively dense population and an elaboration and complexity in social institutions which were impossible for the offal-eating Coahuiltecans or the buffalo-hunting Apaches. The intricate cultural structure that grew from this ample subsistence base is as fascinating and in many ways as exotic as any known in the Americas.

The Caddoes occupied a region which was a bone of contention first between the French and Spanish, then the Spanish and Americans, and finally the Republic of Mexico and the United States. By virtue of this they are also of considerable historical and political importance. But to many Texans their greatest significance lies in the fact that the state name was derived from the Hasinai confederation of Caddoes. The tribes of this confederation called each other *Tayshas*, meaning "allies" or "friends," and the Spaniards, to whom it was also applied, soon came to employ the word for these and other friendly natives. Probably the pronunciation of the term was closer to "Tayshas" or "Taychas" than to "Texas."[1]

Origins and Early History. The modern Oklahoma Caddoes are considered to be a single tribe, but when they first appeared in the historic arena there were more than two dozen tribes, most of them joined loosely together into one or another of three confederacies. The largest of these was the Hasinai (variously called Asenai, Assoni, Asenay, Cenis by earlier explorers and writers), occupying the upper reaches of the Neches and Angelina river valleys. Originally the Hasinais appear to have been composed of eight tribes—the Hainai, Neches, Nacogdoche, Nacono (or Nacao, Naconish), Namidish (Nabiti, Nawidish), Nasoni, Anadarko, "and perhaps Nabedache, two of which, the Nasoni and Anadarko, were not reckoned as original Hasinai tribes while two others, the Nacono and Namidish, were represented by divisions outside of the Hasinai." (Swanton, 1942: 12)

[1] Swanton, 1942: 3. This work, a voluminous source of information on Caddo history and culture, provides the main source of information for this chapter. Parsons (1941) has also been extensively used.

280

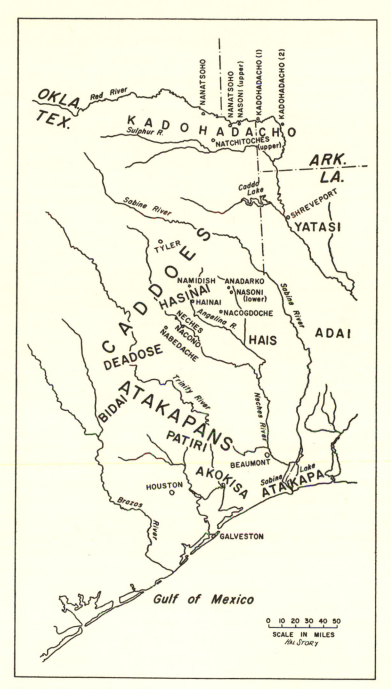

MAP 4.   Texas Tribes of the Southeast Culture Area

The second group, the Kadohadachos or Caddo proper, occupied the great bend of the Red River in northeastern Texas and southwestern Arkansas. When visited by Europeans in 1687, four tribes made up this confederacy: the Kadohadacho proper, the Nanatsoho, the Nasoni, and the upper Natchitoches. The Cahinnios of the Ouachita River in Arkansas are sometimes included with this group, and in later times doubtless joined them. (See Map 4.)

The third group, known as the Natchitoches, lived in the vicinity of the present, namesake town, Natchitoches, Louisiana. Between the Natchitoches and the Kadohadachos was an independent tribe, the Yatasi, which split during the early historic period, one segment joining the Natchitoches, the other the Kadohadachos. Other independent Caddo tribes were the Adais, north of the Natchitoches on Red River, and the Eyeish (or Hais) near San Augustine, Texas.

These tribes and confederacies shared a common language, Caddo, with but minor dialectal differences separating them. The Caddoan linguistic stock, named for the Caddo, includes three other mutually unintelligible languages—Pawnee, Wichita, and Kitsai (or Kichai). Caddo is the most divergent Caddoan language, while the deviation among the other three is about equidistant one from another. (Lesser and Weltfish, 1932: 1) Despite their linguistic affiliations with tribes to the north and west, the Caddoes faced east in a cultural sense, sharing a distinctive cultural tradition with the Creeks, Chickasaws, Choctaws, Cherokees, and Natchez. The Caddoes were more like the Natchez of the lower Mississippi than the others of this Southeast culture area, and the Natchez are regarded as one of the most typical and representative of these tribes. (Kroeber, 1947: 62)

That there was a connection between the tribes of the Southeast culture area and the cultures of the Circum-Caribbean area is apparent. But when, for how long, and what the nature of this association was, is poorly understood. The similarities were so extensive that it seems highly improbable that they could have resulted from sporadic contact between alien cultures. There must have been a migration of people from the Caribbean to some point on the Gulf Coast. It has already been suggested in Chapter 1 that this migration was seaborne and did not come overland through Texas.

282

All the complexities and relationships of Caddo archeology, to say nothing of that of the Southeast in general, have not yet been resolved, but enough is known to draw some fairly broad conclusions. First, Caddo civilization was no Johnny-come-lately. Its beginnings may well go back a thousand years before the beginning of the written history of the region. Second, there are indications that the culture of the historic Caddoes was in some respects the disintegrating shadow of something which had once been more spectacular. By historic times, for instance, the Caddoes had ceased building the imposing flat-topped earthen temple mounds which so conspicuously marked the cultures of their archeologic ancestors. The same comments have been made about the Natchez—that they too were a decadent relict of something which was once more splendid. Perhaps primitive farming techniques had exhausted the soil; possibly climatic factors were to blame. Whatever the cause or causes, by the sixteenth century the members of the Southeast culture area were apparently slipping backward into a more primitive, a less productive and less highly organized, way of life.

From what is known and from what may be reasonably inferred, it is probable that sometime before A.D. 500 a vigorous and advanced people had established themselves somewhere along the Gulf Coast of the United States. In this new land the transplanted culture was highly successful; the people multiplied and spread, perhaps by conquest. In time this cultural pattern spread to the Trinity River in Texas on the west, to the Atlantic Coast on the east, and its influence was felt hundreds of miles to the north. To archeologists this cultural development is known as the Mississippi pattern. It was characterized by a well-developed, productive agriculture, and in consequence, by what must have been a rather high population density. Large ceremonial centers, clustering around temple mounds, were one of its conspicuous features. These mounds vary considerably in size and shape, but they are always earthen, usually square or rectangular with flat tops, and ordinarily have a stairway on at least one side. The prodigious labor that went into building them suggests that subsistence operations were productive enough to afford a considerable proportion of the people time to work on the mounds. They

283

further suggest that there was a well-developed political system which could induce, direct, and organize the populace into fashioning these vast structures. It is believed that these mounds were used for religious ceremonials, which were conducted by priestly castes, and it is assumed that society was stratified or otherwise divided along occupational, hereditary, or similar lines.[2]

The lands of the Caddoes were geographically, as they were culturally, a single, uniform region. All of east Texas is subhumid, low-lying land, has a mild climate, and is part of the coastal plain physiographic region. The actual coastal strip, or coastal prairie, extends inland less than a hundred miles and was not occupied by Caddoan-speakers, but by Atakapan tribes of a different linguistic grouping. The territory of the Caddoes was in that part of the state familiarly known as the "piney woods." This is gently rolling country, sloping toward the Gulf. Before white men despoiled much of it, the uplands supported vast forests of loblolly, longleaf, and shortleaf pines. In its many valleys were groves of the many species of hardwoods typical of forested lands in the Mississippi Valley and eastward. There were many places, particularly in the alluvial fill of the valleys, where an abundance of agricultural produce could be grown with relatively little effort, and throughout the land wild-plant foods were abundant. This region also supported much wild game—black bear, deer, and toward the west where the forests thinned out, buffalo and other grazing animals. It was a productive, rich land for the Caddoes.

The Caddoes were first encountered by Europeans early in October, 1541. Hernando de Soto and his army were then in southern Arkansas among a non-Caddoan people they called Cayas or Tanico. De Soto sent out from this province a small force to reconnoiter the province to the south known as Tula (probably the Cahinnio of later history). The advance party was attacked with considerable vigor, though unsuccessfully, but the main army met with no opposition as they invested the town of Tula. Once the party was in the town, however, the Indians attacked it in three different squadrons and with great fury. But against Spanish armor and mounted men, the

[2] Suhm *et al.* (1954: 144–161) contains a good condensed discussion of Caddo prehistory.

long wooden lances and bows and arrows of the natives were ineffectual.

During the battle one cavalier climbed to an upper room of a building which served as a granary, and found five women huddled in a corner. The Spanish code of honor did not permit the wanton slaughter of women, and he made motions to this effect as best he could. Realizing the soldier was alone, the five demoniac savages rushed upon him, and seized him by the arms, leg, neck, and penis. In his struggles to free himself one leg crashed through the flimsy floor, reducing the soldier to helplessness. Although his life was in peril, he dared not cry out, since these were but women. At this crucial moment another soldier entered the lower room. He saw the leg dangling from above and was preparing to take a swipe at it with his sword when something prompted him to investigate. Climbing to the upper floor he immediately realized the predicament of his comrade and decided it was the better part of valor to discard his code of honor. (Varner and Varner, 1951: 455–456)

The Spaniards soon withdrew from the land of Tula, but in the following year Luis de Moscoso, De Soto's successor, again penetrated Caddo territory. This time they encountered a group called the Amaye some twenty miles east of the Red River, and then the Naguatex or Nawatesh on the Red River itself. This last province was one of the most flourishing the army had passed through. The Spaniards plundered the natives' granaries in July, and on their return in October found that they had been completely replenished. The Spaniards swung southwest after leaving this people and passed through Hasinai territory. Farther on, they met the Eyeish, then the Guasco, Naquuiscoca, and Nacacahoz, which took them to the Daycao River—apparently the Trinity. More primitive Indians, probably Tonkawas or Atakapans, occupied the far bank. (Swanton, 1942: 31–32)

Following these early and generally unfriendly encounters, Europeans had little further contact with Caddoan tribes for almost a hundred and fifty years. These Indians were not totally lost sight of, however, for in 1650 the expedition of Hernán Martín and Diego del Castillo, with the guidance of some Jumanos, journeyed to the out-

285

skirts of the province of Tejas. A "lieutenant" of the Tejas "king" paid Castillo a visit, but the Spaniards did not proceed farther. (Bolton, 1912: 9–10; Swanton, 1942: 36) The French explorer La Salle was the next European to encounter Caddoes. From Fort St. Louis, La Salle sent out parties to find the Mississippi River, whose mouth the expedition had so badly overshot. The first party left the little fort on the coast in the spring of 1686 and in early summer reached a Hasinai town, probably Nabedache. The French continued their exploration beyond this town, but La Salle and his nephew fell ill, and the party was forced to turn back. The Hasinais were so friendly and agreeable that several Frenchmen deserted to join them.[3]

In January of the following year, La Salle and sixteen others again set out for the Mississippi. But La Salle was murdered by some of his companions before they had reached the main Hasinai towns. The survivors continued on through the principal Hasinai town and on to the Nasoni, where further discord among members of the party led to more violence. The survivors returned to the main Hasinai town, and some of them accompanied their Indian friends on a war party against the Kanoatino (probably the Wichitas). A few of the French set out for and eventually reached the Mississippi; others returned to Fort St. Louis.

News that the French were present in Texas soon reached the Spaniards and almost immediately an expedition under Alonso de León set out from Monclova (March 23, 1689) to visit the razed French fort and to capture any surviving Frenchmen. This expedition failed to penetrate Caddo territory, although it did meet a small party of Hasinais. Continued rumors that the French were present in Caddo territory, and, in fact, the expedition of Henri de Tonti to rescue any survivors of La Salle's ill-fated fort, stimulated the Spanish to further efforts in the lands of the Caddoes. In the spring of 1690 an expedition left Monclova, again under the command of Alonso de León, and including four friars led by Father Damian Massanet. A mission, San Francisco de los Tejas, was established in Hasinai territory, and more were proposed by De León and Massanet.

[3] Cox, 1905, I: 231–236. This volume is also the source for the quotation used at the beginning of this chapter (pp. 249–250).

Early in 1691, Domingo Terán de los Rios was empowered to establish four missions among the Kadohadachos, two among the Hasinais, and one on the Guadalupe outside Caddo territory. In the meantime, in 1690, Fray Francisco Casañas de Jesús María, had founded another mission, Santísimo Nombre de María, on the Neches River about five miles east of the original mission. Terán arrived at San Francisco de los Tejas in August of 1691, and already the natives were becoming hostile to the teachings of the priests. Nevertheless, Terán set out in the fall to explore the country; the Kadohadacho confederacy was reached and the Red River explored. But because the party lacked supplies, none of the four missions could be established. And Spanish interest in these east Texas missions was slackening, principally because the French threat seemed to be less than had been anticipated, and the Caddoes were proving much more difficult to convert than had been supposed. In 1693, Captain Gregorio de Salinas Varona, who had been dispatched with supplies for the missions, found that the missionaries were about to abandon the country. Santísimo Nombre de María had already been deserted because of a flood, and Casañas and his companions were at the other mission. Massanet sent back a recommendation that the mission be abolished, but before this could become official policy, Massanet and his fellow workers were forced by the natives to forsake their mission. In March of 1694 the viceroy of Mexico formally recognized the state of affairs by ordering the abandonment of the province of Tejas.

But by the end of the century the French were establishing colonies in Louisiana and were soon exploring the lower Mississippi. They journeyed far up the Red River, and throughout the early years of the eighteenth century were increasingly active among the Caddoes. By August, 1715, the Spanish had decided to re-establish the missions in east Texas, and late in September Diego Ramón set out to reoccupy the region. Instead of rebuilding the Mission of San Francisco de los Tejas, another site four leagues farther inland and on the other bank of the Neches River was chosen. Here a mission was established under Fray Hidalgo to serve the Neches, Nabedache, Nacogdoches, and Nocono tribes. Nearby the Mission Nuestra Señora de la Purísima Concepción was established among the Hasinais under

287

Father Vergara, some twenty-odd miles northeast of the first mission. Because of its strategic location this mission became the headquarters of the province of Texas. A mission was also started for the Nacogdoches and Nacao, called Nuestra Señora de Guadalupe, in the Nacogdoche village, and another, San José de los Nazonis, for the Nadaco (Anadarko) and Nasoni a few miles from the present village of Cushing.

While Spain was improving its position the French were not idle. Their post at Natchitoches was strengthened in 1717, and in 1718 Bernard de la Harpe was empowered to build a post in Kadohadacho territory and to carry on explorations in this region. He soon built a stockaded post close by the Nasoni village on the south bank of the Red River. Shortly after the post was completed La Harpe was told by Indians that France and Spain were at war. In 1719 a French party attacked the Adaes mission, and as a consequence the Spaniards withdrew to the far side of the Trinity, and soon to the *villa* of San Fernando de Bejar, site of present San Antonio.

With Spanish competition diminished, La Harpe explored to the northwest and soon was in contact with the Wichitas. This and other activities of the French induced the Spaniards to send another expedition under Marquis de San Miguel de Aguayo to east Texas. In the summer of 1721 they crossed the Trinity and were met by a Hasinai chief and eight other chiefs. In midsummer the commander of the French forces, Louis Juchereau de St. Denis met Aguayo on the banks of the Neches at the Mission of San Francisco de los Tejas. Aguayo agreed to observe the truce which was then in force between the two countries if the French would withdraw completely from Texas, including Los Adaes. Aguayo then crossed the Angelina and proceeded to the Mission of La Purísima Concepción, the only mission not yet destroyed, and subsequently built a fort and re-established the mission at Los Adaes (near present Robeline, Louisiana). Los Adaes became the capital of the province of Texas, and continued so for more than fifty years. But despite the vigorous re-establishment of Spanish domination in east Texas, the missions were a failure. In 1731 three of them were refounded in or near San Antonio.

Los Adaes was now an isolated post in east Texas, and the fact that the French post at Natchitoches was also isolated resulted in friendly, neighborly relations between the two. While there were occasionally official hard feelings—as when the French moved their post to the west side of the Red River in 1735—the inhabitants of these lonely posts themselves never seem to have been unfriendly. French influence grew, however, at the expense of the Spanish, because the French maintained a liberal trade-policy with the Indians, in contrast to the narrow policy of the Spaniards. The competition between these two great European nations ended in 1762 when the French ceded Louisiana to Spain. With the competition of the French removed, there was little purpose in supporting the presidio and mission of Los Adaes, and in 1772 the decision was made to move the capital to San Antonio de Bejar. In 1803, after having passed once again to France, Louisiana was purchased by the United States.

Appearance and Dress. Almost all Europeans, upon first encountering Caddoes, were moved to make rather startled remarks about their appearance and behavior. Garcilaso de la Vega, one of the chroniclers of the De Soto Expedition, for example, observed that the Tula (Cahinnio) were "naturally well featured" but made themselves "hideous" by artificial cranial deformation in which their heads were elongated and made to "taper off toward the top," and by tattooing. (Varner and Varner, 1951: 457–458) Artificial cranial deformation may not have been universally practiced by Caddoes, but the custom was an old one, observed prehistorically in this area. At the Sanders site near the Red River in Lamar County, for example, multiple burials have been found in which the skulls show that strong frontal deformation was in vogue. (Krieger, 1946: 265 and Plate 21)

Almost a century and a half after the De Soto Expedition, Joutel (Cox, 1905, II: 139–140), one of La Salle's men, reacted to the Caddoes in much the same way as had De la Vega, finding their tattooes particularly repulsive. The Caddoes used needles or other sharp-pointed objects to prick the skin until the blood flowed, and then rubbed powdered charcoal into the wounds. When the wounds healed, the charcoal remaining under the skin made striking tattooes. They tattooed "scores or streaks on their faces, from the top of the forehead down the nose to the tip of the chin," and intricate plant and animal designs were tattooed on their bodies. Joutel thought the women "would not be disagreeable did they adhere to nature" but they were tattooed as much as the men, perhaps more extensively, adding tattooes at the corners of the eyes, "and on other parts of their bodies, whereof they make more particular show on their bosom, and those who have the most are reckoned the handsomest, though that pricking in that part be extremely painful to them."

In addition to tattooing, faces and bodies were painted for special occasions. The women painted themselves "from the waist up to the shoulders in various colored streaks, particularly the breasts." (Casañas, 1927: 285) Men painted their bodies for war, especially with a vermilion color combined with bear grease. Shells, bones, feathers, and pretty stones were worn in the ears, nose, hair, and as necklaces, armlets, wristlets, and at the knees. The Caddoes forsook many of these old ornamental materials when glass beads, metal trinkets, and other gew-gaws became obtainable from European traders.

Hair styles varied from tribe to tribe, and even among the members of one tribe. Commonly a man's hair was allowed to grow about two inches long all over his head except for a small patch on top. The hair on this spot was encouraged to grow to waist length, and feathers were attached to it. Another popular style was a roached form in which all the hair was shaved or plucked out except for a narrow band extending over the head from the forehead to the neck. The hair was greased, and for special occasions the down from swans or ducks was stuck to it, or the hair was dyed. The hair styling of the women was much simpler than that of the men. The hair was parted in the middle and "carefully combed, and dressed like a queue." After gathering it into a knot, "they tie it into a curious knot at the neck with a red rabbit skin which they have colored for the purpose with an herb which grows throughout the whole region." (Espinosa, 1927: 177)

From the European point of view, the most disquieting behavior of Caddoes was their custom of weeping and wailing when they met strangers. Not only women but men too seem to have wept a greet-

290

ing to strangers. Caddo women also wept in the face of impending death, and the French and Spanish soon learned to watch for tears that might presage their own death. The shedding of tears is, of course, an unlearned emotional reaction. Infants and adults of both sexes can cry, but many cultures have restricted, limited, or channeled crying in various ways. Welcoming strangers with tears—and meeting a strange human being is somewhat of an emotional shock—is probably no less natural than virtually prohibiting adult males from crying, as many cultures do. In fact, the proscription on male tears, insofar as tears clear the air and relieve tension, is not only unnatural but probably harmful. What won't the male do in order not to be thought a sissy!

The leaders of French and Spanish expeditions were often greeted with considerable pomp and ceremony. When, for example, La Salle first visited the Hasinais (apparently the Nabedache tribe), he was met by several chiefs and a retinue of warriors, bearing a calumet, or ceremonial pipe. The French party was ceremoniously escorted to the village where La Salle "was received as if in triumph and lodged in the great chief's cabin. There was a great concourse of people, the young men being drawn out and under arms, relieving one another night and day, and, besides, loading us with presents and all kinds of provisions." (Cox, 1905, I: 232) Henri de Tonti, after learning of La Salle's death, journeyed overland from the Illinois country to search for survivors. When he encountered the Kadohadachos, their chief, who was a woman, and other important persons of this "nation" paid him a visit. The woman wept over him, demanding that he seek revenge for the death of her husband and another man who had died at the hands of the Osages. Tonti was forced to agree, and then he was escorted to their temple. "After the priests had invoked their God for a quarter of an hour they conducted me to the cabin of their chief. Before entering they washed my face with water, which is a ceremony among them." (Cox, 1905, I: 46)

Tanned deerskin provided the material for most Caddo clothing. These Indians were expert tanners, using deer and buffalo brains in a process that turned out a lustrous black leather. Garments were fringed or decorated with small white seeds, pierced and sewed on.

291

Moccasins, leggings, breechclouts, and shirts of deerskin or buffalo-hide were worn in winter. In summer the men often stripped down to the comfortable breechclout. Dress-up clothing was richly painted and ornamented, and some of their special clothing was made of turkey feathers. Women also wore breechclouts under their clothing, made of grass and straw. Like other Indians of the Southeast, the more socially prominent Caddo women wore skirts fashioned from cloth woven from nettles or made from mulberry bark.

Subsistence and Material Culture. The Caddoes were agriculturists first and foremost and, except in infrequent drought years, raised an abundance of garden produce. Their principal crops were corn, beans, squash, sunflower seed, and tobacco. Two varieties of corn were raised, an early-maturing variety called "little corn" by the Louisiana French, and "flour corn" that matured later. The little corn was planted toward the end of April after the rainy season was over, and it matured in about a month and a half or less. Following its harvest, flour corn was planted in the same fields. It matured in about three months, so the Caddoes were able to raise two crops of corn on the same piece of ground in a year's time. The best ears of corn were selected and hung in their houses in a place where they would become well smoked. Enough of this seed corn was preserved as a safeguard against crop failure for two successive years' plantings. Beans were also an important article in the diet, and they had five or six varieties, including pole beans.

Both men and women worked in the gardens, the men doing the heavier tasks and leaving much of the remainder to the women. As with other Southeasterners, putting in the crops was a communal enterprise. Groups of men and groups of women, working separately, prepared and planted the garden plots. They began with the plot of the politico-religious leader (the *xinesi*), the only person who did not do any productive labor. Then they planted the crops of the next highest officials, and "in this way they continue working from the highest to the humblest until each has planted what he needs for the year." (Casañas, 1927: 217)

Considering the excellent results achieved, planting was done with surprisingly crude tools. Hoes fashioned either from the shoulder blade of a buffalo or from wood were virtually the only tools used. Since such tools could be used effectively only on lighter soils, there must have been many localities considered unsuitable for farming by Caddoes that are productive with modern machinery. Fire was at least occasionally employed to burn over old fields and perhaps to assist in clearing new ones.

Animals never supplied more than a subsidiary part of the food supply. Their only domesticated animals were dogs, and they were eaten only in times of extreme scarcity or possibly on a few ritual occasions. Caddoes were adept imitators of deer, and a hunter disguised with the antlers and hide of a deer was able to approach his quarry closely, and even to attract it to himself.

After the Caddoes acquired horses, buffalo were easier to hunt and hence figured more prominently in their subsistence. They had always hunted buffalo, however, even though some of the more easterly tribes had to go considerable distances to find sizable herds. Bears were one of the favored game animals. They were hunted primarily in the winter months, as were the buffalo, because in this season the bears were fat, the buffalo more numerous, and the crops required no attention from the men. Bears were hunted mainly for their fat, which, rendered, could be stored in pots for long periods. Unlike Plains Indians, the Caddoes used dogs to hunt buffalo and found them particularly useful for routing out bears.

Besides these animals, the Caddoes made use of a large assortment of small birds, mammals, and fish. Wild hogs (javelinas?) were hunted in early days and in later times razorbacks were probably obtainable. They also hunted prairie chickens, ducks, turkeys, other birds, rabbits, mice, and snakes. Fish were used extensively, with no known limitations on variety or size. They were caught in a number of ways, and it is interesting to note that the Caddoes employed trotlines in a manner almost identical to that used today in the same region. Short lines were hung about a foot apart from a long line, each having a hook baited with "dough bait" or meat. One end of the line was weighted down, the other tied to a boat or a tree. Lines were run several times a day, and good-sized fish were taken in this manner—as they are today. It seems likely that the trotline method

293

of fishing is another custom modern America borrowed from her aboriginal inhabitants.

Many varieties of nuts were obtained from the hardwood forests—pecans, acorns, chestnuts, and others. In season many wild fruits were collected, including plums, cherries, mulberries, blackberries, and grapes, whose flavor particularly impressed Europeans. These were the more important fruits, but others were eaten also, to say nothing of various roots and tubers.

Corn was roasted, presumably by placing the green, unhusked ears in a bed of ashes. It was also boiled, either alone or with beans or other vegetables to make a kind of succotash. Dried corn was ground, as were nuts and seeds, in large mortars made from hollowed-out tree trunks. In concert, the women of a household pounded the corn with large wooden pestles. After the pounding, the coarse flour was passed through sieves made of cane. This flour was used in soups and gruel. For the very fine corn meal used for bread and tortillas, the coarse flour was winnowed in small baskets. Corn was preserved by storing it in baskets in which ashes were placed to discourage weevils and other vermin. It has already been noted that seed corn was hung in a smoky part of the house to preserve it, and perhaps some of the corn intended for food was also preserved in this way. Fish were preserved by smoking them, and the meat of animals killed far from home was jerked, either by sun-drying or fire-drying.

Caddo houses were similar if not identical to those of their relatives, the Wichitas, which have already been described in some detail. They varied considerably in size, depending upon the number of occupants and their position in the social hierarchy. Some Kadohadachos seem to have plastered the outside of their grass houses with mud, a common custom among other Southeast tribes.

Housebuilding was, like many other important activities, a communal affair. When a family decided it was in need of a house, the official, known as a *caddi,* was notified. This official set a date for construction and delegated subofficials (*tammas*) to select persons to take part in the project. Some men were appointed to bring poles for the dwelling, others were put in charge of various phases of the work, a number of women were delegated to bring a special coarse

294

grass with which to cover the house, and other people were assigned various other tasks. The *tammas* slept at the site of the new dwelling the night before it was to be erected, and at dawn they called the party together to raise the house. The *caddi* acted as an overseer, and the *tammas* carried supple switches with which they hastened the slow or the tardy. Men who were late, for example, were switched across the breast; women were whipped on their bare shoulders for similar delinquency, but all in a spirit of good will.

The men who had been directed to bring poles came soon after the call went out at dawn, each placing his pole in one of the holes which had already been dug. In the center of this circle of poles they temporarily erected a tall knobby pole to which a crosspiece was fastened at the top. Two men climbed the pole and, working together, lassoed the tops of the poles in the outer circle, pulled them into the center, and tied them together. Other men quickly began to cover the framework with other timbers, and as soon as they had finished, another crew began to apply the thick grass covering, working from the ground upward. So quickly and expertly was the work done that shortly after noon, the grass figure, which always topped a house, was in place and the temporary center pole was ready to be cut off at the ground level.

While the house-raising was in progress the family who were to live in it were preparing a feast of corn and venison. As soon as the house was completed, the workers were fed, first the *caddi*, then the *tammas*, and on down to the lowliest worker. The spirit of such house-raising bees was a festive and congenial one. The gorged workers departed happy in the satisfaction of a job done with dexterity. (Espinosa, 1927: 154–155)

Temples were like ordinary dwellings, though larger, and in early historic times some of them were still reared on the mounds erected by the ancestors of the Caddoes. Fires were kept going at all times in the center of the houses, and if by accident they were extinguished, they were relighted from the temple fire, which was never allowed to die. In 1690, Massanet (Bolton, 1916: 377–378), visiting the house of a Nabedache chief, described it as being furnished with ten beds that occupied one-half of the interior. The beds were made of reed

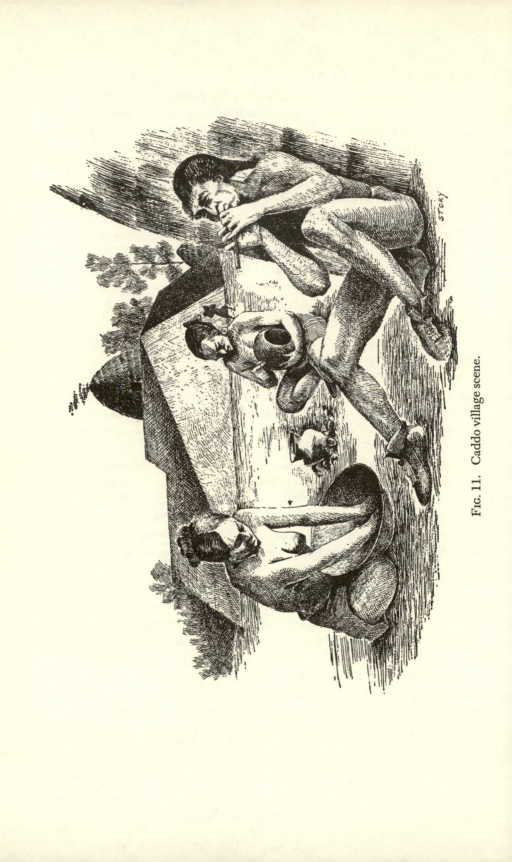

Fig. 11. Caddo village scene.

matting laid on forked sticks, and over this framework were spread buffaloskins. "At the head and foot of the bed is attached another carpet forming a sort of arch, which, linked with a very brilliantly colored piece of reed matting, makes what bears some resemblance to a very pretty alcove." The remainder of the dwelling was taken up with shelves for reed baskets filled with corn, nuts, acorns, and beans, a row of pottery jars, and "six wooden mortars for pounding the corn in rainy weather (for, when it is fair, they grind it in the court-yard)." Ordinary people had, of course, smaller and plainer quarters.

In addition to the temples there were a number of other special buildings. Among the Nabedaches (and probably among all Cad-does) was a smaller structure across a patio from the house of the governor (*xinesi*). This was for the occupancy of only the captains when the governor called them into session. On another side of the patio was a still smaller house in which the "pages" of the captains were lodged while their masters were in conference. From the fore-going it is clear that the dwellings of political leaders formed a central point, but it does not seem that these were in the center of anything resembling a town. Early Spanish and French documents are strange-ly silent on the settlement pattern, but it is assumed that various kin units tended to build their homes near one another, forming a series of hamlets.

The Caddoes are perhaps best known in anthropological circles for their fascinating and varied pottery. Certainly the fame of their pottery is justified, for it was among these Indians that the technical and esthetic aspects of Southeastern pottery reached its climax. Yet, because pottery is virtually indestructible (at least potsherds are), it probably gives us a false impression about the Caddoes' creative and artistic abilities in less durable handicrafts. We know, for ex-ample, that they manufactured all sorts of reed and basketry con-tainers and mats. Early visitors described them as "pretty," "nice," "very brilliantly colored," and Hidalgo (1928: 56) was favorably impressed with their "very curious rugs of reed of different colors which could be used in ladies' drawing rooms." Unfortunately no reed mats or similar handicrafts survive. European articles soon replaced these things and their manufacture became a forgotten art.

297

The Caddoes were also well known in the early days for their bows, one of their important articles of export. The type of bow was apparently no better than others, but the material of which they were made—*bois d'arc* or Osage orange—was superior. They must have made a considerable number of various tools and containers which we are ignorant of. It is known that gourds were used for rattles, and that musical instruments such as flutes and flageolets were made of bird bones and hollow reeds. Drums were made from buried hollow logs, or were pottery jars partly filled with water, over which a hide was stretched.

Social Organization. Caddo men assisted in many tasks which would have been beneath the dignity of their Wichita counterparts, not to mention other Texas Indians. They helped prepare and cultivate the gardens, gangs laboring together. But they had nothing further to do with the women's gardens. They also did most of the housebuilding, and all of the hunting and warfare was exclusively in their hands. They made their own bows and arrows, the hoes used in the gardens, moccasins, and other personal equipment. The women helped cultivate the gardens, and the rest of the care of them fell on their shoulders. They did all the housework, prepared the food, did most if not all of the gathering of nuts, berries, and other wild foods. They also brought in the game their husbands had killed when it had been shot a reasonably short distance from their homes; otherwise, the men lugged their kill part of the way home, and called on the women to carry it the final leg. The women also made the pottery, reed mats, and other domestic utensils. Both men and women tanned skins.

In addition to the sex-based division of labor, there were among the Caddoes a number of full-time occupational specialists. No other Texas tribes had reached a level which allowed the luxury of supporting individuals who did not themselves produce or procure food. Among the Caddoes these specialists were the politico-religious leaders, some members of their hierarchy, and possibly some of the artisans.

Despite the abundance of their crops and the many kinds of things produced by different people, we should not forget that a description

298

of their economy is one that might be summed up as production by a group of relatives for its own consumption. It remained a kinship society and its economic system remained secured to the framework of kinship. Men, for example, worked together with their relatives in the fields, not for their own individual benefit or profit but for the welfare of the whole.

While the Caddoes were economically self-sufficient, they carried on considerable trade with Indians to their west. Cotton blankets and turquoise from the Southwest were found among the Hasinais by the De Soto Expedition, and archeological finds demonstrate that the trade was ancient. In return for these luxuries, the Caddoes traded bow wood and salt. After horses eased the problem of transportation, this trade seems to have expanded. The Jumanos, particularly, played a major role as middleman between the barbaric Caddo confederacies of the East and the Pueblo-Spanish civilization of the Southwest.

When a woman knew that childbirth was approaching, she built herself a small hut on the bank of a nearby creek or river. In the center of the hut she sank a pole or stake to which she could cling during the rigors of childbirth. With the onset of labor she retired to her hut and gave birth unassisted. As soon as the child was born, the mother washed herself and her infant in the stream, even though she might have to break the ice to do so. Apart from bathing, which probably had some sort of religious or symbolical significance, there was no other ritual or ceremony associated with birth. The mother immediately returned to the household with her child and resumed her customary duties. About a week after birth a naming ceremony was held for the child by a priest (Espinosa, 1927: 164):

He comes to the house and takes his particular seat and they place the young child in his arms. He caresses it and talks for a long time into its ear. Next he bathes it all over in a large vessel and asks its parents what name he is to give it. Usually the name they bestow upon it is the diminutive of the name of the parents. If it is a girl this same office is performed by a decrepit old woman who is also a quack [shaman]. . . . To conclude the ceremonies, gifts, in the form of remuneration, are made to those officiating and they that day feast sumptuously on what they secure.

299

This childhood name might be kept throughout life, or it might be dropped for a nickname or that of a guardian spirit. Unlike Lipans and many other Texas Indians, the Caddoes had no fear of using the name of dead persons.

Unwanted children were sometimes destroyed after birth, a practice not regarded as criminal. Children were nursed for at least several years, probably until another child was born. In recent times a five-year-old was referred to as a suckling. (Parsons, 1941: 32)

Boys were hardened and toughened by forcing them to bathe in streams, even icy ones, and were required to undergo a number of other hardships and deprivations. They were also given instruction by older male relatives concerning proper conduct on war parties, and in early times warriors trained the youths by staging foot races. Grandmothers have always had an important role in instructing both boys and girls in correct behavior. The most important relatives, however, in the upbringing of boys were maternal uncles: "Boys were supposed to listen even more to their uncle (mother's brother) than to their father. A boy, whatever his age, was not to answer back to his uncle or father, especially if the senior was a warrior or a doctor." (Parsons, 1941: 28) By the time boys had become skilled hunters, or had shown themselves to be successful warriors, they were considered to be ready for marriage.

Marriage among the Caddoes was conceived in a light somewhat different from the Christian point of view, particularly with respect to the idea that there are few circumstances extenuating enough to dissolve the marriage bond. If a man decided he would like to wed a particular girl he brought her presents, but his energies were mainly directed toward gaining the favor of her parents and brothers. The suitor simply left some venison in front of their door. If they took the meat this was a sign of their assent; if it was rejected, his suit was without favor. Notice of the impending marriage was apparently given to the *caddi,* but there was no further ceremony. The residence of a newly-married couple was apparently matrilocal. In subsequent marriages there was even less formality.

While the Spaniards and French probably were largely ignorant concerning, and certainly contemptuous of, Caddo marriage cus-

300

toms, there seems to be little doubt that marriages were not very stable. Upon the slightest and flimsiest of grounds a couple would separate, "divorce themselves," and seek a marriage with some other partner. Americans have sometimes been accused of practicing a sort of serial polygamy and this may be an accurate appraisal of the customs current in some segments of our society, but it does not approach the turnover of marriage partners among the Caddoes. One early writer (De Solís, 1931: 41–42) also stated that wives were exchanged as well as bartered. The foregoing remarks pertain, however, primarily to the mass of the people. The women of noble families were expected to be faithful, and adultery on their part was punished severely.

While the Caddoes were monogamous after a fashion, this does not mean that polygyny horrified them. They practiced the levirate, in which a man inherited his dead brother's wife, and children if she had any. It is interesting that the marriage bond has remained brittle among surviving Caddoes, although admittedly this may be for completely different reasons. (Parsons, 1941: 30) There were *berdaches* among the Caddoes, but nothing more is known about them.

As with other stages in the life cycle, the final one, death, was an occasion for much or little ceremonial observance, depending upon the social position of the deceased. Immediately following death the body was prepared for burial by bathing it carefully and dressing it in fine clothing. For ordinary persons burial might follow death by only a few hours, but for important personages, such as the grand *xinesi*, it was deferred for two days so that the entire confederacy might gather for the last rites. Before the burial, members of the household displayed their grief by copious weeping. For ordinary persons the grave was dug immediately and the body placed in it, with the head to the west. Large quantities of food and much personal equipment were interred with the body. A man's bow, arrows, knife, and other tools were placed with him; a number of household utensils were placed with a woman's body. For more important personages considerably more ceremonial care seems to have been accorded the corpse. Casañas (1927: 297–299) described in some detail the burial of a leading man. In this case two men served as

301

priests and directors of the last rites. They ordered first that a coffin be made, and when it was completed they put tobacco, another herb, and a bow and arrows in it. "All these things they move about over the coffin from one place to another while they walk to and fro around about the coffin. They keep talking in a low voice as if they were praying. Their mode of speaking is so strenuous that they perspire even though it be cold." When they had completed this portion of the rite they went to the place where the body was to be buried. Once again they spoke in a low voice and the grave was dug only after they had determined where its exact position should be. This done, they returned to the house and directed the placing of the corpse in the coffin. Saying they were going to speak with God, they then went off a little way, returning after a while to relate to the corpse their conversation with God. Then another, a very old priest, appeared and spoke at length of the outstanding nature and behavior of the dead man—what a great warrior and hunter he had been and how hard-working. He admonished the crowd to mourn—weep—for him. When he had finished he sat down near the corpse and repeated to him all the things he had told the living. Finally, he assured the corpse that everybody loved him, that they were weeping for him, but that he must go peacefully to "that other house" to join the other dead, and take up their life. When the elder had completed his homily, the body was taken to its grave at once, accompanied by volleys of arrows shot into the air to arouse the keeper of the house "on the other side." After the mourners had wept over the closed grave, some left to fetch tobacco, fire, and a pot of water to be left on the grave.

Caddoes believed, at least in recent times, that the soul did not leave the vicinity of the body until six days after death. This belief was probably associated with their tenet that souls of the newly-dead were weak, so the living had to supply them with food. And, of course, the things left on the grave were for the soul's use. In modern times, and likely reaching back to early times, there was also the custom of mourners passing the hands over a corpse from head to toe and then over their own bodies. If a person arrived for the funeral too late to do this, he ran his hands over the grave and then

302

over his own body. Messages could be sent through a recently-deceased person to dead relatives, and apparently the custom of running the hands over the corpse and then one's self was associated with this belief. (Parsons, 1941: 36–37)

What we know of the Caddoes' political organization is much more intelligible to people of Western civilization than that of many other Texas Indians. This is not because it closely resembles modern democracies or other well-known political systems, but because it was a bureaucracy containing a series of graded offices—and officers—each with specific duties to perform. Every confederacy was headed by a man with the title of *xinesi* (probably pronounced "chenesi" or "shenesi"). This office was hereditary in the male line, at least in the Hasinai confederacy, and probably in the others. It normally passed to the oldest son. If there were no male heirs the position apparently fell to the *xinesi's* brother. If the new *xinesi* was a child, one of the principal men, probably one of the *caddices* acted for him until he was old enough to assume the responsibility of the office. The *xinesi* was treated with a great deal of respect, and Casañas (1927: 218) went so far as to say that "everybody tries . . . to keep him satisfied by giving him something . . . for him to feast upon. Finally, in controlling them he has only to say, 'I want this or that done.' All obey because they fear his frown."

Subordinate to the *xinesi* were the *caddices*. These men were the tribal chiefs and, like the *xinesi*, gained their office through inheritance. If a *caddi's* tribe was a large one, there were a number of sub-tribal officials, termed *canhas* (or *canahas*), who assisted the *caddi* by taking his place when he had to be absent, by announcing his commands throughout his jurisdiction, and by calling the elders together when the *caddi* so commanded. Under the *canhas* were officials known as *chayas*, who carried out the orders of their superiors. Another group of officials, the *tammas*, had duties roughly similar to those of sergeants-at-arms or sheriffs, one of which, as has already been noted, was that of whipping laggards. A war hero was called an *amayxoya*; he carried and wore special insignia and was set apart as a member of another distinguished group. According to Casañas (1927: 216–217), "the peace and harmony among the of-

303

ficials described is so great that during the year and three months (we have been among them) we have not seen any quarrels—either great or small. But the insolent and lazy are punished."

Sometimes women had great authority, for among the Nabedaches, De Solís (1931: 46) encountered a woman who was addressed by a title which meant "great lady" or "principal lady." She lived in a house of many rooms and was much honored by her tribesmen, who continually brought her gifts. She also had many male and female servants, "and these are like priests and captains among them." Another reference to a "queen" has been recorded for the Kadohadachos, and is reminiscent of the term "white woman" among the Natchez—the mother of the heir apparent, sister of the ruler and often herself a person of great power.

Much of the power and authority of a *xinesi* and a *caddi* derived from their roles as priests and as voices of the gods. Yet in a primitive kinship society, such as was the Caddoes', many if not most of the functions we associate with governmental institutions were performed by kinship units. The Hasinais and probably the Kadohadachos had clans, though little is known about them. Clan members apparently lived together or near one another in the "hamlets" and "cantons" of which the early explorers so often spoke. Of all the Caddo peoples only the Cahinnio, an independent tribe of the early days, lived together in a compact village, probably as a defensive measure. Caddo clans were apparently matrilineal (i.e., traced descent through females). The clans were named after some animal or a natural force, and may have been totemic (meaning that descent was traced from this creature). The clan names known for the Kadohadachos were Beaver, Otter, Wolf, and Lion. Modern clan names remembered by the Caddoes include Buffalo, Bear, Panther, Wolf, Beaver, Eagle, Raccoon, Crow, Thunder, Sun, and Alligator. Some of these may overlap with one another and it is not likely that these represent all the clans originally present.

As elsewhere, these clans functioned as mutual-assistance bodies. Casañas (1927: 217–218), for example, was probably speaking about Hasinai clans when he said:

. . . these Indians help each other in such a manner that if one's house and all his possessions are burned up, they all gather together, build him a new house, and furnish him whatever he needs for his subsistence and comfort. All these things they do together. . . . During sickness, these Indians visit and aid each other with great kindness, trying to give to the sick all possible consolation by taking them something nice to eat. Some of them present the trinkets they own, others lend them. Among them there is no exchange, save by bartering. It seems that everything they own they do not hold as personal property but as common property. Therefore, there is no ambition, no envy to prevent peace and harmony among them.

Early explorers of whatever nation seldom if ever left more than hints about the kinship systems of American Indians, and they made no exception of the Caddoes. When anthropologists began to investigate Caddo society, at the close of nineteenth century, the kinship system was unstable and unquestionably had undergone considerable change.[4] Consequently, there are discrepancies and contradictions in our knowledge of it. Their kinship terminology is apparently the type known as "Iroquois," in which cross-cousins are called by the same terms, but are distinguished from parallel cousins, who in turn are often classified as siblings. (Murdock, 1949: 223, 243–245) In other words, a father's sister's children and a mother's brother's children were brothers and sisters. But modern informants give different terms for these relatives. All sources agree, however, that a father's sister and a mother's brother were distinguished from other parental siblings. In the grandparent generation there was no distinction between maternal and paternal kin.

The sibling terminology is striking because seniority was considered to be of such importance. There were distinguishing terms for an older sister of a woman and for the older brother of a man. Such terminology was also applied to parallel cousins (since they were addressed by sibling terms), but their seniority depended upon the relative ages of their parents, rather than those of the speakers. The same concept was extended to cross-cousins, the principle being

[4] For a more detailed study of Caddo kinship, see Parsons, 1941; Spier, 1924: 258–263, and Schmitt and Schmitt, n.d.: 56–58.

that the children of a sister were considered to be senior to children of a brother.

Like the Wichitas, Caddoes had a joking relationship between affinal relatives of the same generation. A man might joke, for example, more or less obscenely with his brother's wife. Although there was no parent-in-law taboo, a man did not swear or joke about sex in front of his parents-in-law. In many ways this reserve is paralleled in our culture.

The dispersion of Caddo hamlets would lead one to suppose that their inhabitants were not afraid of surprise attacks. But the fact that the Caddoes were mostly grouped into confederacies suggests the contrary—that they were organized for defensive purposes. The confederacies did sometimes fight one another, but there is no historic record of large-scale interconfederacy conflict. The Osages and apparently the Wichitas were age-old enemies, however, and the Apaches attacked the Caddoes savagely when they ventured onto the plains with horses in search of buffalo. Following European contact, the reasons which spurred the Caddoes—as well as other Texas tribes—to war were considerably altered. The former more or less ceremonial, not particularly lethal, warfare became a deadly serious struggle for sheer survival. The appearance of Eastern Indians pushed westward by the advancing frontier and the addition of horses and firearms and similar changes must all have made Caddo warfare considerably more important than it had formerly been.

The two traditional motives which had involved men in warfare were revenge for the slaying of relatives and the quest for personal glory. It should be noted, too, that only some of the men became warriors, and that while warriors formed a somewhat distinct caste and were honored members of society, Caddo culture was not oriented around warfare and the warrior hero.

The Caddo cult of war, if such it may be called, is fascinating not because of its many barbaric overtones but because it had associated with it so many elements which to a non-Caddo seem completely extraneous and nonessential to the business at hand. It prompts us to wonder if many of our own soldierly activities—marching, saluting, and the like—are not also a sort of window dressing. In any event, Caddo preparations for war were elaborate. A special house was built or perhaps an ordinary dwelling was commandeered by the members of a war party. Those men who were bent on going to war assembled in this house and remained in it until they left for the fray. Feasts, dances, prayers, and offerings consumed the seven or eight days necessary to prepare for war. As the emotional intensity grew with each passing day, new recruits joined the war party. Finally, in a furious frenzy the war party's house was burned to the ground. One of the warriors was elected to lead the war party, and once elected, the party's members obeyed his commands implicitly. Scouts were sent out in all directions so that the party would not be surprised, and sentinels were posted whenever the little army camped. They communicated with each other by smoke signals, and in peacetime, distant hamlets could be quickly alerted by these signals. Communication was good enough that the Spaniards were usually unable to surprise them.

Caddo wars, like those of many other American Indians, consisted of hit-and-run-raids, with no pitched battles or masses of men pitted against one another. Dying a hero's death was not a customary type of Caddo behavior. "Flight at the sight of an enemy is not a dishonor. The warrior who brings any spoils from battle, though he got them through treason, or bad faith, is a hero." (Morfi, 1932:52–53) This does not mean, however, that the Caddoes could not defend themselves and their homes with great vigor. The wholehearted, tenacious, though mostly fruitless, defenses Caddo tribes threw before the army of Hernando De Soto are a case in point.

The Caddoes took scalps, removing most of the skin and hair from the heads of their victims, in contrast to the small-sized scalps which Plains Indians traditionally lifted from their victims. Scalps either were tanned and worn by the victorious warriors, or were hung on the doorways of their houses as a token of the occupants' valor.

Captives, particularly men, but often women and children, were slain. Frequently captives were brought back by a returning war party so that the women could wreak their vengeance upon them, and the Caddoes possessed a number of fiendish ways of torturing captives. The women tortured their victims by amputating fingers,

307

cutting off bits of flesh (which some other captive might be forced to eat), gouging out eyes, and similar barbarities, before finally killing them. In another form of torture, and apparently one with ritual overtones, prisoners were suspended from horizontal bars so that their feet did not touch the ground. A stake was driven in the ground beneath their feet, a rope tied from their feet to the stake, and their bodies stretched tightly. The victims were tied to this frame in the morning to face the rising sun and again in the evening to face the sunset. They were released from its tortures for the remainder of the day, although without being given food the first day. On the morning of the second day, the victims were again strung up, and this time four old men slashed incisions in their arms, thighs, and legs. The blood which dripped from their wounds was caught by the old men and passed to two other old men, who cooked it and gave it to the women and children to eat. After the victims were dead, they were cut up, cooked, and eaten by members of the village.[5] While this specific form of torture and cannibalism was practiced by the Kichais, other Caddoes were equally bloodthirsty and ingenious in their devices of torture. This ritual cannibalism was shared with other Southeasterners and, as we have noted, almost all of the Texas Indians were in some degree cannibalistic (the Jumanos and Comanches being the only exceptions so far as we can tell).

A few Caddo sports, such as foot racing, were regarded as training for war, but most games were apparently played for amusement alone. One favorite game was a form of hockey, and another was the widespread Indian game of "hoop and pole," in which a pole or arrow was thrown at a rolling hoop. The Caddoes also played a number of guessing games and games which resemble dice. These games, too, were for simple amusement. There is little evidence that the Caddoes, unlike many Texas Indians, were inveterate gamblers.

Supernaturalism. Like other Indians of the Southeast the Caddoes believed in an omnipotent deity. This supreme fig-

[5] Kroeber (1947: 62) says of the Natchez who shared this custom: "Captive torture on the frame is another trait that looks like a worn-down survival in the light of Mexican captive sacrifice, sometimes also performed on a frame."

308

ure was thought to have been the creator of the universe and all within it. Moreover, some Caddoes believed that he rewarded good behavior and punished bad. There are several versions of how this god was created, but all share the belief that in the beginning there was but one woman. She had two daughters, one of whom was a virgin; the other was pregnant. One day while the two girls were alone they were attacked by a hideous, giant monster. The monster tore the pregnant girl apart and ate her, but the virgin escaped by climbing a tree. When the monster began to tear down the tree the maiden dived into the water and again escaped, despite his drinking the water dry in an attempt to find her. The virgin told her mother about the horrible event and mother and daughter returned to the spot where the pregnant girl had been slain. Here they found a drop of the girl's blood in an acorn shell. The mother covered the shell with another and carried it home in her bosom. When they reached their home the shell with its drop of blood was placed in a small jar, and its mouth covered. During the night they heard a gnawing sound in the jar and the next morning when the mother opened it she found that the drop of blood had turned into a perfectly-formed boy the size of a finger. The mother, overjoyed, again covered the jar, and the next morning she again heard the gnawing sound. This time the little boy grew into a full-sized man. After being equipped by his grandmother, the man defeated the monster, and then with his grandmother and aunt went to the sky from where he ruled the world.

Although this male deity reigned supreme, the Caddoes were not monotheists. They believed that the world was or could be inhabited by multitudes of supernaturally powerful creatures, and very possibly by large amounts of nonanimistic, impersonal supernatural power. Their number and importance probably varied from tribe to tribe.

Some individuals had supernatural partners or helpers, acquired without the guardian-spirit quest so common among the Plains Indians. Having a supernatural partner did not necessarily mean that a person would become a shaman, although some persons undoubtedly did. Not only animals, but inanimate objects and natural phenomena and events (sun, cyclones, lightning, and clouds) could become supernatural helpers.

The religious practices of the Caddo confederacies were focused on temples—temples attended by the spiritual and temporal rulers of the Caddoes, the *xinesis*. As was mentioned earlier, the temples were similar to ordinary dwellings, but larger. A temple was furnished with an altar made of reed mats, various other reed mats, and benches to one side of the door; in front of a bed and raised slightly above the ground was a square, four-legged wooden bench upon which tobacco, a pipe with feathers, and pottery vessels used to burn offerings of fat and tobacco stood in readiness. At the sides of the altar were two small boxes into which the *xinesi* always placed portions of the gifts brought to the gods. In the center of the temple burned a perpetual fire, fed with four heavy logs that pointed in the cardinal directions.

Near the temple were two small houses belonging to the *coconicis*, two boys whom the supreme being had sent to help the Caddoes. These two boys are among the most fascinating creatures of Caddo belief. They served as intermediaries and oracles between the supreme god and the *xinesi*. They spoke to him (in his own disguised voice) and told him—and he in turn informed the people—what was expected of them. No one was allowed to see these children, for to do so would have brought instant death. If the *xinesi* felt that the people were not bringing him a sufficient amount of food, he announced that these children were angry and would not speak to him about the welfare of the people. He might even go so far as to predict great misfortune and disaster, such as crop failure and defeat by their enemies.

Occasionally, perhaps in an annual ceremony of renewal, the *xinesi* summoned the tribes of the confederacy, and called into the temple the tribal leaders and elders. When all were seated, having disrobed before entering, the *xinesi* took some coals from the fire and burned some buffalo fat and tobacco as an offering. Then he shut the door and put out the fire, leaving the temple in somber darkness. The throng outside sang and danced, but those inside maintained perfect silence as

310

they listened to the *xinesi* speak with the *coconicis*. He used two voices, one like that of a child, the other somewhat like his normal voice. In the latter voice he spoke to the boys, asking them to inform God that the people were going to reform, pleading that they be granted bountiful harvests, fine hunting, good health, success in war, many women to serve the men, and other things. When he had concluded his prayer he cast a gourd rattle on the ground. If it made no sound, God was angry with them. And a silent rattle frightened the throng to the extent that the *xinesi* could extract all sorts of promises from them. When the throng had made the promises the *xinesi* desired, the voice of one of the children was heard. The voice said that God was speaking, that if the promises they had made were kept, the Caddoes would be given everything they had asked for, that the people must be told what he had said, and that their needs should be made known to him through the *xinesi*. When he had finished, the *xinesi* in his natural voice repeated what the child had said, concluding by sending the people out to fulfill their promises. (Espinosa, 1927: 160–162) It is not difficult to imagine how in prehistoric times a *xinesi*, desiring to raise his temple closer to the heavens could have had the "little ones" command the tribes under his jurisdiction to build a temple mound.

Besides the priests, of whom there were relatively few, in every tribe there was a large group of medicine men or shamans. They were primarily devoted to the curing of illness, although being able to control and eliminate supernaturally-caused illnesses and hence being in close contact with the supernatural world, their powers and social importance were often something more than just that of a healer. There were societies or guilds of medicine men, of which Beaver, Mescal-bean, and Yuko are remembered. (Parsons, 1941: 34) These medicine societies held public initiations for neophytes. Dressed in their special regalia, shamans gathered together and summoned the prospective practitioners. They gave drinks of certain herbs and large quantities of tobacco to the candidates. In time the candidates passed out, and remained unconscious or in pretended unconsciousness for twenty-four hours. Regaining consciousness, they related the dream experiences they had had—the journeys their souls had taken. Their experiences were cast in song, and for eight days the neophytes by turns sang their songs. These occasions seem to have been popular social events during which the onlookers feasted and were entranced by the songs and dances of the new medicine men.

The belief behind shamanistic curing was that sickness was usually (perhaps always) caused by witches. Witches sent insects, arrows, or other foreign objects magically into a victim's body. Logically, then, treatment of the sick generally consisted of sucking affected areas of the body, sweating the patient, or in sleight-of-hand tricks in which these various foreign objects were extracted. Extracted objects were magically thrown back to their source, and it is easy to see how struggles between shamans (one or both of whom might be witches) could develop. Each shaman had his own particular cures, differing slightly from others of his own shamanistic fraternity. The always interesting Espinosa (1927: 165) said of these practices:

To cure a patient, they build a big bonfire and provide an abundance of fifes and an abundance of feathers. Their instruments are polished sticks with slits like a snake's rattles. These rubbed on a hollow skin make a noise nothing less than infernal. Before playing they drink their brewed herb, covered with foam. They then, without moving at all, begin to dance to this infernal music and the songs of the condemned, for to this alone can the chanted jargon of the medicine men be likened. The ceremony lasts from the middle of the afternoon until near dawn. The medicine man stops his singing at intervals to apply cruel treatment to the patient whom they have sweating on a grate over many coals that are kept burning under the bed. . . . In the midst of the piteous complaints, the medicine man explains that the treatment he is giving is very mild. The doctors continue to suck and to spit. They put into their mouths a worm or blood which they have previously provided and declare that they took it from the body of the patient.

Some of the remedies used by the shamans seem to have been effective. Sucking snakebites, for instance, was a fairly successful method of dealing with this malady; some of the herbs used were also efficacious. If, however, a shaman was having continued misfortune in curing his patients, he was sometimes slain by his own

relatives. While shamans functioned mainly as healers, they also foretold events, blessed new houses, named new-born children, and
consecrated the crops.

The most important religious ceremonies of the Caddoes were the
first-fruits rites marking the beginning of the harvest. At this time
the *caddices* and the *xinesi* were honored with great feasts. But
while the merriment, feasting, and dancing went on, the *xinesi*
went without food, drink, or sleep, spending a number of days
praying, thanking the gods for the harvest, and attempting to ensure
good fortune for the future. In late winter other ceremonies were
held which looked forward to the new planting season, and were primarily concerned with forecasting the nature of the coming season.
Old men, perhaps elderly shamans, drank a tea of laurel leaves
(*Sophora secundiflora?*) and with the aid of eagle wings and tobacco
cast upon a fire, forecast the nature of the coming season. In the
spring, "festivals" were held in which young men were trained for
war by running races. Besides these seasonal ceremonies there were
clan rituals and perhaps other religious performances held by various
groups.

THE MIGHTY are sometimes brought as low as the
humble with as much or even more ease by conquering powers. This
was the case with the Caddo Indians of east Texas, although their
conquest seems to have been primarily brought about by epidemics
rather than by war. The collapse of these confederacies was so rapid,
and their decline in numbers so great that the onrushing American
frontier hardly took notice of the Caddoes, the dregs of what had
been two centuries earlier rich, splendid, barbaric theocracies. Although it is true that even as early as the seventeenth and eighteenth
centuries the Caddoes appear to have passed their zenith, they remained, nonetheless, the most productive, advanced, and populous
peoples of Texas.

313

CHAPTER 12

The Provincial Atakapans

> When they returned, they threw this Indian on the
> prairie. One of them cut his head off and another one
> cut the arms off, while they skinned him at the same
> time. Several of them ate the yellow fat, which was
> still raw, and finally they devoured him completely.
>
> Simars de Bellisle (1719)

Between the Caddoes and the coast, and occupying a stretch of
territory from Louisiana across the Sabine as far as the Trinity and
San Jacinto rivers, lived a number of poorly-known Atakapan-speaking
Indians. These tribes are generally classed as belonging to the
Southeast culturally, but they were peripheral or marginal, and
some had much in common with the Karankawas of the Western
Gulf culture area. But by and large, the Texas Atakapans can be
thought of as a provincial reflection of Caddo grandeur.

The Atakapa proper—and the word means "man-eaters" or "cannibals"
in the Choctaw language—occupied southwestern Louisiana
but extended across the Sabine to the vicinity of Sabine Lake. In the
mideighteenth century their two westernmost villages were on either
side of the Nueces River near present Beaumont. (Swanton, 1946:

315

216; Bolton, 1915: 334) The Akokisas (called also Arkokisa, Orco-quisac, etc.), perhaps signifying "river people," dwelled on the lower Trinity and San Jacinto rivers and along the eastern shores of Galveston Bay. In the eighteenth century they lived in four or five scattered villages in this area. To their north in the San Jacinto river valley lived the Patiris, known to us by little more than a name. Upstream in the Trinity valley were the Bidais—meaning "brushwood" in Caddoan—and to their north the Deadoses, apparently a subdivision of the Bidais. These Atakapan people were not numerous; taken all together they probably numbered less than thirty-five hundred persons. Considering the extent of territory they occupied, this was a very low population density. (Swanton, 1946: 93)

The language of these tribes—Atakapan—was once thought to be an independent language stock, but it has recently been related to that of the Chitimachas, who lived to their east in Louisiana, and to that of the Tunicas of the lower Yazoo above present Vicksburg, Mississippi. These languages form the Tunican language stock. (Swanton, 1952: 197–198)

The marshy coast northeastward from Galveston Bay is subhumid and low-lying, with much of the land subject to salt-water flooding. For the Indians—and still true of much of it today—agriculture there was impossible. Proceeding inland, though prairies and into more heavily-timbered areas, agricultural potentialities improve. Throughout the region game was plentiful, particularly deer and bear, and bison were present sporadically in the prairie sections. In general, it was a region rich in game, fish, and wild plants, but its agricultural potentialities for Indians were deficient.

Origins and Early History. The Atakapans occupied a land which was largely bypassed and overlooked by early Europeans. It is a region also long neglected by archeologists, and it has been only recently that they have given us some clues about its prehistory. A few miles west of Houston nine sites have been investigated in the Addicks Basin. (Wheat, 1953) On the strength of these, a Galveston Bay Focus, encompassing an ill-defined strip of territory from the Sabine to the Brazos, has been proposed. (Suhm *et al.*, 1954: 128–130) Another site near Houston and one on the

316

Bolivar Peninsula some twenty-five miles northeast of Galveston have since been found to belong to the Galveston Bay Focus or have some affiliations with it. (Walley, 1955; Campbell, 1957)

The people of the Galveston Bay Focus were hunters, gatherers, and fishermen, making use of deer, bison, antelope, shellfish, and other wild foods. No indication of agriculture has been discovered, but in such a humid region evidences of farming practices are not likely to be preserved. The Galveston Bay people appear to have roamed the area in small groups, probably moving in a seasonal rhythm. The Galveston Bay Focus may reach back in time as far as A.D. 500, but its duration is unknown. At the Caplen site on the Bolivar Peninsula, where there are affiliations with the Galveston Bay Focus, there is a possibility that occupation lasted until historic times. The Focus has been described as basically Southeastern, though marginal, a summation which applies equally well to historic Atakapans. (Wheat, 1953: 246)

The Hans, among whom Cabeza de Vaca found himself in 1528, may have been one of the coastal tribes of Atakapans, probably the Akokisas (see Chapter 2). Swanton (1946: 85; see also Hodge, 1907b: 54 n. 4) argues for such an affiliation, saying that "the name given being perhaps a snynonym of *añ*, the Atakapa and Akokisa word for 'house.' " Whatever the linguistic affinity of the Hans, culturally they seem to have been more closely affiliated with the Western Gulf culture area and the Karankawas than with the Southeast.

Apart from De Vaca's possible contact with Atakapan peoples, there is little other early mention of them. La Salle must have crossed their territory, as also did the Spaniard Alonso de León, but neither they nor other seventeenth-century explorers left anything more than passing references to them. The first extensive account of Atakapans, and among the most enthralling of such accounts to be found anywhere, was left by a young French officer, Simars de Bellisle. In 1719 a French ship, the *Maréchal d'Estées*, landed five officers on Galveston Bay to refill its water casks. For some unexplained reason the peculiar captain failed to pick up his shore party. One by one, four of the men died from starvation, only the sturdy and determined De Bellisle managing to survive. Several weeks after his last com-

317

panion had succumbed, De Bellisle, while searching for edible worms, spied some Indians collecting bird eggs on an island. Joining them, he was made captive and stripped of his possessions and clothing. But he was fed. As a captive and an outsider he was the victim of many indignities. But the natives, who were Akokisas, eventually supplied him with a wife, or from their point of view, provided a servant and quasi husband for a widow. His account of life with these Indians gives us a fair picture of life on the coast in the eighteenth century; his tale of escape in 1721 through the intercession of Hasinai Caddoes, his domestic arrangements with the Hasinai woman Angelica, and his other experiences comprise an almost unbelievable real-life adventure.[1] Shortly after his escape De Bellisle returned to Galveston Bay as a guide for Bernard de la Harpe. Nine of the Akokisas whom De Bellisle had known during his captivity were taken to New Orleans, where the captain of the ship, Jean Béranger, took down a vocabulary of their language, thus establishing for later students their identity as Akokisas.

The French continued their explorations and expanded their trade contacts in the Atakapan area throughout much of the first half of the eighteenth century. Finally, in 1745, Captain Joaquín de Orobio Bazterra was sent by the Spanish Crown to investigate this French activity. He was able to confirm the fact that French traders were in the region, bartering for deerskins and bisonskins, but learned that they had established no settlements. A rumor that the French were planning to found permanent settlements brought Bazterra back the following year, and in 1749 the missions of San Francisco Xavier, Nuestra Señora de la Candelario, and San Ildefonso were established on the San Gabriel River in central Texas, near present Rockdale. These missions attracted mainly the more inland Atakapans—Bidais and Deadoses—but also some Akokisas from the coast. Father Santa Ana noticed that the Bidais, Deadoses, and Akokisas spoke the same language, camped together, and were interrelated by marriage, and wisely placed the two hundred and two Atakapans in the Mission of San Ildefonso. But Spanish success with the Indians was short-lived;

[1] De Bellisle's "Relation" as reproduced by Margry (1897) has been translated in full by Folmer (1940).

318

Apache attacks and dissension between the religious and military personnel forced the abandonment of these missions in 1755. (Bolton, 1915: 198, 49–55)

In the next year a presidio, San Agustín de Ahumada, was established a few miles above the mouth of the Trinity near the Indian town of El Orcoquisac. Fifty families of Tlascalan Indians were brought from central Mexico to the presidio in an attempt to placate or pacify the Akokisas more successfully. A mission, Nuestra Señora de la Luz, was started south of the present town of Liberty, but as in the missions on the San Gabriel, internal strife and dissension caused the abandonment of the presidio and mission in 1771. (Bolton, 1915: 342–374)

The Bidais, while ostensibly friendly to the Spanish, seem to have been leagued with enemies of the Spanish after 1770. They secured firearms from the French and traded them to the Lipan Apaches, who at this time were the object of Spanish and Comanche vengeance. They were also responsible for an alliance between the Hasinais and Lipans. (Bolton, 1914a, I: 65–66, 93–99) The Spanish sent agents among the Bidais, and their efforts, combined with epidemics, soon reduced this tribe to impotence. Some joined Akokisa remnants, who in turn died out or joined other Atakapans in Louisiana. A settlement of Akokisas is said to have been situated on the west side of the Colorado early in the nineteenth century, but this group subsequently disappears. Perhaps they became extinct; possibly they joined other tribes. (Sjoberg, 1951: 395; Swanton, 1946: 86) Some Bidais are said to have intermarried with the Koasatis, and their descendants, if any, on the Alabama-Coushatta Indian Reservation in Polk County are the only Texas natives who remain in the state today. (Abel, 1922: 96) In the 1830's the Bidais numbered only one hundred men, and were characterized as good deer hunters who planted and reaped "good crops of corn," and were honest and peaceful. (Sibley, 1832: 722) Some of the Bidais also joined Caddo remnants, only to be moved first to the Brazos Reservation in 1854, and subsequently to their reservation in Oklahoma.

Appearance and Dress. There are a few trustworthy accounts of Atakapan physique and appearance. J. O. Dyer

319

(1917. No pagination), who compiled a fragmentary ethnography of the Atakapas of Lake Charles from word-of-mouth sources early in this century, said that they were "dark skinned, with dirty, short, coarse black matted hair; their bodies stout, stature short, and heads of large size placed between the shoulders. The ears were very large, as were the mouths, and the cheek bones and nose prominent." One of his sources of information believed they resembled Akokisas, but Dyer argued that "they were much stouter and their necks shorter." Another of his sources (Dyer, 1917) claimed that the Lake Charles Atakapas were

of short stature, large heads, dark skins, and prominent facial features of an unpleasant cast; especially noticeable were the high cheek bones and protruding lips. Their teeth were stained from the various leaf substitutes they used for tobacco. Head deformation, cuts on the nose and chin, and tattooing, were noticeable, especially in the older members.

The Bidais were reported to have deformed heads, but whether as a result of intention or accident is not known. They also tattooed the face and body. (Dyer, 1916: 3; Sjoberg, 1951: 399) Two drawings of purported Atakapas by A. DeBatz, an eighteenth-century Louisiana Frenchman, do little to enlighten us concerning their physical appearance. (Bushnell, 1927: Plates 4, 6) They are not significantly different from Indians of other tribes in his illustrations. His two sketches do, however, give us a clue to the Atakapas' attire. In both, the warriors are barefooted and breechclouts are the principal article of clothing. In the first a calumet, or ceremonial pipe, is held in the right hand, a small pipe in the left, and a quiver of arrows can be seen over the left shoulder. Earrings are discernible, and the coiffure might be described as on the "bushy" side, much of the hair standing upright. The second illustration, presumed to be of an Atakapa, shows a man in winter attire, which consists of a buffalo robe, painted on the inside with red and black geometric designs. The tail of the buffalo, left on the skin, trails behind. Otherwise, the figure is barefooted and breechclouted like the first, although the hair style is different, and what appears to be a small stuffed animal has been shoved into the top of the breechclout.

320

The women's clothing was as skimpy as the men's so far as we can tell: "The skirt of the women was very primitive. A skin was trimmed into circular shape; in its center a circular hole was cut, and the garment was slipped over the head and fastened around the waist with thongs." (Dyer, 1917)

Subsistence and Material Culture. It is apparent, despite the fact that our knowledge of Atakapan tribes is fragmentary, that they differed somewhat in their cultures, depending upon their geographical location and their proximity to other peoples. The coastal tribes, specifically the Akokisas, were the least Southeastern in culture. Their coastal situation, the relative ease with which they could obtain fish and shellfish, and the difficulty if not impossibility of raising corn, led them toward a way of life very like that of the nearby Karankawas. With the Akokisas, then, we have come almost full circle: back to a fishing, gathering, hunting life along the Gulf littoral. The Bidais, Deadoses, and perhaps to a lesser extent the Patiris and Atakapa proper were much more closely associated with the neighboring Caddoes and the Southeast in general. Their geographic situation allowed them to farm, if less intensively than did the Caddoes, and the example of these culturally-advanced neighbors must have been powerful and persuasive. For many years the Bidais were, in fact, thought to be a Caddo tribe, and they, as well as other Atakapans, spoke Caddo, the lingua franca of east Texas.

The Akokisas who captured Simars de Bellisle seem to have spent spring and summer on the coast, split up into small family groups. In these seasons they made use of shellfish, fish, bird eggs, what Bellisle calls "wild potatoes" (probably the American lotus or water chinquapin [*Nelumbo* sp. var.]), and undoubtedly other wild plants and animals. They had pirogues, or dugout canoes, so they were able to venture as far as the offshore islands. As winter approached, the families gathered in somewhat larger groups in small, probably semi-permanent villages in the interior. (Bolton, 1915: 334) During this season they did considerable hunting. De Bellisle's band, for example, followed this practice:

When the beginning of winter came, we all left to join a band of their people who were waiting for us at the end of the bay. . . . After a few days

STORY

FIG. 12.   Atakapan in a dugout canoe.

had passed, they told me that all the men were going to hunt buffaloes and were going to war against their enemies.[2]

De Bellisle was taken along, the Indians riding, the unfortunate Frenchman walking and trotting along barefooted. In three days' time they reached a prairie covered with bison, and the next day the mounted hunters killed fifteen or sixteen with their bows and arrows. It was while on this expedition that they killed and ate one of their enemies, a Toyal or Tojal (Tonkawa?) Indian. But the next day the party turned homeward with little meat, for within four days' time they were again searching for food. Sometimes they appear to have killed bison closer to the coast, and in the 1830's they were said to kill a great many deer. They were able to go without food for a number of days, Bellisle remarking (Folmer, 1940: 216–217):

When it rains no one goes out to look for food, and they pass easily two or three days in this manner without food, drinking only water and throwing it up without any effort. They told me to do the same and that this was good.

De Bellisle stated specifically that the Akokisas did not raise any crops, and if all Akokisa bands spent the summer months on the coast, this sounds reasonable. Bolton (1915: 334) has suggested, however, that they raised "superfine maize." Even if this is correct, it could have played only a minor role in their subsistence.

What little information is available for Atakapas in the vicinity of Lake Charles in Louisiana suggests a life of fishing, hunting, and gathering similar to that of the Akokisas (Dyer, 1917):

The tribe were skilled fishermen, but their dugouts being frail, they never ventured into the Gulf for any distance. They did not use the bow and arrow to any extent in fishing, but depended upon darts and spears, which they were able to fling with unerring accuracy. . . . [They hit] small fish but ten inches long at a distance of twenty paces. The darts tipped with bone were used for short distances and floated, while the heavier flint tip harpoon had a wooden floater attached to a thong, which enabled them to

[2] Folmer, 1940: 217–218. The excerpt at the head of this chapter is from *ibid.*, 219.

retrieve their weapons, as well as tire out a wounded fish. Flounders were speared by torch light, with a short-handled dart, tipped with a bundle of sharp fish bones.

Flounders and perhaps other fish were baked in pits, and fish were preserved by smoking. A small oily fish, smoked and salted, was used as an article of barter with inland tribes. Another method of catching fish was by cutting off tidal lagoons with crude brushwood traps. Shamans also sprinkled dried, powdered roots and herbs of certain unknown plants on lagoons to stupify fish, the fish being killed with paddles when they rose to the surface. Oysters were "dragged from the shell bottoms with rakes made of two strong poles, curved at the ends and interlaced with strong vines." (Dyer, 1917) Alligators were speared through the eye, and the oil obtained from these reptiles was used on the skin to repel mosquitoes, a practice often cited as the chief cause of the coastal natives' repulsive odor. Many other wild foods, both plant and animal, must have been utilized, there being no known food taboos.

The Bidais and presumably the other, more inland Atakapans were agricultural. Maize was the principal crop and in some years was raised in quantity. But hunting was important, rivaling gardening. Deer were the most frequently-hunted game animal, but excursions to the westerly prairies were made to hunt bison. Their well-prepared deerskins were highly regarded by Europeans. As with the Caddoes, bears were hunted for their skins and for their fat, which, rendered, could be stored for long periods, but the flesh was apparently not eaten. (Dyer, 1916: 6) The Bidais also secured a number of smaller animals by using cane traps. They ate the seeds and rhizomes of the water chinquapin, which grew in marshes and shallow water; acorns, from which the tannin had to be leached out before eating; and undoubtedly many other wild plants. They took fish whenever the opportunity presented itself.[3]

The type of dwelling the Akokisas used is unknown, De Bellisle recounting that they possessed no cabins or fields. They may, how-

[3] Sjoberg, 1951: 396–397. Mrs. Sjoberg has drawn together in this short article all information presently available on the Bidais.

324

ever, have used temporary brush huts or possessed some sort of movable shelters which he might not have regarded as "cabins." Dyer (1917) learned something of the dwellings of the Lake Charles Atakapas:

This [hut] was extremely filthy, filled with vermin, and in one corner were the remains of human excreta; its sides were made of poles interwoven with vines, and the conical top was open in the center to allow the smoke from below to escape; the fireplace of oyster shells (a mere pit) being in the middle of the dirt floor. Only one opening was provided, serving as door and window, and closed by a heavy hide suspended from a crossbar.

Shamans' huts and those of headmen were placed on higher ground, often on the tops of old shell and refuse heaps. The common people had to take less desirable, lower, and often wetter locations for their dwellings. Nothing is known about the older Bidai dwelling; in later, more nomadic times, they used bearskin tents in the winter months.

Little else is known about the remaining material culture of the Atakapan tribes. The coastal tribes manufactured some pottery, and also obtained some by trade from nearby areas. Dyer (1917), for example, recorded that their pottery "was made by tribes to the north of them, except a few of the globular or conical oil jugs of the Carancahuas, so serviceable, fitted in cane frames, to the canoe voyager." Skin containers and wooden bowls and dippers have been recorded for the Bidais, and were probably made by all Atakapans. The bow and arrow was the chief weapon of Atakapan men before the French supplied them with firearms, and it has been reported that the Bidais also employed long, antler-tipped spears. Bidai women manufactured cane baskets of a peculiar type, used both domestically and for trade with other tribes.

Social Organization. Very little of a coherent nature is known about Atakapan social organization. The Akokisas were divided into four or more bands, each having a headman or chief. There appears to have been no paramount tribal chief, and it is unlikely that the dispersed bands ever all came together. During part of the year, as we have seen, even the members of a band were scattered in small family groups.

The Atakapa proper seem to have had roughly the same rudimentary political organization, although they were less dispersed and lived in more or less permanent villages. Dyer (1917), reporting on visits made to an Atakapan village between 1817 and 1819, said it "contained forty miserable, dirty huts, the chief's and shaman's being on an oyster mound, and somewhat larger in size. They had no temple." The Bidais, like other Atakapans, were composed of a number of bands. They were briefly united into a single tribe in the 1770's, but the Spanish were responsible for this, appointing a man named Gorgoritos as chief of the tribe and of a Bidai-Akokisa confederacy. (Bolton, 1915: 232)

The Akokisas may have shared the Caddoes' custom of "wailing" greetings. De Bellisle (Folmer, 1940: 216), when he first encountered what appears to have been this custom, was in fear for his life:

When morning came, they made me embark with them and they took me to the shore, which was visible, and where their wives and other Indians were. When I arived there, I heard these people, and even those with whom I had come, yell frightfully. This made me tremble and I thought they would kill me any moment.

Several days later other Akokisas arrived:

They also came from the end of the bay and landed where I was. At their arrival the same yelling occurred as before. I did not know what it all meant, though later learned that it was their custom to yell as well for good as for bad news.

Expectant Atakapa women were isolated in specially-built huts where they were attended by a number of "old crones of the village." New-born babies were strapped to a piece of bark, bent to fit the child's body (Dyer, 1917):

The head was left free, so that the mother could pick up the strapped bundle and hold it to the breast to nurse. The infant was removed from its cage twice daily, fresh moss being placed between the legs to absorb the natural discharges.

326

Children's heads were accidentally deformed by the type of cradle they were placed in. Also from Dyer we learn that the men changed their names upon the birth of a male heir or when their sons became famous. This widespread practice, known as teknonymy, names a parent after the child, the parent becoming known as father (or mother) of So-and-So. Among the more eastern Atakapas, a father resumed his old name if a child died. (Swanton, 1911: 13) Teknonymy is a reflection of the social milieu and is not entirely foreign in Western culture. A woman, for example, frequently feels too close to her parents-in-law to refer to them as "Mr. and Mrs. Jones" but feels that the use of their given names shows undue familiarity. Using the circumlocution "Junior's grandpa" or some similar appellation is an acceptable if somewhat tortured compromise. There are, of course, other reasons for practicing teknonymy. It may be a reflection of male dominance in which a woman is not privileged to use her husband's given name; and other reasons could be cited. What was behind Atakapan teknonymy we know not.

Not much else is known of Atakapan social institutions. Dyer makes a casual reference to women's being bartered, implying that their position was an inferior one. And among the eastern Atakapas, the women built the mounds upon which the chiefs' houses were reared, and the "women alone are charged with the labors of the field and of the household." (Swanton, 1911: 363)

De Bellisle's candid comments quoted at the head of this chapter leave no doubt that the Akokisas practiced cannibalism, but it is not known whether all Atakapans did so or not. It is not reported for the Bidais, nor is it clear whether the custom was practiced by the Akokisas because of religious beliefs or ghoulish appetites. Taking into account the fact that most of their neighbors and most other Texas natives practiced cannibalism occasionally for magical reasons, it seems a logical conjecture that the anthropophagy of the Akokisas was of a similar type. When the Akokisa hunting party of which De Bellisle was a member returned from the hunt and their cannibalistic feasts, he records (Folmer, 1940: 220) that the women "began to dance for joy, and continued to do so without halting a moment during two days, holding in their hands a bone or a nail of one of their

327

enemies which their husbands had killed." Perhaps they had cause for joy if Morfi (1932: 2) was correct in his appraisal of them: "The nation is not very populous, and it is very cowardly. They only use their arms against wild beasts and those who are so unfortunate as to be shipwrecked on their shores."

Supernaturalism. Our knowledge of Atakapan religious and magical beliefs and practices is as sketchy as that of other facets of their culture. An early nineteenth-century manuscript, describing Eastern Atakapa beliefs, is probably applicable to the Texas Atakapas (Swanton, 1911: 363; also 1907):

The Atacapas pretend that they are come out of the sea, that a prophet or man inspired by God laid down the rules of conduct to their first ancestors (*pères*) which consisted in not doing any evil. They believe in an author of all things: that those who do well go above, and that those who do evil descend under the earth into the shades. They speak of a deluge which swallowed up men, animals, and the land, and it was only those who resided along a high land or mountain . . . who escaped this calamity.

Dyer's account of Atakapan creation is essentially like Swanton's. According to his information the Atakapans believed they had first come from the sea, "being cast up in large oyster shells, from which the first men grew." They also believed that "men that were eaten by men, and those that died from snake bite, were believed to be incapable of entering a second life, hence were eternally damned." (Dyer, 1917) Ensuring the eternal damnation of the enemy may have been the *raison d'être* for Akokisa cannibalism.

Atakapa shamans held a somewhat special position in society, if the location of their dwellings on mounds is any indication. But apart from the cures they performed, we know nothing of their activities. Dyer (1917) recounts that in the first quarter of the nineteenth century Colonel Graham, who had been forced to stay in an Atakapa village because of dysentery, was treated by a shaman:

The shaman took charge of Graham, and started in by giving him hot decoctions of a red root, so astringent that he said "he felt his insides pucker up." His bed was a slightly raised platform of drift wood, covered with moss and skins. A fire was kept up day and night and water poured on the

328

hot oyster shells of the fireplace, keeping the hovel steaming hot [and] . . . his diet was confined for some days to a broth made from shell fish.

Bidais also treated dysentery with boiled roots and berries; other diseases, such as European-introduced typhoid fever, they treated by placing the patients on scaffolds under which smudge fires were built. (Sjoberg, 1951: 399) The Akokisas used yaupon leaves in a drink consumed upon ceremonial occasions, but apparently not in the quantity drunk by Karankawas. The Lake Charles Atakapas had ceremonial dances similar to those of the Karankawas.

ALTHOUGH WE KNOW distressingly little about Atakapan culture, it is apparent that its provincial, peripheral relationship to other Southeastern tribes was basically a matter of adjustment to a distinctive coastal environment. It did not permit the intensive type of farming practiced by the Caddoes or other Southeasterners. Along much of the Gulf Coast there were many tribes of different languages and cultural affiliation who could not live like their relatives in the interior. To be successful along the coast they had to utilize fish and shellfish, and the methods developed to do this were shared by a number of otherwise diverse tribes. It should be mentioned, too, that the beach-combing, more or less scavenger type of existence led by such tribes as the Akokisas was an old one along the Gulf Coast. It goes back to Archaic times, at least, but the indications are that it was no single people who originally populated the coast, but portions of inland tribes who gradually worked out their fish-shellfish and hunting exploitation. None of them ever became truly seafaring, or gave up their ties with their inland relatives. None came close to fully exploiting the potential of marine subsistence.

PART V
Bitter Bread of Banishment

STORY

CHAPTER 13

Extermination and Oblivion

> Texas was generous in respect to its aboriginal in-
> habitants, being ever willing to give its Indians to
> any one who might want them. In fact, the Texas
> mandate, though not recorded in the statutes, was,
> "Go elsewhere or be exterminated."
>
> Edward S. Curtis—*The North American Indian*

THOSE WHO WRITE of the near-extermination of American Indians
generally take sides. Some tell of the brutal butchery and the economic and political exploitation of the Indian by the white man;
others recall the raised tomahawk, the slain child, the scalped mother,
the plundered frontier cabin. Unfortunately, but naturally, many of
the histories written by Americans (and especially Texans) have
obscured, twisted, or rationalized the facts in favor of the white man.
Recently there has been a trend in the opposite direction, and admittedly it has been fostered by social scientists biased in favor of
native peoples. The present account is not an apology or rationalization for either side; it is, rather, an attempt to provide a realistic
over-all view of what happened when Anglo-American civilization
came into contact and inevitable conflict with the Indian cultures of

333

Texas.[1] The facts of history are plain: Most Texas Indians were exterminated or brought to the brink of oblivion by Spaniards, Mexicans, Texans, and Americans who often had no more regard for the life of an Indian than they had for that of a dog, sometimes less. What happened during this era is largely a tale of bloodshed and massacre, yet it is also part of a larger unfolding, that of the emergence of a powerful industrial nation. If some of the Spaniards, Mexicans, Texans, and Americans appear utterly brutal and degraded in this account, it is because historic facts make them so, and not because I presume to pass judgment upon them. Nor is an objective appraisal of why Indian cultures had to perish a rationalization for the white man; it is, instead, a commentary upon cultural life and death.

We have already considered the contact of the Spanish and French with the various tribes of Texas Indians during the colonial period. But before turning to the final chapters of the story, it would be well to sum up the results of these earlier relationships, and to note the nature of the various tribes and nations arrayed against each other early in the nineteenth century when Americans first entered Texas. Spain had been in contact with and influenced Texas Indians for more than three centuries. The effects of Spanish presence upon these peoples varied tremendously, but generally the tribes that had the closest relations with this colonial power were weakened the most. Those who had had little direct contact either had not been weakened, or had benefited from it. Spain had not explored all of Texas, of course, particularly the plains regions of the state. They were not attractive to the Spaniards because they had no gold, no mines, and no sedentary population that could be exploited or missionized. Their vast expanses of treeless surface were also forbidding and confusing to the Spaniard. Spain never seriously tried to colonize the plains, and after 1720 was probably incapable of doing so in the

[1] This chapter relies upon many sources, but the greatest debts are owed to Rupert N. Richardson's *The Comanche Barrier to South Plains Settlement* (1933); Walter P. Webb's *The Texas Rangers: A Conflict of Civilizations* (1935) and *The Great Plains* (1931); and James Mooney's *Calendar History of the Kiowa Indians* (1898).

face of the growing menace of mounted Apaches and Comanches. By the end of the Spanish reign the Comanches were in the ascendancy and had, in fact, pushed back the frontier. (Webb, 1931: 138)

French influence on Texas Indians was briefer and much less extensive than the Spanish, only the Caddoes, Atakapans, and Wichitas becoming intimately involved with them. The French also treated the natives very differently than did the Spaniards. Unlike Spaniards, they came as traders, and their control over native peoples depended upon trade relationships. And from the time of La Salle onward, they married and settled among the Caddoes. Following the Louisiana Purchase early in the nineteenth century, the French ceased to be a factor in the history of Texas.

The Jumanos and Coahuiltecans, being on the southern margins of the state, had early been exposed to Hispanic civilization. By the nineteenth century the Jumanos, as we have seen, had been exterminated. The Coahuiltecans just seem to have faded away. The Spanish established missions among them early, disease took its toll, and by the beginning of the nineteenth century most Coahuiltecans either were already destroyed, had moved southward into Mexico, or had joined other Indian groups. The coastal Karankawas, while no longer numerous, had become merciless and inveterate enemies of Europeans of whatever stamp. They were a serious, if temporary, threat to weak young colonies. The Tonkawas were still culturally a going concern at the opening of the new century but were weak and impoverished. The Comanches and other tribes were their constant enemies, and for self-protection the Tonkawas became habitual allies and helpers of the Anglo-American settlers. The Lipans were not numerous, were disorganized politically, were harried by Comanches, and, like the Tonkawas, were usually at the beck and call of the settlers. The Caddo confederacies had sporadically been exposed to Spanish mission influence, their lands had been a bone of contention between France and Spain, and the high incidence of epidemic diseases had combined to reduce their strength drastically. They were relatively peaceful to boot, and would have quietly continued their slide to oblivion if Texans had left them alone. The Wichita subtribes—the Wacos and Tawakonis—were militant and were allied

335

with the Comanches, but they were weak numerically. In brief, all of these Texas tribes were for one reason or another incapable of withstanding for long the onslaughts of a determined foe. It was only the Comanches and their allies (Wichitas in early days; later, Kiowas and Kiowa Apaches, Cheyennes, and Arapahoes) who were strong in numbers and aggressive by nature, people who would sell their land and independence dearly. The nineteenth-century struggle for Texas was, then, basically a three-sided affair. In the west were the Comanches and their allies, on the south the Mexicans, and in the east the Anglo-Americans. The location of all tribes, historic sites, and geographical features mentioned in this chapter are shown on Map 3.

Although we have discussed Comanche culture at length, it will be helpful to review here some of its military weaknesses and strengths. The Comanches had just been tested by a century of conflict with Spaniards and diverse Indian tribes. They had emerged the victor, a conquering, warlike horde. Every man was a warrior, wily, intelligent, and, when necessary, courageous in the extreme. Before the enthusiastic adoption by Texas Rangers of Samuel Colt's new revolver in 1839 or 1840 (Webb, 1931: 173), the Comanches had few peers as fighting men in the plains. Even after the Rangers obtained these "equalizers" the Comanches cannot be characterized as their inferiors. They could outride the white men, and their bows and arrows were scarcely less effective than the cap-and-ball rifle. The Indian could loose a dozen or more arrows for every rifle shot, although from a shorter distance and perhaps with less accuracy. Add the facts that the Comanches knew the land intimately, fought only when and where they chose, and were steeped in a warrior tradition of fantastic pluck, and it is easy to understand why Texans came to regard them with hatred and terror.

Whatever military defects the Comanches had, they were not to be found in the character of her warriors. Their weaknesses were of a different kind and ultimately of a more serious nature. Divided as the Comanches were into a number of autonomous bands, lacking completely a single leader or a unified leadership, they were incapable of fighting either tribal or national wars. Instead of attacking

336

with organized armies, they were limited to volatile war parties, and although occasionally these numbered several hundred warriors, they were normally much smaller. With no tribal organization there could be no tribal purposes or goals. They could not join together for concerted action against their enemies, nor could they ally themselves with either of their principal antagonists—Mexican and Texan —to defeat one or the other of them. Another liability, particularly in the struggle with Americans, was the Comanches' nomadic mode of life. A particular piece of land might be within a band's favored range, yet there might be no Comanches on it for long periods of time. American settlers felt free to move onto unoccupied land, and quite naturally the natives resented it. Lastly, Comanches were ignorant. They had no way of knowing or finding out important facts about their adversaries. They could not comprehend, for example, how Texans could be fighting Mexicans one day and be at peace with them the next. In all the twists and turns of Texan and American action, the Indians could only be perplexed, and consequently were unable to take advantage of favorable situations to attack their enemies at propitious times.

Very nearly the same comments can be made about the Kiowas and the associated Kiowa Apaches. Individually, they were bold and fearless warriors, and for a number of years held American soldiers in fine contempt. It was perhaps this attitude of superiority which enraged Americans and gave the Kiowas a particularly unsavory reputation. Unlike Comanches, the Kiowas and Kiowa Apaches could function as a tribal unit, but their numbers were so few that this gave them no advantage. Since many of the events of later Kiowa and Kiowa Apache history occurred outside the borders of Texas, they are less important to our story than the Comanches. But it should be kept in mind that they were long-time allies of the Comanches and made innumerable raids along the Texas frontier with them.

The second force in the three-sided struggle for Texas was the Mexican. In many ways the basic nature of this Latin-Indian civilization is the most difficult of the three to judge. This is so because the struggle for Texas came at a time when Mexico was shaking herself free from the grip of Spain, and was changing rapidly. The new na-

337

tion was politically unstable, economically weak, and in a poor position to withstand Indian or Texan attacks on her northern borders. Her residents were a hodgepodge of Spanish and Indian, the Indians of many tribes and degrees of assimilation. Nineteenth-century Mexico had also inherited a rigid, class-structured, Church-oriented society: at the top was the Spaniard or his descendants; at the bottom, a usually inert mass of Indian peons. It is not surprising that the northern sector of this depressed, unarmed, exploited, poorly-assimilated populace was for many years at the mercy of the warriors of the Texas plains. In contrast to the other contenders for Texas, Mexico was laconic, usually unaggressive, and relatively soon yielded up her stake in the state.

The third force in the nineteenth-century struggle for Texas—the Texan—is also difficult to appraise realistically, but for different reasons. So much has been written about Texans by their spiritual if not actual descendants that to separate fact from fiction is perhaps impossible. But several cultural traits, when they are contrasted with those of the other contenders for Texas, stand out. The paramount one stems from the fact that after her revolution Texas became an independent nation. We may say that Texans came into being with the victory at San Jacinto. They came to regard themselves as a breed apart, perhaps, too, a chosen people in a chosen land. Their belief in themselves could not be matched by Mexicans and probably not consciously by any Indians. Their infatuation with themselves and their land resulted at times in noble deeds. At others, it sank to provincialism, stupidity, and self-satisfaction. But say what you may, this infatuation was guileless, ever passionate, and a great advantage in the winning of Texas.[2]

Besides the *esprit de corps* of the pioneers, there were several other factors which weighed heavily in the Texans' success. For one, they

[2] These remarks are not intended to apply to modern Texas residents. The old-time Texan, the old Texas subculture, is passing from the scene, particularly in the mushrooming metropolitan districts. The influx of Americans from everywhere, the ease of communciation with the rest of the world, is submerging or has submerged the old-style Texan. Cowboy boots that have never touched the flanks of horseflesh and Stetson hats more accustomed to hotel hatracks than to the open air are not here regarded as indicative of *the* Texan.

338

were purposeful, especially when contrasted with the other contenders for Texas. Their goal was the possession of all that is Texas today, perhaps more, and there was never any wavering from it. If other, "inferior" people were in their way, it was their misfortune. These others could escape if they were bright, or stay and eventually become second-class citizens, or they could be exterminated. By way of contrast, Indian goals were aimless or inconsistent, those of the Mexican, defensive or revengeful. Stubborn, single-minded purposefulness was an inestimable Texan asset.

Texans were also fortunate in having inherited a society that was young, vigorous, and mostly unencumbered by rigid, anachronistic institutions. It was a society exploding by virtue of the industrial revolution of the nineteenth century let loose in an unexploited land. It was a society that rewarded the man who boldly grappled with the elements and bested them, natural and human. Although Texans were individualistic, they could, when pressed by events, quickly join together in the pursuit of given aims. They did not, at least in the early days, have to wait for higher governmental authority to initiate their wars or other actions. Their small communities were democratically run, and for want of powerful, centralized, well-established political institutions, were adaptable and adjustable to exigencies as they arose. But the atomistic, individualistic nature of frontier society was also a weakness as well as a strength. Following an Indian raid, for example, ably-led troops or posses could rapidly be organized, but when the crisis had passed, support for such bodies —whether Rangers or others—waned, and again the pioneers scattered to their individual parcels of land, defenseless targets for Indian attacks.

Whatever else the early Texans were—brutal, single-minded, grasping—they were also intelligent, if this means the ability to adjust quickly to new situations. To settle Texas and particularly the plains region, to subjugate its lands, to wrest it from Mexico and the Indians, the woodsman from the East had to learn from the Indian and the Mexican. It is a credit to him that he did, that he learned to fight like the Indian, ride like the Mexican, and finally whip them both. But we must not overemphasize the qualities of the man pro-

339

duced on the frontiers of Texas. It is almost always overlooked that by 1830 there were more Anglo-Americans in Texas than there were Mexicans and Indians combined, and their numerical superiority soon became everwhelming. (Webb, 1935: 10) In addition, the leaders of Texas were smart enough or lucky enough never to have had to fight both of their principal adversaries at the same time. A weak Texas force wrested independence from a nation in the throes of revolution. Despite crushing superiority in numbers and military might, the best that Texas and the United States could do was to defeat the Comanches and their allies by logistic strategy. When the Comanches' ponies and food supply gave out, they had to give up; they were not defeated in battle in the strict sense of the term.

It must be borne in mind that the American advance into Texas was a very different kind of movement, and by a civilization with very different motivation, from what the Spanish one had been. Spain's fourfold purpose was to conquer, convert, exploit, and incorporate the native. (Webb, 1931: 88) The American came to exploit, too, but to exploit what the land itself had to offer. Natives were often "taken" but this was a minor by-product of the American advance, and is not to be confused with the virtual enslavement of the Indians in the Spanish system of *encomiendas*. The reduction and enslavement of an alien people had no place in the American advance. Amalgamation with native peoples was likewise undesirable and, for most Texans, unthinkable. Conversion might be desirable from the point of view of the various Protestant sects who trotted in the wake of the frontier's advance, but no padre, no minister, accompanied Lewis and Clark, Pike, or the other American explorers. It is as if the native people were not considered by frontiersmen—all eyes were on the land. The Indians were simply an obstacle to be removed or swept aside, like a rock or a briar patch in a farmer's field. The American settlement of Texas was different, too, in that it was the advancing colonization of a whole people—a nation—pushing slowly, yet inexorably, westward. Men came with their families and belongings to claim and live on land they were going to work themselves, not as conquistadors who hoped to reap a fortune and return to their distant homes.

From the very first there were conflicts between the American colonists and the Texas Indians. Some of Austin's colonists, for example, arrived by boat in 1821. Their schooner, the *Lively*, was wrecked on the coast, and most of the survivors were killed by Karankawas. Others, strangely, were escorted by these Indians to their destination. (Huson, 1953, I: 38) Perhaps their treatment of Americans should be viewed in light of their past relations with Europeans, and of the fact that a few years before, the Karankawas on Galveston Island had had difficulties with the pirate Lafitte. Some of Lafitte's men had captured an Indian woman, and in retaliation several pirates were slain. Lafitte then collected a force of several hundred men and two artillery pieces, and in a desperate battle forced the natives to withdraw with the loss of about thirty men. (Thrall, 1879: 135–136)

Once hostilities had begun, enduring peace was impossible. And shortly, the enmity between Austin's colonists and the Karankawas was extended to the colonies of Green C. DeWitt and Martín de León. By 1825, Austin was forced to undertake a campaign against the Karankawas. He defeated them badly and pursued them to the coast. The Indians appealed to the priests and civil authorities at Goliad, and a peace treaty was signed. Some Karankawas, however, continued to harass the colonists. (Huson, 1953, I: 38) The Mexican government finally sent Captain General Anastacio Bustamante and a body of troops to assist the colonists. In the ruthless campaign which followed, the troops and the colonists defeated the Indians completely. They were driven to Matagorda Bay, some even into the bay, where they drowned. About half of the Cocos and Karankawa proper were killed, and the remainder sued for peace. (Gulick *et al.* [eds.], 1922–27, IV, Pt. I: 245–246) In 1827 a treaty was signed with them, marking the end of the Karankawas as a barrier to the colonization of Texas.

After the 1827 treaty the decline and disappearance of the Karankawas is harder to follow, partly, no doubt, because their reduced number made it impossible for them to do more than get into relatively minor scrapes with Texans. During the Texas Revolution they seem to have switched sides several times, but without deriving any benefit from the struggle. They were quiet during the early years of the Republic, and as President Lamar in his Second Annual Message to Congress said: "The Carronchawas inhabiting the coast, the remnant of a once powerful race, but now too few to be formidable, have given us no uneasiness or any cause of complaint." (Gulick *et al.*, 1922–27, III: 159)

Scattered Karankawan remnants persisted along the coast for some years. In 1843 a band apparently gained permission from the Mexican government to settle west of the Nueces. Others may have moved south of the Rio Grande, and apparently a band lived on Padre Island. A Mexican ranging company under Captain Trinidad Aldrete almost annihilated a band living some fifty miles southwest of Corpus Christi in 1844. (Huson, 1953, I: 43) In 1858 some Karankawas fled back across the Rio Grande from Mexico and were exterminated by a party of ranchers.

While the major campaigns of the Mexicans and Texans against the Karankawas were unqualified successes, the efforts of the whites to wipe them out were not always crowned with success. Noah Smithwick (1900: 20–21), for example, recounts one fiasco:

Martin De Leon had settled his grant with Mexicans, most of them being his peons and vaqueros. He had a large stock of both horses and cattle, and between the Comanches, who stole his horses, and the Cronks, as the Karankawas were called, who killed his cattle, he had a troublesome time of it. Becoming exasperated at the constant depredations of the Cronks, he determined to take matters into his own hands. He organized his retainers into an army, and mounting a four-pounder swivel gun on a jackass, set out to annihilate the tribe. He ran them to cover, brought his artillery to bear and touched it off, but he did not take the precaution to brace up the jackass, and the recoil turned him a flying sumersault, landing him on top of the gun with his feet in the air, a position from which he was unable to extricate himself. The Mexicans got around him and tried to boost him, but the jackass had had enough of that kind of fun and philosophically declined to rise until released from his burden, so they had to dismount the jackass. By that time the Indians had disappeared and if any were killed they were taken off the field.

Nevertheless, the Karankawas were exterminated; trapped between the sea and white man landward, they had little chance to flee. More than most primitive people, too, they clung tenaciously to their old ways of life, refusing to bow to the material superiority of the white man. Perhaps for this reason the Karankawas came closer to being regarded as subhuman brutes (and hence fair game in all seasons) than did any other Texas tribe.

With the exception of the Karankawas, the young American colonies in Texas were not in mortal conflict with any Indians. The colonies were on the coastal plain, beyond the normal range of the dangerous Comanches.[3] And in the early years there was a ready market in the settlements for the horses the Plains Indians had stolen in Mexico, so the peace was easily kept. Stephen F. Austin was, however, captured by Comanches near the Nueces River in 1822, but when the Indians learned that he and his companions were Americans and not Mexicans, they quickly released them.

Neither the Tonkawas nor the Lipan Apaches were in armed conflict with the fledgling colonies. Before the opening of the nineteenth century the Lipans had become divided into two groups, and the Mexican Revolution had served to fragment them further. The Lower Lipans (so called from their position with reference to the Rio Grande) were neighbors of Stephen F. Austin's colony, and were consistently friendly. During the Texas Revolution they embraced their neighbors' cause, and some even received paying commissions in the Texas Army. Flacco the Elder, their head chief, was a close friend of Sam Houston, president of the Republic. (Sjoberg, 1953b: 79) The Upper Lipans, however, sided with Mexico during the Revolution, and after Flacco's death the Lower Lipans became estranged from the Texans, moving westward and thus blurring the distinction between the two divisions.

The Tonkawas were never a direct threat to the settlers, although their thieving and begging made them nuisances. Their enmity with the Comanches and Wichitas was also a liability so far as the white settlers were concerned. In 1824, for example, nearly two hundred Wacos and Tawakonis invaded the settlements hunting Tonkawas,

[3] Webb (1931: 161) has some interesting remarks on this point. Also see Richardson, 1933: 89.

and such a war party in the midst of peaceful settlements could not be countenanced. In the early 1820's the settlers on the lower Colorado and Brazos tried to solve the Tonkawa problem by gathering them together preliminary to expelling them from the region. In the nick of time, however, a Lipan chief arrived with a letter from Sam Houston stating that the Lipans had agreed to take charge of the Tonkawas. The Tonkawas left the vicinity with the Lipans, but in a few years drifted back towards the coast. (Sjoberg, 1953a: 283; Webb, 1935: 20–21)

In the early years of his colony Austin had the good sense to follow a policy of delay in dealing with the Comanches and Wichitas. The initial friendliness of the Comanches and a treaty made with the Wichitas allowed him to mark time while the colony gained strength and disposed of the troublesome coastal Indians. The Mexican government wanted him to go to war with the Comanches, who were raiding San Antonio and Goliad, but this he wisely did not do. By 1826, however, after forming an alliance with immigrant Cherokees, Shawnees, and Delawares, he was on the verge of campaigning against the increasingly troublesome Wichitas. The Mexican government postponed this campaign, however, to recruit more forces in Mexico.

But eastern Texas was filling up with settlers, and as they probed the borders of the plains, conflict with the powerful Comanches, as well as with the shaky Mexican government, was inevitable. When the Texas Revolution came it presented an unparalleled opportunity for the Comanches to lay waste the weakened and fearful colonies. But the efforts of the Texans to placate the Comanches, plus the Indians' ignorance of what was happening, apparently prevented a major disaster. The only big explosion occurred in May, 1836, when some northern bands of Comanches with Kiowa allies made "one of the most destructive raids ever made along the Texas frontier." (Richardson, 1933: 90) This was an attack on Parker's Fort, some seventy miles east of Waco, near Groesbeck in Limestone County. Under a flag of truce the Comanches learned that there were only five or six men in the stockade. They attacked the fort, killed several persons, and took five captives. But there is reason to suspect that this

344

attack was not unprovoked, for Parker was subsequently accused, though not convicted, of having stolen horses in company with Indians, only to cheat them out of the proceeds. And it is odd that a raid would be made so far east. Included among the captives was Mrs. Rachel Plummer, whose story of captivity is probably the best known of the Comanche captive tales. Its publication in 1839 did much to reinforce the Texan belief that "the only good Indian is a dead one." (Plummer, 1926) Nine-year-old Cynthia Ann Parker, another of the captives, could not be ransomed despite repeated attempts. She lived with, and as, a Comanche for twenty-four years, and her son, Quanah Parker, became one of the best known of later Comanche chiefs.

The victory of the Texans at San Jacinto appears to have shown the Comanches that their foes were not to be attacked without fear of serious consequences. And the southern Comanches remained friendly or neutral throughout the Revolution. Houston was also inclined to do his best to keep the newly-formed republic on friendly and peaceful terms with the Comanches. In 1838 a hundred and fifty Comanche warriors descended upon San Antonio to request that a delegation be sent to their camp some two hundred and fifty miles northward to effect a treaty of peace. A council was held, but since the Comanches insisted upon a boundary line between themselves and the hordes of settlers who were pouring into Texas, and since the citizens of San Antonio had no authority to negotiate such a boundary, the meeting was fruitless. They did agree to another meeting in the spring, at which time General Albert Sidney Johnston refused to bind the Republic to any boundary clause. In effect, the Comanches could have peace, but only so long as they were willing to allow Texans to despoil their hunting grounds and seize their lands freely.

About the time the San Antonio negotiations were going on, another band of Comanches in the vicinity of Austin also attempted to reach an accord with the Texans. Noah Smithwick had a leading part in these councils, and it was at this time that he spent three months in the Comanche camp. He finally persuaded the Indians to go to President Houston with him and sign a treaty. It provided that an

345

agent would be appointed to supervise trade, but the Texans did not keep their promises, ostensibly because the treaty was not ratified in the Senate. It was during these negotiations that Smithwick (1900: 194) reported Houston as saying: "If I could build a wall from the Red River to the Rio Grande, so high that no Indian could scale it, the white people would go crazy trying to devise means to get beyond it."

In 1838, Mirabeau B. Lamar succeeded Houston as president, and an aggressive program to defeat, expel, or exterminate the Indians replaced Houston's conciliatory policy. Lamar wanted to build military posts all along the frontier and garrison them with permanent and efficient forces. (Richardson, 1933: 103–104) The Comanches were already making heavier raids, even into San Antonio, so war was as much forced upon the government as the other way around. An immediate consequence was an expedition against the Comanches. A company of men was formed from Bastrop under Noah Smithwick, who joined a group from La Grange under W. M. Eastland, and two companies were put under the command of Colonel John H. Moore. There had been reports of large settlements of Comanches on the upper Colorado, and on February 15, 1839, these sixty-three Texas volunteers plus sixteen Lipans and Tonkawas surprised a Comanche camp near the mouth of the San Saba. They killed a number of Indians, but were soon attacked by a party of warriors and forced to withdraw. The Comanches, under a white flag, probably the one Houston had given them at the treaty in 1838, requested an exchange of prisoners. But the Lipans had killed all of the Comanche prisoners, so no exchange could be effected. (Winfrey, 1959: 57–59)

In October, 1840, Colonel Moore was more successful, and on the Colorado far upstream from Austin, attacked an unsuspecting Comanche camp. The Rangers estimated that forty-eight Indians were killed in the battle and that eighty more drowned in the river. Two Texans were wounded. In the spring of 1839 another party of Rangers, under Captain John Bird, was not so successful. The thirty-five Rangers were surrounded by a large force of Comanches on Little River, a tributary of the Brazos in central Texas, and before

346

withdrawing with unknown but probably heavy losses, the Indians killed seven Rangers, including Captain Bird. (Webb, 1935: 45–47)

In 1839 the Texans were diverted to some extent from the Comanches since they were busy driving the Cherokees and allied Indians out of the state. Earlier in the century uprooted Indians from the East—Shawnees, Delawares, Kickapoos, Seminoles, Cherokees, and others—had settled on the headwaters of the Sabine, among the remnants of the Caddo confederacies, and in other places in east Texas. These were agriculturally-inclined Indians, and they naturally settled on rich farm lands. As soon as white men began to settle this part of the state they began to agitate for the removal of the Indians. But Houston, ever the Indians' friend, negotiated a treaty on February 25, 1836, which would have provided land for the immigrant Indians in Cherokee, Smith, and adjoining counties. Despite Houston's urging, the 1837 Senate refused to ratify the treaty. Lamar, Houston's Indian-hating successor, appointed a commission, supported it with troops, and sent them to expel the Cherokees. When the Cherokees refused to comply with the commission's request to leave immediately, they were attacked by the troops and defeated in two engagements in July, 1839. Chief Bowles was brutally slain, and the surviving Indians were relentlessly pursued for more than a week. Most of the survivors fled across the Red River into the Choctaw and Chickasaw nations.

Papers had fallen into the hands of the Texas government which indicated that the Mexican government was attempting to ally itself with the Indians of the frontiers for a war against Texas. The Cherokees had undoubtedly listened to Mexican agents, but that they were actively involved in the plot is in serious doubt. Their chief, Bowles, was a sensible man and seems to have realized that to involve his people in war would have been disastrous. The truth of the matter seems to be that Lamar had a convenient excuse for attacking peaceful Indians, and he seldom needed so much as an excuse for such actions.

It was also during this period that the remnants of the Caddo confederacies were removed from their ancestral lands. (Glover, 1935) By the beginning of the nineteenth century most of the remaining

Caddoes had settled on Sodo Creek, near present Shreveport, Louisiana. Following the Louisiana Purchase they had become wards of the United States government, but since they remained on the borders their allegiance was sought by both the United States and Spain. Because white settlers were taking up Caddo lands and difficulties between the Indians and United States citizens were multiplying, the Caddoes, in a treaty made in July, 1835, agreed to sell their lands to the government and move beyond the boundaries of the United States. Spain had made overtures to the Caddoes and set aside land in Texas for them. The Texas Revolution disrupted these plans, however, as the Texas government considered the Caddoes to be unwanted intruders. In effect, the hapless Caddoes had become homeless, with poor prospects of securing a place to settle. Mexican agents now made overtures to the Caddoes, as they had to the Cherokees; the Caddoes obtained guns and ammunition from the United States, and shortly these once peaceful people were raiding the Texas frontier. The Texans retaliated and there matters rested until Houston again become president in 1841.[4] In September, 1843, at Bird's Fort on the Trinity River, a treaty was concluded between the Republic of Texas and a number of Indian tribes—Caddoes, Delawares, Shawnees, and the Wichita subtribes—by which it was agreed that the Indians and Texans would thereafter live in peace and friendship. Thus, the history of the once mighty Caddoes comes nearly to its end, a forlorn remnant joining other remnants in yielding sovereignty and independence to the Republic of Texas.

Texas felt it necessary, of course, to secure its eastern flank so that it could pursue more safely its designs in the west and south. And its defeat and expulsion of the Cherokees and other remnant tribes in east Texas did accomplish this end. But it was neither a glorious nor a humane epoch in the state's history. (Webb, 1935: 47–55; Foreman, 1946: 160–161)

While the immigrant Indians were not welcomed by Texans, except when they could be recruited to fight for them, they were even less welcomed and more despised by the "wild" Indians of the plains.

---

[4] See Jenkins (1958: 21–22) for the kind of treatment accorded Caddoes by Texans.

As early as 1830 the bison range was retreating westward, and the white man and the immigrant Indians of the frontier were chiefly responsible. To the white man and even to the immigrant Indians, the disappearance of the bison was not a serious matter, but to Comanches and other Plains natives it was catastrophic. These immigrant Indians were equipped with the best European weapons, all the deceits of the white man, yet retained all the wilderness skills of their ancestors. They roamed the plains at will and slaughtered the bison, lifeblood of the Plains Indians. Seldom did Plains Indians dare to attack these dangerous intruders, and when they did they were almost invariably defeated. The allegation that the "wild" Plains tribes, particularly the Comanches, were more deadly, dangerous adversaries than these Eastern Indians is sheer myth.[5] The climax of the struggle between the immigrant, "civilized" Indians and the "wild" tribes came in 1854. Approximately fifteen hundred Kiowas, Kiowa Apaches, Comanches, Cheyennes, Arapahoes, Osages, and some Crows set out on an expedition to exterminate the intruders. Near the Smoky Hill River in Kansas these allies met a party of eighty Sauk, Fox, and Potawatomi Indians. The Easterners sought shelter, but were immediately surrounded and charged by their more numerous enemy. In the fight that followed, the accurate rifle fire of the Easterners killed about twenty of the attackers, including a prominent Kiowa war chief, and wounded approximately one hundred more. The "implacable" warriors of the Plains were forced to retreat in ignoble defeat. Six "civilized" Indians were slain. (Mooney, 1898: 297–299)

By 1830 the more southerly bands of Comanches, and probably all the Comanches and Kiowas to some extent, were becoming impoverished through the loss of land and the decline in game. They were forced to increase their forays, both along the Texas frontier and particularly into Mexico. They were raiding as far as the state of Zacatecas in 1840, and in 1842 were walking the streets of Saltillo. Nuevo León was the hardest hit, but San Luis Potosí, Zacatecas, Durango, Chihuahua, Tamaulipas, and Coahuila also felt Comanche might. After Texas became a state and when the borders of the United

[5] See Webb (1931: 59) as an example of these wild, unsubstantiated claims.

349

States were more adequately policed, raiding in Mexico was reduced. By 1857 the raids had decreased further, and by 1860 they were rare. Not only was the United States government barring the way with forts and soldiers, but the Mexican government was also adopting more forceful protective policies. Unfortunately for Texans, stopping Indian raids across the border meant that increasingly-impoverished Comanches and Kiowas stepped up their forays in Texas.

But to return to the chronological order of events. During the winter of 1839–40 a band of southern Comanches again asked for peace, apparently realizing that they would ultimately be defeated. They were invited to San Antonio to parley, and in the spring of 1840 a band of sixty-five men, women, and children came in. The men gathered in the Courthouse, the women and children remaining outside. The Indians had brought along a white captive, as had been stipulated in the arrangements for the council. It is likely that this was the only captive this band had, although other bands or sub-bands of southern (Penateka) Comanches did have other prisoners. When the Indians produced only this one captive, the troops were ordered to take the Indians into custody. In the unequal fight that followed, thirty-five Indians, including three women and two children, were slain. Seven white persons were killed and eight wounded. (Richardson, 1933: 108–111) When word of this massacre reached other bands of southern Comanches they promptly tortured thirteen prisoners to death, and retaliatory attacks occurred all along the frontier. In one of these the Comanches raided as far as the coast, but on their return were defeated at Plum Creek near Lockhart. To follow up the Texan victory a force of ninety white men and twelve Lipans under Colonel John H. Moore marched up the Colorado, nearly three hundred miles northwest of Austin, to make a night attack on an unsuspecting Comanche camp. One hundred and thirty savages were slain and thirty-four women and children were taken prisoner in the worst defeat ever suffered by the Comanches at the hands of Texans.[6] Following this defeat and throughout 1841 the frontier was relatively

[6] See Jenkins (1958: 60–68) for an account of the battle of Plum Creek by a participant, and the subsequent expedition against the Comanches.

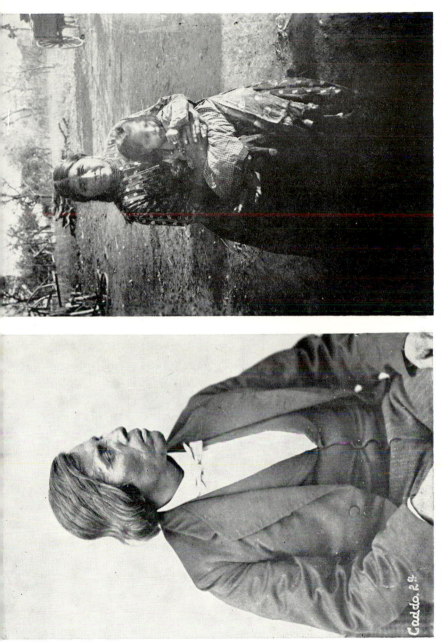

PLATE XII. Caddoes: Nah-ah-sa-nah (known also as Warloupe), for in 1825 near Nachitoches (left). *Photograph by Alexander Gardner, 1872.* Minnie Parton and Charlie Parton (right). *Photograph by James Mooney, 1893. Courtesy of the Smithsonian Institution, Bureau of American Ethnology.*

PLATE XIII. This Comanche was the only member of a twelve-man war party to return from a raid against the Texas frontier (left); A Comanche captive (right). *A. B. Stephenson Collection, courtesy Barker Texas History Center.*

quiet. There were raids in the San Antonio neighborhood, but the Comanches were learning through bitter experience what could be expected from Texans, and were pulling back from the frontier.

When Sam Houston became president again in 1841, Texas returned to a policy of peace. In order to carry out this about-face it was necessary to make treaties with all of the remaining Texas tribes. The small, demoralized tribes responded readily, as we have seen, but the Comanches, too often burned, were difficult to draw into councils. Finally, in 1843, a party was sent out under Colonel J. C. Eldridge, accompanied by Delaware scouts and a Waco chief, to find the Comanches. The party set out in May and in August finally reached the camp of the chief of a band of Penateka Comanches, west of present Lawton, Oklahoma. They were made virtual captives by the Comanches, however, and but for the intercession of the Comanche chief, all would have been slain. (Winfrey, 1959: 210–218, 228–229, 251–275)

In 1844 some Comanches, with representatives from the small tribes, were finally gathered together for a council on Tehuacana Creek (also called Council Springs), near present Mexia, in Limestone County. In one section of the treaty which Houston drew up, there was a clause which provided for a boundary line between the Comanches and the Texans—the long-sought Comanche dream. The boundary line was unacceptable to Buffalo Hump, one of the chiefs, and this clause was striken from the treaty. But even if a boundary line had been agreed upon, it would have done slight good. The Texas government was too weak to hold its settlers behind any line, and Comanche chiefs could not have prevented their warriors from crossing such boundaries to raid.

Treaties between Texas and its Indians were never taken very seriously by any of the signatories. Texans hoped to gain concessions from treaties, but gave little or nothing themselves, and they knew that whatever promises they made would likely be broken. Indians got presents at the councils, but were often unable to abide by the terms of treaties, if in fact they even realized what the terms were. It was also difficult, particularly in the case of Comanches, to know

just how many of the tribe came under the provisions of any particular treaty. One band of Comanches might sign a treaty, but in their
minds this in no way bound other bands.

In 1845 the combination of the news of peace with the Texans and
the appearance of bison far south of their normal range brought the
Comanches back, close to the settlements. Such proximity could only
lead to increased friction. The first trouble was caused by renegade
Delawares, who had frequently aided the Texans in dealing with Comanches. They killed several Comanches, and the Comanches, of
course, swore vengeance on the Delawares and their white allies. Two
white men were soon killed a few miles below Austin, although the
connection between these events may be coincidental. The Delaware
affair was smoothed over, but relations between Texas and the Comanches continued precarious. The Comanches continued to raid
mainly in Mexico, but in passing near or through the Texas settlements some kind of depredation was almost sure to occur. The Indians
could not afford to trust the Texans, and the settlers had to be constantly on guard against the Indians. The Comanches met in council
only when it suited their whim or when they could be confident of
lavish presents. The settlers were ever eager to meet in council but
were equally unwilling to yield anything to the natives. The settlers
continued to slaughter the game on which the Indians depended,
and the frontier continued its glacier-like advance. (Richardson,
1933: 136–137)

When Texas became a state in 1846 the losers were the Indians.
The state kept its public lands, but the Indian problem was inherited by the United States. In a way this sealed the fate of the remaining Texas Indians. The state felt no responsibility for Indians
who were on what it considered to be "its" lands, and the federal
government could not solve the Indian problem without providing
land for them to settle on. In the spring a large number of Penateka
Comanches were gathered together on Tehuacana Creek. Wichitas
and Caddoes were also represented, and the able Indian agent Robert
S. Neighbors was present. The treaty signed at this council provided
that the Indians recognize the jurisdiction of the United States, agree
to trade only with licensed traders, give up prisoners, surrender mur-

352

derers and thieves, and in the future restore stolen horses. For its part the federal government was to build trading stores and agencies, furnish blacksmiths, and at a council give presents in the value of ten thousand dollars.

It was imperative at this time for the government to have peace with the Indians because of the onset of the Mexican War. Through the outstanding service of Neighbors, who personally went directly into Indian territory in an attempt to settle differences, any serious violation of the peace was averted, and some of the Tonkawas and Lipans fought on the side of the Texans. The only major clash between Comanches and Texans was over the settlement of Germans on more than three million acres of land lying between the Llano and Colorado Rivers. (Biesele, 1927: 118, 124–125) Neighbors was able to settle the dispute, at least temporarily, by a treaty in which the Indians were given three thousand dollars' worth of presents. It was during this period that Dr. Ferdinand Roemer, the German scientist, was among the Comanches and Lipans.

A few years after the Mexican War, Ranger stations were set up, and these proved to be a source of great annoyance to the Indians. White men were allowed to cross the boundary line at will, but the Indians were prevented from doing so. This meant that Comanches and Kiowas were sometimes unable to cross into Mexico, their favorite raiding target. They had never agreed to cease raiding the Mexicans, even though the United States in the Treaty of Guadalupe Hidalgo had agreed to prevent such activities. In 1849, when the Whigs came into control, Neighbors, a Democrat, was removed from his post, even though he must be given most of the credit for having maintained the uneasy peace.

Again, then, the Indian situation was on the verge of bloody chaos. In 1848 the southern Comanches were hit by smallpox and cholera, and two chiefs, Old Owl and Santa Anna, who had counseled peace, died. The new agent, John H. Rollins, was old and did not meet the Indians in the field as had Neighbors. Raiding increased and conditions grew worse. Rollins was able, however, to sign a treaty with the Penateka Comanches in 1850, its one new feature being the Comanches' concession not to cross to the south side of the Llano

River without permission from an army officer. The treaty also resulted in the surrender of captives, and it is plain that these southern Comanches were a defeated people. But the more northern Comanches were shortly upbraiding their southern kinsmen for releasing prisoners without ransom, and conditions cannot be said to have improved, even though the southern Comanches were no longer the strong, proud warriors they had once been.

By the middle of the nineteenth century the tidal wave of white advance was on the verge of engulfing the unreconstructed but outnumbered Comanches. In the earlier years of the century the southern Comanche bands had taken the brunt of the frontier's advance. But by 1849, when the first great migration swept across the southern plains, almost all Comanches, as well as the Kiowas and Kiowa Apaches, had been brought into contact with the Americans. And in Texas the old problem remained (Richardson, 1933: 166–167):

The Indians and the Indian problem were federal matters, but the land belonged to the state. If the citizens of the state proposed to occupy the lands, and if the Indians objected, it was the duty of the United States either to remove the Indians or keep them from harassing the settlers. . . . The Indians were troublesome, said the Texans, and the federal forces ought to make war on them; they shed the blood of helpless women and children, and should be punished; they were in the way of expansion, and should be pushed back; really they had no right to remain in Texas, and the United States should remove them just as it had removed other Indians from Florida and Georgia.

Finally, in 1854, in a move to settle the Indian problem, the Texas Legislature authorized the United States government to select land for Indian reservations in Texas. One site was chosen on the Brazos near the mouth of the Clear Fork, the other about forty miles away on the Clear Fork along the present boundary of Haskell and Throckmorton Counties. The Brazos Reservation was to be used by the small, remnant tribes; the one on the Clear Fork, by Comanches. The Brazos Reservation finally gave a home to destitute bands from several tribes—Delawares, Shawnees, Tonkawas, Wichitas, and Caddoes. Several years earlier some Tonkawas had sought assistance from the forts in southern Texas, Fort Inge and Fort Clark. Most Tonkawas, however, seem to have moved from their camps along the Colorado to the Brazos Reservation. It was probably during this period that some of the Tonkawas crossed the Rio Grande to join Mexican-based bands of Lipans, and these bands caused trouble along the border for years, slipping across the river to steal livestock and quickly escaping to their inaccessible mountain bases in Coahuila and Chihuahua.

The plight of the Caddoes and Wichita subtribes—the Wacos and Tawakonis—had by this period become desperate. Some of them, particularly the Wichita subtribes, were skilled thieves and raiders, but their numbers were too few and their decline had proceeded too far for them to pose a serious menace to settlers. They had occupied land coveted by white settlers in the Brazos River valley, and from time to time had been forced by white pressure to move higher up the stream. (Richardson, 1933: 213–214) The reservation held out to them a promise of much-needed security.

The Wichita proper, as well as some of the northern Comanche bands, had been first officially contacted by the United States government in 1834, when Colonel Henry Dodge, leader of the Dragoon Expedition, held a council in one of the Wichita villages on the North Fork of the Red River in southwestern Oklahoma. In the three-day council the Comanches, Kiowas, and Wichitas were urged to live in peace with the Osages and their other eastern neighbors. As a result of this council a treaty was signed in the summer of 1835 at Camp Holmes, near the Canadian River in southcentral Oklahoma, by representatives of tribes from the eastern parts of Indian Territory (including the Osages) and by the northern Comanches and Wichitas. It bravely promised an impossible era of peace and friendship between the tribes. (Wright, 1951: 121–122, 258)

The Wichita proper were regarded as friendly to the United States after this treaty, and seem to have been so. In 1837 a smallpox epidemic swept through many of the tribes on the plains, and the Wichitas were among the hardest hit, reducing the likelihood of any hostile acts on their part. It has been said that sickness was so widespread the dead could not be removed from their houses. (Foreman, 1926: 234–238) By 1850 the remnants of the Wichita proper were located in the Wichita Mountains and in the vicinity of Fort Sill. And in 1859 the Wichita proper began to move to their agreed-upon reservation south of the Canadian River.

The impatient Kiowas had left the council at Camp Holmes in 1835 before a treaty was signed, but in 1837 they, as well as the Kiowa Apaches and Tawakonis, journeyed to Fort Gibson, where on May 26, 1837, they signed their first treaty with the United States. Like the Camp Holmes treaty it provided for peace with the Osages, the Creeks, and the United States. But "Texans" had always been distinguished from "Americans" by Kiowas and to a lesser extent by Comanches. And the Kiowas had consistently looked upon Texans as enemies, but tended to be friendly toward Americans. Soon after their treaty was signed with the United States, the Texan Santa Fe Expedition of 1841 was manhandled by the Kiowas in northwestern Texas to prove the point. They killed six members of the expedition and ran off a number of horses. (Mooney, 1898: 277–279)

By 1853 traffic was so heavy over the Santa Fe Trail, running through the lands of the Comanches and Kiowas, that the United States government thought it necessary to ensure its safety. A treaty was signed by Comanches, Kiowas, and Kiowa Apaches at Fort Atkinson in Kansas, allowing the government to build roads and forts in their country. In return they were to receive eighteen thousand dollars a year for ten years. While the Indians were not exactly eager to agree to the construction of roads and forts, they were even less willing to cease raiding in Mexico, a concession which the government also tried to obtain at this time. (Mooney, 1898: 173–174) The treaty seems to have lessened tensions along the Arkansas River for a few years, but by 1855 travelers were again paying a toll to use the Santa Fe Trail, and the Kiowas were becoming increasingly hostile and, as Americans termed it, insolent.

To return to affairs in Texas, we find that the Texas reservations established in 1854 were never a success, and they lasted but four years. The Indian agents failed to get along with the United States Army, and the citizenry never seems to have become reconciled to their existence. Only a small proportion of the Comanches were ever on their reservation, and of those who were, a few may have joined

356

raiding parties of off-reservation Comanches. But by and large, the Indians on both reservations were at peace, and the Brazos Reservation Indians in particular were of great help in supplying scouts for the United States Army and the Rangers. Nevertheless, by 1856 the Indian problem was serious and by 1858 some parts of the frontier were suffering heavily from Indian raids. Webb (1935: 151) has said that "there was more fighting and bloodshed in Texas in the two years, 1858–1859, than in any other similar period save only that of the Revolution in 1836." The more numerous Indian raids in 1858 stung the army and the Texas Rangers into action. And for the first time white forces penetrated the heart of Comanche country and defeated the Indians there.

In January, 1858, Governor Hardin R. Runnels appointed an experienced Ranger, John S. (Rip) Ford, to the command of the state's forces. By April Ford had collected a force of a hundred and two men, plus wagons and pack mules, and was soon joined by a hundred and thirteen Indian warriors, under Captain Shapley P. Ross, from the Brazos Reservation. This formidable force crossed the Red River and near the Canadian River attacked a Comanche camp. Iron Jacket, famed among Comanche chiefs for the Spanish mail he wore and for his presumed invulnerability, was among the first to fall. But the battle, or series of battles, lasted most of the day, the Comanches being decisively defeated. Ford estimated that he had fought three hundred warriors. His force killed seventy-six Indians and took eighteen captives, mostly women and children, as well as more than three hundred horses. The Texans lost two killed and two wounded. (Webb, 1935: 151–157) Seldom did the Comanches allow themselves to be caught by such a force as Ford had. It is probable that the Comanches felt secure outside of Texas, never even considering that Ford would pursue them beyond its borders. It should also be noted that the Indians of the Brazos Reservation—Shawnees, Delawares, and the Wichita subtribes particularly—probably made success possible. They located the Comanches in the first place (which likely the Texans could not have done), and bore a large share of the fighting in the second.

A second defeat of northern Comanche bands took place in October, 1858. These Comanches had just concluded a friendly council with United States officials and were on the way to their homes. They had camped near a Wichita village, situated near Rush Springs in what is now Oklahoma. Unexpectedly they were attacked by four companies of the Second United States Cavalry under Captain Earl Van Dorn, as well as by a hundred and twenty-five of the faithful Brazos Reservation Indians. In the brief but furious battle which ensued, fifty-six Indians were killed, the survivors dispersed, their lodges destroyed, and three hundred horses captured. The Cavalry lost five men, including two officers. Ross, the leader of the Brazos Indians, and Van Dorn were also wounded. Van Dorn was undoubtedly ignorant of the band's recent council with his government, but such engagements could only reinforce the Indian conviction that white men were masters of deceit.

Despite the defeats at the hands of the Texas Rangers and United States troops, the Indians did not stop their raids on the frontiers. They could not, for the Comanches had only the choice of raiding or starving. Naturally enough, the citizens of Texas soon became hostile to all Indians and especially directed their antagonism toward the obvious target—the peaceful Indians on the reservations. By 1859 the situation on the reservations was intolerable. All sorts of claims, mostly unfounded, were being made against the Indians. White persons killed innocent Indians. Indian stock was stolen, and but for the protection of the United States Army the reservations would have been attacked by mobs of white men. The federal government had to give in, and on July 31, the Indians from both reservations began their trek to Indian Territory and the Wichita Reservation near Fort Cobb, escorted by United States cavalry and infantry.

During the Civil War the Wichitas and most of the associated Indians lately from the Brazos Reservation fled to Kansas after signing a treaty with Confederate forces whose terms the South subsequently failed to carry out. After the war they left Kansas, and the town named for them, and returned to Indian Territory. Their agency was established near Anadarko, and a consolidated group known as "Wichita and Affiliated Tribes" was formed, composed of the Wichita proper, Tawakoni, Waco, Kichai, and Caddoes, as well as Dela-

358

wares, Shawnees, and some Penateka Comanches. (Wright, 1951: 258–260; Foreman, 1946: 302–304)

The Tonkawas, alone among the Indians of the Wichita Reservation, chose not to flee to Kansas during the war, and in 1862 suffered a disaster at the hands of other tribes. In this "Great Massacre" more than half of the Tonkawas were slaughtered. Why they were so served by their fellow Indians has never been made entirely clear. Thomas Battey (1876: 58–59), the Quaker agent of the reservation, believed the Tonkawas had eaten "a couple of Shawnees" and in revenge

The Shawnees, having collected a force composed of Shawnees, Creeks, and Delawares, pursued and overtook them there [near Fort Sill]. Taking them by surprise, they slew over one half of them, losing in the conflict some of their own men, so nearly two hundred human beings perished on that occasion. The allied force took care of their own dead, while those of the Tonqueways, who were thoroughly routed, were left on the ground, to be consumed by wolves and buzzards. Two or three years afterwards most of their bones were gathered up and buried; but some still remain to mark this scene of former barbarities.

It seems, however, that their continued allegiance to the South and their refusal to fight Texans were more likely the causes of their massacre. (Thrall, 1879: 449) A number of the survivors fled to Fort Arbuckle, and in 1863 moved to Fort Belknap in northern Texas. For the next decade the remaining Tonkawas roamed through central and northern Texas, often serving as scouts and guides for the federal army. In 1874 a few Lipans joined them and in 1884 the combined Tonkawa-Lipan group were moved to Indian Territory. They were first located on the Iowa Reservation, but in 1885 were removed to the Oakland Agency in northern Oklahoma. By 1944 but fifty-six Tonkawas remained, and this number included some Lipans. (Wright, 1951: 250) A few Tonkawas were reported in 1927 to live near Sabinas, in northern Coahuila. (Nance, 1952)

The later history of the Lipans is obscure, mainly because they had become so widely dispersed. By 1865, however, some of them had moved to Indian Territory, where they finally joined the Kiowa Apaches at Fort Sill. Other Lipans as late as the 1870's were still

359

roaming west of the Pecos. Some of these joined the Mescalero Apaches in southern New Mexico in 1879; others who had their headquarters in Coahuila and Chihuahua were rounded up by the United States government and placed on the Mescalero Reservation in 1905.

To return to the final destruction of the Comanches, we find that fortunately for them and the other southern Plains Indians, the Civil War gave them a breathing spell in which to regroup their forces and regain some of their depleted strength. Neither the North nor the South seriously attempted to enlist their active support, both sides being content to keep them neutral. But by 1864 the Comanches were strong enough to resume raiding the weakly-defended frontiers of Texas. And in the fall of 1863 it is believed that some sort of alliance was made by most of the southern Plains tribes—Comanches, Kiowas, Kiowa Apaches, Cheyennes, and some Arapahoes and Dakotas. Presumably they were to start a general war the following spring, but although Indian raids in Texas, and all up and down the plains, were common and devastating in 1864, there was no general war. (Mooney, 1898: 176–177) The situation was no better the following year throughout the plains, although it was clear by the fall of 1865 that the Indians desired peace. After a preliminary meeting in August, Kiowas, Comanches, and Kiowa Apaches signed a treaty in October at the mouth of the Little Arkansas, the site of present Wichita, Kansas. By the treaty the Kiowas and Comanches agreed to give up their claims to Colorado, Kansas, and New Mexico, and to occupy a reservation in southwestern Oklahoma and the Staked Plains of Texas. The Kiowas, alone among these tribes, seem to be the only ones to have violated the peace soon afterwards by making a raid in Texas. But the government also failed to live up to the terms of the treaty, and the combination of military campaigns against the Cheyennes and Dakotas and increasing unrest and hostility among the southern tribes resulted in the appointment of a federal peace commission.

As a result the Comanches, Kiowas, and Kiowa Apaches were called to a council on Medicine Lodge Creek, in Kansas, seventy miles south of Fort Larned. In signing what proved to be their last treaty

360

with the government the Comanches, Kiowas, and Kiowa Apaches were officially confederated and agreed to move to their reservation. Of more import, the treaty marked the end of these tribes as free and independent peoples. Probably a third of the Comanches did not sign the treaty, and it is doubtful whether the Kiowas understood its ramifications. The Indians could not easily settle on the land they were assigned in southwestern Oklahoma, for the government had made no preparations for them, and the waning supply of game in the region could not sustain them. Partly in consequence, the winter of 1867–68 saw as many depredations in Texas and Indian Territory as ever. But by the summer of 1868 the beginning of the end was in sight. If the Indians went on the reservation there was not sufficient food for them; if they remained away they were attacked by troops.

It was in 1869 that Congress authorized President Grant to set up a Board of Indian Commissioners. He appointed Quakers to the board, and a Quaker, Laurie Tatum, became the Kiowa and Comanche agent at Fort Sill. The Quakers believed that honesty and kindness could solve the Indian problem, but in the Comanches' case two-thirds of the tribe were not on the reservation, and Tatum could scarcely provide for those he had. Understandably the Comanches and Kiowas continued their raiding for several more years. In 1874, symptomatic of the decline and disintegration of the Comanches, a prophet appeared among them, promising peace and prosperity if they would but kill off the white men. The culmination was an attack on Adobe Walls, a buffalo hunters' camp on the South Canadian in the Texas Panhandle, where, in defiance of government promises that such practices would be halted, white hunters from Dodge City, Kansas, were slaughtering thousands of buffalo on the guaranteed hunting grounds of the Indians. Even with severe loss the Comanches, Kiowas, and Cheyennes were unable to overpower the camp. But they continued to raid and plunder and by the middle of summer large numbers of Comanches, Kiowas, and Cheyennes were at war. Finally, permission was granted the United States Army to attack the Indians on their reservations. The Indians were harried mercilessly, and while few were slain they were forced to surrender because their horses and supplies were exhausted. By the end of 1875

Comanche and Kiowa life, free and wild on the plains, had come to an end.

By the Medicine Lodge Treaty 2,968,893 acres had been set aside for the Comanches, Kiowas, and Kiowa Apaches between the Red and Washita Rivers in southwestern Oklahoma. By 1868, Comanches were setting up their camps, and the following year the Kiowas followed suit, but the last band to arrive, Quanah Parker's Quahadi, did not come in until June 24, 1875. In 1892, against their wishes, their land was allotted in severalty, each person receiving one hundred sixty acres, and the surplus land was opened to white settlement. Their defeat and submergence in a white world had become complete.

It has been possible to mention in this chapter only some of the major events in the nineteenth-century history of the Texas Indians, but for our purposes this is ample. The essentials of the history are simple: early in the nineteenth century three forces came into contention for Texas. One, the Mexican, was relatively soon defeated by the Texans. The second, the Indian, primarily Comanches, remained in conflict for parts of Texas until the last quarter of the century. But the Anglo-American Texans were eventually victorious, and the Texas Indian cultures were obliterated by the onrushing frontier. The few Indian tribes that managed to survive have done so as faltering, harassed enclaves outside the borders of Texas.

Perhaps nothing more should be said about the near-extermination of Texas Indians. Certainly any interpretation of the events in this history runs the risk of biased rationalization, either in defense of the savage tribes, or of their Texan-American conquerors. But even at this risk, one comment cries out to be made. It is that the actions of cultural bodies, whether savage tribes or literate, civilized states, should not, cannot, be judged in terms of individual morality. Cultures are not and never have been "moral" in their dealings and relations with one another. Their treatment of one another is and has been ultimately determined by their relative strengths and the nature of their cultures, not by whatever their internal ethical or moral institutions happen to be. Usually, of course, even the incorrigibly moral indi-

362

vidual, of whatever society, is easily convinced that his nation's course is correct, and he may be coerced into actions against the enemy which are, according to the internal moral code of his society, grossly immoral. Thus, the law-abiding citizen becomes a soldier, and no matter what he does to the enemy it is not "murder." On the contrary, if he is effective at his butchery he receives society's accolades. The frontiersman might shoot a Comanche squaw, dash a child's head against a rock, but it was not murder (to Texans). When the tables are turned, the enemies' deeds are painted black by putting them within one's own moral magnetic field. Hence, Comanches were said by Texans (and many historians) to "murder" and "massacre" peaceful citizens.

To view the events of Texas history from any such moralistic, narrow standpoint, as most histories have done, is to miss the magnitude and meaning of what happened. Briefly, the obliteration of Texas Indians was but a small part, a footnote really, to the nineteenth-century development and emergence of a new, and in technological terms, a tremendously powerful nation-state. Given the accelerating industrial revolution of the United States, its spurting population growth, and the vast empty spaces of the West, inhabited mostly by a few Stone Age tribes of Indians, the inevitability of what had to happen becomes clear. The dynamism of a new America, then as now, swept up willy-nilly its inhabitants, white and Indian, as a spring torrent sweeps up leaves and twigs for a journey to an unknown fate.

But the newness—the size and the potentialities of the America which sprang so rudely and rapidly into being—was in one sense not unique. It was an oldness, a tale often repeated in human history. A new and mighty civilization blossomed upon the sere stalks of the brittle, outmoded nations of past seasons. It took much from the old, and rested heavily upon the contributions of American Indians. In replacing the the old, trampling it under the conquerors' boots, it borrowed from its victims, learned from them, and prospered greatly. Such events are old to history; the new feast upon the old, the new grow old, a newness is born, the once-new fade, are destroyed, and disappear.

BIBLIOGRAPHY

Abel, Annie Heloise (ed.)
   1922. A Report from Natchitoches in 1807, by Dr. John Sibley. Museum
      of the American Indian, Heye Foundation, *Indian Notes and
      Monographs*. Vol. 25.
Atkinson, Mary Jourdan
   1935. *The Texas Indians*. San Antonio.
   1958. *Indians of the Southwest*. San Antonio.
Bandelier, Adolph F. A.
   1890. Final Report of Investigations Among the Indians of the South-
      western United States. *Papers of the Archaeologic Institute of
      America*. American Series III, Part I.
Battey, Thomas C.
   1876. *Life and Adventures of a Quaker Among the Indians*. Boston.
Beals, Ralph L.
   1932. The Comparative Ethnology of Northern Mexico Before 1750.
      Ibero-Americana, Vol. 2: 92–225.
Bedichek, Roy
   1950. *Karánkaway Country*. Garden City, N.Y.
   1956. *Educational Competition*. Austin.
Biesele, R. L.
   1927. The Relations Between the German Settlers and the Indians in
      Texas, 1844–1860. *Southwestern Historical Quarterly*, Vol. 31:
      116–129.
Bolton, Herbert E.
   1911. The Jumano Indians in Texas, 1650–1771. *Quarterly of the Texas
      State Historical Association*, Vol. 15: 66–84.

1912. The Spanish Occupation of Texas, 1519–1690. *Southwestern Historical Quarterly*, Vol. 16: 1–26.

1914a. *Athanase de Mézières and the Louisiana-Texas Frontier, 1768–1780.* 2 vols. Cleveland.

1914b. The Founding of the Missions on the San Gabriel River, 1745–1749. *Southwestern Historical Quarterly*, Vol. 17: 323–378.

1915. *Texas in the Middle Eighteenth Century.* Berkeley.

1916. (ed.) *Spanish Exploration in the Southwest, 1542–1706.* Original Narratives of Early American History. New York.

Brant, Charles S.

1949. The Cultural Position of the Kiowa-Apache. *Southwestern Journal of Anthropology*, Vol. 5: 56–61.

1953. Kiowa Apache Culture History; Some Further Observations. *Southwestern Journal of Anthropology*, Vol. 9: 195–202.

Bushnell, David I.

1927. Drawings by A. DeBatz in Louisiana, 1732–1735. *Smithsonian Miscellaneous Collections*, Vol. 80, No. 5: 1–14.

Campbell, Thomas N.

1947. The Johnson site; type site of the Aransas Focus of the Texas Coast. *Texas Archeological and Paleontological Society Bulletin*, Vol. 18: 40–75.

1952. The Kent-Crane site; a shell midden on the Texas Coast. *Texas Archeological and Paleontological Society Bulletin*, Vol. 23: 39–77.

1956. Archeological Materials from Five Islands in the Laguna Madre, Texas Coast. *Bulletin of the Texas Archeological Society*, Vol. 27: 7–46.

1957. Archeological Investigations at the Caplen Site, Galveston County, Texas. *Texas Journal of Science*, Vol. 9: 448–471.

1958a. Archeological Remains from the Live Oak Point Site, Aransas County, Texas. *Texas Journal of Science*, Vol. 10: 423–442.

1958b. Origin of the Mescal Bean Cult. *American Anthropologist*, Vol. 60: 156–160.

Casañas, Fray Francisco

1927. Descriptions of the Tejas or Asinai Indians, 1691–1722. Translated from the Spanish by Mattie Austin Hatcher. In four parts. Parts I and II: Fray Francisco Casañas de Jesús Mariá to the Viceroy of Mexico. *Southwestern Historical Quarterly*, Vol. 30: 206–218, 283–304.

Catlin, George

1841. *Letters and Notes of the Manners, Customs, and Condition of the North American Indians.* 2 vols. London.

366

BIBLIOGRAPHY

Cook, John R.
　1907. *The Border and the Buffalo*. Topeka, Kan.

Cox, Isaac Joslin (ed.)
　1905. *The Journeys of Rène Robert Cavelier, Sieur de La Salle*. 2 vols. New York.

Crook, Wilson W., Jr., and R. K. Harris
　1958. A Pleistocene Campsite near Lewisville, Texas. *American Antiquity*, Vol. 23: 233–246.

Curtis, Edward S.
　1930. *The North American Indian*. 20 vols. Vol. 19. Norwood, Mass.

Dennis, T. S., and Mrs. T. S. Dennis (eds.)
　1925. *Life of F. M. Buckelew, the Indian Captive, as related by Himself*. Bandera, Texas.

De Solís, Fray Gaspar José
　1931. Diary of a Visit of Inspection of the Texas Missions Made by Fray Gaspar José de Solís in the Year 1767–1768. Translated by Margaret K. Kress. *Southwestern Historical Quarterly*, Vol. 35: 28–76.

De Voto, Bernard
　1947. *Across the Wide Missouri*. Boston.

Dobie, J. Frank
　1952. *The Mustangs*. Boston.

Dodge, Richard I.
　1882. *Our Wild Indians: Thirty-three Years' Personal Experience among the Red Men of the Great West*. Hartford, Conn.

Dorsey, George A.
　1904. *The Mythology of the Wichita*. Carnegie Institution of Washington. Publication No. 21.

Dyer, Joseph O.
　1916. *Comparisons of Customs of Wild Tribes Near Galveston A Century Ago, with Ancient Semitic Customs*. Galveston.
　1917. *The Lake Charles Atakapas Cannibals. Period of 1817–1820*. Eight-page pamphlet, not numbered. Galveston.

Espinosa, Fray Isidro Felis de
　1927. Descriptions of the Tejas or Asinai Indians, 1691–1722. Translated from the Spanish by Mattie Austin Hatcher. In four parts. Part IV: Fray Isidro Felis de Espinosa on the Asinai and their Allies. *Southwestern Historical Quarterly*, Vol. 31: 150–180.

Ewers, John C.
　1955. *The Horse in Blackfoot Indian Culture*. Bureau of American Ethnology, Bulletin 159. Washington, D.C.

367

Fewkes, J. Walter
1902. The Pueblo Settlements Near El Paso, Texas. *American Anthropologist,* Vol. 4: 57–75.

Folmer, Henri
1940. De Bellisle on the Texas Coast. *Southwestern Historical Quarterly,* Vol. 44: 204–231.

Foreman, Grant
1926. *Pioneer Days in the Early Southwest.* Cleveland.
1946. *The Last Trek of the Indians.* Chicago.

Garretson, Martin S.
1938. *The American Bison.* New York.

Gatschet, Albert S.
1891. The Karankawa Indians. *Archaeological and Ethnological Papers of the Peabody Museum.* Vol. 1, No. 2.

Glover, William B.
1935. A History of the Caddo Indians. *Louisiana Historical Quarterly,* Vol. 18: 872–946.

Gulick, Charles Adams (ed. with others)
1920–27. *The Papers of Mirabeau Buonaparte Lamar.* 6 vols. Austin.

Gunnerson, Dolores A.
1956. The Southern Athabascans: Their Arrival in the Southwest. *El Palacio,* Vol. 63: 346–365.

Hackett, Charles W. (ed.)
1923–26–37. *Historical Documents Relating to New Mexico, Nueva Vizcaya and Approaches Thereto, to 1773.* Collected by Adolph F. A. Bandelier and Fanny R. Bandelier. Carnegie Institution of Washington, Publication 330. I, II, III.
1931. *Pichardo's Treatise on the Limits of Louisiana and Texas.* Vol. I.

Haines, Francis
1938a. Where Did the Plains Indians Get Their Horses? *American Anthropologist,* Vol. 40: 112–117.
1938b. The Northward Spread of Horses Among the Plains Indians. *American Anthropologist,* Vol. 40: 429–437.

Hammond, George P., and Agapito Rey
1927. The Rodríguez Expedition to New Mexico, 1581–1582. *New Mexico Historical Review,* Vol. 2: 239–269.
1929. Expedition into New Mexico Made by Antonio de Espejo, 1582–1583, as Revealed in the Journal of Diego Pérez de Luxán, a Member of the Party. *Quivira Society Publications,* Vol. 1.

Harper, Elizabeth Ann
1953a. The Taovayas Indians in Frontier Trade and Diplomacy, 1719–

1768. *The Chronicles of Oklahoma,* Vol. 31: 268–289. (Article 1)

1953b. The Taovayas Indians in Frontier Trade and Diplomacy, 1769–1779. *Southwestern Historical Quarterly,* Vol. 57: 181–201. (Article 2)

1953c. The Taovayas Indians in Frontier Trade and Diplomacy, 1779–1835. *Panhandle Plains Historical Review.* Vol. 26: 41–72.

Harrington, J. P.
1910. On Phonetic and Lexical Resemblances between Kiowan and Tanoan. *American Anthropologist,* Vol. 12: 119–123.
1940. Southern Peripheral Athapaskawan Origins, Divisions, and Migrations. In *Essays in Historical Anthropology of North America, Swanton Anniversary Volume, Smithsonian Miscellaneous Collections,* Vol. 100: 503–532.

Hidalgo, Fray Francisco
1928. Description of the Tejas or Asinai Indians, 1691–1722. Translated from the Spanish by Mattie Austin Hatcher. In four parts. Part III: Fray Francisco Hidalgo to Fray Isidro Casañas. *Southwestern Historical Quarterly,* Vol. 31: 50–62.

Hill, A. T., and George Metcalf
1941. A Site of the Dismal River Aspect in Chase County, Nebraska. *Nebraska History,* Vol. 22: 159–226.

Hodge, Frederick Webb
1910. The Jumano Indians. *Proceedings of the American Antiquarian Society,* n.s., Vol. 20: 249–268.
1907a. (ed.) *Handbook of American Indians North of Mexico.* Bureau of American Ethnology, Bulletin 30, Parts 1 and 2. Washington, D.C.
1907b. (ed.) The Narrative of Álvar Núñez Cabeza de Vaca. In *Spanish Explorers in the Southern United States, 1528–1543* (pp. 12–126). New York.

Hoijer, Harry
1933. Tonkawa: An Indian Language of Texas. In *Handbook of American Indian Languages,* edited by Franz Boas. Part 3. New York.
1938. The Southern Athapaskan Languages. *American Anthropologist,* Vol. 40: 75–87.
1952. Tonkawa Indians. In *The Handbook of Texas* (Vol. 2: 788–789), edited by Walter P. Webb. Austin.

Hollon, W. Eugene, and R. L. Butler (eds.)
1956. *William Bollaert's Texas.* Norman.

Hornaday, W. T.
   1887. *The Extermination of the American Bison. Annual Report*, Smithsonian Institution. Part II, pp. 367–548.
Howard, James H.
   1957. The Mescal Bean Cult of the Central and Southern Plains: An Ancestor of the Peyote Cult? *American Anthropologist*, Vol. 59: 75–87.
Huson, Hobart
   1953. *Refugio, a Comprehensive History of Refugio County from Aboriginal Times to 1953.* 2 vols. Vol. 1. Woodsboro, Texas.
Jelks, Edward B.
   1953. Excavations at the Blum Rockshelter. *Bulletin of the Texas Archeological Society*, Vol. 24: 189–207.
Jenkins, John Holland, III (ed.)
   1958. *Recollections of Early Texas*. Austin.
Kelley, J. Charles
   1949a. Notes on Julimes, Chihuahua. *El Palacio*, Vol. 56: 358–361.
   1949b. Archaeological Notes on Two Excavated House Structures in Western Texas. *Texas Archeological and Paleontological Society Bulletin*, Vol. 20: 89–114.
   1951. A Bravo Valley Aspect Component of the Lower Rio Conchos Valley, Chihuahua, Mexico. *American Antiquity*, Vol. 17: 114–119.
   1952. Factors Involved in the Abandonment of Certain Peripheral Southwestern Settlements. *American Anthropologist*, Vol. 54: 356–387.
   1955. Juan Sabeata and Diffusion in Aboriginal Texas. *American Anthropologist*, Vol. 57: 981–995.
Kelley, J. Charles, T. N. Campbell, and Donald J. Lehmer
   1940. The Association of Archeological Materials with Geological Deposits in the Big Bend Region of Texas. *Sul Ross State Teachers College Bulletin*, Vol. 21, No. 3.
Kenney, M. M.
   1897. Tribal Society among Texas Indians. *Quarterly of the Texas State Historical Association*, Vol. I: 26–33.
Krieger, Alex D.
   1946. *Culture Complexes and Chronology in Northern Texas*. University of Texas Publication No. 4640. Austin.
   1948. Importance of the 'Gilmore Corridor' in Culture Contacts between Middle America and the Eastern United States. *Texas Archeological and Paleontological Society Bulletin*, Vol. 19: 155–178.

1953. New World Culture History: Anglo-America. In *Anthropology Today, An Encyclopedic Inventory* (pp. 238–264), edited by A. L. Kroeber. Chicago.

1956. Food Habits of the Texas Coastal Indians in the Early Sixteenth Century. *Bulletin of the Texas Archeological Society,* Vol. 27: 47–58.

N.d. Archeology, Ethnology, and Early Spanish History of the Falcón Reservoir Area in Texas and Tamaulipas. (MS)

Kroeber, Alfred L.
1947. *Cultural and Natural Areas of Native North America.* Berkeley.
1948. *Anthropology.* New edition. New York.

Kuykendall, J. H.
1903. Reminiscences of Early Texas. *Quarterly of the Texas Historical Association,* Vol. 6: 236–253; 311–330.

La Barre, Weston
1960. Twenty Years of Peyote Studies. *Current Anthropology,* Vol. 1: 45–60.

Lehmer, Donald J.
1948. The Jornada Branch of the Mogollon. *University of Arizona Bulletin,* Vol. 19: 1–99.

Lesser, Alexander, and Gene Weltfish
1932. Composition of the Caddoan Linguistic Stock. *Smithsonian Miscellaneous Collections,* Vol. 87: viii–15.

Lowie, Robert H.
1953. Alleged Kiowa-Crow Affinities. *Southwestern Journal of Anthropology,* Vol. 9: 357–368.

McAllister, J. G.
1935. Kiowa-Apache Social Organization. In *Social Anthropology of North American Tribes* (pp. 99–169), edited by Fred Eggan. Chicago.
1949. Kiowa-Apache Tales. In *The Sky Is My Tipi* (pp. 1–141), edited by M. C. Boatright. Texas Folklore Society. Vol. 22.

MacNeish, Richard S.
1947. A Preliminary Report on Coastal Tamaulipas, Mexico. *American Antiquity,* Vol. 13: 1–15.

Margry, Pierre
1879–88. *Découvertes et établissements des Français dans l'ouest et dans le sud de l'Amérique Septentrionale (1614–1698).* Mémoires et documents inédits. 6 vols. Paris.

Marriott, Alice L.
1945. *The Ten Grandmothers.* Norman.

Martin, George C.
  1936. *The Indian Tribes of the Mission Nuestra Señora del Refugio.* San Antonio.
Martin, George C. (ed.)
  1947. *Expedition into Texas of Fernando del Bosque, Standard-Bearer of the King Don Carlos II, in the Year 1675.* Translated from the Spanish by Betty B. Brewster. San Antonio.
Mason, J. Alden
  1935. The Place of Texas in Pre-Columbian Relationships between the United States and Mexico. *Texas Archeological and Paleontological Society Bulletin,* Vol. 7: 29–46.
  1937. Further Remarks on Pre-Columbian Relationships between the United States and Mexico. *Texas Archeological and Paleontological Society Bulletin,* Vol. 9: 120–129.
Mayhall, Mildred P.
  1939. The Indians of Texas: The Atakapa, the Karankawa, the Tonkawa. Unpublished Ph.D. dissertation, University of Texas Library. Austin.
Methvin, Rev. J. J.
  1927. *Andele, or the Mexican-Kiowa Captive.* 4th ed. Anadarko, Oklahoma.
Mishkin, Bernard
  1940. Rank and Warfare among the Plains Indians. *Monographs of the American Ethnological Society.* Vol. 3.
Mooney, James
  1898. *Calendar History of the Kiowa Indians. Annual Report.* Bureau of American Ethnology, Vol. 17, Part I. Washington.
Morfi, Padre Fray Juan Agustín
  1932. *Excerpts from the Memorias for the History of the Province of Texas.* Appendix, prolog, and notes by Frederick C. Chabot.
Morgan, Lewis Henry
  1877. *Ancient Society.* New York.
Murdock, George Peter
  1949. *Social Structure.* New York.
Nance, Berta Hart
  1952. D. A. Nance and the Tonkawa Indians. *West Texas Historical Association Yearbook,* Vol. 28: 87–95.
Newcomb, W. W., Jr.
  1950. A Re-examination of the Causes of Plains Warfare. *American Anthropologist,* Vol. 52: 317–329.
  1956. A Reappraisal of the 'Cultural Sink' of Texas. *Southwestern Journal of Anthropology,* Vol. 12: 145–153.

BIBLIOGRAPHY

Newell, H. Perry, and Alex D. Krieger
   1949. The George C. Davis Site, Cherokee County, Texas. *Memoirs of the Society for American Archaeology*. No. 5.
Nye, Wilbur S.
   1937. *Carbine and Lance: The Story of Old Fort Sill*. Norman.
Olmsted, Frederick Law
   1860. *A Journey Through Texas; Saddle-trip on the Southwestern Frontier*. New York.
Opler, Morris E.
   1936. The Kinship Systems of the Southern Athabaskan-Speaking Tribes. *American Anthropologist*, Vol. 38: 620–633.
   1940. Myths and Legends of the Lipan Apache Indians. *Memoirs of the American Folklore Society*. Vol. 36.
   1945. The Lipan Apache Death Complex and Its Extensions. *Southwestern Journal of Anthropology*, Vol. 1: 122–141.
   1946. *Childhood and Youth in Jicarilla Apache Society*. Frederick Webb Hodge Anniversary Publication Fund, Southwest Museum. Vol. 5. Los Angeles.
   1959. Component, Assemblage, and Theme in Cultural Integration and Differentiation. *American Anthropologist*, Vol. 61: 995–964.
Parsons, Elsie Clews
   1941. Notes on the Caddo. *Memoirs of the American Anthropological Association*. No. 57. Menasha, Wis.
Plummer, Rachel
   1926. *The Rachel Plummer Narrative*. Edited by James W. Parker, privately printed.
Richardson, Jane
   1940. Law and Status Among the Kiowa Indians. *Monograph of the American Ethnological Society*. Vol. 1.
Richardson, Rupert N.
   1933. *The Comanche Barrier to South Plains Setlement*. Glendale, Calif.
Roe, Frank Gilbert
   1951. *The North American Buffalo: A Critical Study of the Species in Its Wild State*. Toronto.
   1955. *The Indian and the Horse*. Norman.
Roemer, Ferdinand
   1935. *Texas, with Particular Reference to German Immigration and the Physical Appearance of the Country*. Translated from the German by Oswald Mueller. San Antonio.
Ruecking, Frederick, Jr.
   1953. The Economic System of the Coahuiltecan Indians of Southern

Texas and Northeastern Mexico. *Texas Journal of Science,* Vol. 5: 470–489.

1954a. Ceremonies of the Coahuiltecan Indians of Southern Texas and Northeastern Mexico. *Texas Journal of Science,* Vol. 6: 330–339.

1954b. Band and Bandclusters of the Coahuiltecan Indians. Department of Anthropology, University of Texas. *Student Papers in Anthropology,* Vol. 1: 1–24.

1955. The Social Organization of the Coahuiltecan Indians of Southern Texas and Northeastern Mexico. *Texas Journal of Science,* Vol. 7: 357–388.

Sánchez, José María
1926. A Trip to Texas in 1828. Transcribed from the Spanish by Carlos E. Casteñeda. *Southwestern Historical Quarterly,* Vol. 29: 249–288.

Sapir, Edward
1920. The Hokan and Coahuiltecan Languages. *International Journal of American Linguistics,* Vol. 1: 280–290.

1949. *Selected Writings.* Berkeley.

Sauer, Carl
1934. The Distribution of Aboriginal Tribes and Languages in Northwestern Mexico. *Ibero-Americana,* Vol. 5: 65–74.

Schaedel, R. P.
1949. The Karankawa of the Texas Gulf Coast. *Southwestern Journal of Anthropology,* Vol. 5: 117–137.

Schmitt, Karl, and Iva Osanai Schmitt
N.d. *Wichita Kinship, Past and Present.* University Book Exchange. Norman.

Scholes, F. V., and H. P. Mera
1940. Some Aspects of the Jumano Problem. *Carnegie Institution Contributions to American Anthropology and History,* Vol. 6: 265–299.

Scott, Hugh Lenox
1911. Notes on the Kado, or Sun Dance of the Kiowa. *American Anthropologist,* Vol. 13: 345–379.

Secoy, Frank R.
1951. The Identity of the 'Paduca,' an Ethnohistorical Analysis. *American Anthropologist,* Vol. 53: 525–542.

1953. Changing Military Patterns on the Great Plains. *Monographs of the American Ethnological Society.* Vol. 21. New York.

Sellards, E. H.
1941. Stone Images from Henderson County, Texas. *American Antiquity,* Vol. 7: 29–38.

BIBLIOGRAPHY

1952. *Early Man in America: A Study in Prehistory*. Austin.

Sellards, E. H., Glen L. Evans, and Grayson E. Meade
1947. Fossil Bison and Associated Artifacts from Plainview, Texas. With description of artifacts by Alex D. Krieger. *Bulletin of the Geological Society of America*, Vol. 58: 927–954.

Sibley, John
1832. Historical Sketches of the Several Indian Tribes in Louisiana. *American State Papers, Indian Affairs*. Vol. IV. Washington.

Sjoberg, Andreé F.
1951. The Bidai Indians of Southwestern Texas. *Southwestern Journal of Anthropology*, Vol. 7: 391–400.
1953a. The Culture of the Tonkawa, A Texas Indian Tribe. *Texas Journal of Science*, Vol. 5: 280–304.
1953b. Lipan Apache Culture in Historical Perspective. *Southwestern Journal of Anthropology*, Vol. 9: 76–98.

Smithwick, Noah
1900. *The Evolution of a State or Recollections of Old Texas Days*. Compiled by his daughter, Nanna Smithwick Donaldson. Austin.

Spier, Leslie
1921. The Sun Dance of the Plains Indians. *Anthropological Papers of the American Museum of Natural History*, Vol. 16: 451–527.
1924. Wichita and Caddo Relationship Terms. *American Anthropologist*, Vol. 26: 258–263.

Steward, Julian H.
1947. American Culture History in the Light of South America. *Southwestern Journal of Anthropology*, Vol. 3: 85–107.

Strong, William Duncan
1935. An Introduction to Nebraska Archeology. *Smithsonian Miscellaneous Collections*. Vol. 93, No. 10. 323 pp.

Suhm, Dee Ann
1955. Excavations at the Collins Site, Travis County, Texas. *Bulletin of the Texas Archeological Society*, Vol. 26: 7–54.
1956. Archeological Excavations at the Collins and Smith Sites, Travis County, Texas. Unpublished M.A. thesis, University of Texas Library, Austin.
1957. Excavations at the Smith Rockshelter, Travis County. *Texas Journal of Science*, Vol. 9: 26–58.
1959. The Williams Site and Central Texas Archeology. *Texas Journal of Science*, Vol. 11: 218–250.

Suhm, Dee Ann, with Alex D. Krieger and the collaboration of Edward B. Jelks

375

1954. An Introductory Handbook of Texas Archeology. *Bulletin of the Texas Archeological Society.* Vol. 25. Austin.

Swanton, John R.

1907. Mythology of the Indians of Louisiana and the Texas Coast. *Journal of American Folklore,* Vol. 20: 285–290.

1911. *Indian Tribes of the Lower Mississippi Valley.* Bureau of American Ethnology, Bulletin 43. Washington, D.C.

1915. Linguistic Position of the Tribes of Southern Texas and Northeastern Mexico. *American Anthropologist,* Vol. 17: 17–40.

1940. *Linguistic Material from the Tribes of Southern Texas and Northeastern Mexico.* Bureau of American Ethnology, Bulletin 127. Washington, D.C.

1942. *Source Material on the History and Ethnology of the Caddo Indians.* Bureau of American Ethnology, Bulletin 132. Washington, D.C.

1946. *The Indians of the Southeastern United States.* Bureau of American Ethnology, Buletin 137. Washington, D.C.

1952. *The Indian Tribes of North America.* Bureau of American Ethnology, Bulletin 145. Washington, D.C.

Thomas, Alfred B. (trans. and ed.)

1932. *Forgotten Frontiers: A Study of the Spanish Indian Policy of Don Juan Bautista de Anza, Governor of New Mexico, 1777–1778.* Norman.

1935. *After Coronado: Spanish Exploration Northeast of New Mexico, 1696–1727.*

Thrall, Homer S.

1879. *A Pictorial History of Texas.* St. Louis.

Tylor, Edward B.

1903. *Primitive Culture.* 2 vols. Vol. 1, 4th edition, rev. London.

Varner, John Grier, and Jeannette Johnson Varner (transs. and eds.)

1951. *The Florida of the Inca.* Austin.

Wallace, Ernest, and E. A. Hoebel

1952. *The Comanches, Lords of the South Plains.* Norman.

Walley, Raymond

1955. A Preliminary Report on the Albert George Site in Fort Bend County [Texas]. *Bulletin of the Texas Archeological Society,* Vol. 26: 218–234.

Webb, Walter P.

1931. *The Great Plains.* New York.

1935. *The Texas Rangers: A Century of Frontier Defense.* Boston.

Wedel, W. R.

1940. Culture Sequences in the Central Great Plains. In *Essays in His-*

torical Anthropology of North America, Swanton Anniversary Volume, *Smithsonian Miscellaneous Collections*, Vol. 100: 291–352.

1942. Archeological Remains in Central Kansas and their Possible Bearing on the Location of Quivira. *Smithsonian Miscellaneous Collections*, Vol. 101: 1–24.

1959. *An Introduction to Kansas Archeology*. Bureau of American Ethnology, Bulletin 174. Washington, D.C.

Wendorf, Fred, Alex D. Krieger, Claude C. Albritton, and T. D. Stewart
1955. *The Midland Discovery*. Austin.

Wheat, Joe Ben
1953. *An Archeological Survey of the Addicks Dam Basin, Southeast Texas*. Bureau of American Ethnology, Bulletin 154: 143–252.

Whitaker, Thomas W., Hugh C. Cotter, and Richard S. MacNeish
1957. Cucurbit Materials from Three Caves Near Ocampo, Tamaulipas. *American Antiquity*, Vol. 22: 352–358.

White, Leslie A.
1949a. Ethnological Theory. In *Philosophy for the Future* (pp. 357–384), edited by Roy Wood Sellars, V. J. McGill, and Marvin Farber. New York.

1949b. *The Science of Culture*. New York.

1959. *The Evolution of Culture*. New York.

Winfrey, Dorman H. (ed.)
1959. *Texas Indian Papers, 1825–1843*. Texas State Library. Austin.

Winship, George P.
1896. *The Coronado Expedition, 1540–1542. 14th Annual Report*, Bureau of American Ethnology, Part I. Washington, D.C.

Wissler, Clark
1914. The Influence of the Horse in the Development of Plains Culture. *American Anthropologist*, Vol. 16: 1–25.

Wormington, H. M.
1957. *Ancient Man in North America*. 4th edition, rev. Denver.

Wright, Muriel H.
1951. *A Guide to the Indian Tribes of Oklahoma*. Norman.

Zingg, Robert M.
1939. A Reconstruction of Uto-Aztekan History. *Contributions to Ethnography*, Vol. II. New York. 274 pp.

INDEX

Abandonment of aged: by Comanches, 172; by Kiowas, 205–206

Abel, Annie Heloise: 319

Abriache Indians: location, 234; mentioned, 239. *See* Jumanos

Acubadoes Indians: mentioned, 42. *See* Coahuiltecans

Adais: as independent Caddo tribe, 282

Adobe Walls: attack on, 361

Adultery: among Caddo, 301; among Comanche, punishment for, 176; and method of determining guilt, 176–177; and damages collected from guilty, 177; mentioned, 170; among Lipan Apache, 122. *See also* Divorce

Agave: Coahuiltecan food, 41; appearance of, 115; used for food by Coahuiltecans, Jumanos, Lipan Apaches, 115; preparation of, by Lipan Apaches, 115–116; Jumano use of, 239

Aguayo, Marquis de San Miguel de: expedition under, sent to east Texas, 1721, 288

Akokisas: location, 316; probability that Hans were band of, 317; attracted to missions, 318; De Bellisle captured by, 318, 321; remnants join Bidais, 319; appearance, 320; dugout canoes, 321; similarity to Karankawas, 321; subsistence, 323; dwellings, 324–325; bands, 325–326; greeting customs, 326; cannibalism, 327–328; use of yaupon compared to Karankawan usage, 329; mentioned, 24. *See also* Atakapans

Alabama-Coushatta Indians: possible intermarriage with Bidais, 319; reservation, 319; mentioned, 24

Alamo: mentioned, 37

Aldrete, Captain Trinidad: led slaughter of Karankawas, 342

Amaye Indians: De Soto Expedition's encounter with, 285

Amayxoya: as Caddo war heroes, 303

Amotomancos: Jumano pueblo, 234; compared to Tanpachoas, 235–236; appearance, 237; mentioned (Otomoacos), 235, 239. *See also* Jumanos

Anadarko Indians: as Hasinai tribe, 280; mission established for, 288. *See also* Caddoes

Animals: domesticated in Americas, 17

Annual round: Atakapan, 321–322; Coahuiltecan, 39–40; Karankawa, 66; Wichita, 257–258. *See also* Subsistence

Antelope: in south Texas, 30; Lipan Apaches hunted, by surround, 113; Kiowas and Kiowa Apaches hunted, 197

Antelope band. *See* Quahadi Comanches

Apaches: compared to Paleo-American hunters, 14; hostile to Coahuiltecans, 37; raided Spanish for horses, 87; western subdivision, 103; origin and prehistory, 104–105; raided Jumanos, 231; absorbed remnant Jumanos, 233; Jumanos raided with, 234; as growing menace to Spaniards, 335; numbers, 335; mentioned, 100. *See also* Eastern Apaches; Lipan Apaches

Appearance: Atakapan, 319–320, 327; Caddo, 289–291; Coahuiltecan, 37–39; Comanche, 158; Jumano, 237;

Carancaguacas. *See* Karankawa proper; Karankawas

Carbon 14. *See* Radiocarbon dating

Carlana Apaches: union with Cuartelejos and disappearance, 106. *See also* Apaches; Eastern Apaches; Lipan Apaches

Carrizo Indians: location, 31. *See also* Coahuiltecans

Casañas, de Jesús María, Fray Francisco: founded mission, 287; described Caddo women painting themselves, 290; Caddo planting customs, 292; described Caddo burial, 301–302; on Caddo *xinesi*, 303–304; Caddo clans, 304–305

Castillo (of Narváez Expedition): companion of De Vaca, 34; as shaman, 53

Castillo, Diego del: expedition to Caddo territory, 285–286

Castro (Lipan Apache chief): attire described by Olmsted, 110; mentioned, 112

Catlin, George: on appearance of Comanches, 158; and Kiowas, 195; and Wichitas, 250–251; and Wichita dress, 253; and gardens, 253

Cattle: of Lipan Apaches, 118–119; hunted by Comanches, 163

Catujane Indians: attracted to mission, 36. *See also* Coahuiltecans

Cavas Indians: Tonkawa subdivision, 134; discovered by De León Expedition, 136. *See also* Tonkawas

Cayas Indians: De Soto's encounter with, 284. *See also* Caddoes

Cenis. *See* Hasinai Confederacy; Caddoes

Central Texas Aspect: tentative association with Tonkawas, 134–135

Chayas: Caddo officials, 303. *See also* Caddoes

Cherokees: cultural tradition shared with Caddoes, 282; alliance with Austin's colony, 344; expulsion from Texas, 347–348

Cheyenne Indians: cause of Kiowa and Kiowa Apache migration, 195; wars with Kiowas, 210; tribal medicine of, 214; as allies of Comanches, 336; fight with Eastern Indians, 1854, 349; alliance with other Plains Indians, 360–361; mentioned, 98

Chickasaws: cultural tradition shared with Caddoes, 282; Texas Cherokees flee to, 347

Chiefs: Atakapan, 325; Coahuiltecan, 44–45; Comanche, 174–176; Jumano, 243–244; Karankawa, 71; Kiowa, 207; Lipan Apache, 124–125; Tonkawa, 141; Wichita, 267

Childbirth: Atakapan, 326; Caddo, 299; Coahuiltecan, 48–49; Comanche, 166; Lipan Apache, 119; Tonkawa, 145–146; Wichita, 258–259

Childhood: Atakapan, 326–327; Caddo, 300; Coahuiltecan, 49–50; Comanche, 166–167; Karankawa, 72; Kiowa, 199–200; Lipan Apache, 119–120; Tonkawa, 146; Wichita, 259–261, 275. *See also* Puberty ceremonies

Chiricahua Apaches: western Apaches, 104

Chitimacha: Atakapan language related to, 316

Choctaw Indians: cultural tradition shared with Caddoes, 282

Choctaw nation: Texas Cherokees flee to, 347

Circum-Caribbean area: Southeast culture area related to, 24; connection with Southeast culture area, 282

Clamcoets Indians. *See* Karankawa proper; Karankawas

Clans: Tonkawa, 141–142; Caddo, 304–305

Clear Fork Reservation: established for Comanches, 354

Clovis Fluted point: distribution, 9; characteristic of Llano complex, 9; compared to Folsom point, 10; compared to Plainview point, 11

Coahuiltecan bands: Acubadoes, 42; Aranamas, location, 31; mission established for, 37, 63; probably synonymous with Mariames, 49; Arbadaos, 42; Avavares, tale told to De Vaca by, 55–56; mentioned, 53; Borrados, as coastal Coahuiltecans, 60; Cacaxtles, 36; Carrizos, 31; Catujanes, 36; Cotzales, 36; Kesale, 39; Malaquite, 60; Milijaes, 36; Tilijaes, 36; Yguazes, 46, 49

Coahuiltecans: members of Western Gulf culture area, 21, 29; extinction of, 25, 335; environment, 30; language, 30; Karankawas speakers of Coahuiltecan, 30; subdivisions, 30–31; origins, 31–32; development related to, 32; related to Hokan languages, 32; as "fossil" culture, 33; colonial history, 33–37; endurance, 37; appearance, 37–39; cultural summary, 56–57; development compared to that of Northern Shoshones, 156

—subsistence and material culture: dress, 39; annual round, 39–40; variability of wild foods, 39–40; hunting, 40–41; wild-plant foods, 41–42; preparation of food, 42–43; dwellings, 43; utensils and weapons, 43–44

—social organization: territories of, 39; bands, 44–45; kinship system, 44–45; polygyny, 45; infanticide of girls, 46, 48–49; warfare, 46–48; cannibalism, 48; childbirth, 48; couvade, 48; pregnancy, 48; puberty ceremonies, 49–50; tattooing, 49–50; divorce, 50; levirate, 50; marriage, 50; sororate, 50; berdaches, 51; death and mourning, 51; quarrels over women, 51; coastal bands, 60

—supernaturalism: beliefs, 51–52; curing, 52; mitotes, 52, 53–55; shamans, 52; mythology, 55–56

Coaque Indians: Karankawa band, 59. See Karankawas

Cobanes Indians. See Kopano; Karankawas

Cochise (Apache chief): mentioned, 103

Coco Indians: Karankawan band, 59, 136; killed by Bustamante, 341. See also Karankawas

Coconicis: Imaginary Caddo oracles, 310–311. See Caddo: supernaturalism

Colonies, American: lack of conflict with Indians, 343–344

Colorado Museum of Natural History: discoverers of Folsom site, 10

Colt, Samuel: mentioned, 336

Comanche Reservation. See Clear Fork Reservation

Comanches: Texas Plains tribe, 22; reservation Indians, 25; hostile to Coahuiltecans, 37; appearance in New Mexico, 87–88; as horsemen, 88–89; horse race with soldiers and Kickapoos, 89; conflict with Apaches, 98, 101, 106, 107, 114; appearance compared to that of Tonkawas, 137; pre-empt Tonkawa hunting grounds, 138; Tonkawas use names of, 148; eaten by Tonkawas, 150–151; why synonymous with Indian to many Texans, 155–156; as invaders of southern plains, 156; language, 156; early history, 156–157; origins, 156–157; bands, 157–158; appearance, 158, 250; cultural summary, 191; name for Kiowas, 193–194; relations with Kiowas, 194–195; relations with Wichitas, 248–249, 257, 268; raid San Saba mission with Wichitas, 254; compared to Wichitas, 265; trade with Wichitas, 258; as Lipan Apache enemies, 319; as growing menace to Spaniards, 335; as Tonkawa enemies, 335, 343; condition at beginning of nineteenth century, 336; review of military potentialities, 336–337; final defeat, 340; young American settlements beyond range of, 343; relations with Austin's colony, 344; attack on Parker's Fort, 344–345; relations with Republic of Texas, 345–346, 349, 350–352; raids, 346; fight with eastern Indians, 1854, 349; forays into Mexico, 349–350; battle at San Antonio Courthouse, 350; Battle of Plum Creek, 350; Penateka band, 350–353; difficult to draw into councils, 351; increased friction with

Cox, Isaac Joslin: 76, 87, 135, 286 n., 289, 291

Cradleboard: Lipan Apache, 119; Tonkawa, 146

Cranial deformation: Atakapan, 327; Caddo, 289

Creeks: cultural tradition shared with Caddoes, 282; Fort Gibson treaty affects, 356; participate in Tonkawa massacre, 359

Crook, Wilson W., Jr., and R. K. Harris: 9

Crow Indians: Kiowa association with, 194; fight with Eastern Indians, 1854, 349

Crow kinship system: 143

Cuartelejo: relationship with Jicarilla Apaches. See Apaches; Eastern Apaches; Lipan Apaches

Culture: understanding of, depends on knowing past, 3; evolution of, 3–4; relation of one to another, 362–363

Curing: Atakapan (Bidais), 328–329; Caddo, 312–313; Coahuiltecan, 52; Comanche, 187–188

Curtis, Edward S.: 251 n., 270, 273, 333

Dakotas: conflict with Kiowas and Kiowa Apaches, 195; alliance with other Plains Indians, 360; mentioned, 98

Dallas Archeological Society: 9

Deadose Indians: Atakapan subdivision, 24; subdivision of Patiris, 316; attracted to missions, 318; relationship to Caddoes, 321. See also Atakapans

Death and burial: Caddo, 301–302; Comanche, 172–173; Karankawa, 74; Kiowa, 206; Lipan Apache, 122–123; Tonkawa, 146–149; Wichita, 263

DeBatz, A.: 320

De Bellisle, Simars: on Atakapan cannibalism, 315, 327; and captivity among Atakapans, 317–318, 318 n.;

and fasting among Atakapans, 323; and Atakapan greetings, 326; mentioned, 321, 324

Deities: Caddo, 309; Comanche, 189–190; Karankawa, 78–79; Kiowa, 210–211; Tonkawa, 149; Wichita, 270–271

De la Harpe, Bernard. See Harpe, Bernard de la

Delawares: immigrants to Texas, 24, 347; alliance with Austin's colony, 344; treaty with Republic of Texas, 1843, 348; scouts for Colonel Eldridge, 351; renegade kills Comanche, 1845, 352; settle on Brazos Reservation, 354; join Rangers to attack Comanches, 357; final settlement on reservation, 358–359; participants in Tonkawa massacre, 359

De León, Captain Alonso: destruction of Fort St. Louis, 36, 62–63, 76, 286; encountered Tonkawas, 135–136; probably crossed Atakapan territory, 317

De León, Martín: conflict of colony with Karankawas, 341

De Mézières, Athanase: on industriousness of Wichitas, 247; visited Wichitas in 1757, 249; on division of labor among Wichitas, 257; and Wichita government, 268; and view of Wichita supernaturalism, 270

Dennis, T. S., and Mrs. T. S. (eds.): 109, 112, 113, 116, 117, 118, 119, 120, 121, 126, 130

De Solís, Fray Gaspar José: on Coahuiltecan appearance and hardiness, 39, 64–65; account of, compared to Father Morfi's, 64 n.; on Karankawa appetite, 67; and Karankawa wife exchange, 74; and mitotes, 79–81; and Karankawa warfare and religion, 89; and Caddo wife exchange, 301; observed eminent Nabedache woman, 304

De Soto, Hernando: expedition of, possibly encountered Tonkawas, 135; encounter with Caddoes, 1541, 284–285; expedition of, found evidence of trade with Southwest among Caddoes, 299; conflict of army with Caddoes, 307; mentioned, 289

De Vaca, Álvar Núñez Cabeza: on physical abilities of Coahuiltecans, 29; and life among south Texas Indians, 33–34, 33–34 n.; and appearance of Coahuiltecans, 37; and hunting customs of Coahuiltecans, 40; and food habits of Coahuiltecans, 41; and division of labor of Coahuiltecans, 46; and marriage customs of Coahuiltecans, 50–51; adopted Coahuiltecan curing customs, 52; as shaman among Coahuiltecans, 52–53; recounted Avavare mythology, 55–56; on appearance of Karankawas, 63; described shipwreck, 65; as trader among Indians, 70–71; mentioned lack of chiefs among Karankawas, 71; on Karankawa love of children, 72; and Karankawa horror at Spanish cannibalism, 77; noted yaupon tea of Karankawas, 79; described Karankawa mitote, 81; possible encounter with Tonkawas, 135; visited Jumano Indians, 225; termed Jumanos "Cow Nation," 229; noted drought among Jumanos, 231; first European to meet Jumanos, 236; described Jumano stone-boiling, 241; mentioned Jumano dwellings, 241, 317; mentioned, 59 n., 60, 62, 66

De Voto, Bernard: viii

DeWitt, Green C.: 341

Dismal River culture: 105

Division of labor: Caddo, 298; Coahuiltecan, 46; Kiowa, 201–202

Divorce: Caddo, 301; Coahuiltecan, 50. See also Social organization

Dobie, J. Frank: 88

Dodge, Richard I.: 89, 155, 250, 355

Dog: appears in Archaic stage, 15; barkless, of Coahuiltecans, 30

Dorantes (De Vaca companion): 34

Dorsey, George A.: 251 n., 259, 263, 264, 270

Douay, Father Anastasius: possible encounter with Tonkawas, 135; described lavish greeting by Caddoes, 279

Dragoon Expedition: Catlin as a member of, 158, 195, 250; council of, held at Wichita village, 355

Dress: Atakapan, 320–321; Caddo, 291–292; Coahuiltecan, 39; Comanche, 158–160; Jumano, 237; Kiowa and Kiowa Apache, 196; Lipan Apache, 110; Tonkawa, 137–138; Vaqueros, 109; Wichita, 253

Dwellings: Atakapan (Akokisa, Atakapa), 324–325; Caddo, 294–295; Coahuiltecan, 43; Comanche, 164–165; Jumano, 241; Karankawa, 68; Kiowa, 198; Lipan Apache, 116–117; Tonkawa, 140; Wichita, 255–256

Dyer, Joseph O.: 319–328, *passim*

Eagle dance: of Comanches, 188

Eagle Shields: shamanistic society of Kiowas, 205

Eastern Apaches: conflict with Comanches, 98; tribes, 104; early history, 105–109; eighteenth-century decline, 107–109; divergence of culture, 109; trade with pueblos, 114; dispersion, 194; Jumanos merge with, 234; Wichita conflict with, 268; mentioned, 162. See also Lipan Apaches; Apaches

Eastland, W. M.: 346

Edwards Plateau Aspect: artifacts, 15; mentioned, 135

Eldridge, Colonel J. C.: 351

Elephant, Columbian (*Elephas columbi*): hunted by Llano man, 7, 9; found with carved stone heads, 12; mentioned, 14

Elopement: practiced by Comanches, 169; and by Kiowas, 201

Emet Indians: Tonkawa band encountered by De León Expedition, 136; mentioned, 134. See also Tonkawas

Environment: as barrier to cultural stimulus from south into Texas, 19;

dians, 19; possibility of migrations through Texas, 19–20

Nuestra Señora de Guadalupe: Spanish mission established for Nacogdoches and Anadarkos, 288

Nuestra Señora de la Candelario: Spanish mission established for Atakapans, 318

Nuestra Señora de la Luz: Spanish mission established near Liberty, Texas, 319

Nuestra Señora de la Purísima Concepción: mission established among Hasinais, 287, 288

Nuestra Señora del Refugio: Spanish mission built for Aranama Indians, 63

Nye, Wilbur S.: 196

Old Owl (Comanche chief): 353

Olmsted, Frederick Law: on Lipan Apache dress, 110, 112; and Lipan Apache warfare, 125

Omaha Indians: tribal medicine of, 214; relation to Wichitas, 276

Oñate, Don Juan de: colonizer of New Mexico, 86; on Plains Apaches, 103; exploration of plains, 106; on Apache attire, 109; visited Quivira, 248; on Wichita gardens, 253; and villages, 254; and dwellings, 255; and granaries, 256; and Apache war with Wichitas, 268; mentioned, 105, 116

Opler, Morris E.: 109 n., 120, 121, 122, 126, 127, 128

Orcoquisac. See Akokisas; Atakapans

Orejon Indians: location, 31. See Coahuiltecans

Origins: Apache, 104–105; Atakapan, 316–317; Caddo, 20, 283–284; Coahuiltecan, 31–32; Comanche, 156–157; Jumano, 229–231; Karankawa, 61–63; Kiowa, 194; Kiowa Apache, 193; Tonkawa, 134–135; Wichita, 248

Origin tales: Atakapan, 328; Caddo, 309; Kiowa, 219–220; Wichita, 275–276

396

Osage Indians: capture Kiowa *taime*, 214; enemies of Wichitas, 248, 257, 268; relation to Wichitas, 276; enemies of Kadohadachos, 291; enemies of Caddoes, 306; fight with Eastern Indians, 1854, 349; sign Camp Holmes Treaty, 1835, 355; Fort Gibson Treaty effects, 356; mentioned, 189

Oto Indians: relation to Wichitas, 276

Otomoacos Indians. See Amotomancos; Jumanos

Pachal band. See Coahuiltecans

Padoka: French term for Apaches, 108

Paleo-American stage: life of people, 4–5; racial connections, 4–5; nomadic hunters, 6; extinct animals associated with, 7, 91; number of sites, 7; distribution of sites in Texas, 9–15; inferences about, 13–14; disappearance, 14–15

Paloma Apaches: mentioned, 106. See Apaches; Eastern Apaches; Lipan Apaches

Pani Pique. See Wichitas

Panipiquets. See Wichitas

Panis. See Wichitas

Panis Noirs. See Wichitas

Parker, Cynthia Ann: captured by Indians, 345

Parker, Quanah: son of Cynthia Ann Parker, 345; chief of Quahadi Comanches, 362

Parker's Fort: attack on, 344–345

Parsons, Elsie Clews: 280 n., 300, 301, 303, 305 n., 311

Patarabueye: as Jumano subdivision, 227; named by Spanish slavers, 232, 234; mentioned, 23, 239. See also Jumanos

Pataraguey Indians. See Patarabueye; Jumanos

Patiris: as Atakapan tribe, 24; location of, 316; relation to Caddoes, 321. See also Atakapans

Pawnee Picts. See Wichitas